FPCC

DEC 1 9 1991

INVENTORY 98

 St. Louis Community College

Forest Park
Florissant Valley
Meramec

Instructional Resources
St. Louis, Missouri

*DICTIONARY OF
CONCEPTS IN
RECREATION AND
LEISURE STUDIES*

Recent Titles in
Reference Sources for the Social Sciences and Humanities

Research Guide for Psychology
Raymond G. McInnis

Dictionary of Concepts in Human Geography
Robert P. Larkin and Gary L. Peters

Dictionary of Concepts in History
Harry Ritter

A Research Guide to the Health Sciences: Medical, Nutritional, and Environmental
Kathleen J. Haselbauer

Dictionary of Concepts in Physical Geography
Thomas P. Huber, Robert P. Larkin, and Gary L. Peters

Dictionary of Concepts in the Philosophy of Science
Paul T. Durbin

Dictionary of Concepts in General Psychology
John A. Popplestone and Marion White McPherson

Research Guide for Studies in Infancy and Childhood
Enid E. Haag

DICTIONARY OF CONCEPTS IN RECREATION AND LEISURE STUDIES

Stephen L. J. Smith

Reference Sources for the Social Sciences and Humanities, Number 9
Raymond G. McInnis, Series Editor

Greenwood Press
New York • Westport, Connecticut • London

Library of Congress Cataloging-in-Publication Data

Smith, Stephen L. J., 1946–
    Dictionary of concepts in recreation and leisure studies / Stephen
L. J. Smith.
        p.   cm. — (Reference sources for the social sciences and
humanities, ISSN 0730–3335 ; no. 9)
    Includes bibliographical references.
    ISBN 0–313–25262–9 (lib. bdg. : alk. paper)
    1. Recreation—Dictionaries.   2. Leisure—Dictionaries.
I. Title.   II. Series.
GV11.S57   1990
790'.03—dc20   89–78447

British Library Cataloguing in Publication Data is available.

Library of Congress Catalog Card Number: 89–78447
ISBN: 0–313–25262–9
ISSN: 0730–3335

First published in 1990

Greenwood Press, 88 Post Road West, Westport, CT 06881
An imprint of Greenwood Publishing Group, Inc.

Printed in the United States of America

∞

The paper used in this book complies with the
Permanent Paper Standard issued by the National
Information Standards Organization (Z39.48–1984).

10   9   8   7   6   5   4   3   2   1

Contents

Series Foreword

In all disciplines, scholars seek to understand and explain the subject matter in their area of specialization. The object of their activity is to produce a body of knowledge about specific fields of inquiry. As they achieve an understanding of their subject, scholars publish the results of their interpretations (that is, their research findings) in the form of explanations. Explanation, then, can be said to organize and communicate understanding. When reduced to agreed-upon theoretical principles, the explanations that emerge from this process of organizing understanding are called concepts.

Concepts serve many functions. They help us identify topics that we think about, help classify these topics into related sets, help relate them to specific times and places, and provide us with definitions. Someone has observed that without concepts, "man could hardly be said to think."

Like knowledge itself, the meanings of concepts are fluid. From the moment an authority introduces one into a discipline's vocabulary and gives it specific significance, that concept has the potential to acquire a variety of meanings. As new understandings develop in a discipline, inevitably the concepts change.

Although this pattern in the formation of the meaning of concepts is widely recognized, few dictionaries—certainly none in a consistent manner—trace the path a concept takes as it becomes embedded in a research topic's literature.

This dictionary makes accessible brief, authoritative discussions of major concepts in recreation and leisure studies. Like all other concept dictionaries in this series, entries uniformly consist of four parts.

The first briefly defines a concept's current meaning and/or meanings. The second locates a concept's origins in the vocabulary of recreation and leisure studies and, paragraph by paragraph, traces to the present how its various meanings developed. The third cites fully all references discussed in the preceding part.

For needs not met by information in parts one through three, the fourth part provides sources of additional information for further investigation about the concept. Primarily these additional information sources consist of references for extensive literature reviews, major articles, and other specific discussions considered essential to a comprehensive understanding of the concept.

Entries in this dictionary are deliberately designed to meet different levels of needs. Among the four parts of each entry, the first is perhaps characteristic of what we associate with most specialized, or "subject field," dictionaries. When you need only to learn the current meaning of a concept, you can confine your use of the dictionary to this part of an entry.

Other, more comprehensive research needs are met in parts two and three of each entry. In these parts, you can "tune in," so to speak, at the level of discussion of the concept you wish, and then proceed to the level of understanding that meets your particular needs. Parts two and three of each entry make up this dictionary's major contributions. That is, each entry's second and third part add, uniquely, a significant feature about how meanings of concepts develop and evolve. This feature has heretofore only been included in a few reference works, and if they occur at all it's more by accident than design. Yet, when we consider how desirable these characteristics of dictionaries are, we can only wonder why, in the past, these characteristics have not been featured in subject-field dictionaries.

Finally, as a departure point for more intense investigation, the last part of each entry gives suggestions you need to explore the discussions in the literature of specific concepts to whatever detail required.

Raymond G. McInnis

Preface

This dictionary is a map of the new world of recreation and leisure studies. Although university departments devoted to the study of recreation and leisure have been around for over a half century, there has never been a comprehensive concept dictionary written for the field. The volume in your hands is a modest attempt to fill this gap.

Like all maps, this "verbal" map simplifies and abstracts a complex reality. Certain features are highlighted, while others are merely suggested. Still others are ignored. Of equal importance to identifying key features is noting their relationships. You will find in the discussion of each concept links between that concept and others listed in the dictionary. This is indicated by using CAPITAL LETTERS for the term cross-referenced. The discussions are generally organized chronologically, emphasizing the evolution of the term and its interpretation or application. I have usually selected only one preferred definition for each concept (although two or three definitions are given for a few concepts). Even though I have emphasized one definition you will find a discussion of alternative definitions where relevant. Numerous references and suggestions for further reading will allow you to pursue any topic in more detail.

The concepts included here may be grouped into four broad, overlapping categories. First, there are elemental concepts—those ideas that form the intellectual bedrock of the field. Elemental concepts include "fun," "play," "environment," and, of course, "recreation" and "leisure." Second, there are theoretical concepts. These are scholarly models or interpretations of the patterns and processes seen in recreation and leisure. Examples include "agon," "conspicuous consumption," and "perceived freedom."

Research or methodological concepts make up the third category. These represent the conceptual tools used to analyze various phenomena. "Gravity model," "product life cycle," and "time budgets" are typical of these. Professional concepts are the final category. These represent some of the basic ideas inherent in the service side of the field. Professional concepts include "advocacy," "community development," and "carrying capacity."

The selection of the concepts was an involved process. I consulted with colleagues, examined index of books and journals, and—to some extent—allowed myself to be drawn on to identify certain concepts by the logical relationships and insights that emerged from the definition of more basic concepts. I believe the final selection represents the key idea of our field. Additional concepts are imbedded with the highlighted concepts. For example, "autotelic behavior" is included under "intrinsic motivation"; "distance decay" is described under "gravity model." Nonetheless, time and space limitations forced the omission of some concepts. Among the more obvious omissions are broad professional terms such as "management," "planning," and "marketing." If there is sufficient demand for a second edition of the dictionary, these omissions might be filled.

I received generous gifts of time, insight, and criticism from many colleagues. These include (in alphabetical order): Barbara Brown, Linda Caldwell, Paul Eagles, George Francis, Wendy Frisby, Don Getz, Adrienne Gilbert, Bob Graham, Lloyd Heywood, Ron Johnson, Leslie June, Roberta Kay, Ron McCarville, Roger Mannell, Bruce Mitchell, Bryan Smale, Daniel Stynes, Carlton Van Doren, and Jiri Zuzanek. And I want to thank Elfi Barnett who typed and retyped every word in this volume. If I have overlooked anyone—my sincere apologies. It was not due to ingratitude but to acute mental failure at the conclusion of this four-year labor of love.

Any errors of omission, commission, or interpretation are mine alone. If confronted by evidence of mistakes, I plan to follow the example of Samuel Johnson, lexicographer of the first modern English language dictionary in 1755. When challenged to explain why he incorrectly defined "pastern" as the "knee" of a horse, he could only answer, "Ignorance, madam, pure ignorance."

A

ACCESSIBILITY. 1. The characteristics of a recreation resource, facility, or program that make it available to potential users. 2. A measure of the degree to which a recreation resource, facility, or program is available to potential users.

The idea of accessibility is closely related to concerns over the quality of life and the provision of recreation services. At a superficial level, the greater the degree of accessibility to desired services, the better the quality of life. Quality of life, of course, depends on many other factors besides just accessibility. Everything else being equal, though, greater rather than lesser accessibility to services and RESOURCES provides greater satisfaction to individuals.

Accessibility is an issue of concern in THERAPEUTIC RECREATION and recreation planning. In the context of therapeutic recreation, accessibility is based on the principles of NORMALIZATION and the DEINSTITUTIONALIZATION movement (Wolfensberger, 1972). Recreationists interested in these specializations usually identify two types of accessibility: (1) program and (2) physical (Mace, 1980). In each case the goal is to reduce BARRIERS to a recreation resource so that both able-bodied and disabled individuals may use it. Reduction in barriers may be accomplished either in the original design of a program or facility or through modifications to existing programs or facilities.

Three separate issues are addressed to ensure appropriate levels of accessibility. The first is physical design. The provision of ramps, curb cuts, wider doors, elevators, and nonskid surfaces are examples of improvements in physical designs. Such modifications are, of course, specific to facilities and sites; improvements in accessibility can also be achieved through the use of individualized physical equipment. Examples of this type of equipment include electronic aids for seeing, speaking, and hearing. Decoders for closed captioning on television have also been developed. There is even some experimental work on computer-controlled gait simulators for paraplegics. These have the effect of improving accessibility by providing personalized aids for the individual.

A second issue associated with improving accessibility is that of policy decisions. Accessibility to some sites can be increased by certain management or policy actions. A restauranteur, for example, may admit Seeing Eye dogs in a dining establishment where animals are normally prohibited. A PARK manager may open a trail to motorized wheelchairs that had been previously closed to motorized vehicles.

The third area of concern is that of personnel resources. Sometimes improvements in accessibility require the provision of sign language interpreters, aides to help with registration forms, or drivers for vans and buses.

The current practice and implementation of accessibility principles was mandated in the United States by two major federal acts. Public Law 90–480, the Architectural Barriers Act of 1968, requires that any building receiving federal funds for construction or leasing be made "accessible" in accordance with the terms of Section A117.1 of the American National STANDARDS Institute (ANSI). The ANSI guidelines regarding accessibility were first formulated in 1941 and updated in 1971 and again in 1980. Although no ANSI guidelines have been established expressly for recreational facilities, they do exist for many general facilities such as walkways, doorways, and washrooms.

The second major federal law regarding accessibility in the United States is Public Law 93–112, the Rehabilitation Act of 1973. Whereas PL 90–480 applies to facilities, PL 93–112 sets out guidelines for accessibility to federally supported programs and services.

One question occasionally raised in connection with accessibility is the possibility of providing separate but equal facilities and programs for disabled individuals (Mace, 1980). Such a strategy is generally considered contrary to the intent (if not the letter) of existing accessibility legislation. It remains, however, a difficult issue in some circumstances. Some recreation facilities offer, by their very nature, limited accessibility. These include caves, WILDERNESS areas, certain historic properties, and some highly specialized and potentially dangerous facilities such as large power dams. It can be argued that modifications to permit easy accessibility to all visitors regardless of ability is either practically impossible or, if technically feasible, would destroy the essential qualities of the facility. In such cases provision of audiovisual INTERPRETATION services may be an acceptable alternative.

With respect to recreation planning, accessibility refers to the proximity of recreation resources to a potential user population. It may be measured either in terms of the supply of resources, such as acres of parkland or number of campsites, surrounding a given population center or in terms of the total population within a certain distance of a given recreation resource. Three general types of accessibility may be estimated regardless of the particular perspective (site specific or population specific) by the planner. These three types are (1) point accessibility, (2) linear accessibility, and (3) areal accessibility.

Point accessibility applies to the distribution of resources around a discrete population center or the distribution of a population around a discrete recreation facility. In either case, one assumes that the center of facility can be represented by a dimensionless point on a map. One then maps and counts the total number of people (or facilities) within a given distance of a facility (or population center). This type of measure is closely related to the concept of SERVICE AREAS. Alternatively, one can estimate the average distance between each user or group of users and the nearest facility. Relative accessibility for different users can be determined by comparing these mean distances. Kenneth Mladenka and Kim Hill (1977) provide an illustration of the application of point accessibility in their assessment of the distribution of parks and libraries in Houston, Texas. They found that higher income neighborhoods had greater accessibility (smaller distances) to libraries while lower income neighborhoods had greater accessibility to city parks. Accessibility was measured by determining the mean distance from five randomly selected points within each census tract sampled and the nearest library and city park.

Another measure of point accessibility has been defined by John Wright, William Braithwaite, and Richard Forster (1976). Their measure, known as the normal relative accessibility (NRA), is an index that quantitatively describes the degree of accessibility a given residence has to a particular open space facility:

$$\text{NRA} = 100 \times e^{-(d/r)^2}$$

Where r = range or extent of service area of facility
d = distance between the residence and the facility
e = natural logarithm base, approximately 2.718

The values of NRA are interpreted through the following table:

NRA	Relative Accessibility
80–100%	Excellent
60–79	Good
40–59	Fair
20–39	Poor
0–19	Very Poor

Linear accessibility is a less common form of accessibility measurement. One of the first planners to introduce it to recreation analysis was Allan Patmore (1971) in his study of accessibility in NATIONAL PARKS. In one instance, Patmore mapped lines parallel to and 1 mile on either side of the major highways in Yellowstone National Park. He then reviewed the availability of sites and attractions within these corridors of travel as well as the percentage of park area that fell outside these corridors. His findings were compared to national park developments in Wales to identify certain important political and social differences in park design, usage, and accessibility of park attractions between the United States and Great Britain.

Linear accessibility can also be measured in terms of travel time. All those locations surrounding a population center within, perhaps, 15, 30, 45, and 60 minutes could be plotted and delineated by isochrones. Isochrones typically extend outward from population centers along major highways, reflecting the greater ease of travel associated with highways, and shrink back toward the population centers in areas served only by secondary roads.

Areal accessibility is also known as regional potential. This is the most complex of the types of accessibility described here. It reflects the interaction of DEMAND for recreation with the supply of recreation resources over a large REGION. Regional potential is usually expressed in the form of a contour map. Peaks are associated with a combination of abundant supply and low demand while the valleys on the map reflect areas of high demand and low supply. The elevations on the map are a function of areal variations in the capacity of various recreation facilities, the total number of those facilities, the distance between each facility and each population center, and the spatial distribution and size of these centers. John Ross and Gordon Ewing (1976) mapped the recreation potential for the Windsor, Ontario, to Quebec City, Quebec, corridor in Canada. The highest potentials were located in the vicinity of large provincial and national parks while the lowest potentials were found around large urban areas with limited outdoor recreation sites in the immediate vicinity.

The measurement of accessibility is often an early step in the total evaluation of the adequacy of recreation resources. The level of accessibility a planner measures is ultimately a function of prevailing technology and social conditions. Changes in the available transportation technology, the cost of travel, the freedom of travel, and various psychological, political, or perceptual barriers can be as important in limiting accessibility as shortages in physical supply.

REFERENCES

Mace, Ron. 1980. "Facilities and Equipment/Program accessibility." In *Focus on Research: Recreation for Disabled Individuals,* 131–137. Washington, D.C: Regional Rehabilitation Institute on Attitudinal, Legal, and Leisure Barriers, George Washington University. A general discussion of the legal issues and principles of accessibility for disabled people.

Mladenka, Kenneth R., and Hill, Kim Q. 1977. "The Distribution of Benefits in an Urban Environmental: Parks and Libraries in Houston." *Urban Affairs Quarterly* 13(1): 73–94. Presents a measure of accessibility to urban recreation services and compares levels of accessibility between social groups.

Patmore, J. Allan. 1971. "Routeways and Recreation." In *Recreational Geography,* ed. Patrick Lavery, 70–96. London: David and Charles. Contains a description of linear accessibility measures in national parks.

Ross, John H. C., and Ewing, Gordon O. 1976. "Potential Functions in Evaluating the

Need for Recreation Facilities." In *Canadian Outdoor Recreation Demand Study*. *Vol. 2, The Technical Notes*. Ottawa, Ont.: Parks Canada. Defines and illustrates the use of a regional potential measure in recreation planning.

Wolfensberger, Wolf. 1972. *The Principle of Normalization in Human Services*. Toronto: Leonard Crainford. A basic reference on the concept of normalization, deinstitutionalization, and accessibility.

Wright, John R., Braithwaite, William M., and Forster, Richard R. 1976. *Planning for Urban Recreational Open Space: Towards Community-Specific Standards*. Guelph, Ont.: University of Guelph, Centre for Resources Development. A comprehensive examination of the use of standards in recreation planning; defines and illustrates the use of an index of accessibility: normal relative accessibility.

SOURCES OF ADDITIONAL INFORMATION

One of the first formal expressions of the normalization principle was by Bengt Nirje, in "The Normalization Principle: Implications and Comments" (*Journal of Mental Subnormality* 16: 62–70, 1970). A review of some perceptual barriers to improved accessibility is found in Diane Richler's "Access to Community Resources: The Invisible Barriers to Integration," (*Journal of Leisurability* 11:4–11, 1984). A discussion of the practical implications of American legislation in terms of a specific leisure facility, museums, may be found in Larry Molloy's "The Case for Accessibility" (*Museum News* 56:15–17, 1977). More extensive information on this topic may be found in Alice P. Kenney, *Access to the Past* (Nashville, TN: American Association for State and Local History, 1980).

An overview of some measures of accessibility in recreation planning and recreation trip forecasting are found in Stephen L. J. Smith, *Recreation Geography* (London: Longman Group, 1983, 45–63, 137–138. Sture Öberg evaluates several different measures of physical accessibility from a geographic perspective in his *Methods of Describing Physical Access to Supply Points* (Lund Series in Geography, ser. B, no. 43, Lund, Sweden: Department of Geography, Royal University of Lund, 1976). One particular measure of accessibility developed by geographers is based on network theory and is referred to simply as the accessibility index. A description of the index and its uses can be found in Robert Hammond and Patrick McCullagh, *Quantitative Techniques in Geography*. (Oxford: Clarendon Press, 1974, 43–46).

ACTIVITY ANALYSIS. A procedure for identifying and examining the essential characteristics of a RECREATION activity, GAME, or SPORT to determine the behavioral requirements needed for enjoyable and successful participation.

The development of activity analysis as a strategy in THERAPEUTIC RECREATION and ADAPTIVE PROGRAMMING is often associated with Elliott Avedon (1974). Avedon argued that there were ten elements common to all activities: (1) the purpose or aim of the activity, (2) the procedures or actions involved in participation, (3) the rules of play, (4) the number of participants, (5) the roles or functions of each participant, (6) the results or payoff of the activity, (7) the skills required for play (including physical, cognitive, and emotional), (8) social interaction patterns, (9) the physical setting of the activity, and (10) the required equipment. Clear indication and understanding of each of these ten elements is necessary, according to Avedon, if a therapeutic recreationist was to successfully involve a client in participation in a given activity. One of the responsibilities of the therapeutic recreationist, therefore, was to either ensure that the potential participant could meet the requirements implicit in the ten elements or to modify the elements so that the requirements could be met.

Application and refinement of the concept of activity analysis was encouraged by the requirements of Medicaid and Medicare, Public Law 94–142, and various hospital and institutional accreditation standards. Generally, these have required the development of individualized treatment plans or individualized education plans, which are closely related to the concept of activity analysis. Carol Peterson (1976), building on the work of Avedon, helped to formalize and articulate in greater detail the concept of activity analysis in keeping with the requirements of these health care and social service initiatives.

She noted that activity analysis may be approached from two different perspectives: instructional and rehabilitative. In the first perspective the therapeutic recreationist focuses on identifying the skills and behaviors an individual must be able to master as part of participation in an activity, such as the need for eye-foot coordination in soccer. In the second, the recreationist identifies those activities that provide the opportunities to practice certain skills the individual needs to develop to overcome certain disabilities or limitations. The use of some forms of card games, for example, can promote verbal exchange between two players and might promote social interaction and verbal exchange skills.

Peterson's model identifies four sets of activity behaviors: (1) physical, (2) cognitive, (3) emotional, and (4) social. An activity analysis requires identification of the specific characteristics of an activity in each of these categories. Physical characteristics include the specific parts of the body employed in participation, the types of movement required, necessary forms of coordination, strength, endurance, and flexibility. Cognitive skills include the ability to remember and follow formal rules, to concentrate on the action, spatial awareness of a board or field position of players or game pieces, and the planning of game strategy.

Emotional characteristics are typically expressed in terms of six basic emotions: joy, guilt, pain, anger, fear, and frustration. Unlike the physical and cognitive skills required for successful participation, the emotional behaviors refer to likely emotional responses that may be encountered as a result of play. Contact sports may arouse anger; intense COMPETITION in a team sport might engender feelings of guilt in one player if he perceives himself as "letting the team down."

Social skills include the ability to cooperate on a team, to compete while constrained by formal rules and in socially acceptable forms, engage in appropriate levels of physical contact or to refrain from physical contact if such contact is inappropriate, and to participate in a form that is either appropriate to the participant's sex role or to function appropriately in a sex-integrated environment.

Activity analysis provides the therapeutic recreationist with a better understanding of the benefits of participation in specific activities, which can be used to enhance the effectiveness of a rehabilitation program. It also provides a detailed appreciation of the complexity of an activity and its appropriateness for an individual or group with specific needs or limitations. Such information can be a valuable aid in providing a base for modifying activities to permit or encourage participation in activities that may provide therapeutic benefits for the participants.

REFERENCES

Avedon, Elliott M. 1974. *Therapeutic Recreation Service*. Englewood Cliffs, NJ: Prentice Hall. Chapter 11 is one of the first articulations of the concept of activity analysis.
Peterson, Carol Ann. 1976. "State of the Art: Activity Analysis." In *Leisure Activity Participation and Handicapped Populations: Assessment of Research Needs*, 81–93. Arlington, VA: National Recreation and Park Association. Extends and elaborates earlier ideas of activity analysis and presents a model for application.

SOURCES OF ADDITIONAL INFORMATION

Gerald S. O'Morrow and Ronald P. Reynolds, *Therapeutic Recreation: A Helping Profession* 3rd edition (Englewood Cliffs, NJ: Prentice Hall, 1989) offers some personal perspectives on the place of activity analysis in recreation leadership and in the development of therapeutic recreation. Dan Kennedy, David Austin, and Ralph Smith, in Chapter 6 of *Special Recreation: Opportunities for Persons with Disabilities* (Philadelphia: Saunders College, 1986) contains a good overview on activity analysis as part of program planning. Other overviews of the concept may be found in Marcia Jean Carter, Glen Van Andel, and Gary Robb, *Therapeutic Recreation: A Practical Approach* (St. Louis, MO: Time Mirror/Mosby, 1985); Claudine Sherrill, *Adapted Physical Education and Recreation: A Multidisciplinary Approach* (Dubuque, IA: William C. Brown, 1986); and Jay Shivers and Hollis Fait, *Special Recreational Services: Therapeutic and Applied* (Philadelphia: Lea & Febiger, 1985).

ACTIVITY CLUSTERS. Groupings of recreation activities on the basis of shared characteristics, usually participation patterns or perceptual qualities.

The concept of activity clusters developed as a response to the need to find a sense of order and simplicity in the great diversity of free TIME activities available to people. The development of such clusters also contributes to LEISURE EDUCATION and recreation planning. For example, a recreation planner or programmer could compare the activities available at a particular facility with the total range of activities as summarized by a listing of activity clusters to identify any gaps in RECREATION offerings. A leisure taxonomy based on activity clusters could also be used by leisure counselors to introduce and describe possible activities to their clients.

Activity clusters contain specific activities that offer similar recreational experiences or benefits to participants. This key characteristic of activity clusters also could be of benefit to park managers in certain situations. If snowmobiling, for example, were considered to be an inappropriate activity in a PARK, a park manager could use activity clusters to identify if there were the potential for the SUBSTITUTION of activities that would be acceptable to both the park's visitors and management.

The earliest attempts to formally articulate a classification scheme for activity clusters include Max Kaplan (1960: 268–270) and Sebastian de Grazia (1962: 168–169). Kaplan suggested five categories: social activities, GAMES and SPORT, art, movement, and immobility. De Grazia proposed classifying all activities in terms of six polar dimensions: active/passive, participant/spectator, solitary/social, indoor/outdoor, in-home/outside-home, and sedentary/on-the-feet. Neither of these two classification systems, however, was based on an objective analysis of leisure activity patterns. They were based, instead, on the intuition of the authors. Despite the potential weaknesses in classification schemes developed subjectively, these early proposals encouraged subsequent quantitative analysis to define new and objective schemes.

One of the first quantitative studies of activity clusters was that by Charles Proctor (1962) for the Outdoor Recreation Resources Review Commission. Proctor's research design became the archetype for one of the two major methodological designs associated with the study of activity clusters: "participation analysis." His basic approach was to conduct a survey of a sample of recreationists to determine the frequency of participation in a series of preselected activities. The participation data were then factor analyzed to identify a series of dimensions composed on several activities. He next examined the names of these activities and suggested a label for each cluster of activities associated with each dimension.

Proctor obtained his data through a nationwide recreation survey of over 3600 Americans. Fifteen outdoor activities were specified and frequency of participation data obtained for every respondent. Factor analysis of the data produced four clusters that Proctor identified as water recreation, passive recreation, backwoods recreation, and active recreation.

Subsequent authors have followed the same general design with variations in the emphasis of each study. Doyle Bishop (1970), for example, analyzed the participation patterns of adults in four communities to examine the stability of the factor structure in different social settings. Peter Witt (1971) carried out a related analysis in those communities, focusing on teenage patterns. Other authors have experimented with different statistical procedures. Thomas Burton (1971) compared factor analysis with cluster analysis; David Duncan (1978) compared R-mode factor analysis (in which the activities are analyzed) with Q-mode factor analysis (in which the participants are factor analyzed). Robert Ditton, Thomas Goodale, and Per Johnsen (1975) studied the effect of including environmental variables with participation variables in their factor analysis. Lawrence Allen, Maureen Donnelly, and Donald Warder (1984) examined the stability of activity clusters between seasons.

The "participation analysis group" has been criticized by other researchers on several grounds. One of the more important of these criticisms is based on the interpretation of the activities that form the clusters defined through factor analysis. These clusters are based on groups of activities participated in by the same individuals. As noted previously, this feature is often used as the basis for determining the substitutability of activities. Participation in two different activities by the same group may not indicate substitutability however, but rather COMPLEMENTARITY. For example, picnicking and attending outdoor events appeared together in one of Proctor's clusters. Their joint appearance reflects the fact that people who attend outdoor events also tend to picnic while attending those events. The two activities are not substitutable—they are linked together in the same experience.

Another criticism of the use of participation data is that participation rates do not necessarily reflect just the preferences of individuals for different activities; they also reflect the opportunities for participation. Low participation in some activity by a particular group may be due either to a lack of interest or a lack of opportunity (BARRIER). To overcome this problem, other researchers have suggested using attitudinal or perceptual data as the basis for defining clusters. This approach may be described as an "attitudinal analysis." Among the first researchers to experiment with attitudinal data were John Neulinger and Miranda Breit (1969). Neulinger and Breit examined the attitudes of a group of respondents toward selected activities, regardless of their own history of participation. The attitudinal scores were then factor analyzed and interpreted in much the same way as with the "participation analysis" group.

Variations in this design included analysis of the perceived similarities of activities, rather than any attitudinal or psychological valuations of activities (Ritchie, 1975). Boris Becker (1976) examined the use of nonmetric multidimensional scaling as an alternative to factor analysis of attitudinal information. Howard Tinsley and Thomas Johnson (1984) experimented with the use of diverse leisure and avocational activities to develop a leisure activity taxonomy for counseling purposes.

The "attitude analysis group" has not avoided criticism, either. One of the most basic objections to the use of psychological data in defining activity clusters is the question whether one can reliably infer a direct linkage between attitudinal measures and actual behavioral patterns (Becker, 1976). Recently, several researchers have begun to systematically examine the strengths and weaknesses of both research designs. They have collected data on both participation and perception for the same activities from the same groups of respondents. Their results suggest that similar, but not identical, activity clusters are defined with either approach (Chase and Cheek, 1979; Gudykunst et al. 1981; Allen and Buchanan, 1982).

Although most of the work conducted on defining activity clusters is associated with either the "participation analysis" or the "attitude analysis" groups, other authors have proposed activity clusters based on other schemes.

Kaplan (1975:292–313) presented a subjectively defined LEISURE typology based on social psychological concepts. This typology, credited to Joffre Dumazdier by Kaplan, is based on five major divisions of activities: physical activities, intellectual activities, artistic activities, sociable activities, and practical activities. Each of these is then divided into two subcategories. The resulting ten clusters were used as the classification system for a seven-nations TIME BUDGET study of leisure behavior.

Michael and Holly Chubb (1981:281) describe an activity classification system based on the types of RESOURCE used in association with different activities. This system begins by dividing activities according to whether they are associated with dry land, water and shorelines, or ice and snow. Each category is then divided into intensive use activities and extensive use activities. Several of these divisions are further subdivided according to more specific criteria. For example, extensive dry land activities are divided into three subcategories based on whether the use of a machine is essential, the use of an animal is essential, or neither. This type of classification can be of value for planning resource allocation and use, but is less relevant when the focus is not on resource planning. Furthermore, some activities may involve combinations of resources not easily accounted by this system.

One of the basic tasks of any science is to develop classification systems or taxonomies of the phenomena studied. This is part of the continuing interest in the development of activity clusters. It is likely, however, that no single system appropriate for all uses will ever be developed. Unlike biological species or chemical compounds, there are probably no naturally occurring activity groupings. Any grouping is ultimately based on the needs and perspectives of the researcher or theoretician developing the system.

REFERENCES

Allen, Lawrence, and Buchanan, Thomas. 1982. "Techniques for Comparing Leisure Classification Systems." *Journal of Leisure Research* 14:307–322. Describes methods for comparing factor structures based on participation data with those based on perceptual data.

Allen, Lawrence, Donnelly, Maureen, and Warder, Donald. 1984. "The Stability of Leisure Factor Structures Across Time." *Leisure Sciences* 6:221–238. Compares activity groups in summer and fall and notes significant changes.

Becker, Boris. 1976. "Perceived Similarities among Recreational Activities." *Journal of Leisure Research* 8:112–122. Tests the usefulness of nonmetric multidimensional scaling as a clustering tool for activity groups.

Bishop, Doyle. 1970. "Stability of the Factor Structure of Leisure Behavior: Analysis of Four Communities." *Journal of Leisure Research* 2:160–170. Identifies four stable structures for adults in different communities.

Burton, Thomas. 1971. "Identification of Recreation Types through Cluster Analysis." *Society and Leisure* 1:47–65. Examines the use of cluster analysis as an alternative to factor analysis in defining activity groups.

Chase, David, and Cheek, Neil. 1979. "Activity Preferences and Participation: Conclusions from a Factor Analytic Study." *Journal of Leisure Research* 11:92–101. Compares the factor structures of attitudinal and participation data.

Chubb, Michael, and Chubb, Holly. 1981. *One Third of our Time?* New York: Wiley. An introductory, near-encyclopedic text for recreation studies.

de Grazia, Sebastian. 1962. *Of Time, Work, and Leisure*. New York: Doubleday Anchor. An important and influential work on social aspects of leisure: proposes an intuitive system for classifying activities.

Ditton, Robert, Goodale, Thomas, and Johnsen, Per. 1975. "A Cluster Analysis of Activity, Frequency, and Environmental Variables to Identify Water-Based Recreation Types." *Journal of Leisure Research* 7:282–295. Expands traditional approaches by including environmental variables in defining activity clusters.

Duncan, David. 1978. "Leisure Types: Factor Analyses of Leisure Profiles." *Journal of Leisure Research* 10:113–115. Compares R-mode and Q-mode factor analyses as procedures for defining activity clusters.

Gudykunst, William, Morra, John, Kantor, Wayne, and Parker, Howard. 1981. "Dimensions of Leisure Activities: A Factor Analytic Study in New England." *Journal of Leisure Research* 13:28–42. Examines the relationship between factor structures based on participation data and those based on perceptual data.

Kaplan, Max. 1960. *Leisure in America: A Social Inquiry*. New York: Doubleday. One of the first proposals to create an activity classification scheme.

Kaplan, Max. 1975. *Leisure: Theory and Policy*. New York: Wiley. The author presents a sociological theory of leisure, with particular attention to public policy issues.

Neulinger, John, and Breit, Miranda. 1969. "Attitude Dimensions of Leisure." *Journal of Leisure Research* 1:255–261. An early examination of attitudinal data as a base for defining activity clusters.

Proctor, Charles. 1962. "Appendix A," In *National Recreation Survey, ORRRC Study*, report 19. Washington, DC: U.S. Government Printing Office. Analysis of a major national survey of recreation patterns, including an early example of factor analysis of participation data.

Ritchie, Brent. 1975. "On the Derivation of Leisure Activity Types: A Perceptual Mapping Approach." *Journal of Leisure Research* 7:128–140. Uses similarity data rather than attitudinal data to identify substitutable activities.

Tinsley, Howard, and Johnson, Thomas. 1984. "A Preliminary Taxonomy of Leisure Activities." *Journal of Leisure Research* 16:234–244. Study based on psychological benefits perceived by participants.

Witt, Peter. 1971. "Factor Structure of Leisure Behavior for High School Age Youth in Three Communities." *Journal of Leisure Research* 3(4):213–219. Identifies five stable activity clusters for teenagers in different communities.

SOURCES OF ADDITIONAL INFORMATION

A review of the substitutability concept and its role in the development of activity clusters is provided in John Hendee and Rabel Burdge, "The Substitutability Concept: Implications for Recreation Research Management" (*Journal of Leisure Research* 6:155–162, 1974). A comment on this article appears in Jay Beaman, "Comments on the Paper 'The Substitutability Concept' by Hendee and Burdge" (*Journal of Leisure Research* 7:146–152, 1975). Another example of the definition of activity clusters may be found in Gerald Romsa, "A Method for Deriving Outdoor Recreational Activity Packages" (*Journal of*

Leisure Research 5:34–46, 1973). A further comparison of two methods, factor analysis and multidimensional scaling, used for defining activity clusters is Morris Holbrook, "Representing Patterns of Association among Leisure Activities: A Comparison of Two Techniques" (*Journal of Leisure Research* 12:242–256, 1980).

ADAPTIVE PROGRAMMING. The modification of recreation activities, GAMES, or SPORTS on the basis of an explicit recognition of the needs and abilities of potential participants and ACTIVITY ANALYSIS to permit or encourage participation in an activity by individuals who would otherwise be discouraged or prohibited from participating without these modifications.

Adaptive programming, a type of RECREATION PROGRAMMING, is an important strategy for professionals working in general recreation or in THERAPEUTIC RECREATION. Although adaptive programming is usually associated with physically or mentally disabled individuals, adaptive programming can also be applied to other populations such as children or seniors. The purpose of adaptation is to promote participation among individuals or groups who would otherwise probably not participate due to the demands of the activities. These demands include the need for physical strength or endurance or the ability to perform complex motor skills. The modifications to be made in activities are based on an activity analysis, or the identification of the inherent characteristics of the activity. Such characteristics are classified as psychomotor skills, cognitive behaviors, and affective behaviors. Potential modifications are then identified so that the target population or clientele group can successfully participate in the activity.

The modifications can include

1. Changes in the size and shape of the playing area. For example, the size of a baseball diamond can be reduced to accommodate limited physical mobility.
2. Changes in the time required or permitted for play. The length of time associated with a hockey or football game might be shortened or the time permitted to carry out certain plays might be lengthened.
3. Specialized or modified equipment might be developed. Lighter bowling balls, lower basketball hoops, and smaller soccer nets are a few examples.
4. Changes in the size or structure of a team. More players might be added to a volleyball team, for example, to permit greater coverage of the floor.
5. Changes in the rules. This can include the breaking of complex motor skills into a series of simpler skills, such as the use of a tee for baseball as opposed to a pitcher or the use of a pitcher from a player's own team instead of from the competitor's team.

There may also be changes in the emphasis of COMPETITION or in the structure of teams to encourage full participation by all participants (and to discourage the emergence of a "star" to the detriment of the other players). These types of modification, however, are usually reserved for those settings in which the benefits of participation in a noncompetitive environment outweigh the benefits and pleasures associated with competitive play. This form of activity modification thus is closely associated with the concept of new games. Many adapted sports and games are still highly competitive. In fact, one objective of adaptive programming is to permit participation in a game by individuals with widely varying levels of ability. Some forms of adaptive programming could thus be employed to permit relatively equal competition between able-bodied and disabled participants or between mentally retarded and non-mentally retarded participants.

An important principle in adaptive programming is to retain the essential quality of the activity being modified. Wheelchair basketball, for example, is still essentially basketball but with certain rule changes to permit play in wheelchairs. Another principle is to not overadapt activities. Some element of challenge or competition should be retained to simulate interest and enjoyment in the successful playing of the game. Virginia Frye and Martha Peters (1972) suggested the following guidelines for modifying activities: (1) analyze the essential physical, social, cognitive, and perceptual skills required for participation; (2) identify those qualities that make the activity enjoyable; (3) analyze the nature and limitations of the needs of the potential participants; and (4) identify those modifications that will make the activity available and enjoyable to the target population.

Adaptive programming is an especially useful practice in institutions, rehabilitation facilities, hospitals, transitional programs, and MAINSTREAMING programs in the community.

REFERENCE

Frye, Mary Virginia, and Peters, Martha. 1972. *Therapeutic Recreation: Its Theory, Philosophy, and Practice*. Harrisburg, PA: Stackpole Books. A fundamental reference on the practice of adaptive programming.

SOURCES OF ADDITIONAL INFORMATION

Four additional sources for useful information on the principles and practices of adaptive programming are David Auxter and Jean Pyfer, *Principles and Methods of Adapted Physical Education and Recreation* (St. Louis, MO: Mosby, 1985); Scout Lee Gunn and Carol Ann Peterson, *Therapeutic Recreation: Program Design, Principles, and Procedures,* Englewood Cliffs, NJ: Prentice Hall, 1984); Richard Kraus, *Therapeutic Recreation Service, Principles, and Practices* (New York: CBS College, 1983); and Dan Kennedy, David Austin, and Ralph Smith, *Special Recreation: Opportunities for Persons with Disabilities* (New York: Saunders College, 1987).

ADVOCACY. 1. The representation of the interests of a client who is unable to represent himself effectively to those empowered to make decisions affecting the client. 2. The promotion of a cause or principle.

The concept of advocacy is ancient. Its roots can be traced back to the Roman republic when *advocati,* volunteer patricians skilled in oratory and points of law, were called to appear before a magistrate to provide advice on particular cases and legal precedents. These volunteers eventually became paid professionals in the Roman Empire. After the fall of Rome, the concept of advocacy continued in the Catholic Church as part of the practice of canon law (which is derived largely from Roman civil law). Advocates are still used in various tribunals in the Catholic Church, such as canonization proceedings or hearings on petitions for marriage annulments and to ensure the soundness of evidence and the orthodoxy of procedures and arguments. (The notion of the "devil's advocate" comes from the actions of an advocate attempting to find flaws in a case for canonization.)

Advocates were also used in the Early and High Middle Ages to help settle certain criminal and civil disputes including trial by combat involving members of the nobility or conflicting claims over a widow's inheritance. In the first case, it was generally considered inappropriate to expect members of nobility to endanger themselves in a physical fight to settle a dispute, so they found advocates who believed their claims and were willing to fight for them. In the case of widows, women were normally not granted legal standing to permit them to speak before a magistrate; to protect her rights, a woman had to enlist the services of an advocate.

The modern profession of attorney, a special type of advocate, began in the late twelfth century as a learned individual who was called to provide expert advice in judicial proceedings and to assist a jury in interpreting evidence and arguments (comparable to the Roman *advocatus*). By the early fourteenth century, this form of advocacy had evolved into service representing one client's special interests in a trial or hearing.

The basic notion behind advocacy (in the first definition, above) is that a person is better able to win a claim if he enlists the aid of another individual who is more skilled in pressing a claim. This skill typically involves ability and experience as a negotiator; oratorical talents; political influence; or specialized knowledge of the law, political change processes, or bureaucratic procedures.

Advocacy in the realm of social and recreation services became organized in the mid–1960s as one aspect of the COMMUNITY DEVELOPMENT movement. An oft-cited reference in the history of "citizen advocacy" (as advocacy in social services is sometimes known) is Paul Davidoff (1965). Davidoff introduced advocacy planning as a strategy for obtaining justice for minority groups and the poor. He saw advocacy planning as a way of ensuring the fuller participation of these groups in the power structure of a pluralistic society. Advocacy planners see their activity, therefore, as a dialectical or confrontational process.

Alan Ross and Robert Guskin (1971) identify several different roles the advocacy planner must fill as part of this dialectical process. The first, and sometimes most difficult, is that of community organizer. This stage requires that the advocate and a large number of individuals agree on the nature of the problem to be attacked, reach a consensus on specific objectives and basic values, develop the conviction that joint action with the advocate is more likely to produce results than each individual working alone, and—as a result—begin to think of themselves as a group rather than as a collection of individuals.

Once a community group has been organized, the advocate begins to function as a liaison-spokesman for the group—attempting to translate the anger and anguish the group may feel into acceptable and productive bureaucratic responses. This process may also involve work as a negotiator between factions of the community group as well as between the community group and the power structure they are attacking. Finally, the advocate may be required to collect and interpret data to support the group's case.

Ross and Guskin (1971) also identify several value orientations shared by advocate planners. They observe a strong emotional and personal orientation toward the individuals or groups advocates represent. The relationship between the advocate and the client is not simply professional, but personal and political. Ross and Guskin believe that ideally there is no distinction between the planner's beliefs and values and his work as an advocate. Advocate planners also strongly believe in the right of the client group to have greater political power and to participate in decision making that affects their lives. This greater participation is often seen not just as a means to an end, but a legitimate end in itself. The third value orientation is an emphasis on early victories. While long-term political changes may be desirable, successful advocacy planning must provide early successes. These successes help to cement the commitment of the client group to the advocacy process (and to the advocate). Finally, advocacy planners have a fundamental suspicion of existing bureaucracies and power structures. This mistrust fuels their belief that confrontation and risk taking are the only methods that will produce desirable social changes.

The concept of advocacy in recreation and leisure studies is also an important one in THERAPEUTIC RECREATION, particularly with respect to MAINSTREAMING and NORMALIZATION. The roles and values of therapeutic recreation advocates are generally similar to those of advocacy planners, although some authors label as "advocates" individuals in roles that do not conform to the traditional sense of advocate. For example, Wolf Wolfensberger (1973) identifies foster parents, adoptive parents, and friends as "advocacy roles." To the extent that a foster or adoptive parent might function as a legal guardian, representing the child to protect the child's health or property rights, this role would conform to the meaning of "advocacy." Wolfensberger's usage, however, is less persuasive when the foster or adoptive parent exercise power to make decisions for the child. The role of an advocate is, by denotation, limited to representing or speaking for the interests of another person—not the exercise of power over that person. Wolfensberger fails to explain why he does not see advocacy as a part of the role of natural parents, although they may act in ways that are consistent with the role of an advocate. Wolfensberger also fails to convincingly explain how advocacy is a role of friends. The support and psychological benefits provided by friends would seem to be justifiable in their own right, without artificially recasting these in the mold of advocacy.

Other authors have identified still other forms of advocacy. John Lord (1981), for example, suggests: (1) self, (2) individual, (3) agency, and (4) group advocacy. *Self-advocacy* refers to an individual representing his own needs before an agency. While such actions occur regularly, Lord does not offer an explanation of why this represents a form of advocacy. Again, the role of an advocate is, by denotation, to represent another individual. Self-advocacy would appear to be self-contradictory.

Individual advocacy conforms closely to the traditional concepts of an advocate. This is the relationship between an attorney and a client, or a legal guardian and a ward with respect to legal proceedings. A parent may also act as an advocate for his or her child when seeking special programs or assistance from a department of recreation or a school board.

Agency advocacy is represented by advocacy planning—a form that Lord criticizes. He believes that "the nature of professionalism is generally contradictory to the concept of advocacy" because professionals are "trained to 'know best' and to 'do for' their clients" (Lord, 1981:10). Furthermore, he expresses his belief that planners are trained to "emphasize success over support and nurturing" (Lord, 1981:10). Lord appears to misunderstand the origins and nature of advocacy. An individual has traditionally turned to an advocate precisely because the advocate was better trained or more able to "do for" the client and thus more likely to be successful in the struggle for justice.

Group advocacy (also known as collective advocacy) involves the organization of a group to promote the interests of a larger group. For example, a group of parents and knowledgeable, concerned citizens might organize to promote the integration of physically disabled children into a community recreation program or to provide enrichment programs for gifted children.

The second definition (above) of advocacy is also used in the RECREATION field. In this context, an advocate functions essentially as a lobbyist, a patron, or an apologist for a cause such as greater support for the arts or the protection of WILDERNESS. Advocacy, in this sense, is less frequently discussed in recreation and leisure studies than is the first definition.

Advocacy, as the act of representing a client, has been the subject of numerous authors in therapeutic recreation and is an important tool in normalization and mainstreaming. The literature on advocacy, however, suffers from several problems. Authors often appear uncertain whether advocacy is an end in itself or a means to a larger end. Perhaps as a result of this, there is widespread carelessness and imprecision in the use of the term. Some authors also remain vague or imprecise about the makeup of the client group they purport to represent. The advocates of advocacy tend to write only descriptions of their interpretation of the concept or testimonies supporting their personal beliefs. They have largely failed to conduct any objective and careful analyses of the dynamics of groups in communities, the organization and functioning of power in political and community systems, the relative merits of individual versus collective action, and the role of special interest groups and pressure groups in a democracy. Considering the potentially vital role advocacy groups can play in society, it is unfortunate that the subject has not been more competently examined.

REFERENCES

Davidoff, Paul. 1965. "Advocacy Planning and Pluralism in Planning." *Journal of the American Institute of Planners* 32:331–337. Considered to be one of the first articles on the concept of citizen advocacy.

Guskin, Alan E., and Ross, Robert. 1971. "Advocacy and Democracy: The Long View." *American Journal of Orthopsychiatry* 41:43–57. Examines role of advocacy in context of community organization; considers the roles and values of advocacy planners.

Lord, John. 1981. "Advocacy for Change." *Leisurability* 8(1):4–12. An essay promoting advocacy as a tool for social change; outlines several different forms advocacy may take.

Wolfensberger, Wolf. 1973. "Citizen Advocacy for the Handicapped, Impaired and Disadvantaged: An Overview." In *Citizen Advocacy and Protective Services for the Impaired and Handicapped*, ed. Wolf Wolfensberger and Helen Zahua, 7–34. Toronto: National Institute on Mental Retardation. Outlines a strategy for advocacy and support services for disabled individuals.

SOURCES FOR ADDITIONAL INFORMATION

A representative collection of articles on advocacy for individuals with special needs is Wolf Wolfensberger and Helen Zahua's collection, *Citizen Advocacy and Protective Services for the Impaired and Handicapped* (Toronto: National Institute on Mental Retardation, 1973). The *Journal of Leisurability* also contains essays supporting the concept of advocacy. Typical examples in that journal include Jill Owen, "Advocacy with Instead of for Consumers" (8 no. 3:19–22, 1981); Patricia Anthony, "The Recreation Practitioner as Change Agent and Advocate for Disabled Persons" (12 no. 1:19–23, 1985); and Barbara Fraser, "The Role of Voluntary Advocate Associations in Facilitating Leisure Services" (10 no. 3:25–31, 1983). Peggy Hutchison and John Lord promote advocacy in *Recreation Integration* (Ottawa: Leisurability Publications, 1981, see 85–93).

AGON. 1. The spirit of competition in games; most closely associated with SPORT contests, but it can apply to other games of skill such as chess. 2. The struggle for personal supremacy.

Roger Caillois (1961) used agon to refer to one of the four basic types of GAME. Agon applies to games based on skill as opposed to those based on chance (ALEA), imitation (MIMICRY), or vertigo (ILINX). The experience of agon in a game implies more than just COMPETITION between two opponents. It also presupposes a period of sustained attention to the game by the players, a period of training prior to the contest, sustained effort and discipline aimed at victory, and the conscious desire for victory. As a game quality, agon also implies the existence of agreed-on rules and limits governing the time, place, and actions of the competitors.

John Loy and Graham Hesketh (1984) elaborated the concept of agon by distinguishing it from the "agon motif." To Loy and Hesketh, agon refers to a specific contest or system of contests whereas the agon motif refers to the processes and products of agon. The motif is composed of three themes: (1) a pronounced spirit of rivalry, (2) a stress on individualism, and (3) an emphasis on pursuing fame and glory through competition. The agon motif is most explicitly expressed in contemporary Western cultures through sporting contests, but it has been the dominant cultural theme in earlier civilizations. Military aristocracies such as Sparta in ancient Greece, the chivalric order of medieval Europe, and the Samurai of feudal Japan were essentially agonistic societies. The agon motif was also dominant in tribal warrior cultures such as the Zulus in pre-Empire South Africa, the Bedouin of the Middle East, and some Plains Indians of North America.

Loy and Hesketh suggest that the agon motif may be viewed as a four-step quest for superiority: (1) becoming the best through training, (2) testing the best through repeated competition, (3) beating the best in a decisive agonal contest, and (4) being the best and accepting public fame and recognition.

Loy and Hesketh have also coined other terms related to the basic concept of agon: *agonomics*, the study of agonetic behavior; *agonetic behavior*, the display of physical ability through competition; and *agonetic activities*, specific occurrences of PLAY activities used for competition.

REFERENCES

Caillois, Roger. 1961. *Man, Play and Games*. New York: The Free Press. An important study of the sociology of games. Chapter 2 describes in detail Caillois's classification of games.

Loy, John W., and Hesketh, Graham L. 1984. "The Agon Motif: A Prolegomenon for the Study of Agonetic Behavior." In *Contribution of Sociology to the Study of Sport*, ed. K. Olin, 31–50. Jyvaskyla, Finland: University of Jyvaskyla Press. A good review of the concept of agon in sport and anthropology. Presents a detailed model of the concept of agon motif and its social structure.

SOURCES OF ADDITIONAL INFORMATION

Another view of agon motif may be found in W. R. Morford and S. J. Clark, "The Agon Motif" (*Exercise and Sport Sciences Review* 4:169–193, 1976). Studies that have examined agon as a cultural theme include A. W. Gouldner, *Enter Plato* (New York: Basic Books, 1965); M. G. McNamee, *Honor and the Epic Hero* (New York: Holt, Rinehart & Winston, 1960); I. Nitobe, *Bushido* (Burbank, CA: Ohara, 1979); N. K. Sidhanta, *The Heroic Age of India* (London: Kegan, 1929); P. G. Turvill, *The Heroic Age of Scandinavia* (London: Hutchinson, 1951); and M. Vale, *War and Chivalry* (Athens: University of Georgia Press, 1981).

ALEA. 1. The spirit of chance in game-playing. 2. Games of chance or gambling.

Alea is a Latin word referring to gambling GAMES, especially dice. Roger Caillois (1961) adopted the term to refer to one of four basic types of game. In this sense it stands in contrast to AGON (games of skill), MIMICRY (games based on imitation), and ILINX (games based on vertigo or dizziness).

The spirit of alea implies an emphasis on destiny or fate and, in contrast, a denial of merit or skill as basis of COMPETITION. In its pure form, it has the effect of making all players absolutely equal and passive. Although alea is usually seen as diametrically opposite to agon, Caillois suggests an underlying similarity. Both provide a type of equality often denied in real life. In the case of agon, all players have the same possibility of proving their superiority; in the case of alea, all players have the equal probability of being favored by chance. In either event, the players are able to escape a complex real world and enter, temporarily, an artificial world with simple and consistent rules for everyone.

REFERENCES

Caillois, Roger. 1961. *Man, Play and Games*. New York: The Free Press. An important study of the sociology of games. Chapter 2 describes in detail Caillois's classification of games.

SOURCES OF ADDITIONAL INFORMATION

Some of Roger Caillois's ideas about play and games were first explored in his *Man and the Sacred* (New York: The Free Press, 1959). A classic study of play and games, which also greatly influenced Caillois, is Johan Huizinga, *Homo Ludens* (Boston: Beacon Press, 1955). Another philosophically directed study of games and the spirit of game playing is David Miller, *Gods and Games* (New York: Harper Colophon, 1973).

ALLOCENTRIC. A category of TOURISTS characterized by a strong interest in discovery, uniqueness, challenge, and experimentation.

Allocentric tourists were first described by that name by Stanley Plog (1974) as part of a study into the motivations and BARRIERS that affected the DEMAND for airline travel. Plog suggested that tourists could be placed on a spectrum ranging from allocentrics to PSYCHOCENTRICS, with intermediate groups known as near-allocentric, mid-centric, and near-psychocentric.

The primary characteristics of allocentrics include

1. A preference for exotic, little-known destinations.
2. Enjoyment of a sense of discovery and of "being first."
3. A high level of activity and involvement in various events or opportunities in their travel.
4. Prefer adequate to good-quality accommodation and food services, but avoid franchise or "touristy" operations.
5. Enjoy meeting and dealing with people from different cultures.
6. Prefer flexibility in tour planning and enjoy doing much of travel arranging independently.

Plog further elaborates his allocentric/psychocentric model by suggesting that tourism destinations begin by being discovered by allocentrics. The allocentrics' enthusiasm for a new destination slowly builds the destination's reputation, so that it becomes an increasingly fashionable destination. This leads, then, to an expansion of the TOURISM infrastructure and services at that destination, accompanied by a growth in the number of near-allocentrics that are attracted. As the destination matures, with increasing commercialization and mass marketing, the area draws more mid-centrics and some near-psychocentrics. The allocentrics, who discovered the destination, lose interest or are repelled by the changing nature of the destination and have moved on to other areas. The process of evolution continues until the destination area appeals only to the most conservative and cautious tourists, the psychocentrics.

Plog also suggests that the distribution of tourists belonging to each category on the allocentric/psychocentric spectrum approximates a normal distribution. Only a small percentage of tourists are either allocentrics or psychocentrics, while a greater number are near-allocentrics and near-psychocentrics. The largest number are mid-centrics. This aspect of Plog's model resembles Everett Rogers's (1962) model of product adoption (a version of the PRODUCT LIFE CYCLE). Rogers's model is also approximately a normal curve with a small number of "innovators" and "laggards" on the extreme ends. "Early adopters," "early majority," and "late majority" make up the central part of the curve. One of the differences between Plog's curve and Rogers's curve is that Plog's model is explicitly based on personality or psychological traits while Rogers's model is based only on the timing of product adoption. Conceptually, though, Rogers's adoption groups are shaped by psychological differences; and, as noted, Plog's psychological groupings imply the relative order of adoption of destinations as tourism products. Both models, therefore, may be viewed as different aspects of a more general model of commodity adoption and diffusion.

REFERENCES

Plog, Stanley C. 1974. "Why Destination Areas Rise and Fall in Popularity." *Cornell Hotel and Restaurant Administration Quarterly* 14 (4):13–16. The original reference for the concept of allocentrics.
Rogers, Everett M. 1962. *Diffusion and Innovation*. New York: Free Press of Glencoe. Presents a model of consumers based on a continuum running from "innovators" to "laggards."

SOURCES OF ADDITIONAL INFORMATION

Robert McIntosh and Charles Goeldner provide a good discussion of the concept in *Tourism: Principles, Practices, Philosophies* (New York: Wiley, 1986, 135–141). Stephen Smith describes an empirical test of Plog's model in "A Test of Plog's Allocentric/ Psychocentric Model: Evidence from Seven Nations" (*Journal of Travel Research*, 1990, 27 [4]:40–42).

AMATEUR. One who participates, for intrinsic satisfaction only, in an activity
(1) that requires a level of skill, education, or practice and (2) in which others
participate for financial reward.

The term *amateur* is derived from *amator,* "one who loves." An amateur is
popularly defined, therefore, to be one who engages in an activity for the love
of it. Such simplicity, however, presents problems. It may be seen as implying
that paid workers never experience INTRINSIC MOTIVATION in their work. This,
of course, is not always true. Amateur is also employed as a value judgment,
as in "amateurish effort." Robert Stebbins (1977, 1982) has examined the
concept of amateurism and related terms including hobbyism and VOLUNTEERISM
as forms of a growing phenomenon he labels "serious leisure." As part of his
review, Stebbins notes that the popular uses of amateur are imprecise, vague,
and sometimes contradictory. Given his perception that serious LEISURE is increasingly important as a social phenomenon, he proposes a more sophisticated
and precise conceptualization of amateur.

The starting point for Stebbins's definition is his notion of a "professional–
amateur–public system" (P–A–P). The basic idea behind P–A–P is that amateurs
exist only for those activities for which there are also professionals—as the term
is usually applied by occupation sociologists such as Edward Gross (1958) and
Talcott Parsons (1968). Furthermore, these activities are conducted for clients
or "publics" who are external audiences, consumers, or arbiters of performance.

Activities for which amateurs exist have a number of important qualities that
distinguish them from other leisure activities. Besides their association with
professionals and a public, amateur activities occasionally involve the need for
the participant to persevere through times of drudgery, tedium, or unpleasant
effort. The activities are not always relaxing, enjoyable, or FUN. Second, the
amateur finds the motivation to persevere through difficult times in the durable
benefits the activity provides, such as SELF-ACTUALIZATION and the opportunity
for social interaction. Third, amateur activities require the application of special
effort based on knowledge, training, or skill. The acquisition and application of
this knowledge, training, or skill produces over time a sense of "career," the
fourth quality. Because of these four qualities, amateurs share a subculture or
ethos governing their values, beliefs, and performance standards (the fifth
quality). Finally, amateurs identify strongly with their activity and take pride in
it, sometimes to the point of obsessiveness.

Amateurs, to Stebbins, differ from hobbyists in that hobbyists exist outside
the P–A–P system. Basically, a hobbyist is a recreationist engaged in an activity for which there is no comparable profession (they may be paid workers,
but they are not true professionals). Furthermore, while amateurism implies a
strict lack of financial reward, hobbyists may earn income from their activity,
as long as the dominant motivation is intrinsic and the money does not represent a major source of the person's income. Volunteers may participate in
activities in which paid professionals also work, but are distinguished from

amateurs in that their activities are undertaken largely for the benefit of others. Although volunteer activity may provide a strong sense of satisfaction through service, volunteer activities are usually seen as essentially unpaid work rather than recreation.

Stebbins's work represents some of the most sophisticated analysis of the phenomenon of amateurism in leisure available. His conceptualization of amateurism, however, still has some problems. The lexicographic linkage of amateurs with professionals is one. While the requirement that the term *amateur* be used in connection with those activities for which other people are paid makes sense and conforms to conventional understanding (one speaks of amateur athletes but not amateur television viewers), the restriction to professional-caliber activities seems too narrow. For example, sports do not meet the criteria established by many authors for professions. There is no formal accreditation process for SPORT that is linked to educational attainment, as in the case of medicine, dentistry, law, theology, and (more recently) recreation and parks (Schein, 1972). Thus under Stebbins's criteria, there could be no amateur athletes. As another example, the author classifies all collectors as hobbyists on the grounds that there are no professional collectors. While one could debate whether stamp and coin dealers could be called collectors (they would normally not be considered professional in any event), many museum curators and directors of museum acquisitions are clearly both collectors and professionals. The point here is not to debate specific examples but to highlight the practical difficulty of applying Stebbins's restrictive criteria in classifying people as either amateurs, hobbyists, or professionals.

Stebbins's conceptualization of amateur also has hints of elitism. For example, he does not believe children can be true amateurs, and that only those adults who are committed, proficient, skilled, knowledgeable, and regular participants in their activity should be considered as amateurs. The rest of the participants are defined as "novices" or "dabblers." While there is reason for expecting some minimum level of education or skill for participation in certain activities— one cannot be an amateur conchologist without being able to identify a variety of shells and mollusks or be an amateur pianist without knowing how to play the piano. The level of skill necessary to be able to play many amateur sports, for example, is not that great. Many of Stebbins's ideas about amateurism are useful, however, and have been incorporated into the above definition.

While Stebbins's conceptualization hints at elitism and invidious distinctions, definitions of amateur in the athletic world have been much more blatant. Concern over the definition of amateur status in athletics date from nineteenth-century England, especially in the context of rowing (although other sports officials struggle with the same issue). Typical of early definitions of an amateur in the latter half of the 1800s is the "Putney Definition" (developed at a conference of rowing club representatives held at Putney, England, in 1878). An amateur was defined as:

an officer of Her Majesty's Army, or Navy, or Civil Service, a member of the Liberal Professions, or of the Universities or Public Schools, or of any established boat or rowing club not containing mechanics or professionals [and] who must not have competed in any COMPETITION for either a stake or money, or entrance-fee, or with or against a professional for any prize; nor even taught, pursued, or assisted in the pursuit of athletic exercises of any kind as a means of a livelihood, nor have ever been employed in or about boats, or in manual labour; nor be a mechanic, artisan, or labourer. (Eric Halladay, 1987)

The ostensible purpose of these rules was to exclude individuals who, by virtue of their employment in manual occupations, would be much stronger than gentlemen who did not work daily with their muscles (women, of any class, were systematically excluded from athletic competition). In application, however, the distinction excluded any man involved in menial duty, whether or not physically demanding. A perception of the real intent of such rules, held then as well as now, was that they were designed to limit club membership to the traditional aristocracy (Pleket, 1978). H. W. Pleket attributed this desire to the growing fear of the older, land-based aristocracy that they were losing social and political influence to an increasing number of nouveaux riches, particularly industrialists and entrepreneurs. Because club membership may have been seen as a way of controlling access to the network of influential social leaders.

Public indignation with class-based definitions of amateurs grew through the 1880s and 1890s. Social-class clauses slowly disappeared in response to this pressure, finally being eradicated in 1937 when the Amateur Rowing Association removed the last such clause from their eligibility criteria.

Although the equation, "amateurs = gentlemen," has long been discredited, another aspect of the nineteenth-century definitions—abstention from any financial reward for athletic participation—has been much more durable. It has also generated even more controversy. A leading proponent of the ideal of amateurism uncontaminated by money was Pierre de Coubertin, the founder of the modern Olympic Games. The original eligibility rules for Olympic athletes not only excluded anyone who had received money for participation in his sport, but for participation in any sport. De Coubertin's Olympic ideals, however, were without historical validity. Although extensive documents from the ancient Olympic Games are scarce, Pleket (1978) summarized much of the evidence available surrounding the social class and prize structures of Olympic participants. He noted that although most of the best athletes would not have considered themselves professionals in the sense that they depend on sport for their livelihood— because they were independently wealthy—they expected and received substantial financial rewards for Olympic victories.

The expectation among athletes that they should be paid for their successes has existed in many other cultures throughout history. As recently as the first half of the nineteenth century, English amateurs expected that they should be entitled to money for an athletic victory. Halladay (1987:40), for example, quotes a comment by an amateur oarsman in one British Club who refused to "row a gentleman of the Dolphin Club for 'nothing at all' " on the grounds that "public interest in the river as well as the spirit of racing would soon cease if all contests were for honour only.''

De Coubertin's philosophy, nonetheless, exercised a strong emotional appeal for many sports officials for the better part of the twentieth century. Avery Brundage, a key figure in the International Olympic Committee until his death in 1975, was one of the strongest forces in perpetuating de Coubertin's rigid and simplistic notion of amateurism. This notion, however, was subject to a steady increase in pressure for change, starting with at least the 1936 Olympics when Jesse Owens was disqualified after a series of dramatic track and field victories in the Berlin Olympics on the grounds that he had once played semi-professional baseball. The pressure was stepped up in 1952 with the entrance of the Soviet Union and the German Democratic Republic (GDR) in the Olympics with the resulting challenge to the concept of amateurism so profound that it has not yet been adequately resolved.

The challenge created by the participation of these two countries is that the distinction between amateur and professional sport is meaningless in a communist economy. Responding to complaints from Western sports officials, sports officials from the Soviet Union and the GDR argued that their athletes were treated the same as all other citizens. Housing, food, transportation, medical treatment, and other goods and services are provided by the state to elite athletes, but they are provided to all citizens. Athletes from communist countries do not *earn* their living from sports because they cannot earn their living from sports: they are entitled to their support by virtue of being a citizen in their country. Sports officials in Western countries counter that the top athletes are identified early in their careers and allowed to devote virtually full-time effort year-round, with the possible exception of military duty for a few weeks each year, to their sport while other citizens do hold employment positions. This makes the athletes functionally professionals.

Reet Howell (1978) has suggested calling athletes from communist countries ''state amateurs.'' This suggestion provides a potentially neutral label for the athletes, but it does nothing to resolve the perception of fundamental unfairness in differences in the support state amateurs are able to claim on the basis of their country's political and economic system.

In response to the success of state amateurs in international competition, other countries, both Western as well as Third World, began to develop government-supported mechanisms for their best athletes. These systems do not pay athletes for competition, but do provide support in the form of travel costs, equipment, living expenses, assistance in finding suitable employment, compensation for wages lost due to time taken off for competition, and so on. Different levels of support may be provided on the basis of the relative ranking of the athlete in his or her sport.

Another challenge to Olympic amateurism has come from the growth of professional sports, particularly in the United States, into a multimillion-dollar industry. Some sports organizations and promoters can offer exorbitant contracts as well as opportunities for substantial income from endorsements, appearances, licensing, and promotions. Gambling, legal and illegal, can provide still other sources of income. Only the most naive individual could expect superior amateur athletes to remain totally free during their athletic careers of financial payoffs in some form or other. One need only look at the scandals that have hit many American universities in their amateur varsity athletic programs to appreciate the pressures and temptations inherent in all aspects of elite amateur sport.

The result of these forces, according to John Lucas (1984), is that the International Olympic Committee finally revised its charter in 1983. The revisions included replacement of the word *amateur* by *nonprofessional*. The charter revisions also permitted nonprofessionals, subject to approval by Olympic officials, to earn money from endorsements, public appearances, and other activities in connection with their sport. The only exclusion was the signing of a professional sports contract. Money received from approved activities is put into escrow, but it can be drawn on for liberally defined living expenses.

Even these changes in the concept of amateur have not been enough, however. Tennis was added to the 1984 Los Angeles Olympics as an experimental event, with permission given to allow professional players to compete. This exemption was repeated for the 1988 Seoul Olympics. A limited number of professional hockey players were allowed to join national teams in the 1988 Calgary Olympics. A future exemption is likely to be made for soccer, a sport whose top players compete in the World Cup are routinely excluded because of the issue of amateurism. With more exemptions, pressure will finally rise to the point where any traditional conception of amateur status in future Olympics will be eliminated.

Although the development of "serious leisure" described by Stebbins and the evolution of amateurs in the Olympics to nonprofessionals are contemporary issues, they were anticipated by Johan Huizinga (1955:197) nearly a half-century ago:

Now, with the increasing systematization and regimentation of sport, something of the pure play-quality is inevitably lost. We see this very clearly in the official distinction between amateurs and professional (or "gentlemen and players" as used pointedly to be said). . . . The spirit of the professional is no longer the true play-spirit; it is lacking in spontaneity and carelessness. This affects the amateur too, who begins to suffer from an inferiority complex. Between them they push sport further and further away from the play-sphere proper until it becomes a thing *sui generis:* neither play nor earnest. . . . However important it may be for the players or spectators, it [had become] completely sterile.

REFERENCES

Gross, Edward. 1958. *Work and Society.* New York: Thomas Crowell. An early text on occupational sociology; provides a discussion of the concept of professionalism.

Halladay, Eric. 1987. "Of Pride and Prejudice: The Amateur Question in English

Nineteenth-Century Rowing.'' *International Journal of the History of Sport* 4:39–55. Examines the evolving definition of amateurism in connection with rowing clubs; an excellent historical study of an important aspect of the concept of amateurism as applied in sport.

Howell, Reet. 1978. ''The Western World and Sport: National Government Programs.'' In *Comparative Physical Education and Sport*, ed. Uriel Simri, 176–187. Netanya, Israel: Wingate Institute for Physical Education and Sport. Defines ''state amateur'' and describes various national programs of support for athletes.

Huizinga, Johan. 1955. *Homo Ludens*. Boston: Beacon Press. The classic study of play; includes a critique of the decline of the play element in amateur sport.

Lucas, John. 1984. ''No More Amateurs—Only Nonprofessional Athletes in the Olympic Games.'' *Journal of Physical Education, Recreation, and Dance* 55(2):22–23. A personal essay describing some of the forces that may have led the International Olympic Committee to revise eligibility rules.

Parsons, Talcott. 1968. ''Professions.'' In *International Encyclopedia of the Social Sciences*, Vol. 12, ed. David Sills, 536–547. New York: Crowell, Collier, and Macmillan. A sociological perspective on the concept of professions.

Pleket, H. W. 1978. ''The Ideology of Athleticism.'' In *Sport International Relations*, ed. Benjamin Lowe, David Hanin, and Andrew Strenk, 207–223. Champaign, IL: Stipes. Examines historical conceptions of amateurism in ancient Greece; discusses the problem of professionalism versus amateurism.

Schein, Edgar H. 1972. *Professional Education*. New York: McGraw-Hill. Examines the nature of professions as well as the structure and function of professional education and accreditation systems. Identifies elements common to all professions.

Stebbins, Robert A. 1977. ''The Amateur: Two Sociological Definitions.'' *Pacific Sociological Review* 20:582–606. Develops two ''definitions'' of amateur that are actually complex descriptions of the characteristics of amateurism; the first focuses on the relationship between amateurs, professionals, and ''publics'' while the second addresses attitudes typical of amateurs.

Stebbins, Robert A. 1982. ''Serious Leisure: A Conceptual Statement.'' *Pacific Sociological Review* 25:251–272. Describes concept of ''serious leisure''; relates to phenomena of amateurism, hobbies, and volunteerism.

SOURCES OF ADDITIONAL INFORMATION

Robert Stebbins has probably produced the single greatest opus associated with the study of amateurism in the recreation and leisure field. His works include *Amateurs: On the Margin between Work and Leisure* (Beverly Hills, CA: Sage, 1979); '' 'Amateur' and 'Hobbyist' as Concepts for the Study of Leisure Problems'' (*Social Problems* 27: 412–417, 1980); and ''Science Amators? Rewards and Costs in Amateur Astronomy and Archaeology'' (*Journal of Leisure Research* 13: 289–304, 1981). J. Van Til has written on the concept of volunteerism in ''In Search of Volunteerism'' (*Volunteer Administration*, 12: 8–20, 1979); A. Lauffer and S. Gorodezky have also addressed this topic in *Volunteers* (Beverly Hills, CA: Sage, 1977). A Marxist perspective on amateurism in athletics may be found in Sada Morikawa's ''Amateurism—Yesterday, Today, and Tomorrow'' (*International Review of Sport Sociology* 12(no. 2: 61–68, 1977).

ATTRACTIVITY. A quantitative measure of the ability of a site or destination to draw visitors; normally used in the context of recreation trip modeling.

Attractivity was developed as a concept by recreation trip modelers in the context of forecasting future travel patterns and in explaining historical patterns of recreation site use levels. Many recreation trip models are based on the assumption that there are three basic variables or forces that influence the number of visitors to a particular destination: population characteristics of one or more origins that produce the visitors, the distance between these origins and the destination, and the attractiveness of the destination. The GRAVITY MODEL, one of the first models developed for predicting recreation travel, clearly illustrates this assumption:

$$T_{ij} = \frac{GP_iA_j}{D_{ij}^a}$$

where T_{ij} = number of trips from an origin, i, to destination, j
  P_i = population of origin, i
  A_j = attractivity of destination, j
  D_{ij} = distance between i and j
  a and G = statistically estimated coefficients

The notion of attractivity, however, is not specific to the gravity model but has been included in some form or another as a component in virtually all recreation travel models. Four separate approaches may be used to develop estimates of destination attractivity: (1) simple exogenous, (2) complex exogenous, (3) inferred exogenous, and (4) endogenous.

The simple exogenous approach involves the selection of one or more site attributes directly related to a hypothetical or theoretical model of the ability of a PARK or other destination to attract visitors. One common type of attribute is the capacity of a site, measured as park acreage (Grubb and Goodwin, 1968) or the number of campsites (Wennergren and Nielsen, 1970). The simple exogenous approach can also utilize multiple variables, entered separately into a model such as James Mak and James Moncur's (1980) study of the length of stay of visitors to each of four separate Hawaiian islands. Noting that most tourists to Hawaii were interested in a sunny, warm climate and well-developed resort facilities, they used two independent measures of attractiveness: average annual rainfall and the number of hotel rooms per 1000 acres for each island.

The complex exogenous approach also uses two or more variables as a measure of a site's attractiveness. The difference is that the complex approach combines the variables into a single, composite index while the simple approach keeps the variables separate. Jack Ellis and Carlton Van Doren's (1966) forecasting work for campers at Michigan State parks combined recreation RESOURCE variables related to climate, vegetation, topography, recreational facilities, and water resources using a combinatory rule arbitrarily developed by the authors. On a community scale, Lisle Mitchell (1968) combines a variety of urban park and playground features, such as the availability of picnic areas, tennis courts, and wading pools into a measure of the attractiveness of urban parks.

A characteristic common to both the simple and exogenous approaches is that both require the researcher to specify the site variables to be studied and the methods by which these are to be measured, weighted, or combined. An alternative to this direct specification of site variables by the researcher is the inferred exogenous approach. A researcher using this design typically begins with an observed measure of preference, such as a direct ranking of sites or through a comparison of levels of use. One early example of this approach was W. R. Catton's (1966) use of the psychological method of paired comparisons to the rank of the relative attractiveness of a selection of U.S. NATIONAL PARK sites using a sample of National Park officials. Although Catton was able to develop a consistent and reliable measure of site attractiveness, he did not relate the ranked preferences to site features nor did he address the question of whether the site preferences of the officials matched the preferences of the park visitors those officials are expected to serve.

John Ross (1973) used an innovative modification of the paired comparisons method to derive measures of the attractiveness of parks in Canada. Noting that some travelers would bypass a park close to their home to visit a more distant park, Ross argued the explanation for this behavior was that the more distant park must be more attractive. Although one might not know exactly what features made the more distant park more attractive, it is possible to determine relative attractiveness levels of a system of parks serving the same population by examining patterns of origin-destination flows. Ross applied his method, sometimes known as the revealed preference method, to the Saskatchewan provincial park system as well as to two urban parks systems in Sarnia and London, Ontario. Gordon Ewing and Terrance Kulka (1979) have also used the revealed preference method in their study of the attractiveness of Vermont ski resorts. Ewing and Kulka, however, discovered that this method is vulnerable to bias introduced by certain spatial patterns of parks and origins. The authors compared the results of the revealed preference method with the results of a more standard survey method (the stated preference method) in which the skiers were asked directly to rank ski resorts by order of preference. Although somewhat more costly and difficult to administer, the stated preference approach was preferred because the results appeared to be more stable and reliable.

Hym Kwai Cheung (1972) inferred the attractiveness of parks for day-use in Saskatchewan by examining a combination of the popularity of different recreational activities, the facilities available at individual parks to support those activities, and the overall attendance at those parks. His formulation of attractivity, which was developed as part of a forecasting model, was not as accurate as it might have been because he relied on a national survey of recreation activity participation rates, which missed some significant provincial variations. Cheung was also unable to separate the effects of distance from attractivity in examining attendance levels, nor could he correct for variations in activity participation rates due to variations in the supply of facilities as opposed to variations in the DEMAND for those activities. Despite these limitations, his model has been cited by many authors as providing the stimulus for similar formulations of inferred attractivity, including Robert Lloyd and Robert Ader (1980) who successfully applied a Cheung-type model to predicting market shares of urban parks in Columbia, South Carolina.

Still another example of an inferred exogenous approach is Winston Husbands's (1982) analysis of the TOURISM attractiveness of a sample of eleven countries. Using a statistical technique called nonmetric multidimensional scaling and the pattern of TOURIST flows between each of the eleven countries, Husbands derived a measure of the relative attractiveness of each country. He then compared the attractiveness ranking to a measure of the relative economic development of each country. He concluded that tourist attractivity was directly related to the extent that each country was "central" or "peripheral" in the core of economically developed nations. The more peripheral a country, the more attractive it was to tourists from developed or central countries. He then interpreted this finding in light of a Marxist view of international relations. Stephen Smith (1985), however, observed that Husbands had failed to account for differences in population sizes among his study countries and for the distance between pairs of origin and destination countries. After adjusting Husbands's data for these omissions, Smith showed that the resulting level of attractiveness of each country was more closely tied to the country's climate than level of economic development: the warmer and sunnier the country, the more popular the country was as a destination.

The fourth approach to estimating attractiveness, the endogenous approach, treats attractivity as a coefficient in a travel forecasting model to be statistically estimated rather than as a variable to be defined prior to its use in a model. In the context of the gravity model (above) attractivity (A_j) would be combined with the coefficient G to form a single new coefficient rather than be defined as a separate variable. Frank Cesario (1973, 1974, 1975) was one of the first researchers to develop and use this approach. A typical Cesario model would use observed levels of recreational travel between specific origin-destination pairs and a measure of travel cost as the primary exogenous variables. The attractiveness of the various destinations and the emissiveness of the origins were statistically calibrated as model coefficients. M. J. Baxter (1979) has also explored this approach, arguing that attractivity and distance effects should be combined into a single, composite coefficient whose values may be inferred from observed travel patterns.

REFERENCES

Baxter, M. J. 1979. "The Interpretation of the Distance and Attractiveness Components in Models of Recreation Trips." *Geographical Analysis* 11:322–315. Argues that attractivity should be combined with distance and that the combined component should be estimated statistically, rather than exogenously.

Catton, W. R. 1966. *From Animistic to Naturalistic Sociology.* New York: McGraw-Hill. Uses a National Park example to illustrate method of paired comparisons for assessing site attractiveness.

Cesario, Frank J. 1973. "A Generalized Trip Distribution Model." *Journal of Regional Science* 13:233–248. Defines attractivity as a statistical coefficient; introduces concept of emissivity as measure of the propensity of origins to generate travel.

Cesario, Frank J. 1974. "More on the Generalized Trip Distribution Model." *Journal of Regional Science* 14:389–397. Extends discussion of his 1973 model.

Cesario, Frank J. 1975. "A New Method for Analyzing Outdoor Recreation Trip Data." *Journal of Leisure Research* 7:200–215. Another look at his 1973 model for a recreation and leisure studies audience.

Cheung, Hym Kwai. 1972. "A Day-Use Visitation Model." *Journal of Leisure Research* 4:139–156. Describes a forecasting model for day-use parks that includes an attractivity variable inferred from activity preferences and participation rates as well as on-site facility inventories.

Ellis, Jack B., and Van Doren, Carlton, S. 1966. "A Comparative Evaluation of Gravity and Systems Theory Models for Statewide Recreational Flows." *Journal of Regional Science* 6:57–70. An important, early article in recreation trip modeling; defines attractivity as a composite of natural and man-made site features in Michigan State parks.

Ewing, Gordon O., and Kulka, Terrance. 1979. "Revealed and Stated Preference Analysis of Ski Resort Attractiveness." *Leisure Sciences* 2:249–276. Applies Ross's "revealed preference approach" to Vermont ski resorts; discovers a potential bias problem in the revealed preference model and suggests possible solutions.

Grubb, H. W., and Goodwin, J. T. 1968. *Economic Evaluation of Water-Oriented Recreation,* report 84. Austin, TX: Texas Water Development Board. Describes a method for assessing recreational value of reservoirs; includes a proposed measure of park attractiveness based on capacity.

Husbands, Winston. 1983. "Tourist Space and Touristic Attraction: An Analysis of the Destination Choices of European Travelers." *Leisure Sciences* 5:289–307. Develops an inferred definition of attractivity from the pattern of origin-destination flows; offers a Marxist interpretation of attractivity.

Lloyd, Robert, and Ader, Robert. 1980. "A Cognitive Model for Recreational Spatial Behavior in an Urban Area." *Southeastern Geographer* 20:145–159. Applies Cheung's attractivity method (with modifications) to parks in Columbia, South Carolina.

Mak, James, and Moncur, James. 1980. "The Choice of Journey Destinations and Lengths of Stay: A Micro Analysis." *The Review of Regional Studies* 10(2):38–47. Develops an explanatory model for length of stay at each of four Hawaiian islands on basis of tourists' characteristics and site features.

Mitchell, Lisle S. 1968. "The Facility Index as a Measure of Attendance at Recreation Sites." *Professional Geographer* 20:276–278. Proposes a simple index for combining selected urban park facilities into a single attractiveness measure.

Ross, John H. C. 1973. *A Measure of Site Attraction,* occasional paper no. 2. Ottawa, Ont.: Environment Canada. Uses a modification of paired comparison methodology (revealed preference approach) to analyze patterns of travel to near versus distant parks to derive a measure of park attractiveness.

Smith, Stephen L. J. 1985. "Comments on 'Tourist Space and Touristic Attraction.' "

Leisure Sciences 7:65–71. Critiques Husbands's definition of tourist attractiveness and offers a reanalysis and reinterpretation of results.

Wennergren, E. Boyd, and Nielsen, Darwin B. 1970. "Probability Estimates of Recreation Demands." *Journal of Leisure Research* 2:112–122. Describes a stochastic park use prediction model; attractiveness is defined in terms of park capacity.

SOURCES OF ADDITIONAL INFORMATION

The literature on attractivity is intimately tied up with recreational travel modeling. Most recreational travel models include some attempt to define attractivity in a way consistent with the researcher's hypotheses about the forces affecting travel. Some examples of attractivity measurement that illustrate the approaches described here include Frank Cesario's "A Combined Trip Generation and Trip Distribution Model" (*Transportation Science* 9:211–223; 1975) and George Peterson, John Dwyer, and Alexander Darragh's "A Behavioral Urban Recreation Site Choice Model" (*Leisure Sciences* 6:61–82, 1983). Two variables that can significantly influence the perceived level of attractiveness of a site are crowding (user density) and familiarity. The role of potential user familiarity with a site in influencing site use is described by Daniel Stynes, "The Role of Information in Recreation Site Selection," in *Forest and River Recreation: Research Update* (misc. pub. 18, Minneapolis: University of Minnesota Agricultural Experiment Station, 1972). Crowding has been addressed by many researchers, including Jerry Vaske, Maureen Donnelly, and Thomas Heberlein in "Perceptions of Crowding and Resource Quality by Early and More Recent Visitors" (*Leisure Sciences* 3:367–382, 1980) and Robert Ditton, Anthony Fedler, and Alan Graefe, "Factors Contributing to Perceptions of Recreational Crowding" (*Leisure Sciences* 5:273–288; 1983).

AUTHENTICITY. 1. A desired experience or benefit associated with visits to certain types of TOURISM destinations. It is presumed to be the result of an encounter with true, uncommercialized, everyday life in a CULTURE different than that of the visitor. Authenticity is contrasted with the experience associated with visits to commercial attractions, staged events, reconstructed sites, theme parks, resorts, or other artificial or contrived manifestations of culture, entertainment, or life. 2. The genuineness of a tourist environment.

The quality of authenticity is a difficult one to measure or to describe precisely, but it is nonetheless a frequent topic of commentators on modern tourism. While similar to ATTRACTIVITY in that both are based on qualities that attract visitors to destinations, authenticity refers more to the subjective experience enjoyed by the TOURIST on-site while attractivity refers to some objective quality of the site that can be measured or inferred by a researcher.

One common view of the nature and significance of authenticity may be found in the passage from Daniel Boorstin (1964): "One of the most ancient motives for travel, when men had any choice about it, was to see the unfamiliar. Man's incurable desire to go someplace else is a testimony to his incurable optimism and insatiable curiosity. We always expect things to be different over there. 'Traveling,' Descartes wrote in the early seventeenth century, 'is almost like conversing with men of other countries.' "

The desire to see the unfamiliar, to enjoy the sense of a different place, to "converse with men of other countries" is one summary of the desire for authenticity. Boorstin and other authors such as Louis Turner and John Ash (1975) lament that this desire has all but disappeared among modern tourists. Tourists now seek, they argue, the familiarity of large hotel chains, the speed and comfort of jet travel, the convenience of organized tours, and the easy understanding of popular guidebooks.

The views of these commentators, though, have been challenged by other authors such as Roy Buck (1977) and Eric Cohen (1979) as being nothing more than travel snobbery. These cynical travel commentators, they retort, are guilty of trivializing an important, legitimate, and personally rewarding social behavior enjoyed by tens of millions of people every year. Furthermore, as Dean MacCannell (1976) suggests, modern tourists actually do seek authenticity but are frequently frustrated in their search.

MacCannell's work is probably the basic reference for the study of authenticity in tourism. Drawing on a qualitative sociological tradition that emphasizes the search for personal meaning—exemplified by the writings of Thorstein Veblen (1953) and David Riesman (1961)—MacCannell develops an argument for the significance of authenticity as a major force behind modern tourist behavior. The success or failure of their search for authenticity, however, is largely determined by the structure of tourism settings. MacCannell's interpretation of the structure of tourism settings is drawn directly from Erving Goffman's (1959) analysis of social establishments and environments. Goffman postulated the existence of a "front stage" and a "back stage" for most social environments: the front stage is a contrived, artificial setting lacking local significance or meaning; the back stage is the ENVIRONMENT in which the locals live and carry out their personal and social affairs in the privacy of their own community or families.

MacCannell adopted Goffman's notion of front and back stage settings and elaborated his model by adding four more stages:

1. Stage I. Goffman's front stage.

2. Stage II. A front stage given some cosmetic work to convey a sense of atmosphere or authenticity.

3. Stage III. A front stage setting rebuilt to resemble a back stage setting.

4. Stage IV. A highly modified back stage that is open to visitors.

5. Stage V. A back stage that has been cleaned up or modified to accommodate occasional visitors.

6. Stage VI. Goffman's back stage.

Although MacCannell presents these six stages as conceptually distinct environments, it is difficult to make empirical distinctions between any two adjacent stages, especially for Stages II through V. These intermediate stages are sometimes grouped together and characterized as (to use MacCannell's phrase), "staged authenticity."

MacCannell's model is based on the hypothesis that tourists enter a destination region typically through a Stage I setting. They desire to penetrate deeper in search of authenticity, but may be blocked for any number of reasons, including intentional actions on the part of the hosts. Buck (1978), for instance, described how the tourism businesses in Lancaster County, Pennsylvania, the site of an Old Order Amish Community that attracts a large number of tourists, keep visitors limited to the first four stages, protecting Amish families from unwanted, closer contacts with outsiders.

Although MacCannell's work on the stages of authenticity is widely quoted in the tourism literature, it has been rarely applied in any objective, quantitative studies. Buck's use of MacCannell's model, for example, did not empirically validate the model but simply borrowed it as a device for presenting his own views of the structure of tourism in an Amish community. In another study, Richard Chalfen (1979) interpreted tourist photography as evidence of their desire to move further back stage in their search for authenticity. Although Chalfen's work is illustrated with a series of anecdotes, his analysis is still primarily intuitive rather than scientific.

Cohen (1979), noting the lack of scientific research either testing the validity of MacCannell's model or extending its applications, has suggested modifications that might stimulate such new work. Because empirical distinctions between Stages II through V are difficult to define reliably, Cohen suggested returning to the two original stages proposed by Goffman. Cohen proposed, furthermore, that the tourist's perception of the tourism settings should also be recognized. The result of these two modifications is a four-cell model of tourist situations:

Tourists' Impressions of Scene:

		Real	Staged
Nature of	Real	A. Authentic and seen as such.	C. Authentic but suspected as faked.
Scene:	Staged	B. Faked but perceived as authentic.	D. Faked setting recognized as such.

Graham Dann (1981) has also argued for the importance of dealing with tourists' perceptions as part of the analysis of authenticity in tourism settings. He suggests that the central issue in authenticity is not simply whether or not a scene encountered by a tourist is real, but how a tourist perceives the setting and whether or not he cares about authenticity.

Dann's point about whether or not tourists care about authenticity raises again the continuing debate in tourism commentary: whether or not tourists seek "real life" in their chosen destinations or if they want artificial settings and staged events. Stanley Plog (1974), in a paper that did not directly address the topic of authenticity as a tourist motivator, proposed a model that is also widely cited by tourism authors. Plog suggested that tourists (and the settings that appeal to them) could be placed on a continuum running from PSYCHOCENTRIC to ALLO-CENTRIC. Psychocentric tourists desire familiarity, security, and predictability in their travel, usually preferring to return to the same comfortable, well-serviced tourism destination year after year. Their opposites, allocentric tourists, seek novelty, challenge, uniqueness, and new experiences. Although the terms are not synonymous, allocentric tourists would likely include those who value authenticity. Dann (1981) concurs that tourists' motivations cover a spectrum of interests that includes the "search for meaning," a phrase that implies a desire for authenticity. As a group, tourists range from (to use Dann's terminology) "alienated cultural dopes" to "modern pilgrims."

As noted previously, most authors who have written on the concept of authenticity and tourist motivational types have not based their conclusions on objective evidence. They have relied, instead, on personal interpretations of anecdotal evidence. Paul Vallee (1987), in one of the few quantitative studies of authenticity, examined the self-reported importance of a series of statements describing a range of potential travel motivations and benefits, including specifically several indicators related to authenticity (e.g., "Desire to experience new and different lifestyles"). Vallee's tentative conclusions are that both the cynical tourism commentators, represented by Boorstin, as well as the more sanguine group, represented by MacCannell, have probably overstated their cases. A significant number of tourists appear to seek authenticity (contrary to Boorstin), but this number is far from a strong majority (contrary to MacCannell). Vallee also found evidence that authenticity as a factor in tourism motivations may be composed of two elements: a behavioral component and a situational component. Authenticity implies a combination of both an appropriate setting, representing a back stage social environment, and a set of appropriate actions by the visitor, such as speaking the local language, eating local foods, and meeting local residents on a friendly and respectful basis.

Philip Pearce and Gianna Moseardo (1986) have also discussed the potential importance of meetings between tourists and local residents as a source of authenticity. Pearce and Moscardo introduced their arguments by relating authenticity to Abraham Maslow's (1954) notions of SELF-ACTUALIZATION and Martin Heidegger's (1962) philosophical views of the nature of authentic human experience. Their basic argument is that authenticity can be experienced when tourists meet "authentic" people in certain contexts that are not necessarily related to a front stage or back stage setting. Drawing on the work of Pearce and Marie Caltabiano (1983), an examination of 400 individual tourists' accounts of personal vacation experiences, Pearce and Moscardo proposed an expansion of Cohen's four-cell model into a nine-cell model, incorporating "front stage people" and "back stage people" with front and back stage settings and the relative importance (high versus low) the tourist places on the setting and the people:

1. The tourist values meeting back stage people in a back stage setting.

2. The tourist values meeting front stage people in a front stage setting.

3. The tourist values meeting front stage people in a back stage setting.

4. The tourist values meeting back stage people in a front stage setting.

5. The tourist values meeting back stage people regardless of the setting.

6. The tourist values meeting front stage people regardless of the setting.

7. The tourist values the back stage setting with little interest in the people he meets.

8. The tourist values the front stage setting with little interest in the people he meets.

9. The tourist values his vacation regardless of the setting or the people he meets.

The Pearce-Moscardo model offers two features that previous models did not. First, of course, is the addition of the personal interaction component. The second is inclusion of the tourist's preferences for certain types of setting or personal contact. Whereas Cohen's four-cell model utilized the tourist's perception of the tourism setting, Pearce and Moscardo use the tourist's preferences. On the other hand, Pearce and Moscardo lose Cohen's explicit reference to the tourists' perception of reality of the setting by assuming, implicitly, that tourists are able to accurately perceive what is a front stage or back stage setting (or individual). Their formulation also fails to provide any greater insight into how front stage and back stage settings (or people) might be operationally distinguished from each other.

Authenticity, despite its definitional and measurement challenges, is a provocative concept in TOURISM and should be examined more fully and with greater emphasis on verifiable, objective data and definitions.

REFERENCES

Boorstin, Daniel. 1964. *The Image: A Guide to Pseudo-Events in America*. New York: Harper & Row. An early and well-known criticism of modern mass tourism.

Buck, Roy C. 1977. "Towards a Synthesis in Tourism Theory." *Annals of Tourism Research* 4:110–121. Suggests tourists do seek authenticity in their travels; criticizes views of Boorstin.

Buck, Roy C. 1978. "Boundary Maintenance Revised: Tourist Experience in an Old Order Amish Community." *Rural Sociology* 43:221–234. Applies MacCannell's model to an ethnic-based tourism destination.

Chalfen, Richard M. 1979. "Photography's Role in Tourism." *Annals of Tourism Research* 6:435–447. A phenomenological interpretation of cameras and photography in tourism.

Cohen, Eric. 1979. "Rethinking the Sociology of Tourism." *Annals of Tourism Research* 6:18–35. Introduces a four-cell model of tourism situations combining reality and perception.

Dann, Graham M. S. 1981. "Tourist Motivation: An Appraisal." *Annals of Tourism Research* 9:127–131. Personal interpretation of role of authenticity, or the lack of it, in tourism.

Goffman, Erving. 1959. *The Presentation of Self in Everyday Life*. New York: Doubleday. A social psychological study of the nature of individual identity in a social world.

Heidegger, Martin. 1962. *Being and Time*. Oxford: Blackwell. A classic philosophical work concerned with the individual's sense of being.

MacCannell, Dean. 1976. *The Tourist: A New Theory of the Leisure Class*. New York: Schocken Books. A major reference for the concept of authenticity.

Maslow, Abraham H. 1954. *Motivation and Personality*. New York: Harper & Row. A well-known psychological text that introduces concept of self-actualization.

Pearce, Philip L., and Caltabiano, Marie. 1983. "Inferring Travel Motivation from Traveller's Experiences." *Journal of Travel Research* 22(2):16–20. Reviews 400 reports of travelers accounts of recent vacations.

Pearce, Philip L., and Moscardo, Gianna M. 1986. "The Concept of Authenticity in Tourist Experiences." *Australian and New Zealand Journal of Sociology* 22:121–132. Argues for including personal interactions as a source of authenticity in travel experiences.

Plog, Stanley C. 1974. "Why Destination Areas Rise and Fall in Popularity." *Cornell Hotel and Restaurant Administration Quarterly* 14(4):13–16. Proposes a spectrum of tourist psychological types and relates it to various popular destinations.

Riesman, David. 1961. *The Lonely Crowd*. New Haven, CT: Yale University Press. A well-known sociological work that examines the loss of identity in urban societies.

Turner, Louis, and Ash, John. 1975. *The Golden Hordes: International Tourism and the Pleasure Periphery*. London: Constable. A critical look at social impacts of mass tourism on foreign destinations.

Vallee, Paul. 1987. Authenticity as a Factor in Segmenting the Canadian Travel Market. Unpublished M.A. thesis, Waterloo, Ont., University of Waterloo. Reviews authenticity as a concept and attempts to measure quantitatively the relative importance of authenticity as a tourist motivation.

Veblen, Thorstein. 1953. *The Theory of the Leisure Class*. London: Unwin. A reprint of the turn-of-the century classic sociological text that examines the social functions of leisure, travel, tourism, consumption, and work.

SOURCES OF ADDITIONAL INFORMATION

A focused discussion of authenticity as a tourism phenomenon may be bound in Dean MacCannell's "Staged Authenticity: Arrangements of a Social Space in Tourist Settings" (*American Journal of Sociology* 79:589–603, 1977). More general discussions in which authenticity is considered implicitly include Eric Cohen "A Phenomenology of Tourism" (*Sociology* 13:179–201, 1979), W. Sutton "Travel and Understanding: Notes on the Social Structure of Touring" (*International Journal of Comparative Sociology* 8:218–223, 1967); Graham Dann "Anomie, Ego-Enhancement and Tourism" (*Annals of Tourism Research* 4:184–194, 1977); John Foster "The Sociological Consequences of Tourism" (*International Journal of Comparative Sociology* 12:217–227, 1972; and D. L. Redfoot "Touristic Authenticity, Touristic Angst, and Modern Reality" (*Qualitative Sociology* 7:291–309, 1984). Valene Smith also examines the intricate relationships between visitors and the culture they encounter in her text *Hosts and Guests: The Anthropology of Tourism* (Philadelphia: University of Pennsylvania Press, 1977). Roger Mannell and Seppo Iso-Ahola offer a speculative link between authenticity and ''true leisure'' in ''Psychological Nature of Leisure and Tourism Experience'' (*Annals of Tourism Research* 14:291–309, 1987).

AUTOTELIC BEHAVIOR. See FLOW.

B
_____

BARRIER. Any impediment to an individual's participation in an activity or use of a facility; the impediment may affect frequency, duration, or quality of participation or usage.

The concept of barriers is closely related to CONSTRAINTS and is essentially the opposite of ACCESSIBILITY. While accessibility refers to the characteristics of facilities or programs that render them available for use, barriers are those characteristics that render them unavailable for use. Unlike accessibility, however, barriers may also include personal characteristics such as attitudes or health problems that limit participation in certain activities. Barriers are also closely tied to NONPARTICIPATION. Nonparticipation is not simply the lack of participation, in the context of leisure research, but a potentially serious problem (or symptom of another problem) that should be addressed and corrected, if possible. The generic reason for nonparticipation is usually conceived to be some form of a barrier. Whether the barrier is the fundamental problem or the cause of nonparticipation, which is then considered to be the fundamental problem, is largely a matter of perspective and interpretation.

Although several researchers have proposed different classification schemes for barriers (McGuire, 1984), no single classification scheme has emerged as being widely acceptable. Thus although other groupings are possible, barriers can be categorized as being physical, programmatic, social, or personal.

Physical barriers include gates, locks, and fences intentionally designed to protect people or property by limiting access. Such barriers, while important to facility managers, are relatively trivial as a concept in recreation and leisure studies. More significant physical barriers include architectural design features that have the effect of unintentionally excluding people from facilities who should

have access to them. While much work remains to be done in removing architectural barriers from recreation facilities in North America, the Architectural
Barriers Act of 1968 (Public Law 90–480) has gone a long way toward helping
to reduce such barriers. This legislation requires that any facility or building
supported by federal funds be made accessible in accordance with the terms of
Section A117.1 of the American National Standards Institute. (ANSI).

Other physical barriers, however, are not necessarily subject to amelioration
by public law. WILDERNESS areas, underwater environments, caves, and some
special interest facilities such as heritage buildings or hydroelectric dams may
have physical barriers that are inherent features. They could not be removed
without destroying the very facility one would hope to make accessible. Other
facilities that have no immediately obvious architectural barriers can acquire
physical barriers when they become filled to capacity with users.

Recreation facilities are usually located some distance away from potential
users. Distance itself can be a physical barrier, as the phenomenon of distance
decay suggests. The importance of distance as a barrier may be related directly
to the physical distance separating the potential user from the facility, but other
aspects of distance may also be relevant. For example, Norbert Dee and John
Liebman (1970) used the number of street crossings as a measure of the barrier
separating children from urban playgrounds. S. L. Edwards and S. J. Dennis
(1976) measured the barrier of distance as a function of fuel costs, fuel consumption, distance driven, and the value of the travel time of the travelers
(estimated as a fraction of their hourly salary). In the context of international
travel, Stephen Smith (1984) estimated the distance equivalence of the international border as a barrier to cross-border travel between Canada and the United
States.

Program barriers are characteristics of recreation programs that reduce the
ability of potential participants to attend. Common program barriers include the
scheduling of a program during hours that potential participants have other
commitments, high admission or equipment costs, and limits on the number of
registrants the program can accommodate. Some programs also have restrictions
on access tied to attainment of a certain skill level or the possession of a proper
certificate, such as a certificate showing proficiency with scuba equipment.

Social barriers can have widespread influence on participation patterns, but
they are often covert. Attitudes toward appropriate and inappropriate activities
for teenagers, females, seniors, upper-class professionals, or any other social
group promote participation in certain activities by those groups and discourage
participation in other activities. These attitudes may exist in the mind of the
participant or may be externally imposed by the opinions of others. The role of
attitudes and motivations as barriers has been addressed in the leisure studies
literature, but usually in connection with an examination of the role of other
barriers as well. Peter Witt and Thomas Goodale (1981), for example, examined
the effect of attitudinal and motivational barriers on leisure participation at different stages in the HUMAN LIFE CYCLE and found that they play different roles

depending on whether the person is a teenager, a single adult, a parent with young children, or a senior.

Gerald Romsa and Wayne Hoffman (1980) examined the effect of different barriers, including attitudes, on the leisure participation patterns of different socioeconomic groups. In their study they hypothesized that economic barriers would be more important for lower income groups than for higher income groups; higher income groups would cite supply factors or time limitations as the leading barriers. Their results failed to support this hypothesis. They found, in particular, that the major reason cited by lower income individuals for not participating more in activities was a lack of interest. This may be taken at face value, or it may indicate a more deep-seated resignation that some activities are not appropriate for them and thus they are "not interested." Different experiences or different SOCIALIZATION patterns in youth may have led to different attitudes and thus different patterns or participation and barrier perceptions.

Racial barriers are another form of social barrier that have been virtually eliminated officially from recreation facilities and programs in North America, but age, sex, religion, linguistic, and nationality barriers may still be found in many private clubs and facilities. These can be viewed as invidious by the people they exclude, but they may also represent a positive force for maintaining and promoting a sense of group or cultural identity among the members, such as in the case of an ethnic club or a church-based youth group. Many fitness clubs are also sex specific or have sex-segregated programs catering to the preferences of many women and men to participate in fitness classes with members of their own sex exclusively.

Finally, personal barriers in some form affect virtually everyone. Limitations in time or money are among the most commonly cited reasons for individuals not participating more in their favorite activities (Fitness Canada, 1986; Searle and Jackson, 1985; Francken and van Raaij, 1981). Jackson (1983) notes, however, that there may be significant variations in the way these general barriers affect participation. He found, for example, that "cost barriers" were of different importance to different groups for different activities depending on whether the operational definition of *cost* was in terms of equipment costs, fees and charges, or transportation costs. Lack of skill, lack of a partner for participation, inadequate knowledge of available opportunities as well as health, injury, or disabilities (Fitness Canada, 1986) also affect many people.

Most of the research conducted on barriers has been descriptive and empirical: the researcher surveys a group of participants or would-be participants and asks what barriers they perceive. Their responses are then correlated with other personal characteristics to derive a more informed understanding of why people may not participate as much as they would like. More recently, however, Crawford and Godbey (1987) have proposed an outline of a model of different types of barrier and the way they block participation. They propose a three-part classification system: intrapersonal barriers (such as attitudes, emotional health, perceived self-skills), interpersonal barriers (such as lack of an appropriate partner or spousal conflicts), and structural (such as supply, income, time limits). They relate their model to social exchange theory. This theory hypothesizes, basically, that individuals attempt to minimize costs and to maximize rewards that satisfy individual goals—barriers, in this sense are viewed as costs to be avoided or minimized. Whether this particular view will result in significant advances in reconceptualizing barriers remains to be seen. Regardless of the actual outcome, Crawford and Godbey's work does emphasize the significance of further research into the role of barriers in leisure studies. This work has already contributed to our understanding of some of the forces that shape participation patterns, and it has the potential to contribute to a better theoretical understanding of human leisure behavior as well as to enhancing the quality of life for all people.

REFERENCES

Boothby, John, Tungatt, Malcolm F., and Townsend, Alan R. 1981. "Ceasing Participation in Sports Activities." *Journal of Leisure Research* 13:1–14. An examination of the reasons former athletes gave for ceasing activity; concludes that most reasons are associated with (1) changes in the physical ability or health of the participant and (2) changes in the relationship between the former participant and his sporting environment, including the development of social and economic constraints and changes in his social group, such as loss of participation partners.
Crawford, Duane W., and Godbey, Geoffrey. 1987. "Reconceptualizing Barriers to Family Leisure." *Leisure Sciences* 9:119–128. A conceptual paper describing a generic approach to classifying barriers; offers suggestions for further research.
Dee, Norbert, and Liebman, John. 1970. "A Statistical Study of Attendance at Urban Playgrounds." *Journal of Leisure Research* 2:145–159. Develops a model of playground use in a large urban area; defines distance in terms of street crossings.
Edwards, S. L., and Dennis, S. J. 1976. "Long Distance Day Tripping in Great Britain." *Journal of Transport Economics and Policy* 10:237–256. Develops a valuation method for determining economic value of pleasure travel; defines distance in terms of a complex function of fuel costs and time costs.
Fitness Canada. 1986. *Physical Activity among Activity-Limited and Disabled Adults in Canada*. Ottawa: Fitness Canada. One in a series of reports based on the Canada Fitness Survey; focuses on disabilities, but covers other barriers as well.
Francken, Dick A., and van Raaij, W. Fred. 1981. "Satisfaction with Leisure Time Activities." *Journal of Leisure Research* 13:337–352. Examines relationships among expressed levels of satisfaction with leisure activities, perceptions of different types of barrier and socioeconomic status.
Jackson, Edgar L. 1983. "Activity-Specific Barriers to Recreation Participation." *Leisure Sciences* 6:47–60. Examines variation in types of barrier cited with respect to desired participation in different activities; argues that precise definition of barriers is important for accurate understanding of role of barriers.
McGuire, Francis. 1984. "A Factor Analytic Study of Leisure Constraints in Advanced Adulthood." *Leisure Sciences* 6:313–326. Examines the perceptions of a sample of adults (forty-five years and over) toward thirty constraints; groups constraints into five general categories.

Romsa, Gerald, and Hoffman, Wayne. 1980. "An Application of Nonparticipation Data in Recreation Research: Testing the Opportunity Theory." *Journal of Leisure Research* 12:321–328. Examines relative importance of different barriers for lower versus higher income groups.

Searle, Mark S., and Jackson, Edgar L. 1985. "Socioeconomic Variations in Perceived Barriers to Recreation Participation among Would-Be Participants." *Leisure Sciences* 7:227–249. Found that work, overcrowding, and lack of partners were the key barriers to further participation; the poor, elderly, and single parents were most likely to be affected by barriers.

Smith, Stephen L. J. 1984. "A Method for Estimating the Distance Equivalences of International Boundaries." *Journal of Travel Research* 22(3):37–39. Describes a regression-based procedure for determining the effect of international borders on reducing tourist travel between adjacent countries.

Witt, Peter A., and Goodale, Thomas L. 1981. "The Relationship between Barriers to Leisure Enjoyment and Family Stages." *Leisure Sciences* 4:29–49. Observed differences in perceptions of major barriers on the basis of position in the life cycle.

SOURCES OF ADDITIONAL INFORMATION

A collection of readings on the issue of barriers and nonparticipation is Michael Wade's, ed., *Constraints on Leisure* (Springfield, Ill: Charles C. Thomas, 1984). Edgar Jackson and Mark Searle cover some conceptual issues associated with the identification and analysis of barriers in their "Recreation Non-Participation and Barriers to Participation: Concepts and Models" (*Leisure and Society* 8:693–707, 1975). The same authors report on some empirical research related to nonparticipation in "Recreation Non-Participation: Variables Related to the Desire for New Recreational Activities" (*Recreation Research Review* 10 no. 2:5–12, 1983). A nonempirical management perspective is offered by Searle and Jackson in "Recreation Non-Participation and Barriers to Participation: Considerations for the Management of Recreation Delivery Systems" (*Journal of Park and Recreation Administration* 3:23–35, 1985). Geoffrey Godbey examines the role of lack of information as a factor in nonparticipation in his "Nonuse of Public Leisure Services: A Model" (*Journal of Park and Recreation Administration* 3:1–12, 1985). Edgar Jackson provides a good overview of the literature on constraints and the distinction between constraints and barriers in "Leisure Constraints: A Survey of Past Research" (*Leisure Sciences* 10:203–215, 1988). Another good literature review is Gary Elles and Craig Rademacher, "Barriers to Recreation Participation," in *A Literature Review: The President's Commission on America's Outdoors* (Washington, DC: U.S. Government Printing Office, 1986, Motivation-33–Motivation-50).

BENEFITS. See VALUE.

BIOSPHERE RESERVE. An area representative of one of the world's biogeographical provinces, formally designated by UNESCO and managed under the laws of the nation in which it is located. Key features of biosphere reserves include the presence of a protected core landscape surrounded by one or more buffer zones of modified landscapes and a management system that emphasizes research, RESOURCE monitoring, and education related to conservation and the use of resources for sustainable development.

In 1964, the International Biological Program (IBP) was established by the International Council of Scientific Unions with a ten-year mandate to accomplish two goals: (1) to promote basic research on ecosystems and (2) to encourage nations to establish protected natural areas for ongoing research and resource monitoring. This initiative reflected growing worldwide concern over CONSER-VATION, the quality of the ENVIRONMENT, and protection of the world's major ecosystems. These same concerns led UNESCO to convene in 1968 the International Conference of Experts on the Scientific Basis for Rational Use and Conservation of the Resources of the Biosphere (usually known simply as the Biosphere Conference). One principal recommendation, among a very large number of recommendations arising from that conference was that UNESCO extend the work of the IBP after IBP's termination in 1974, especially the designation of protected landscapes. An implementation plan was drawn up by representatives from the Biosphere Conference to create the International Co-ordinating Council (ICC) in 1970, which was subsequently approved by the UNESCO General Conference.

The ICC subsequently designed a flexible scientific program based on a continuation and expansion of the IBP's objectives. This plan became known as the Man and the Biosphere Program (MAB). MAB was based on the assumption that nations would voluntarily cooperate on joint scientific projects related to environmental conservation, exchange information and experience, and dedicate some of their internal resources and institutional activities to the protection of designated areas. The criteria for specifying biosphere reserves were first spelled out in 1974 (UNESCO/MAB, 1974). Consistent with IBP's philosophy, the initial emphasis was on the protection of an undisturbed core of WILDERNESS combined with basic research on the biophysical resource base. Over time, however, the concept evolved to the contemporary view that places the emphasis on conservation rather than preservation. More precisely, the concept of a biosphere reserve implies the following (Francis, 1985):

1. The reserve should be representative of one of the world's biogeographic provinces (the terrestrial surface of the world has been divided by ecologists into 227 biogeographic provinces) (see Udvardy 1975, 1984).

2. Each reserve should have a relatively undisturbed landscape core large enough for it to function as a self-sustaining ecosystem. The core should be surrounded by one or more buffer zones that shield the core from direct human impact and illustrate the effect of different resource uses on the landscape represented by the core. These buffer zones may have a variety of human activities located within them, ranging from RECREATION and TOURISM to human settlement.

3. Interdisciplinary research, resource monitoring, and education should be integral parts of the management process of each reserve. Special attention should be given to establishing baseline data for monitoring ecosystem change, measuring the effects of

different types of resource use including recreation and tourism on the ecosystem, the effects of pollution on the ecosystem, the effectiveness of reclamation or resource rehabilitation projects, and strategies to permit use of the ecosystem in accordance with the principles of sustainable development.

4. Each reserve must be established and managed in accordance with local agencies and regulations, and in such a way as to ensure cooperation and support from the various groups of people who will ultimately influence the success of the reserve and its projects.

While these points represent the dominant view of the biosphere reserve in the 1980s, George Francis (1985) also identifies two variants that may be important as the concept is implemented in countries around the world. The first concerns the principle of a relatively undisturbed core area. In many long-settled parts of the world, there is no part of the landscape that can be considered to be even relatively undisturbed. Thus while such cores are desirable and possible in some biogeographic provinces, the requirement for an undisturbed core simply could not be achieved in other parts of the world, such as parts of Europe, southeast Asia, and Africa. This problem is not viewed as an insurmountable deterrent to the creation of biosphere reserves, because as W. J. Lusigi (1984), H. L. Morales (1984), and Michel Maldague (1984) point out, the key role of biosphere reserves is not protection of wilderness but ecologically balanced development.

The other departure from the consensus concerns the assumption that the typical reserve consists of a core surrounded by one or more buffers. In some circumstances, as Jerry Franklin (1977) has argued, the various components of a reserve might actually be spatially disaggregated from each other—with one or more core areas separated at some distance from one or more areas of greater human impact. In fact, this variant may provide an increasingly common model for the worldwide system of biosphere reserves in the future (Francis, 1985).

By 1987, a total of 223 biosphere reserves had been established in seventy countries, representing 101 of the 227 biogeographic provinces. The majority of these have been created by designating previously established NATIONAL PARKS or other protected areas, and most still have not yet developed the full complement of cooperative program policies and projects intended by the MAB program (Miller, 1983; Eidsvik, 1984a).

Biosphere reserves are still a relatively new concept in the recreation and leisure studies field, and even in the conservation and resource management profession. Eidsvik (1984b) has described the concept as the latest step in the evolution of thinking about wildland management. In the opening years of the twentieth century, the emphasis was generally on preservation—the establishment of tracts of land set aside as preserves for the future. This gradually evolved to an emphasis on protection, with the development of a system of park or game wardens. These were eventually replaced by managers who worked on-site and who were guided by park master plans. Biosphere reserves represent the emergence of a new perspective—integrated management—that places the protection and management of the reserves in a larger regional and economic context. This does not mean that the concept of a wilderness preserve is becoming out of date, but rather reflects the growing maturity of the conservation movement in recognizing that resource protection and economic development can be integrated in many areas, with some undisturbed tracts of land set aside as wilderness preserves and other tracts of severely degraded resources subjected to a program of rehabilitation.

REFERENCES

Eidsvik, Harold K. 1984a. "Future Directions for the Nearctic Realm." In *National Parks, Conservation, and Development: The Role of Protected Areas in Sustaining Society*, ed. Jeffrey A. McNeely and Kenton R. Miller, 546–549. Washington, DC: The Smithsonian Institution Press. Reviews implementation techniques for biosphere reserves with special reference to the far north.

Eidsvik, Harold K. 1984b. "Evolving a New Approach to Biosphere Reserves" In *Conservation, Science, and Society*, 73–80. Minsk, Byelorussia/USSR: First International Biosphere Reserve Congress. Describes development of biosphere reserves as a stage in the evolution of resource management philosophy and practice.

Francis, George. 1985. "Biosphere Reserves: Innovations for Cooperation in the Search for Sustainable Development." *Environments* 17:24–36. Excellent overview of biosphere concept; includes status report on Canadian reserves.

Franklin, Jerry F. 1977. "The Biosphere Reserve Program in the United States." *Science* 195:262–267. A status report on U.S. reserves; includes review of history of the concept.

Lusigi, W. J. 1984. "Mt. Kulal Biosphere Reserve: Reconciling Conservation with Local Human Population Needs." In *Conservation, Science, and Society*, 459–469. Minsk, Byelorussia/USSR: First International Biosphere Reserve Congress. Describes an example of a biosphere reserve managed explicitly to demonstrate how conservation practices can improve living standards of nomadic tribes.

Maldague, Michel. 1984. "The Biosphere Concept: Its Implementation and Its Potential as a Tool for Integrated Development." In *Ecology in Practice*, ed. F. di Castri, 376–401. Dublin, Ireland: Tycooly International. Presents a view similar to that of Lusigi.

Miller, Kenton R. 1983. "Biosphere Reserves in Concept and Practice." In *Towards the Biosphere Reserve: Exploring Relationships Between Parks and Adjacent Lands*, ed. Robert Scace and Clifford Martinka, 7–21. Denver: U.S. National Park Service. Review article on the implementation of biosphere reserve concept; notes most are simply redesignation of existing parks.

Morales, H. L. 1984. "For a Self-Sustained Development." In *Conservation, Science and Society*, 478–485. Minsk, Byelorussia/USSR: First International Biosphere Reserve Congress. A position paper emphasizing the role of local public participation in biosphere reserve management.

Udvardy, Miklos D. F. 1975. *A Classification of the Biogeographical Provinces of the World*, IUCN occasional paper 18. Morges, Switzerland: International Union for the Conservation of Nature. Introduces the regional classification system used for biosphere reserves.

Udvardy, Miklos D. F. 1984. "The IUCN/UNESCO System of Biogeographical Provinces in Relation to the Biosphere Reserves." In *Conservation, Science, and Society*, 16–19. Minsk, Byelorussia/USSR: First International Biosphere Reserve Congress. Relates IUCN/UNESCO ecological classification system specifically to biosphere reserves.

UNESCO/MAB. 1974. *Final Report of the Task Force on Criteria and Guidelines for the Choice and Establishment of Biosphere Reserves*. Paris: UNESCO. The first formal articulation of the biosphere reserve concept.

SOURCES OF ADDITIONAL INFORMATION

Many of the published papers on biosphere reserves are located in "fugitive" sources—government documents, United Nations and IUCN documents, and conference proceedings. Sources that may be more generally available include a special issue of *Ambio: A Journal of the Human Environment* (10:2–3, 1981) was devoted to the biosphere reserve concept. Additional overview articles may be found in Michel Batisse's "The Relevance of MAB" (*Environmental Conservation* 7:179–184, 1980) and "The Biosphere Reserve: A Tool for Environmental Conservation and Management" (*Environmental Conservation* 9:101–111, 1982) and Gonzalo Halffter's, "Biosphere Reserves and National Parks: Complementary Systems of Natural Protection" (*Impact of Science on Society* 30:269–277, 1980).

C

CARRYING CAPACITY. 1. A measure of the ability of a recreation site to support sustained use at a specified level of quality. 2. A management concept used to express the perceived need to set limits on visitor levels to protect both the biophysical ENVIRONMENT and the quality of the recreational experience.

The introduction of the concept of carrying capacity into the field of recreation and leisure studies is usually attributed to E. P. Meinecke (1929), a plant pathologist who wrote of the threat posed by increasing numbers of tourists to the redwood forests of California. Other researchers and planners working in recreation soon adopted carrying capacity as an argument for limiting recreational use in environmentally sensitive areas. Until about 1959 the emphasis in the concept was primarily biological. Recognition of the potential effects of heavy use on the users' experience (as opposed to the natural environment) was, at best, implicit and, at worst, totally absent.

In 1959, the National Advisory Council on Regional Recreation Planning suggested that the focus on biological impacts of recreation was too narrow. Some increased recognition should be given to understanding the legitimate concerns of recreationists for the quality of the RECREATION experience. The council argued that "carrying capacity may also be [defined] as the maximum human use that is compatible with the quality of recreation experience desired by the user."

The relationship between a biological emphasis and a user emphasis in carrying capacity research was formalized by Wilbur LaPage (1963) who suggested that the concept of carrying capacity should be understood to be composed of (1) a biotic component and (2) an aesthetic component. Alan Wagar (1964) added to the concept by explicitly arguing that researchers need to consider management objectives as well as resource and user characteristics. Wagar also emphasizes the role of crowding in determining user satisfaction. This was the first major attempt to link the quality of a recreational experience with the number and type of user contacts.

Much subsequent research attempted to measure more precisely the relationship between the number, type, and context of user contacts on one hand and the degree of user satisfaction, on the other. Robert Lucas's (1964) work on the carrying capacity of the Quetico-Superior Area and his evaluation of the effects of user contacts on canoeists' satisfaction is widely considered to be seminal. Other research and opinions on carrying capacity published during the 1960s and 1970s refined the philosophical basis of carrying capacity and introduced new terms designed to reflect shades of meaning in the use of the more general term *carrying capacity*.

The body of research designed to identify the relationship between crowding (or user density) and user satisfaction has produced mixed results. Some researchers such as Charles Cicchetti and Kerry Smith (1973), George Stankey (1973), and Robert Manning and Charles Ciali (1980) found evidence supporting the commonly held notion that satisfaction declines as crowding increases. Others, however, found different patterns. T. Heberlein and B. Laybourne (1978) and Thomas Heberlein, John Trent and Robert Baumgartner (1982) observed that deer hunter satisfaction actually increased with user density (over the range of actual user densities reported in field studies). Kenneth McConnell (1977) observed that crowding had a negative effect on many forms of wilderness recreation, such as backpacking, but had positive effects on more social forms of recreation, such as "singles" beach use. It seems plausible that one user's reaction to the presence of other users will not always be a monotonic function. In other words, user satisfaction on a beach may increase with the number of users to some optimal density and then decrease as that density is exceeded.

Work on clarifying the terminology of carrying capacity and on expanding the philosophical basis of the concept has produced mixed results. Numerous definitions were proposed, with each author correcting what he perceived to be weaknesses in other definitions. Wagar (1964), for example, defined carrying capacity to be the level of recreational use an area can withstand while providing a sustained quality of experience. R. Held, S. Brinkler, and A. Wilcox (1969) specified that capacity should be measured in man-days of use that can be tolerated without irreversible deterioration of the physical environment and without user satisfaction declining to the point where it failed to be pleasurable. The Conservation Foundation (1973) defined carrying capacity as the ability of a system to absorb outside influence and to retain its essential character. They suggested three types of capacity be recognized: (1) physical capacity, which is primarily a function of available space, (2) ecological capacity, which is similar to LaPage's "biotic component," and (3) psychological carrying capacity, which was described as the effect of other visitors on an individual visitor's mind. T. W. Suder and J. M. Simpson (1972) emphasized that carrying capacity should be considered to be a derived dependent characteristic of a site that is subject to precise definition only after the details of site development have been spelled out. In contrast to the Conservation Foundation, Suder and Simpson suggested three other types of capacity: (1) design capacity, which is the absolute number of spaces allotted for users in a park plan, (2) maximum capacity, which is the upper limit of users that can be accommodated regardless of any environmental deterioration, and (3) optimum capacity, which is the level of use that permits maintenance of a site at some specified level and retains the economic value of man-made facilities.

Gordon Hammon et al. (1974) concluded that, at the time they were writing, not only was there no agreement on the definition of carrying capacity, there were very few practical guidelines about how the concept could be used in management. Their criticism can be read as a harbinger of a new connotation of the term (described below) that emphasizes carrying capacity as a "process concept" rather than a "product concept." Hammon et al. identified five factors a manager needs to consider in estimating the carrying capacity of a site: (1) administrative issues, such as the objectives of the facility, the level of development, and permissible managerial procedures; (2) biological characteristics, including the health, type, diversity, and tolerance of species on-site; (3) physical characteristics such as the areas, climate, and nature of the surface material on-site; (4) social issues, including the motivations of users, their values, and the size and composition of user groups; and (5) temporal factors such as the daily length of use and length of season.

A recent development has been to deemphasize the notion of carrying capacity determination as the search for a single number or range of numbers, and to reinterpret the concept as a managerial process. George Stanley (1979) described carrying capacity as, "in my view, [it] is not a scientific concept, but a management notion. . . . While research can help managers who are concerned with carrying capacity, it cannot supply answers about what the carrying capacity of a site is or should be." Bo Shelby and Thomas Heberlein (1984) described two components of carrying capacity as (1) the descriptive component and (2) the evaluative component (cf. Wagar, 1964) and suggested that the process of determining carrying capacity was actually the managerial integration of both components. The descriptive component required a manager to identify the number and nature of users, the managerial options available, and the real or expected environmental impacts associated with different levels of use and different types of management. The evaluative component provides the manager with information about how the site should actually operate. It implies knowledge of social and political values, the types of experience the site is expected to provide, and the quality associated for each type of experience desired.

One likely reason for the shift in definition of carrying capacity from the search for a number to a management procedure is the historical difficulty of finding reliable and valid functions relating use levels and environmental and social effects. If one accepts that any recreational use will cause some change in the environment and influence other users, the task of the manager may be conceived as the monitoring of those changes and the management of the site in such a way as to ensure any changes are within acceptable limits. This type of reasoning has been formalized by George Stankey and Stephen McCool (1984) as the LIMITS OF ACCEPTABLE CHANGE planning process.

REFERENCES

Cicchetti, Charles J., and Smith, V. Kerry. 1973. "Congestion, Quality Deterioration, and Optimal Use: Wilderness Recreation in the Spanish Peaks Primitive Areas." *Social Science Research* 2(1):15–30. A good example of research relating user density and user satisfaction; observed an inverse relationship.

Conservation Foundation. 1973. *National Parks for the Future*. Washington, DC: Conservation Foundation. Offers a broadly based philosophical definition of carrying capacity and relates it expressly to national park policy.

Hammon, Gordon A., Cordell, Harold K., Moncrief, Lewis W., Warren, M. Roger, Crysdale, Richard A., and Graham, John. 1974. *Capacity of Water-Based Recreation Systems*, report 90. Raleigh, NC: Water Resources Research Institute. Reviews carrying capacity research and proposes a conceptual model of carrying capacity in context of managing water-based recreation.

Heberlein, T., and Laybourne, B. 1978. *The Wisconsin Deer Hunter: Social Characteristics, Attitudes, and Preferences for Proposed Hunting Season Changes*, working paper 10. Madison WI: Center for Resources Policy Studies and Programs. A good example of research relating user density and user satisfaction; observed positive relationship.

Heberlein, Thomas, Trent, John N., and Baumgartner, Robert M. 1982. "The Influence of Hunter Density on Firearm Deer Hunters' Satisfaction: A Field Experiment." *Transactions of the 47th North America Natural Resource and Wildlife Conference* 47:665–676. Elaboration and updating of research reported in Heberlein and Laybourne (1978).

Held, R. B., Brinkler, S., and Wilcox, A. T. 1969. *A Study to Develop Practical Techniques for Determining the Carrying Capacity of Natural Areas in the National Park System*, report to the U.S. National Park Service. Fort Collins: Colorado State University. Suggested techniques and units of measurement for estimating carrying capacity; emphasized role of economic, social, political, and aesthetic limits in determining feasibility of environmental regeneration.

LaPage, Wilbur F. 1963. "Some Sociological Aspects of Forest Recreation." *Journal of Forestry* 60(5):319–321. A brief but important article arguing for greater recognition of the sociological issues in carrying capacity research.

Lucas, Robert C. 1964. *The Recreation Capacity of the Quetico-Superior Area*, research paper LS-15. St. Paul, MN: USDA Forest Service. An important and influential work examining user contacts and determinants of conflicts between wilderness users.

McConnell, Kenneth. 1977. "Congestion and Willingness to Pay." *Land Economics* 53:185–195. A good example of research relating user density and user satisfaction. Observed nature of relationship varies with activity.

Manning, Robert E., and Ciali, Charles P. 1980. "Recreation Density and User Satisfaction: A Further Explanation of the Satisfaction Model." *Journal of Leisure*

Research 12:329–345. A good example of research relating user density and user satisfaction; inverse relationship observed.

Meinecke, E. P. 1929. *The Effect of Excessive Tourist Travel on California Redwood Parks*. Sacramento: California State Printing Office. Possibly the first publication using the concept of carrying capacity in the context of recreation management.

National Advisory Council on Regional Recreation Planning. 1959. *A User-Resource Recreation Planning Method*. Loomis, CA: Hidden Valley. An early monograph arguing for reinterpreting carrying capacity in terms of user needs, not just biological constraints.

Shelby, Bo, and Heberlein, Thomas A. 1984. "A Conceptual Framework for Carrying Capacity Determination." *Leisure Sciences* 6(4):433–451. Describes components of carrying capacity estimation procedures and suggests "rules" to follow for such estimations.

Stankey, George H. 1973. *Visitor Perception of Wilderness Recreation Carrying Capacity*, research paper INT-143. Ogden, UT: USDA Forest Service. A good example of research relating user density and user satisfaction; inverse relationship observed.

Stankey, George H. 1979. "A Framework for Social Behavior Research—Applied Issues." In *Long Distance Trails: The Appalachian Trails—A Guide to Future Research and Management Needs*, ed. W. R. Burch, 43–53. New Haven, CT: Yale University Press. Describes carrying capacity as a tool for managers, not merely as a research question.

Stankey, George H., and McCool, Stephen F. 1984. "Carrying Capacity in Recreation Settings: Evolution, Appraisal, and Application." *Leisure Sciences* 6:453–473. Traces historical evolution of carrying capacity research and introduces the concepts of "limits of acceptable change."

Suder, T. W., and Simpson, J. M. 1972. *Recreational Carrying Capacity of the National Parks*. Washington, DC: Office of Natural Science, National Park Service. A planner and designer's view of carrying capacity in a park setting.

Wagar, J. Alan. 1964. *The Carrying Capacity of Wildlands for Recreation*, Forest Science monograph 7. Washington, DC: Society of American Foresters. An early and important exploration of the relationship between crowding and recreational quality; exercised significant influence on subsequent carrying capacity research for the next decade.

SOURCES OF ADDITIONAL INFORMATION

Useful introductions to research in carrying capacity may be found in B. Mitchell, *Geography and Resource Analysis* (London: Longman, 1979); Alan Jubenville and Roland Becker, "Outdoor Recreation Management Planning: Contemporary Schools of Thought," in Stanley Lieber and Daniel Fesenmaier, eds., *Recreation Planning and Management* (State College, PA: Venture, 1983, 303–319); Alan Graefe, Jerry Vaske, and Fred Kuss, "Social Carrying Capacity: An Integration and Synthesis of Twenty Years of Research" (*Leisure Sciences* 6:395–431, 1984).

Surveys critical of much existing research may be found in William Burch, "Much Ado about Nothing—Some Reflections on the Wider and Wilder Implications of Social Carrying Capacity" (*Leisure Sciences* 6:487–496, 1983) and Raymond Washburne, "Wilderness Recreational Carrying Capacity: Are Numbers Necessary?" (*Journal of Forestry*

80:726–728, 1982). An introduction to application of carrying capacity to tourism may be found in Donald Getz, "Capacity to Absorb Tourism Concepts and Implication for Strategic Planning" (*Annals of Tourism Research* 10:239–263, 1983). A more recent and more comprehensive review of carrying capacity as a management concept is Bo Shelby and Thomas Heberlein, *Carrying Capacity in Recreation Settings* (Corvallis: Oregon State University Press, 1986).

CATCHMENT AREA. See SERVICE AREA.

COGNITIVE DISSONANCE. A psychological tension resulting from simultaneously holding mutually incompatible cognitions (items of knowledge, belief, perception, or commitment).

The theory of cognitive dissonance was developed by Leon Festinger (1957, 1964) as a theory of motivation. Festinger noted that an individual occasionally finds himself in a situation where he holds two or more mutually incompatible ideas or an attitude that is incompatible with a behavior. Such a circumstance normally cannot be maintained for long and the individual must find some mechanism for reducing the dissonance or conflict. Dissonance is thus seen as a dynamic concept rather than as a structural concept because it represents a temporary mental condition. Researchers tend not to measure dissonance directly, but rather infer it from observed actions or statements of belief.

Cognitive dissonance is most likely to arise in structures of limited complexity—perhaps involving only two or three cognitions—and with a high degree of emotional involvement. The magnitude of dissonance is a function of the number and importance of dissonant cognitions compared to the total number of cognitions. The greater the magnitude of dissonance, the greater the efforts of the individual to resolve that dissonance through any of several different strategies, some of which are not necessarily obvious. For example, the resolution of cognitive dissonance is a possible explanation of the so-called Stockholm effect in which hostages of political kidnappings sometimes begin to take sides with their kidnappers. Opposition to the kidnappers' values, resentment to being held, and the reality of captivity create a powerful psychological tension in the minds of a victim. Because the reality of captivity cannot be changed, some hostages eventually "decide" that their captors have a legitimate grievance and may go so far as to decide to stay with them.

Cognitive dissonance is often used in environmental psychology as an explanation for residents continuing to live in flood-prone or earthquake-prone areas (Kates, 1962; Burton, 1972). The desire to avoid loss of life and property while continuing to live in hazardous areas are a simple form of cognitive dissonance. The resolution for many residents is to deny the probability of future disasters, while continuing to live in the area. In the field of RECREATION and LEISURE, cognitive dissonance is sometimes used to explain the rationale of participation in recreation activities carrying high degrees of risk, such as skydiving or spelunking. Participants, especially those who belong to clubs, have made a com-

mitment to participate. This commitment can be reinforced by social pressure
of other club members to continue one's participation. The combination of a
personal commitment to the activity, the social pressure to honor that commitment, and a perception of the risk of the activity creates a degree of cognitive
dissonance. The simplest resolution is often to reduce the assessment of risk
below that supported by empirical evidence. A further strategy for reducing
cognitive dissonance is to persuade friends and other participants that the risk
is low and to pressure them into participating as well—thus offering "confir-
mation" of the "safety" of these activities.

In a less dramatic context, Robert Adams (1973) used cognitive dissonance
theory to examine the behavior of recreationists under conditions of uncertainty.
His problem was this: if someone decides to go to a beach for swimming and
sunbathing and then learns that the forecast is, for example, a 60 percent chance
of rain, he is put into a state of cognitive dissonance. A commitment to a course
of action has been made, but other information suggests that the desired outcome
may be thwarted. Two strategies are possible. The beach goer may cancel his
trip. This action reduces dissonance, but it can cause disappointment. Alternatively, the interpretation of the weather forecast can be altered mentally to a
more favorable forecast. This also reduces dissonance and avoids disappointment.
Adams predicted the latter strategy for reducing dissonance would be more
common, and he conducted an experiment to test the prediction. The results
indicated that potential travelers often did distort the interpretation of the weather
forecast so that their actions could be consonant with their commitment and
desires.

REFERENCES

Adams, Robert L. A. 1973. "Uncertainty in Nature, Cognitive Dissonance, and the
     Perceptual Distortion of Environmental Information: Weather Forecasts and New
     England Beach Trip Decisions." *Economic Geography* 49:287–297. An experi-
     mental study of the effect of weather uncertainty on the decision to make or cancel
     trips to beaches for swimming and sunning.
Burton, Ian. 1972. "Cultural and Personality Variables in the Perception of Natural
     Hazards." In *Environment and the Social Sciences,* ed. J. F. Wohwill and D. H.
     Carson. Washington, DC: American Psychological Association. Examines a va-
     riety of social psychological variables and their influence on cognitive dissonance
     resolution strategies in the context of flood perception.
Festinger, Leon. 1957. *A Theory of Cognitive Dissonance.* Evanston, IL: Row, Peterson.
     The classical articulation of cognitive dissonance theory.
Festinger, Leon. 1964. "The Motivating Effect of Cognitive Dissonance" and "The
     Psychological Effects of Insufficient Rewards." In *The Cognitive Processes,* ed.
     Robert J. G. Hersper, Charles C. Anderson, Clifford M. Christenson, and Steven
     M. Hunkin, 509–523, 524–538. Englewood Cliffs, NJ: Prentice Hall. Two ex-
     perimental illustrations of the application of Festinger's theory.
Kates, Robert W. 1962. *Hazard and Choice Perception in Flood Plain Management,*
     research paper 78. Chicago: University of Chicago Press, Department of Geog-

raphy. A well-known early study of the role of cognitive dissonance in environmental psychology.

SOURCES OF ADDITIONAL INFORMATION

Jack Brehm and Arthur Cohen, *Explorations in Cognitive Dissonance* (New York: Wiley, 1962) provide a good introduction to the theory of cognitive dissonance as well as detailed examination of many technical details and applications of the theory from a traditional psychological perspective. Glenn Shippee, Jeffrey Burroughs, and Stuart Wakefield, in "Dissonance Theory Revisited: Perception of Environmental Hazards in Residential Areas" (*Environment and Behavior* 12: 33–51, 1980), examine the influence of distance of residence from the site of a disaster of forms of cognitive dissonance resolution. Their work draws especially from earlier studies by D. Sinha, "Behaviour in a Catastrophic Situation: A Psychological Study of Reports and Rumours" (*British Journal of Psychology* 43:200–209, 1957) and J. A. Prasad, "Comparative Study of Rumours and Reports in Earthquakes" (*British Journal of Psychology* 41:129–144, 1950). Rick Rollins and Gordon Bradley, "Measuring Recreation Satisfaction with Leisure Settings" (*Recreation Research Review* 13:23–27, 1986) refers to cognitive dissonance as one possible explanation for the shifting of evaluations of the importance of selected hiking variables on trip satisfaction before and after an outing.

COMMUNITY DEVELOPMENT. 1. A process for economic and social progress based on local initiatives. Its success depends on the full participation of the community, the development of community awareness of its needs and their possible solutions, and the acquisition of volunteers or workers with appropriate technical skills including negotiation and mediation techniques. 2. An ideology that emphasizes the development or empowering of community-based groups for political, social, and/or economic goals.

Community development has its origins in local self-help programs that arose in the United Kingdom, the United States, Canada, and other nations in the 1930s Great Depression. The initial emphasis was to provide local solutions for problems of unemployment and political instability in a period in which existing governmental structures were inadequate to provide remedies. Although many countries experimented with forms of community development projects, the programs in Great Britain were arguably among the most advanced. The Depression had strained the government's ability to support the remnants of the British Empire as well as its domestic population, so the government turned to an expanded program of indirect colonial administration. Local initiatives were started under the leadership of colonial administrators to identify specific community needs and to coordinate the acquisition and use of resources to meet those needs. A prerequisite for this process was the education of local residents so they could assist in the planning and operation of their own projects. Consequently, an early term for the process that was to become known as community development was *adult education* (Lotz, 1987).

Following World War II, many of the remaining British colonies began to push harder for greater self-rule and eventual independence. The Labour Government, which came to power in the United Kingdom after the war, committed itself to supporting these movements and adopted community development as part of their strategy of promoting stable and effective government in their colonies. One of the first appearances of the term *community development* in an international context occurred in this period at a 1948 conference in Cambridge (Lotz, 1987). Over the next decade, community development became an increasingly common model for international aid. The concept also began to be more fully examined and discussed as an area of policy analysis. Two definitions are typical of this period. First, "A movement designed to promote better living for the whole community with the active participation and, if possible, on the initiative of the community, but if this initiative is not forthcoming spontaneously, by the use of techniques for arousing and stimulating it in order to secure the active and enthusiastic response of the movement" (HMSO, 1954). And the 1955 United Nations definition expressed in *Social Progress Through Community Development:* "Community development can be tentatively defined as a process designed to create economic and social progress for the whole community with its active participation and the fullest reliance upon the community's initiative" (quoted in Lotz, 1987:42). The key features of these and other definitions of the 1950s and early 1960s are an emphasis on process, service to the entire community, and a combination of economic and social improvement. Although not explicit, *community* was generally understood to be geographically defined, usually an urban or limited rural area and most often located in the former colonies of the European powers.

Through the 1960s the community development movement expanded to include projects in North American urban areas, such as the Model Cities Program in the United States. The international context, however, also continued and included the Peace Corps program of President John Kennedy. Despite the ideals and promise of the movement, common problems continued to trouble many community development projects domestically and internationally. The residents of many local areas lacked the skills to implement successful programs, without a lengthy period of education or training. This, of course, was recognized as a need from the beginning of the "adult education" movement in Great Britain in the 1930s. Many community development projects were seen as examples of the inevitable failure of projects run by well-meaning and enthusiastic but unskilled AMATEURS. The usual solution suggested to this problem was to bring in an "expert," either at the initiative of a central government or at the initiative of the local community. In the first instance, such experts sometimes attempted to take control of local programs, subverting the philosophy of community development as a local initiative. In the latter instance, where the community brought in its own expert, the community often brought in only a single individual rather than a team. The result, again, was often failure because successful community development programs normally require the skills of many different types of individual. As Lotz (1987) suggests, the minimum for a community development team should include an "ideas person" who can provide conceptual and creative guidance for the identification of activities and projects, a development officer to identify and obtain resources, a communications specialist to provide liaison between the project leaders and the community, and a general manager to coordinate the overall program and associated workers. This team is usually supplemented by a battery of volunteers, technical people, and other workers who actually do the work of developing facilities and operating programs.

The community development model was adopted more widely by North American communities throughout the 1970s. The basic concept of community development did not significantly change through this period. Definitions such as those of Peter Du Sautoy (1964), David Brokensha and Peter Hodge (1969), and James Draper (1971) are very similar to those written two decades earlier. A less obvious development, however, was the evolution of the concept of community. As community development strategies were applied to the problems of large, pluralistic urban areas of North America, it became clear that these geographical entities were quite politically and socially different than the more homogeneous rural communities and towns of developing nations. Some authors, such as Hayden Roberts (1979), went as far as suggesting that modern cities in North America were not real communities.

Communities, according to Roberts, must share common values, political views, and social objectives. Such unity is often found in certain ethnic or economic classes, he believes, and in small settlements in Third World countries. North American cities, however, generally do not qualify as real communities.

Regardless of how one chooses to define community, many groups with shared values did adopt community development methods as part of their political strategy. One of the best examples is the rise of local activist groups in the environmental movement of the 1970s. Their reliance on local initiatives, use of volunteers, education and "consciousness-raising" efforts, and local community action parallel closely the traditional community development programs. The same strategy has also been used increasingly by senior citizens, physically disabled individuals, labor groups, and others. Observing these developments, Roberts (1979: xiv) has suggested that now "community development has to do with such notions as authority, power, leadership, human relations, and social change."

The extension of community development strategies to recreation and leisure services in the 1970s and 1980s is another illustration of the diffusion of community development into new contexts. The concept is explicitly linked by recreationists to both geographical communities, primarily neighborhoods, as well as special interest communities such as amateur athletics supporters or senior citizens. The connection between the concept and the field of recreation is summarized by the following observation made by Donald Getz, Robert Graham, and Robert Payne (1984) in an update to the Kitchener, Ontario, Parks and Recreation Master Plan: "Community development is a process which seeks to identify, foster, and support leadership qualities possessed by people in order that those people may be able to direct their own lives. For individuals, such a process offers a great deal in terms of belonging to social groups, contributing to social welfare, and developing leadership competence. By promoting such psychological benefits as these, community development offers an effective approach to recreation and leisure service.''

The authors also emphasize the importance of education to prepare local residents to assume greater leadership responsibilities for the provision and maintenance of services and facilities in their neighborhoods. Community development must occur simultaneously with what the authors describe as ''organizational development.'' Recreation and leisure service departments in North America traditionally have operated as centralized organizations with varying but limited degrees of public input. A community development model of the provision of park and recreation services necessarily has implications for the internal organization of the recreation department. Much time and effort is needed to make appropriate changes in the perceptions of the recreation staff, to prepare them to work as FACILITATORS, to modify agency goals and objectives, and to adjust the policies and procedures of the department to support the community development approach. Special attention must also be given to recruiting, training, and managing volunteers and citizen advisory boards to work as mediating structures between the community and the municipal agency.

As the Getz quotation notes, the application of community development methods to recreation and leisure services is based on the philosophy that recreation is much more than just the provision of programs and the operation of facilities. Recreation is seen as a social movement that helps to build a sense of community and promotes personal growth (Murphy, 1975; D'Amore, 1977). James Murphy and Louis D'Amore, among other recreationists, see a long-term trend in leisure services away from the traditional roles of program and facility management toward promotion of citizen participation in public services and programs in all areas. Furthermore, these authors believe that the community development strategy will help to break down the barriers between various professions and agencies that share a common concern for promoting human welfare and community improvement. This breakdown will occur by placing the initiative for and ultimate control of the programs and agencies in the hands of the local community.

Citizen participation in recreation and leisure services is not just an either-or situation. Sherry Arnstein (1969) has described an eight-rung ''ladder'' that ranges from governmental manipulation of the community to total control and responsibility by the community. While Arnstein's model was developed with regard to citizen participation in local public affairs generally, Richard Pine (1984) has explicitly linked it to leisure services and policies. Pines's work also illustrates another aspect of community development and leisure services. He describes how community development strategies have been applied in cultural policy formation and application in Finland, England, and Ireland. These policies, developed in the context of the ''cultural democracy movement'' (Simpson, 1976), concern the planning and provision of broadcasting, publishing, and fine/performing arts facilities and programs in local communities.

In sum, community development is a way for people to help themselves. Over time, the application of the concept has evolved from its emphasis on recovery from economic depression and the assistance to former colonies in becoming self-sufficient to the acquisition and use of political power by special interest groups and the decentralization of public planning and service management to the community.

REFERENCES

Arnstein, Sherry. 1969. "A Ladder of Citizen Participation." *Journal of the American Institute of Planners* 35 (July): 216–224. Strongly worded argument for citizen participation; introduces a "ladder" model of participation levels.

Brokensha, David, and Hodge, Peter. 1969. *Community Development: An Interpretation.* San Francisco: Chandler Press. Review of history of community development and its role in economic and social progress. Includes personal reflections on specific examples of community development projects.

D'Amore, Louis. 1977. Community Development and Public Leisure Services. Seminar notes prepared for the Canadian Parks/Recreation Association, Ottawa. Unpublished collection of notes and quotations for a workshop on community development.

Draper, James (ed.). 1971. *Citizen Participation: Canada.* Toronto: The New Press. Collection of readings offering different models of and arguments for citizen participation in the provision of services and in the political process. Strong Canadian orientation.

Du Sautoy, Peter. 1964. *The Organization of a Community Development Programme.* London: Oxford University Press. Presents guidelines for developing and managing a community development program, with special reference to the author's experiences in Africa.

Getz, Donald, Graham, Robert, and Payne, Robert. 1984. *Master Plan Update: City of Kitchener Parks and Recreation.* Kitchener, Ont.: Department of Parks and Recreation. Contains a major section discussing concept of community development and its application to municipal services; recommends specific policies for implementation.

HMSO. 1954. *Report of the Ashbridge Conference on Social Development.* London: Colonial Office. Proceedings of one of the first international conferences that focused on Community development in developing nations.

Lotz, Jim. 1987. "A Short History of community Development." *Journal of Community Development* 1(2): 40–47. Examination of community development as a worldwide movement, but with special reference to developments in Canada.

Murphy, James. 1975. *Recreation and Leisure Services.* Dubuque, IA: W. C. Brown. An introduction to the philosophy and role of public recreation service organizations.

Pine, Richard. 1984. "Community Development and Voluntary Associations." *Leisure Studies* 3:107–121. Reviews Arnstein's "ladder" and presents three case studies of community development for cultural policy.

Roberts, Hayden. 1979. *Community Development: Learning and Action.* Toronto: University of Toronto Press. Describes a politically and educationally based model for community development. A major point of the book is criticism of economic focus of traditional community development programs.

Simpson, John A. 1976. *Towards Cultural Democracy*. Strasbourg, France: Council of Europe. The classic statement of the meaning and importance of public involvement in development of cultural policies and programs.

SOURCES OF ADDITIONAL INFORMATION

Community development is a separate field with its own jargon, experts, and literature. Some important journals for articles on community development are the *Journal of Community Development, Community Development Journal*, and the *International Review of Community Development*. The December 1986 issue of *Recreation Canada* contains several articles directly related to the theme of community development and recreation services. Paulo Freire, *Pedagogy of the Oppressed* (New York: Herder and Herder, 1972) is an articulate discussion of the role of education in social and economic progress. A useful collection of readings that includes articles on different approaches to community organization, models of the complex structure of communities, and the strategies of practitioners is Fred M. Cox, et al., eds., *Strategies of Community Organization* (Ithaca, IL: F. E. Peacock, 1970). Ralph Kramer and Harry Specht have also prepared a collection of useful readings in their *Readings in Community Organization Practice* (3rd edition, Englewood Cliffs, NJ: Prentice Hall, 1983).

COMPETITION. A social process involving the objective comparison of the performance of two or more individuals against each other or against some other standard of performance.

Competition has attracted the attention of social scientists, philosophers, educators, athletes, and many others for generations. While competition is a concept used in the context of free enterprise, travel modeling, consumer decision making, and other areas, the term is most closely associated with physical activity, especially GAMES and SPORT, in leisure studies. As early as 1901, W. I. Thomas (1901) examined the role of competition in society, offering subjective evidence that competition was not only vital to a healthy and productive society but was a human instinct. His work, of course, was not the earliest examination of competition. Thomas's view, in fact, was largely a recapitulation of conventional wisdom in North America and in Great Britain that competition in sport, with its combination of cooperation and self-discipline for the good of the team, is a driving spirit and a noble ideal in society. This belief, too, had still earlier precedents. Jacob Burckhardt (1963) propounded a thesis that the ancient Greek civilization rose to prominence because of its unique competitive spirit, of which the ancient Olympics was only one manifestation.

The voluminous literature on competition may be viewed as forming three major themes: ethnology, philosophy, and psychology. Each has a rather long history of development, although the level of current research activity appears to vary substantially among them. Ethnological research focusing on competition has not been significantly active for perhaps two decades. Philosophical articles (which include opinion pieces and personal essays) continue to be a popular format, but they generally are not based on empirical research and tend to appear in collections of readings, conference proceedings, and popular or trade journals rather than in research journals. Articles examining the psychology and social psychology of competition are by far the most numerous in social scientific and physical education research journals. They display a history of hypothesis formation, testing, and cumulative knowledge formation.

In contrast to the North American and European tradition of competition as an instinct and social ideal, ethnologists observed that competition was not as pervasive or as homogeneous as originally believed. Among the researchers who reported either variations in the degree of competition in different CULTURES or a virtual absence of competition were Ruth Bunzel (1932) and Ruth Benedict (1961) on their work on the Zuni, Otto Klineberg (1948) on the Hopi, Kenelm Burridge (1957) on the New Guinea Tangu, and Lawrence Frank (1966) on the Navaho. Much of this work is summarized in Brian Sutton-Smith's (1972) cross-cultural study on games.

Opinion and philosophical articles typically take a position for or against competition and then rely on anecdotal information, selected research from ethnological or psychological studies, or rhetoric to support the author's position. Essays critical of competition include Arthur Combs's (1957) article in which he identifies and then debunks three myths: (1) we live in a competitive society, (2) competition is a motivating force, and (3) competition promotes quality. George Leonard (1976) continues in a similar vein in an essay titled "Winning Isn't Everything. It's Nothing," is intended to counter Vince Lombardi's creed, "Winning Isn't Everything. It's the Only Thing." A different approach in criticizing competition is Terry Orlick's (1978) text on cooperative games. Drawing on a combination of personal experience, emotional arguments, and selected ethnology and sociology, Orlick attempts to show how competition is a destructive force in society, responsible (in part) for crime, violence, poverty, and other social ills. He promotes a different strategy of PLAY and sport by describing new games that emphasize cooperation rather than competition.

In contrast to these authors are writers such as Gordon Reddiford (1982) who argues that the essence of competition is team work, adherence to rules, and fair play. John Underwood (1984) also writes in support of competition as a positive social and personal force. He acknowledges that competition can become degraded, degenerating into a "win at all costs" mentality; but his point is that competition can be good, and that the task for sports leaders and physical educators is to "purify competition" rather than eliminate it.

More neutral views appear in some philosophical or opinion essays. Scott Kretchman (1975) offers an interpretation of competition in sport as a form of dialogue between two people. He draws parallels between Martin Buber's concept of "I-thou" as an intimate encounter between two people and Buber's concept of "I-it" as a manipulative relationship, on one hand, and different competitive encounters between players, on the other. A significant theme in Kretchman's work is that competition necessarily implies a contest between two or more people. To Kretchman, competition in isolation is a contradiction in terms. Another author, Erich

Segal (1984) offers a useful overview of different attitudes toward competition, providing a taxonomy of sporting attitudes ranging from Lombardi's creed of competition to the spirit of cooperation in Orlick's new games.

Psychological inquiry into competition may be simplistically divided into two subthemes: the effects of competition on performance and the antecedents of competition (how an individual acquires a competitive spirit). Although research may be found on both topics over the last several decades, the effects of competition on performance tend to dominate earlier research while models of the acquisition of competition tend to dominate later studies.

One of the earliest questions physical educators and sport psychologists sought to answer was whether competition improved an athlete's speed and accuracy. Russell Church (1962) and Jacquelyn Gaebelein and Stuart Taylor (1971) found that the speed of performance of standardized physical tasks improved under simulated competitive environments in laboratory settings, while Irving Whittemore (1924), John Dashiell (1930), and Church (1968) found that the accuracy of the task performance was impaired by competition. Rainer Martens (1971) reviewed twenty-five similar studies. He noted that the results generally indicated that competition improved performance on tasks associated with muscular endurance or strength and that are simple and well learned. Complex tasks, including tasks involving accuracy, and tasks that have not been well learned were generally performed more poorly under the stress of competition. Martens then suggested these findings confirmed the notion of OPTIMAL AROUSAL level, or the Yerkes-Dodson Law (Yerkes and Dodson, 1908). This law states that the best level of performance of any task is associated with an optimal level of arousal or stimulation. The relationship between performance and arousal level can be summarized by a simple inverted U-shaped curve:

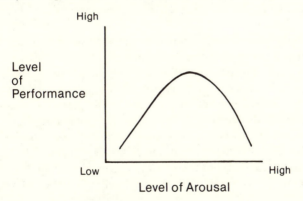

Level of Arousal

More recently, John Gross and Diane Gill (1982) examined both speed and accuracy effects in a dart-throwing competition, and confirmed that speed improved under competition. They failed, however, to support the earlier findings about accuracy, noting that competition had no measurable effects on the accuracy of their subjects' dart-throwing abilities.

A perennial question, more closely related to understanding the very concept of competition, is Whence does the competitive spirit or attitude arise? One of the first designs used to answer this question was to search for particular personality characteristics that might be closely associated with different levels of competitiveness in athletes. E. G. Booth (1958) applied the Minnesota Multiphasic Personality Inventory (MMPI) to a sample of athletes. Scores on various items from the test were correlated with coaches' assessments of the competitiveness of each subject. Both reported highly significant correlations with twenty-two items. Other researchers, however, failed to confirm these initial findings in independent replications (Rasch, Hunt, and Robertson, 1961; Kroll and Peterson, 1966). More recently, Joseph Willis (1982) adopted the same basic design but developed three new scales based on sport-specific statements and found tentative evidence linking personality measures with assessments of competitiveness, including aggression, extraversion, and self-confidence.

Robert White (1959) approached the question of the origin of competitiveness from a different tack. In his theoretical work, White outlined a hypothesis relating competition to other intrinsic motivations, and argued that intrinsic motivation derived from the so-called competence motive, the desire to be competent in one's environment. The same hypothesis was repeated, with tentative evidence cited, by Richard DeCharms (1968) and Jerome Kagan (1971). Edward Deci (1975) also linked competition to the competence motive, but added an elaboration. Deci proposed that children are born with a basic, undifferentiated INTRINSIC MOTIVATION to be self-determining in relation to their environment. As they grow, their experiences and interactions with the environment channel this diffuse drive into more specific motivations such as SELF-ACTUALIZATION and achievement. This process of evolution and differentiation continues over time, further refining the achievement motive into several forms, including competitiveness.

Joseph Verhoff (1973) has proposed a similar, but separate theory relating the development of competitiveness as a form of intrinsic motivation. Verhoff's model posits three phases: acquisition, application, and integration. In the first phase, an individual acquires a sense of autonomy in the mastery of physical skills in which he begins to develop a sense of competence in the performance of certain tasks. In the second state, the individual applies these skills in a "social comparison setting" so that his mastery of the skills may be compared to the abilities of others. The third stage is simply the integration of the first two. The individual develops a sense of self-confidence that allows him to test or compare himself against others in a test of relative excellence, without losing his sense of competence.

Verhoff's model was influential in shaping Tara Scanlon's (1978) model of the acquisition of competitiveness. Scanlon sees competition as being a specific expression of a more general achievement motivation. The achievement motivation is, according to Scanlon, "the striving to increase . . . one's own capabilities in all activities in which a standard of excellence is thought to apply and where the execution of such activities can, therefore, either succeed or fail.''

Scanlon's model, was, in turn, an important influence on Geoffrey Watson's (1981) design for introducing children to competition. Using Verhoff's and Scanlon's work, Watson outlined a process whereby children are first given the opportunity to learn selected physical skills that will be the basis for future competition. In this introductory phase, however, these skills are presented primarily for enjoyment and as an opportunity for self-expression. In the second phase, the children begin using their skills in a group setting, playing with other children at comparable levels of competence. Finally, they are introduced into highly controlled competitive settings in which they have the opportunity to play against each other and to enjoy a sense of accomplishment and mastery.

One of the leading researchers associated with the study of competition in sport is Martens. His text *Social Psychology and Physical Activity* (1975) is still considered a standard reference for the study of sport and competition. He also describes in his text the development and use of a specialized psychological tool for measuring the levels of anxiety associated with competition: the Sport Competition Anxiety Test (SCAT). SCAT has become accepted as a reliable tool by most sport psychologists for studying competitiveness and the stress associated with performance under competitive situations. It is basically a personality test, like the MMPI, but it performs much better than the MMPI in the study of competition because it is based on sport-related behaviors and statements.

Martens defines competition to be ''a social comparison process which involves individuals comparing their performance with some standard in the presence of other individuals who can evaluate the comparison process.'' As the reader will note, this definition was the inspiration for the definition given in this dictionary. A key feature of this definition is the fact that competition is a social process. As Kretchman (1975) also noted, competition involves a social comparison of the performance of an individual. While Kretchman insisted that competition had to involve two or more competitors, Martens can conceive of competition involving just one person striving to better is own record or that of another person who is not physically present or competing. In such cases, however, the evaluation must be made by an independent, objective observer. Self-evaluation of a solo performance does not represent meaningful competition. This notion of the social qualities of competition have also been emphasized by earlier researchers including Louis Festinger (1954), Roland Radloff (1966), and Joseph Verhoff (1973).

Beyond this definition, Martens sees four stages of competition. Initially, the individual confronts an objective competitive situation. This is the objective or factual condition in which one individual's performance will be compared to the performance of some standard (perhaps the performance of another competitor) in the presence of an independent evaluator. Second, this objective situation is perceived and interpreted by the potential participant; this phase is the subjective competitive situation. In the third phase, the potential competitor decides whether to accept the challenge of competition or not. If he does, he then enters the fourth stage, the consequence of competition. Here the individual has elected to compete, and his performance will be judged by others against some standard of excellence. His performance and their evaluation will then become an influence on how he interprets and responds to future objective competitive situations.

Competition has been and continues to be a popular topic for social scientists, philosophers, social critics, and the general public. Like many other social and psychological concepts, it is difficult to define and analyze in a valid and reliable fashion, and so will remain a challenge for social scientists. Furthermore, the significance of competition in Western society and its fundamental role in sport mean that this concept will continue to be an actively researched topic.

REFERENCES

Benedict, Ruth. 1961. *Patterns of Culture*. Boston: Houghton Mifflin. An ethnological study that includes a review of competition in selected primitive cultures.

Booth, E. G. 1958. "Personality Traits of Athletes as Measured by the MMPI." *Research Quarterly* 29:127–138. Correlates scores on the MMPI with coaches' assessments of the degree of competitiveness of male athletes.

Bunzel, Ruth L. 1932. *Introduction to Zuni Ceremonialism,* report 47. Washington, DC: Bureau of American Ethnology. Describes sport, competition, and cooperation in Zuni culture.

Burckhardt, Jacob. 1963. *History of Greek Culture*. New York: Unger Press. A sweeping overview of Hellenic civilization; proposes a hypothesis that competition was an essential element of the Greek rise to preeminence in the ancient world.

Burridge, Kenelm O. L. 1957. "Disputing in Tangu." *American Anthropologist* 59:763–780. Examines competition and the settling of disputes in a New Guinea culture.

Church, Russell M. 1962. "The Effects of Competition on Reaction Time and Palmer Skin Conductance." *Journal of Abnormal and Social Psychology* 65:32–40. Observes that competition tends to improve reaction time and speed of performance.

Church, Russell M. 1968. "Applications of Behavior Theory to Social Psychology: Imitation and Competition." In *Social Facilitation and Imitative Behavior,* ed. Edward C. Simmel, Ronald A. Hopper, and G. Alexander Milton, 135–168. Boston: Allyn & Bacon. Examines effect of competition on accuracy of skill performance.

Coakley, Jay. 1978. *Sport in Society*. St. Louis, MO: C. V. Mosby. Introduction to sociology of sport, with an emphasis on contemporary issues such as competition, role in childhood development, professionalism, and the relationship between sport and sex or race.

Combs, Arthur W. 1957. "The Myth of Competition." *Childhood Education* 33:264–268. Examines and debunks three myths related to competition in society; argues competition is overvalued.

Crandall, Virginia C., and Battle, Esther S. 1970. "The Antecedents and Adult Correlates of Academic and Intellectual Effort." In *Minnesota Symposium on Child Psychology,* Vol. 4., ed. John P. Hill, 36–93. Minneapolis: University of Minnesota

Press. Suggests that competition is strongly linked to specific types of activity and is not a general achievement motive.

Cratty, Bryant. 1981. *Social Psychology in Athletics*. Englewood Cliffs, NJ: Prentice Hall. Includes a discussion on nature of competition and its role in society; compares competition with cooperation as motivating force.

Dashiell, John F. 1930. "An Experimental Analysis of Some Group Effects." *Journal of Abnormal and Social Psychology* 25:190–199. Examines effect of competition on accuracy of skill performance.

DeCharms, Richard. 1968. *Personal Causation: The Internal Affective Determinants of Behavior*. New York: Academic Press. Relates competition to drive for competence in childhood development.

Deci, Edward L. 1975. *Intrinsic Motivation*. New York: Plenum Press. Examines development and evolution of intrinsic motivation and its relationship to other motivational drives.

Festinger, Louis. 1954. "A Theory of Social Comparison Processes." *Human Relations* 7:117–140. Defines competition as a social comparison between individuals.

Frank, Lawrence K. 1966. "The Cultural Patterning of Child Development." In *Human Development,* ed. Frank Falkner, Philadelphia: Saunders. Includes a description of the attitudes of Navaho Indians toward competition in sport.

Gaebelein, Jacquelyn, and Taylor, Stuart. 1971. "The Effects of Competition and Attack on Physical Aggression." *Psychonomic Science* 24:65–67. Examines effect of competition on reaction time.

Gill, Diane. 1981. "Current Research and Future Prospects in Sport Psychology." In *Perspective on the Academic Disciplines of Physical Education,* ed. George Brooks, 342–378. Champaign, IL: Human Kinetics. Review of research on effects of competition on different aspects of athletes' performance.

Graham, Peter J. 1976. "The Competitive Emphasis in Sport: A Need for Reflection." Paper presented to the International Congress of Physical Activity Sciences, Quebec City, Que. Urges a reconsideration of the form and role of competition in sport and physical activity; recommends more emphasis on nonzero-sum or cooperative games.

Gross, John B., and Gill, Diane C. 1982. "Competition and Instructional Side Effects on the Speed and Accuracy of a Throwing Task." *Research Quarterly* 53:125–132. Tested effect of competition on speed and accuracy of dart throwing; competition seemed to improve speed, but had no effect on accuracy.

Kagen, Jerome. 1971. *Understanding Children: Behavior, Motives, and Thoughts*. New York: Harcourt Brace Jovanovich. Relates competition to drive for competence in childhood development.

Klineberg, Otto. 1948. *Social Psychology*. New York: Holt. Includes a description of the attitudes of Hopi Indians toward competition in sport.

Kretchman, R. Scott. 1975. "Meeting the Opposition: Buber's 'Will' and 'Grace' in Sport." *Quest* 24:19–27. Philosophical examination of sport as a dialogue between two people; based on Buber's "I-thou" concept.

Kroll, Walter, and Peterson, Kay H. 1966. "Cross-Validations of the Booth Scale." *Research Quarterly* 36:66–70. Tests but fails to confirm Booth's findings regarding personality attributes and competitiveness.

Leonard, George B. 1976. "Winning Isn't Everything. It's Nothing." In *Sport Sociology: Contemporary Themes,* ed. Andrew Yiannakis, 84–86. Dubuque, Iowa: Kendall/

Hunt. Essay discrediting Vince Lombardi's creed about the centrality of competition in life.

Lüschen, Gunther. 1970. "Cooperation, Association, and Contest." *Journal of Conflict Resolution* 14:21–34. Examines different types of competition, emphasizing difference between zero-sum and nonzero-sum games.

Maller, Julius B. 1929. "Cooperation and Competition: An Experimental Study in Motivation," Teachers College Contributions to Education report 384. New York: Columbia University Teachers' College. An early psychological inquiry into the nature of competition that was conceived as the striving for sole possession of some object or goal.

Martens, Rainer. 1975. *Social Psychology and Physical Activity*. New York: Harper & Row. An important social psychological analysis of sport, including a hypothesis about the origin of competitiveness.

Mowrer, Orval H. 1950. *Learning Theory and Personality Dynamics*. New York: Ronald Press. Includes a description of competition as a paradox: a self-perpetuating and yet self-defeating behavior.

Orlick, Terry. 1978. *Winning through Cooperation*. Washington, DC: Acropolis Books. Promotes concept of new games, based on cooperation. Includes anecdotal evidence of value of cooperation from other cultures.

Radloff, Roland. 1966. "Social Comparison and Ability Evaluation." *Journal of Experimental Social Psychology* 1 (Suppl.): 6–26. Defines competition as a social comparison process between individuals.

Rasch, Philip J., Hunt, M. Briggs, and Robertson, Port G. 1961. "The Booth Scale as a Predictor of Competitive Behavior of College Wrestlers." *Research Quarterly* 31:117–118. Tests but fails to confirm Booth's findings regarding personality attributes and competitiveness.

Reddiford, Gordon. 1982. "Playing to Win." *Physical Education Review* 5(2):107–115. Apologia for competition; emphasizes role of rules, fair play, and striving for excellence.

Roberts, Glyn C., and Russell, David G. 1977. "The Forgotten Factor: Psychological Processes of Competition." *Australian Journal of Sports Medicine* 9:38–43. Offers an interpretation of competition as an information-processing and motivational strategy.

Ross, Robert G., and Van den Haag, Ernest. 1957. *The Fabric of Society*. New York: Harcourt Brace and World. Offers a distinction between indirect and direct competition (competing against a record or ideal versus competing against another person).

Ryan, Frank J. 1958. "An Investigation of Personality Differences Associated with Competitive Ability." In *Psychosocial Problems of College Men*, ed. Bryant M. Wedge, New Haven, CT: Yale University Press. Examined personality correlates of men judged to be good competitors.

Scanlon, Tara K. 1978. "Antecedents of Competitiveness." In *Children in Sport*, ed. Richard Magill, Michael Ash, and Frank Smoll, 53–75. Champaign, IL: Human Kinetics. Applies Verhoff's and Martens's theories about the acquisition of competitiveness to a model relating competition and the notions of achievement motivation and competance seeking.

Segal, Erich. 1984. "To Win or Die: A Taxonomy of Sporting Attitudes." *Journal of*

Sport History 11(2):25–31. Reviews range of attitudes toward competition from positive to negative.

Skinner, Benjamin F. 1953. *Science and Human Behavior.* London: Collier-Macmillan. An early behavioral text leading to development of stimulus-response psychology; interprets competition in terms of behavioral reinforcement.

Solomon, Daniel. 1969. "The Generality of Children's Achievement-Related Behavior." *Journal of Genetic Psychology* 114:109–125. Examines whether competition is a general achievement motive or if it is limited to only specific activities.

Sutton-Smith, Brian. 1972. *The Folk Games of Children.* Austin, TX: University of Texas Press. Reviews many different studies examining children's play and sports in primitive and developed societies.

Thomas, W. I. 1901. "The Gaming Instinct." *American Journal of Sociology* 6:750–763. An early sociological analysis of the role of competition in society; basically an apologia for competition.

Underwood, John. 1984. "A Game Plan for America." In *Sport in Contemporary Society,* 2nd edition, ed. D. Stanley Eitzen, 416–430. New York: St. Martin's Press.

Verhoff, Joseph. 1973. "Development of Achievement Motivation." In *Achievement-Related Motives in Children,* ed. C. P. Smith. New York: Russell Sage Foundation. An influential model of the acquisition of competitiveness by children: proposes three stages—acquisition, application, and integration.

Watson, Geoffrey G. 1981. "Introducing Children to Attractive Competitive Situations." Paper presented to the fifth World Congress on Psychology of Sport, Ottawa, Ont. Presents a three-stage design for introducing children to competition using Verhoff's model.

White, Robert. 1959. "Motivation Reconsidered: The Concept of Competence." *Psychological Review* 66:297–334. Presents a good case for the origin of intrinsic motives, including competition, as deriving from the desire to be competent in one's environment.

Whiting, Harold T. A. 1972. "Psychology of Competition." In *Readings in Sport Psychology,* ed. Harold T. A. Whiting, 11–25. London: Kingston. Offers a definition of competition based on the notion of striving against others or the environment for personal gain.

Whittemore, Irving C. 1924. "Influence of Competition on Performance: An Experimental Study." *Journal of Abnormal and Social Psychology* 19:236–253. Examines effect of competition on accuracy of skill performance.

Willis, Joseph D. 1982. "Three Scales to Measure Competition-Related Motives in Sport." *Journal of Sport Psychology* 4:338–353. Develops and tests three personality tests designed to identify motives related to sport and competitiveness.

Yerkes, Robert M., and Dodson, Joseph D. 1908. "The Relation of Strength of Stimulus to Rapidity of Habit-Formation." *Journal of Comparative Neurology and Psychology* 18:459–482. Observed an inverted-U function relating arousal level and rapidity of learning.

SOURCES OF ADDITIONAL INFORMATION

A good introduction to the role of competition, personality difference, motivation, and other psychological factors in sport is Richard H. Cox's *Sport Psychology* (Dubuque, IA: William C. Brown, 1985). Edmund Burke and Douglas Kleiber, "Psychological and

Physical Implications of Highly Competitive Sports for Children," in William Straub, ed., *Sport Psychology* (Ithaca, NY: Movement Publications, 1980, 305–313), and Burt S. Rushall, "The Content of Competition Thinking," in William Straub, ed., *Cognitive Sport Psychology* (Lansing, NY: Sport Science Associates, 1984, 51–62) are two, more narrow examinations of aspects of competition in sport. Gary Werner's, *Competition* (Elgin, IL: David C. Cook, 1979), is a personal essay on the benefits and dangers of competition with special emphasis on the relationship between competition and the Fellowship of Christian Athletes' version of Christianity. Rainer Martens's SCAT instrument is described in detail in his *Sport Competition Anxiety Test* (Champaign, IL: Human Kinetics, 1977). Brian Sutton-Smith and John Roberts offer a tripartite description of competitive styles in "Rubrics of Competitive Behavior" (*Journal of Genetic Psychology* 105:13–37, 1960). Diane Gill et al., have examined the effects of sex differences on response to competition in "Sex Differences in Achievement Cognition and Performance in Competition" (*Research Quarterly* 55:340–346, 1984).

COMPLEMENTARITY. The quality of two or more activities such that participation in one activity facilitates or enhances participation in another activity.

The concept of complementarity is a derivative of research into ACTIVITY CLUSTERS and SUBSTITUTION. Much of the original research into identifying substitutable activities was based on factor analyses of participation patterns (Proctor, 1962; Bishop, 1970; Hendee and Burdge, 1974). The premise of this work was that activities that clustered together on statistically derived factors of participation provided similar types of satisfaction for participants, and thus could be substituted for each other.

Other authors, such as Jay Beaman (1975) and Robert Baumgartner and Thomas Heberlein (1981), have noted that activities cluster together on participation-based factors solely on the basis of common participation. While some substitutable activities may be found together on the same factor, other forces can lead to such clustering. These forces include spurious correlations created by unidentified common elements such as social class. William Moss and Stephen Lamphear (1970), for example, found that sailing and dancing clustered together. Another source of clustering is participation in two or more activities that are closely linked: *complementary activities*. Complementary activities are those activities that enhance or facilitate participation in each other such as playing rugby and drinking beer, camping and hiking, or dining out and attending the theater. Participation in one of these is usually directly associated with or preceded by participation in the other, as part of a larger recreation experience. Elimination of one-half of these pairs for some legal or management reason would not lead to increased participation in the other half, as a substitute; rather, participation in the remaining activity would also disappear.

REFERENCES

Baumgartner, Robert, and Heberlein, Thomas. 1981. "Process, Goal, and Social Interaction Differences in Recreation: What Makes an Activity Substitutable?" *Leisure Sciences* 4:443–457.

Beaman, Jay. 1975. "Comments on the Paper 'The Substitutability Concept: Implications for Recreation Research and Management' by Hendee and Burdge." *Journal of Leisure Research* 7:146–151. Presents a methodological critique of Hendee and Burdge; notes their method cannot distinguish between substitutability and complementarity.

Bishop, Doyle. 1970. "Stability of the Factor Structure of Leisure Behavior." *Journal of Leisure Research* 2:160–170. Examines the factor structure of leisure participation in four communities.

Hendee, John C., and Burdge, Rabel J. 1974. "The Substitutability Concept: Implications for Recreation Research and Management." *Journal of Leisure Research* 6:157–162. Describes the concept of substitutability; a basic reference in the history of the concept of substitutability. Presents both conceptual model and empirical evidence of substitutability.

Moss, William T., and Lamphear, Stephen C. 1970. "Substitutability of Recreation Activities in Meeting Stated Needs and Drives of the Visitor." *Environmental Education* 1(4):129–131. Example of an empirical derivation of activity clusters to identify substitutable activities in the context of environmental education and recreation programming.

Proctor, Charles. 1962. "Dependence of Recreation Participation on Background Characteristics of Sample Persons in the September 1960 National Recreation Survey." In *National Recreation Survey, ORRRC Study*, report 19, 77–94. Washington, DC: U.S. Government Printing Office. One of the first examples of a factor analysis of recreation participation.

SOURCES OF ADDITIONAL INFORMATION

Research specifically directed toward complementarity is relatively scarce. One finds the issue discussed in broader articles and chapters examining substitutability. A good theoretical examination of substitutability is Seppo Iso-Ahola's "A Theory of Substitutability of Leisure Behavior" (*Leisure Sciences* 8:367–389, 1985). Iso-Ahola also addresses the topic in his *The Social Psychology of Leisure and Recreation* (Dubuque, IA: William C. Brown, 1980). Jerry Vaske, Maureen Donnelly, and Dan Tweed, "Recreationist-Defined versus Researcher-Defined Similarity Judgments in Substitutability Research" (*Journal of Leisure Research* 15: 251–262, 1983) examine the relative validity of different types of measures of substitutability, including a user-defined estimate that allows a researcher to distinguish between substitution and complementarity in the motivations of the participant.

CONFLICT. The subjective experience of interference, attributed to another person or group, in the pursuit of a RECREATION, LEISURE, or TOURISM goal.

The management or prevention of conflicts between users, potential users, or local residents and visitors is a major concern for managers, policymakers, and planners (Bryan, 1979). Conflicts in recreation, leisure, and tourism tend to arise in two contexts: (1) individuals engaging in incompatible activities or DEPRECIATIVE BEHAVIOR, and (2) individuals pursuing compatible or identical activities that result in immediate competition for scarce resources. This latter context produces conflict when one individual or group loses the competition and blames another for their loss. Conflict thus may sometimes be interpreted as a zero-sum GAME where one party's success comes at the expense of another party's failure. The critical element here is the attribution of blame by one party to the other. If the loss of a recreation opportunity is attributed to "bad luck," there is no sense of conflict. It should also be noted that the accused party does not have to actually be responsible for the perceived loss for a perception of conflict to exist. Perception, rather than reality, is the determinant.

This point about perception illustrates a fundamental characteristic of conflict: it is subjective. Although certain objective situations may almost always lead to a feeling of conflict, such as a motorboater racing through a crowded swimming area, conflict is an interpretation of the objective situation, not the situation, per se. One implication of this is that conflict may be either symmetrical or asymmetrical. In the motorboat example, the boater's behavior may have been provoked by resentment of swimmers near a launching ramp. In such a case, the conflict is symmetrical or mutual.

As an example of asymmetrical conflict, two hikers may pass each other in a WILDERNESS area. One may enjoy meeting a fellow outdoor enthusiast, while the other may resent having his solitude violated. The subjective interpretation of the same event can result in one recreationist perceiving the encounter to be a potentially pleasant encounter while the other sees it as a conflict. A special form of symmetrical conflict in tourism is XENOPHOBIA, an intense disliking of any visitor by local residents.

Gerald Jacob and Richard Schreyer (1980) identify four factors that can lead to feelings of conflict:

1. Differences in activity style. Incompatible differences in the intensity of participation or COMPETITION; blatant and objectionable differences in styles of dress or quality of equipment.

2. Issues of resource specificity. A sense of exclusive ownership of a facility by one user group; symbolic meanings attached to places or activities.

3. Incompatible modes of experiences. Emphasis on movement and action versus emphasis on meditation or aesthetic appreciation.

4. Lifestyle intolerance. Intolerance for different ethnic groups or for individuals who live in other communities; differences in VALUES, particularly as revealed in activities.

Conflict may result in a number of different responses, depending on the intensity of the feelings of conflict, the number of individuals who experience these feelings, and the sociopolitical context of the conflict. In many instances, conflict simply results in DISPLACEMENT (Anderson and Brown, 1984), such as the party experiencing the conflict switching to a different facility. Conflict may also result in COGNITIVE DISSONANCE—the user concludes that the lost opportunity "is not that important." This strategy helps to reduce feelings of frustration or anger. In more dramatic conflicts, the offended parties resort to legal or political remedies, including lawsuits, boycotts, and civil disobedience. These actions may draw other users, the manager, and policymakers into the conflict. Extremely intense user conflicts may even lead to criminal acts and violence.

Existing theoretical and empirical research on conflict in tourism, recreation, and leisure studies is inadequate. Much more empirical research needs to be done defining, measuring, diagnosing, managing, and preventing conflicts if recreation and TOURISM facilities and sites are to be successfully operated.

REFERENCES

Anderson, Dorothy H., and Brown, Perry J. 1984. "The Displacement Process in Recreation." *Journal of Leisure Research* 16:61–73. Examines the displacement process as a social-psychological phenomenon; illustrates with empirical data from the Boundary Waters Canoe Area Wilderness.

Bryan, Hobson. 1979. *Conflict in the Great Outdoors: Toward Understanding and Managing for Divers Sportsmen Preferences*. University, AL: University of Alabama Bureau of Public Administration. A report on some causes of and management strategies for conflict in outdoor recreation.

Jacob, Gerald, and Schreyer, Richard. 1980. "Conflict in Outdoor Recreation: A Theoretical Perspective." *Journal of Leisure Research* 12:368–380. Provides an overview of major conceptual and theoretical issues involved in the analysis of conflicts in recreation.

SOURCES OF ADDITIONAL INFORMATION

A research problem in the study of conflict is the development of a workable operational definition. This issue as well as other difficulties is discussed in Clinton Fink, "Some Conceptual Difficulties in the Theory of Social Conflicts" (*Journal of Conflict Resolution* 12:412–460, 1968). Further information on conceptual issues on the study of conflicts may be found in Vahakn Dadrian, "On the Dual Role of Social Conflicts: An Appraisal of Coser's Theory" (*International Journal of Group Tensions* 1:371–377, 1971) and in Morton Deutsch, "Toward an Understanding of Conflict" (*International Journal of Group Tensions* 1:42–54, 1971). Some conflict studies specific to recreation and leisure are Beverly Driver and John Bassett, "Defining Conflicts among River Users: A Case Study of Michigan's AuSable River" (*Naturalist* 1:19–23, 1975) and Timothy Knopp and John Tyger, "A Study of Conflict in Recreational Land Use: Snowmobiling versus Ski-Touring" (*Journal of Leisure Research* 5:6–17, 1973). A tourism example is Wesley Roehl and Daniel Fesenmeir, "Tourism Land Use Conflict in the United States" (*Annals of Tourism Research* 14:471–485, 1985).

CONSERVATION. The rational use and management of RESOURCES to (1) provide a sustainable yield from renewable resources, (2) maintain the existing stock of nonrenewable resources as long as possible while also maintaining an acceptable quality of life in the society that controls those resources, and (3) preserve rare or significant resources from extinction or disappearance.

Definitions of conservation, particularly in the context of natural resources, are the subject of frequent debate. Differences of opinion stem not just from conceptual differences of competing disciplines or philosophies, but from the recognition that the application of a particular definition by a public agency can have a significant effect on the profitability of individual businesses, on the health of an industry, on a region's or nation's economy, on the quality of the physical ENVIRONMENT, and even on the quality of life in a society and in neighboring societies.

While conservation is basically a modern concept, actions that represent harbingers of the conservation ethic may be found throughout history. For example, Charles Bennett (1983) observed that Assyrian rulers in 850 B.C. practiced a form of game management and that Chinese emperors may have been even earlier practitioners. He also cited evidence that the Incas controlled the hunting of vicuna and regulated the number of predators on vicuna through selective harvesting of the predators. In England, William the Conqueror established the New Forest as a game reserve and implemented stringent penalties for poaching: "Whoever shall kill a stag, wild boar, or even a hare, shall have his eyes torn out." William's actions illustrate an important point about early "conservation" legislation: the motivation for most early game regulations was the desire to protect the privileges of the nobility rather than the integrity of the resource base or the quality of life of the general public.

This rather selfish motivation persisted into the settlement of the New World. For example, forest resources in the Plymouth Colony were placed under royal protection to ensure that the most desirable trees would be reserved for the British navy. By the end of the seventeenth century, however, some public leaders were beginning to recognize the broader social implications of resource protection and the problems that might ensue if resources were not conserved. William Penn, for example, wrote of the potential loss of forests through uncontrolled settlement and agricultural practices. He required, in his 1681 ordinance, that 1 acre of land be left forested for every 5 acres of land that were cleared. A century later, George Washington warned of soil erosion problems and the attendant loss of fertility on his plantation and those of his neighbors.

Conservation of resources, as we understand the concept, began to take form after the American Civil War. The Homestead Act of 1862 that encouraged dispersal of new settlements, the extension of the railroad across the continent, the slow realization that the frontier was disappearing, and the increasingly frequent public accounts of the wanton destruction of wildlife—from the passenger pigeon to the buffalo—helped to stir national concern over the future of America's land, wildlife, forests, and waters. This growing concern led to a series of public actions that helped to increase the momentum of the "conservation movement":

1864   Yosemite Valley, California, reserved as a state park

1871   U.S. Fish Commission established

1872   Yellowstone National Park established

1875   American Forestry Association created

1879   U.S. Geological Survey established

1885   New York State and the Province of Ontario created the Niagara Falls Reservation

1891   Forest Reserve Act approved by Congress

1891   Yosemite National park established

1892   Sierra Club founded

1895   American Scenic and Historic Preservation Society founded

1900   Lacey Act became law making the interstate shipment of game killed in violation of state laws a federal offence

1902   Bureau of Reclamation created

1905   National Audubon Society founded

1906   Antiquities Act permits creation of national monuments

1908   Theodore Roosevelt convened White House Conference of Governors on Conservation

1908   White House Governors' Conference

This chronology can be extended to the present day, but many authors believe that the 1908 White House Governors' Conference was a culminating act in the early history of conservation. It not only raised public awareness of the need for conservation but helped to mobilize the powers of state and federal agencies to work towards conservation goals. It was also about the time of the 1908 Governors' Conference that debates among conservationists began to split the movement into relatively distinct "camps." These camps continue to exist today and continue to shape American conservation debate and policy.

Even the credit for using the term *conservation* in its modern sense is a matter of debate by these camps. Gifford Pinchot, who was an important figure behind the 1908 Conference, claimed this distinction in his *Breaking New Ground* (1947). The significance of his assertion is that he intended conservation to mean, "wise use," not preservation, as his opponents preferred. Samuel Hays (1959), however, observes earlier examples of the use of conservation in the modern sense of resource preservation. Whitney Cross (1953) also discusses the issue of competing claims to the term and concept of conservation.

While many different positions and definitions have been proposed by North American conservationists over the last century, Leonard Ortolano (1984) suggests that conservation definitions can be grouped into three general schools: (1) efficient use of resources; (2) maintenance of harmony between people and nature; and (3) religion, renewal, and rights.

The first school—efficiency—emphasizes the wise use of resources. As noted previously, it is closely associated with Pinchot, a close friend of Theodore Roosevelt. Pinchot was influential in making conservation a political reality and in formulating public policy in a way that balanced the ideals of resource protection with the political and economic realities of his time. In *The Fight for Conservation,* Pinchot (1910:42–50) outlined three principles of conservation.

The first of these, aimed at reassuring those business leaders who feared that conservation meant preservation, stated clearly: "The first principle of conservation is development, the use of natural resources now existing on this continent for the benefit of the people who live here now."

Pinchot's second principle was more general and less controversial: "Conservation stands for the prevention of waste." The third principle expressed the prevailing concern in the federal government over the problem of monopolies in American industry: "The natural resources must be developed and preserved for the benefit of the many, and not merely for the profit of the few."

Implicit in all three principles was Pinchot's belief that conservation practices required the guidance of scientists and technologists. Conservation is not simply a matter of caring about nature, but of collecting data, conducting research, and relying on expertly trained managers to promote the efficient use of resources for social and economic benefits. Much of the conservation literature of the first half of the twentieth century emphasized the need for scientific or technical education as the basis for conservation practice; this issue is examined in greater detail in Samuel Hays (1959).

The efficiency school, represented also by writing of authors such as Orris Herfindahl (1961), Reuben Parson (1964), Henry Clepper (1966), and Bennett (1973), continues to be important today. It is part of the intellectual foundation of benefit-cost analysis and serves as a guiding principle in many public policy decisions about resource protection.

Conservation as a search for "harmony" developed from George Marsh's (1864) *Man and Nature; or, Physical Geography as Modified by Human Action.* Marsh's thesis in this influential text was that *human improvidence* (Marsh's term) could threaten the natural balance and eventually the earth's ability to support human life. Aldo Leopold (1933) advanced the views of Marsh and gave them a more contemporary, scientific foundation. Rachel Carson's (1962) popular *Silent Spring* helped to raise public awareness of this view of conservation, and was an important force in the banning of DDT as a pesticide. Conservation as "harmony" is a philosophy that is popular in general books on conservation and is an integral part of some secondary school programs in environmental studies. It is arguably the dominant public view of conservation—shaping public response to issues of pollution, acid rain, erosion, and the loss of endangered species.

The third philosophy, conservation as a quasi-religion, has evolved from the writings of the English romantic poets William Wordsworth and Samuel Taylor Coleridge, and from the American transcendentalists Ralph Waldo Emerson and Henry David Thoreau. These authors found beauty, renewal, and spiritual growth in WILDERNESS. To them, civilized society was chaotic and corrupt; one could only hope to find moral perfection by returning to nature. The natural environment was to these individuals a form of therapy from people suffering the illness of modernization.

The greatest spokesman for this philosophy was John Muir, a leader in the futile fight to save Hetch Hetchy Valley and the founder of the Sierra Club. While Muir and his followers served an important role in the development of the concepts of wilderness and conservation, their views are probably not in the mainstream of conservation thought in America today. They do, however, still have adherents. Groups such as Friends of the Earth and Greenpeace represent a particularly militant form of this philosophy of conservation. Another aspect of the quasi-religious view of conservation, hinted at by Aldo Leopold and John Muir but openly expressed by some activists, is that animals and possibly vegetation and even inanimate matter should be considered as part of the human moral community. In this view, nonhuman species are presumed to have legal rights. Christopher Stone (1974) advanced this view in his monograph, *Should Trees Have Standing?* This document played a role in the U.S. Supreme Court deliberations on whether the U.S. Forest Service should be permitted to construct a ski resort in the Mineral King Valley Wilderness. While the Supreme Court declined to give nonhuman species legal standing in that dispute, Supreme Court Justice William Black noted that plaintiffs in litigation sometimes appear to speak for an ecological resource, such as a fisherman appearing before a court to testify on behalf of the protection of a fishery.

John Passmore (1974) argued, however, that the notion that nonhuman entities have legal rights is absurd. To accept such a view would, in Passmore's opinion, not only mean that progress would cease, but that human life itself might perish. People exist and societies flourish by utilizing and consuming natural resources. Accepting the hypothesis that plants and animals have a moral right to life would destroy the ability of people to harvest food for their own survival and would be an implicit but profound statement that nonhuman species had rights superior to those of humans.

A more moderate view of the spiritual conception of conservation was expressed by Lyndon Johnson (1965) in his call for a broader interpretation of conservation to meet the challenges faced by American cities and rural areas in the 1960s: "Our conservation must not be just the classic conservation of protection and development, but a creative conservation of restoration and innovation. Its concern is not with nature alone but with the total relationship between man and the world around him. Its object is not just man's welfare but the dignity of man's spirit."

Perhaps the most significant feature of this statement is not the emphasis on the role of conservation as a force for enhancing the "dignity of man's spirit," but the extension of conservation to the entire environment—natural and manmade. This statement was made as part of President Johnson's announcement for a White House Conference on Natural Beauty that helped spark a wave of beautification and restoration projects in both urban and rural areas across the country and helped to crystalize an attitude toward environmental and heritage protection that continues today.

The foregoing discussion repeats a view of conservation that is relatively specific to the United States and Canada. The quasi-religious view of conservation, with its emphasis on preservation of wilderness, is particularly unique to North America. Many developed countries throughout the world no longer have wilderness areas comparable to those in the American west or the Canadian west and north. As a result, the idea of preserving large tracts of unspoiled or unmodified ecosystems for any purpose is simply irrelevant.

A more common and realistic view of conservation in other countries is a synthesis of the efficiency and harmony conceptions of conservation. This synthesis is usually described as "sustainable development." Human actions and the environment cannot be separated: societies must utilize their resources if their people are to live; natural ecosystems must be protected and sustained if the life-supporting capabilities of the environment are to be maintained. BIO-SPHERE RESERVES are intended to provide practical demonstrations of how this can be done in a variety of ecosystems around the world. These reserves, however, are isolated and relatively unique sites. As a strategy to promote the principles of sustainable development and to encourage greater application of the lessons learned from biosphere reserves and other research projects, the International Union for the Conservation of Nature and Natural Resources (IUCN)—in cooperation with the U.N. Environmental Program; the U.N. Educational, Scientific, and Cultural Organization (UNESCO); the Food and Agriculture Organization; and the World Wildlife Fund—undertook the development of the World Conservation Strategy in 1980 (IUCN/UNEP/WWF, 1980). This strategy has three basic objectives: (1) maintenance of essential ecological processes, (2) preservation of genetic diversity of wildlife, and (3) sustainable utilization of ecosystems for human well-being. By July 1987, more than forty countries had adopted or were considering the principles laid out in the World Conservation Strategy and their relevance to a National Conservation Strategy. Gordon Nelson (1987) provides an overview of how the World Conservation Strategy is interpreted and applied in nine different natural settings. The 1980 strategy has been expanded and updated by *Our Common Future* (World Commission on Environment and Development, 1987), also known as the Brundtland Report (after the Norwegian prime minister, Gro Harlem Brundtland who chaired the commission that wrote the report).

The modern concept of conservation is more than a century old. Like many other concepts in this dictionary, conservation is a uniquely human matter. Other species use resources for their survival, but their actions are controlled by a balance of environmental and genetic forces. Humans, however, have developed complex educational, social, and political forces that govern and motivate our use of resources. The issue of conservation of resources is one of the two great themes (the other being human development) in recreation and leisure studies. Many recreation and leisure studies departments can trace their roots back to conservation-related programs in colleges and universities. Conservation issues have dominated and continue to dominate much of the research, education, and service activities of our field.

REFERENCES

Bennett, Charles F. 1983. *Conservation and Management of Natural Resources in the United States*. New York: Wiley. An introductory-level textbook with fairly conventional chapters on major resource groups; special attention is given, however, to some resource problems in the Third World.

Carson, Rachel. 1962. *Silent Spring*. Boston: Houghton Mifflin. A controversial and influential text on the potential dangers associated with pesticide "fallout" and its effect on human health as well as on the balance of nature.

Clepper, Henry. 1966. *Origins of American Conservation*. New York: Ronald Press. A collection of historical essays on natural resources and the rise of the conservation ethic.

Cross, Whitney R. 1953. "W J McGee and the Idea of Conservation," *Historian* 15:148–162. A brief history of the development of the concept of conservation, with particular attention paid to the role of one of Pinchot's associates, W J McGee.

Hays, Samuel P. 1959. *Conservation and the Gospel of Efficiency: The Progressive Conservation Movement, 1890–1920*. Cambridge, MA: Harvard University Press. A history of the conservation movement, with special emphasis on conservation as efficient use of resources.

Herfindahl, Orris C. 1961. "What Is Conservation?" In *Three Studies in Minerals Economics*, ed. O. C. Herfindahl, 1–12. Washington, DC: Resources for the Future. A definitional essay that critically examines contemporary definitions of conservation such as "wise use" and "greatest good for the greatest number." Concludes with a simple definition: Conservation is that "which saves something for future use instead of present use or which saves something for use instead of nonuse."

IUCN/UNEP/WWF. 1980. *World Conservation Strategy*. Gland, Switzerland: IUCN. The definitive statement of the World Conservation Strategy; includes a discussion of conservation and recommendations for national actions.

Johnson, Lyndon B. 1965. "Natural Beauty—Message from the President of the United States." *Congressional Record* 89th Cong., 1st sess., Feb. 8, Vol. 111, pt. 2, 2085–2089. The official call for a conference on natural beauty; generally considered to be one of the landmark events in conservation since World War II.

Leopold, Aldo. 1933. *Game Management*. New York: Charles Scribner's Sons. A landmark study in the conservation of wild animals and of the development of a scientific basis for conservation practice.

Marsh, George P. 1864. *Man and Nature; or, Physical Geography as Modified by Human Action*. New York: Charles Scribner. A classic text on human-environment relationships; influenced many early conservationists.

Nelson, J. Gordon. 1987. "Experience with National Conservation Strategies." *Alternatives* 15(1):42–49. A review of nine nations' responses to the World Conservation Strategy.

Ortolano, Leonard. 1984. *Environmental Planning and Decision Making*. New York: Wiley. An introductory but somewhat technical book on environmental planning.

Parson, Reuben L. 1964. *Conserving American Resources*. Englewood Cliffs, NJ: Prentice Hall. A popular text on natural resource conservation in the 1960s; orientation is a modern version of Pinchot's "wise use" philosophy.

Passmore, John A. 1974. *Man's Responsibility for Nature, Ecological Problems, and*

Western Traditions. London: Duckworth. An interpretation of the conservation
    movement; criticizes the notion that nonhuman species are part of the human moral
    community.
Pinchot, Gifford. 1910. *The Fight for Conservation.* Garden City, NY:Harcourt Brace.
    An important statement of the "wise use" or utilitarian school of conservation;
    this book helped to make conservation a household word.
Pinchot, Gifford. 1947. *Breaking New Ground.* New York: Harcourt, Brace, and World.
    Pinchot's reflections on the origin of the idea of conservation and his role in it.
Stone, Christopher D. 1974. *Should Trees Have Standing?* Los Altos, CA: William
    Kaufmann. A controversial book presenting the case for legal status for nonhuman
    species.
World Commission on Environment and Development. 1987. *Our Common Future.*
    London: Oxford University Press. The final report of the so-called Brundtland
    Commission; sets out an international strategy for conservation and economic
    development to reduce poverty, especially in Third World countries, that will
    protect global environments.

SOURCES OF ADDITIONAL INFORMATION

Literally hundreds of books and tens of thousands of articles have been written on
conservation. Some helpful references that will serve as a starting point for further reading
include the following: Roderick Nash's, *Wilderness and the American Mind,* (Hartford,
CT: Yale University Press, 1967) is a still widely respected history of the wilderness
movement with much relevance to the early struggles of conservationists. Nash has also
prepared a collection of historical essays by many of the noted figures in the history of
conservation from artist George Catlin (1832) to Lyndon Johnson (1965) titled *The
American Environment: Readings in the History of Conservation* (Reading, MA: Addison-
Wesley, 1968). Ian Burton has edited a collection of readings with a more modern and
technical orientation: *Readings in Resource Management and Conservation* (Chicago:
University of Chicago Press, 1965). Still another collection, this one with a mix of more
scholarly articles, popular journalism, and poetry is Robert McHenry's *A Documentary
History of Conservation in America* (New York: Praeger, 1972). A report that is a useful
complement to the Brundtland Report is W. C. Clark and R. E. Munn, eds., *Sustainable
Development of the Biosphere* (London: Cambridge University Press, 1986). Finally, a
popular, well-written, and moving book that has developed nearly a cultlike reputation
is Aldo Leopold's *A Sand County Almanac and Sketches Here and There* (New York:
Oxford University Press, 1949).

CONSPICUOUS CONSUMPTION. The excessive or unproductive consumption of commodities—especially rare, expensive, or desirable commodities—for
the purpose of demonstrating social status.

The concept of conspicuous consumption is usually associated with Thorstein
Veblen. Veblen, a social critic writing in the United States in the closing years
of the nineteenth century and the beginning of the twentieth, described how the
nouveau riche—the LEISURE CLASS, in Veblen's terminology—of industrialized
America used consumption and leisure to distinguish themselves from the masses
of middle- and working-class Americans. Although Veblen's goal was an attack

on the extravagance of parvenus, he also described how conspicuous consumption has been a social phenomenon of virtually every CULTURE since prehistoric times. For example, Veblen suggested that males in primitive societies established their self-presumed social superiority over females by claiming the best and greatest quantity of food, clothing, and ornamentation for themselves. Female consumption of food and clothing was limited only to those goods necessary to ensure their continued productivity for the entire tribe, and not for their own fulfillment or comfort.

Veblen's analysis of American society focused not only on the use of alcohol, narcotics, jewelry, expensive clothing, and elaborate homes as examples of conspicuous consumption, but also on participation in certain types of SPORT and LEISURE activity and patronage of the arts as ways of demonstrating social status or personal dignity. While conspicuous consumption is often thought to be exclusive to the idle rich, Veblen suggested that some form of conspicuous consumption may be found at nearly all levels of society.

Political, social, cultural, and economic changes have created a world at the end of the twentieth century that is quite different from the society Veblen knew; however, conspicuous consumption remains a valid and powerful concept for social scientists concerned with patterns of leisure behavior.

REFERENCE

Veblen, Thorstein. 1899. *The Theory of the Leisure Class*. New York: Macmillan. The classic study of leisure behavior and social life in turn-of-the-century America.

SOURCES OF ADDITIONAL INFORMATION

Conspicuous consumption is discussed in many sociology survey texts. Other authors that have examined the role of consumption in social status and lifestyles include John Kenneth Galbraith, *The Affluent Society* (Boston: Houghton Mifflin, 1984); Gabriel Kolko, *Wealth and Power in America* (New York: Praeger, 1962); Tibor Scitovsky, *The Joyless Economy: An Inquiry into Human Satisfaction* (New York: Oxford University Press, 1976); David Riesman, *The Lonely Crowd* (New Haven, CT: Yale University Press, 1950); and C. A. R. Crosland, *The Future of Socialism* (London: Cape, 1956).

CONSTRAINT. Any factor that precludes or reduced an individual's frequency, rate, or satisfaction level of participating in a recreation activity.

The concept of constraint is closely linked to that of BARRIER and NONPARTICIPATION. Edgar Jackson (1988), however, has argued that constraint is broader than barrier and may be a preferable term when discussing the full range of factors that preclude or reduce recreation participation. Duane Crawford and Geoffrey Godbey (1987) also discuss the breadth of constraint as a concept and note that there is no widely accepted operational definition of the term. Most researchers use a phrase similar to ''any factor which intervenes between the preference for an activity and participation in it'' (Crawford and Godbey,

1987:120). In his review article, Jackson notes that there has not yet been a full cataloging or comprehensive identification of potential constraints. Different authors have proposed a wide range of classification systems and scope of constraints. At one extreme is Gerald Romsa and Wayne Hoffman's (1980) analysis of nonparticipation in which they identify only four factors. At the other extreme, Karla Henderson, Deborah Stalnaker, and Glenda Taylor (1987) identified fifty-five factors. Jackson (1988) believes that there are well over a hundred separate variables that could be labeled as constraints.

Given the uncertainty about the total number of possible constraints, it is not surprising that there is no accepted classification system for constraints. Among the more common systems that have been proposed are "internal" versus "external" (Francken and van Raaij, 1981), "blocking" versus "inhibiting" (Jackson and Searle, 1985), "intrapersonal" versus "interpersonal" (Crawford and Godbey, 1987), "permanent" versus "temporary" (Iso-Ahola and Mannell, 1985), and "subject to management control" versus "not subject to management control" (Howard and Crompton, 1984).

Each system has its advantages and disadvantages—the diversity of the proposed systems highlights both the uncertainty about the conceptual nature of constraints as well as the diverse perspectives researchers bring to bear on their study.

However the concept of constraint is to be defined, it is important to distinguish it from reasons for nonparticipation. The notion of a constraint implies that if something were removed or corrected, participation would occur. One reason for nonparticipation is an absence of interest in participating. Lack of interest, therefore would normally not be considered a restraint. Jackson (1988:211) has expressed this as the formula "all constraints are reasons, but not all reasons are constraints."

REFERENCES

Crawford, Duane, and Godbey, Geoffrey. 1987. "Reconceptualizing Barriers to Family Leisure," *Leisure Sciences* 9:119–127. Discusses the concepts of barriers and constraints; offers recommendations for research.
Francken, Dick A., and van Raaij, Fred. 1981. "Satisfaction with Leisure Time Pursuits." *Journal of Leisure Research* 13:337–352. Explains leisure satisfaction as a function of the discrepancy between actual and desired situations, and of perceived barriers.
Henderson, Karla A., Stalnaker, Deborah, and Taylor, Glenda. 1987. "Personality Traits and Leisure Barriers among Women." Paper presented at the fifth Canadian Congress on Leisure Research, Dalhousie University, Halifax, N.S. An empirical study using one of the most exhaustive lists of constraints developed.
Howard, Dennis R., and Crompton, John L. 1984. "Who Are the Consumers of Public Park and Recreation Services?: An Analysis of the Users and Non-Users of Three Municipal Leisure Service Organizations." *Journal of Park and Recreation Administration* 2:33–48. Offers a classification of constraints in terms of those that managers can influence versus those managers cannot.
Iso-Ahola, Seppo, and Mannell, Roger C. 1985. "Social and Psychological Constraints

on Leisure." In *Constraints on Leisure,* ed. Michael Wade, 111–151. Springfield, IL: Charles C. Thomas. Categories constraints into permanent versus temporary barriers on participation.

Jackson, Edgar L. 1988. "Leisure Constraints: A Survey of Past Research." *Leisure Sciences* 10:203–215. A useful overview of the existing literature and conceptualizations of constraints.

Jackson, Edgar L. and Searle, Mark S. 1985. "Recreation Nonparticipation and Barriers to Participation: Concepts and Models." *Leisure and Society* 8:693–707. A conceptual examination of types of recreation barriers; proposes a distinction between "blocking" and "inhibiting" barriers.

Romsa, Gerald, and Hoffman, Wayne. 1980. "An Application of Nonparticipation Data in Recreation Research: Testing the Opportunity Theory." *Journal of Leisure Research* 12:321–328. Utilizes a simple four-part classification of constraints.

SOURCES OF ADDITIONAL INFORMATION

The bibliographies in the barrier and nonparticipation definitions contain a number of good references for further reading. Some sources that are particularly relevant to this topic include Jacqueline Desbarats, "Spatial Choice and Constraints on Behavior" (*Annals of the Association of American Geographers* 73:340–357, 1983); Michael Wade (ed.), *Constraints on Leisure* (Springfield, IL: Charles C. Thomas, 1985). Geoffrey Godbey, "Nonuse of Public Leisure Services: A Model" (*Journal of Park and Recreation Administration* 3:1–12, 1985); and Francis McGuire, "A Factor Analytic Study of Leisure Constraints in Advanced Adulthood" (*Leisure Sciences* 6:313–326, 1984).

CONSUMER SURPLUS. See TRAVEL COST METHOD.

CONTINGENT VALUATION METHOD. A method for estimating the VALUE of a recreation RESOURCE based on asking directly potential consumers their willingness to pay for a specified change in the supply of that resource.

The contingent valuation method (CVM) is one of three standard methods approved by the U.S. Senate for use in estimating the value of public resources for resource development planning. The CVM received approval from the Senate in 1979. The other two methods are the UNIT DAY VALUE METHOD, approved by the Senate in 1962 (U.S. Congress, 1962) and the TRAVEL COST METHOD (TCM), approved for use in 1973.

The basis of this method is to directly ask the potential consumer what he would be willing to pay for some specified increment or decrement in the supply of or access to a given resource. The method may also be used to determine the value of a recreation experience. The earliest formulations of this method were developed by Robert Davis (1963) in the early 1960s. He originally described the approach as a "bidding game." He presented the respondent with a description of the resource (opportunities for outdoor recreation in a Maine State park), a hypothetical specified increment in resource supply, and a hypothetical method of payment. A price was suggested and the respondent asked if he would be willing to pay that amount. If answered affirmatively, the amount was increased systematically until the respondent answered negatively. The maximum value the respondent was willing to pay was taken as an estimate of the marginal value of the proposed increment in resource supply.

Davis (1963) then related the maximum willingness to pay to a number of respondent characteristics through a multiple regression model. He observed a significant positive relationship between the willingness to pay for outdoor recreation and length of residence in the study area, household income, and previous involvement in outdoor recreation. Judd Hammack and Gardner Brown (1974) also observed a similar pattern in their study of recreationists' willingness to pay for waterfowl and wetland recreation. In addition to understanding some of the forces that affect willingness to pay, such studies may provide a shortcut to further analysis of willingness to pay. If a reliable and accurate model can be developed relating observable population characteristics to the intangible willingness to pay, then it is conceptually simple to collect populationwide information on the significant variables from standard census sources, apply the model, and estimate aggregate population willingness to pay and thus the aggregate value of the resource.

The actual successes in developing such reliable and accurate models have been mixed, however, so most researchers and policy analysts have concentrated on directly asking willingness to pay questions of a representative sample of a study population.

Both bidding (iterative) questions such as those used by Davis and noniterative (single estimated maximum value) questions are used. Bidding formats seem to be preferred by many researchers (Walsh, 1986:208) but these are feasible only in personal interviews. Because many large sample surveys are conducted through the use of a mailed questionnaire, the noniterative question format is more common.

As noted above, the usual content of the question in the contingent valuation approach is how much the respondent would be willing to pay for an increase in the resource supply. Some authors have noted that one might also ask questions about willingness to sell (how much the respondent would expect to be paid in compensation for a loss in the available resource base) as well as willingness to bribe (how much the respondent would be willing to pay to avoid suffering a decrease in the available resource base) (Walsh, 1986; Dwyer, Kelly, and Bowes, 1977; Brookshire, Randall, and Stoll, 1980). These authors also noted that, at the time they were writing, the preferred perspective was willingness to pay. Conceptually, however, the choice of willingness to pay versus willingness to sell may be based on the issue of property rights with reference to the resource under study. If potential users currently do not have a legal basis for the use of a resource, such as obtaining access to privately owned land, the willingness to pay perspective is appropriate. However, if the resource is one potential users already have access to, such as public land or private land to which the user group has entitlement, the willingness to sell perspective may be more relevant.

In addition to the challenges of selecting the proper perspective and of developing a satisfactorily worded question to elicit precisely the information sought, two other problems are frequently noted with this method. The first concerns the hypothetical method of payment (sometimes called the payment vehicle). Some researchers have raised the issue of whether respondents assign different values to a resource increment depending on whether the cost increase is levied in the form of increased taxes, entrance fees, license fees, travel costs, or other form. Alan Randall, Barry Ives, and Clyde Eastman (1979) and Douglas Greenley, Richard Walsh, and Robert Young (1981), among others, have found that the hypothetical payment vehicle does appear to have an effect on willingness to pay. For example, Randall, Ives, and Eastman found that their respondents were willing to pay only one-quarter as much for improved air quality through increased utility bills as compared to a sales tax. Greenley, Walsh, and Young found a similar discrepancy for water quality improvements when comparing results from a hypothetical utility bill increase versus a sales tax.

Another, more general concern is whether any meaningful results can be obtained through this method because the contingent valuation approach is a very crude approximation of the actual market place. In particular, it is noted that respondents may employ a gaming strategy by reporting artificially high values if they do not believe the charge is to be implemented, and is only an exercise to determine public support for protecting a resource. On the other hand, if respondents believe a fee will be implemented, they may tend to report values much lower than the ones they would actually pay, if necessary (Freeman, 1979, 1985). If the form of the questionnaire is carefully designed to present as complete a picture of the valuation problem as possible and to encourage the respondents to think in terms of a marketplace decision, available evidence in the literature suggests the method can overcome this "strategic bias" and produce acceptable estimates (Cocheba and Langford, 1981; Haspel and Johnson, 1982; Randall, Hoehn, and Tolley, 1981).

The problem of deriving reliable and accurate estimates of the value of resources in different applications is a very important concern in resource analysis. While further refinements of the contingent valuation approach are possible, the state of the art of resource and recreation economics suggests that this approach is accepted as one of the most useful for resource valuation studies and is growing in popularity. It is currently the valuation method of choice for assessing the effects of changes in quality in resources on resource values. The CVM is also particularly useful for determining valuation shift due to resource management changes that may not be reflected in travel patterns or that may simultaneously manage value but lower visitation levels (such as the imposition of a rationing system).

REFERENCES

Brookshire, David S., Randall, Alan, and Stoll, John J. 1980. "Valuing Increments and Decrements in Natural Resource Service Flows." *American Journal of Agricul-*

tural Economics 62:478–488. Compares "willingness to sell" with "willingness to bribe" questions as a basis for contingent valuation.

Cocheba, Daniel J., and Langford, William A. 1981. "Direct Willingness to Pay Questions: An Analysis of Their Use for Quantitatively Valuing Wildlife." *Journal of Leisure Research* 13:311–322. Illustrates contingent value method in context of a migratory bird conservation program.

Davis, Robert K. 1963. "Recreation Planning as an Economic Problem." *Natural Resources Journal* 3:239–249. The first published article examining the use of willingness to pay questions.

Dwyer, John F., Kelly, John R., and Bowes, Michael D. 1977. *Improved Procedures for Valuation of the Contribution of Recreation to National Economic Development*, report no. 128. Urbana, IL: Water Resources Center, University of Illinois. A dated but good overview of valuation procedures for public recreation resources.

Freeman, Myrick. 1979. *The Benefits of Environmental Improvement*. Baltimore: Johns Hopkins University Press. Examines strengths and weaknesses of contingent valuation method.

Freeman, Myrick. 1985. "Supply Uncertainty, Option Price, and Option Value." *Land Economics* 61:176–181. Revisits earlier review of contingent valuation method, particularly in context of option value and demand.

Greenley, Douglas A., Walsh, Richard G., and Young, Robert A. 1982. "Option Value: Empirical Evidence from a Case Study of Recreation and Water Quality." *Quarterly Journal of Economics* 96:657–672. Documents effect of payment format on estimated willingness to pay.

Hammack, Judd, and Brown, Gardner. 1974. *Waterfowl and Wetlands: Toward Bioeconomic Analysis*. Boulder, CO: Westview Press. An early application of the contingent valuation method; similar to Davis's work.

Haspel, Abraham E., and Johnson, F. Reed. 1982. "Multiple Destination Trip Bias in Recreation Benefit Estimation." *Land Economics*. 58:364–372. A technical examination of the effect of 2 or more destinations on estimated recreation benefits.

Randall, Alan, Hoehn, John, and Tolley, George. 1981. "The Structure of Contingent Markets: Some Results of a Recent Experiment." Paper presented at the annual meetings of the American Economic Association, Washington, D.C. A test of the accuracy of the contingent valuation approach.

Randall, Alan, Ives, Barry, and Eastman, Clyde. 1979. "Bidding Games for Valuation of Aesthetic Environmental Improvements." *American Journal of Agricultural Economics* 61:921–925. Examines use of contingent value questions; notes effects of payment format on willingness to pay.

U.S. Congress. Senate. 1962. *Supplement No. 1, Evaluation Standards for Primary Recreation Benefits, in Policies, Standards, and Procedures in the Formulation, Evaluation, and Review of Plans for Use and Development of Water and Related Land Resources*. 87th Cong., 2d sess., May 29, S. Doc. 97.

Walsh, Richard G. 1986. *Recreation Economic Decisions*. State College, PA: Venture. A general recreation economics text; Chapter 8 is an excellent overview of valuation methods.

SOURCES OF ADDITIONAL INFORMATION

A text devoted to the contingent valuation method is R. G. Cummings, D. S. Brookshire, and W. P. Schulze's *Valuing Environmental Goods: An Assessment of the Contingent*

Valuation Method (Totowa, NJ: Rowman and Allanheld, 1986). Richard Walsh's 1987 text, *Recreation Economic Decisions* (which is included in the list of references) is a particularly good introduction to recreation valuation approaches; see Chapter 8, "Measures of Benefits." Other useful sources related to nonmarket valuation and the contingent valuation approach include Richard Bishop and Thomas Heberlein, "Measuring Values of Extra-Market Goods: Are Indirect Measures Biased?" (*American Journal of Agricultural Economics* 61:926–930, 1979); Richard Bishop, Thomas Heberlein, and Mary Jo Kealy, "Contingent Valuation of Environmental Assets: Comparisons with a Simulated Market" (*Natural Resource Journal* 23:619–633, 1983); Kevin Boyle, Richard Bishop, and Michael Welsh, "Starting Point Bias in Contingent Valuation Bidding Games" (*Land Economics* 61:188–194, 1985); David Brookshire and Thomas Crocker, "The Advantages of Contingent Valuation Methods for Benefit-Cost Analysis" (*Public Choice* 36:235–252, 1981); John Daubert and Robert Young, "Recreational Demands for Maintaining Instream Flows: A Contingent Valuation Approach" (*American Journal of Agricultural Economics* 63:665–676, 1981); Jack Knetsch and J. A. Sinden, "Willingness to Pay and Compensation Demanded: Experimental Evidence of an Unexpected Diversity in Measures of Value" (*Quarterly Journal of Economics,* 99:507–521, 1984); and U.S. Water Resources Council, "Economic and Environmental Principles and Guidelines for Water and Related Land Resource Implementation Studies" (Washington, DC: U.S. Government Printing Office, 1983). An article that reviews some problems in CVM is Steven F. Edwards and Glen D. Anderson, "Overlooked Biases in Contingent Valuation Surveys" (*Land Economics* 63:168–178, 1987).

CULTURE. The social HERITAGE of a people, including their material artifacts, belief systems, religions, forms of government, customs, language, RECREATION, housing, commercial activity, forms and places of work, education, and science and technology.

Culture is perhaps the broadest concept in this dictionary. Academic debates of the meaning and content of the term often become tedious and heated; political discussions about a nation's culture may generate suspicion and even violence, as the "Cultural Revolution" in China demonstrated in the 1970s. Such experiences prompted the poet Hans Johst to pen his famous observation, "Whenever I hear the word 'culture,' I release the safety-catch on my pistol."

Culture is included in this dictionary because it provides the context for understanding forms of recreation and LEISURE. Recreation and leisure, in turn, often provide valuable insights into the culture of different societies. The term, however, has evolved through several different connotations over the last two centuries, and continues to be given different emphases by different authors. Alfred Kroeber and Clyde Kluckhohn (1952) collected 166 definitions, primarily from the English language, that they grouped into seven categories: descriptive, historical, normative, psychological, structural, genetic, and incomplete. Their list could be easily doubled using definitions published since 1952. Kroeber and Kluckhohn also provided a succinct history of the concept of culture in the eighteenth and nineteenth centuries, from which the next few paragraphs have drawn.

Prior to the middle of the eighteenth century, *culture* and its equivalent in other European languages generally referred to the growth and cultivation of plants and animals. In the second half of the eighteenth century, however, a number of philosophical and historical works began to appear that used the word *culture* in a human context. Among the more influential of the historical works were the histories of Johann Adelung, *Essay on the History of the Culture of the Human Species* (published anonymously in 1781) and Johann Herder (1887), *Ideas on the Philosophy of History of Mankind* (which originally appeared in a series of four installments, 1784 through 1791).

To Adelung and Herder, culture was basically the development of a refined individual moral or spiritual condition, rather than a more general social phenomenon. For example, Adelung defined *cultur* in his 1793 dictionary as "the improvement of refining of the total mental and bodily forces of a person or a people; so that the word includes not only the enlightening or improving of understanding through liberation from prejudices, but also polishing, namely improvement and refinement, of customs and manners" (quoted in Kroeber and Kluckhohn, 1952:38).

By the end of the eighteenth century, the philosophers who had examined culture as an aspect of the development of an informed intellect and superior moral being, began to lose interest in the topic. This waning of interest in culture as a moral or philosophical concept began with Kant and reached its nadir in the nineteenth century with Hegel. Ironically, about the same time philosophers had nearly abandoned all interest in culture, historians and ethnographers had increased their interest and work, pushing their understanding and usage of the term closer to its modern connotation. A leading figure in the development of an historical approach to the study of culture at this time was Gustav Klemm (1943). He argues that the proper subject of history was not lists of kings and battles, but the development of people through their culture. Klemm's work had a profound influence on other historians, especially Edward Tylor (1871) who proposed a definition of culture in *Primitive Society* that is still considered a standard definition: "the complex whole which includes knowledge, belief, art, law, morals, customs, and any other capabilities and habits acquired by man as a member of society."

Although, as has been noted, interest in culture as a philosophical issue had been declining since Kant's day, a few nineteenth-century philosophers maintained a personal interest. Matthew Arnold (1869:525), in *Culture and Anarchy,* described culture as the pursuit of perfection and, in turn (to use Arnold's phrase, which has long since lost its original force and elegance), "the pursuit of perfection . . . is the pursuit of sweetness and light."

Arnold's conceptualization of culture dominated most popular dictionaries until the 1920s, when Tylor's definition began to replace it. Tylor's historical approach eventually became the dominant paradigm for the study of culture in the 1930s. This approach, however, had several weaknesses. Much of the historical writing on culture is merely descriptive, with no attempt made to test possible causal relationships or to identify underlying forces that shaped culture. Furthermore, the historical approach relied heavily on the literary skills and personal observational sophistication of the authors. In other words, the findings of many cultural historians were open to suspicions about the authors' prejudices and misinterpretations of evidence. Dissatisfaction with the historical approach gave rise to the antihistorical or scientific approaches of Bronislaw Malinowski (1944) and Alfred Radcliffe-Brown (1940). Malinowski proposed an approach toward the study of culture that was analogous to economic theory. He argued that it was possible to develop a scientific theory of culture based on a set of fixed laws and principles that would make the descriptive and subjective approaches of other scholars irrelevant. Radcliffe-Brown, while sharing Malinowski's impatience with the failings of the historical approach, disagreed with Malinowski's criticism of comparisons as a research design. Radcliffe-Brown argued that the analysis of social structures could be achieved only through a systematic and objective comparison of structures from different societies.

This debate between the historical approach and the antihistorical approach has its basis in a well-known tension between the humanities and the social sciences. History and the other humanities tend to be concerned with idiosyncratic problems: unique or singular events that require qualitative analysis and subjective interpretations. The social sciences, on the other hand, tend to be concerned with nomothetic problems: the search for regularities and verifiable laws. Kroeber (1944) felt that the solution to the debate was to search for some sort of middle ground for cultural studies. His position was that because the subject matter of cultural studies is largely idiosyncratic, a descriptive and historical approach is necessary. On the other hand, traditional humanists had been too careless in striving for balance and objectivity in their research, too lax in reporting the quantitative characteristics of any surveys or other objective data cited, and have largely ignored the formulation and rigorous testing of possible casual hypotheses for the phenomena they observe. Closer adherence to the rules of data collection and objective analysis must be achieved even in descriptive work. If the entire body of cultural research were surveyed, according to Kroeber, one would come to the conclusion that the humanistic approach has been more successful in producing publishable research and in generating major insights; the scientific approach has produced fewer demonstrable successes, but it has the potential to do much more.

The tension between the humanistic and the social scientific approaches continues today. In recent years, quantitative research designs have dominated the articles appearing in journals such as *Leisure Sciences* and *Journal of Leisure Research,* but there is a strong recognition of the value of qualitative and phenomenological approaches in the study of leisure, especially when studying leisure as a cultural phenomenon.

While the force of scholarship and research on culture has been channeled along both the historical and social scientific paradigms in recent years, the old view of culture as spiritual and moral growth has not totally disappeared. T. S.

Eliot (1948), writing in the aftermath of World War II prepared a difficult and speculative work, *Notes Towards the Definition of Culture,* that explored the close relationship between culture and religion. He described culture as that which makes life worth living and observed that both culture and religion represented a society's way of life—and were thus closely related. Eliot's *Notes,* however, have not been particularly influential in the modern study of culture because he failed to make a strong logical argument for his views. His emphasis on the importance of a social elite in protecting and developing culture (Eliot viewed World War II as a war precipitated by the European masses) has also tended to put some distance between himself and the majority of cultural scholars.

Josef Pieper (1952), too, wrote at the end of World War II on the nature and role of culture in modern life. Pieper's text, *Leisure: The Basis of Culture,* is better known by leisure scholars than Eliot's work, but like Eliot's work, Pieper's views have had relatively little influence on contemporary social science. Pieper's view of LEISURE also tends to be elitist; leisure is for contemplation, reflection, meditation, and joyous celebration. The quality of an individual's leisure is an indication of the quality of his soul. It is from this spiritually based leisure that culture develops and flourishes. To the degree that a society has time for and supports contemplation and spirituality, to that degree its culture will blossom. The more popular forms of recreation and entertainment have, to Pieper, little to do with "true" leisure or culture.

Pieper's implicit distinction between true leisure and its more popular but less lofty forms was a harbinger of a major research emphasis in the 1960s and 1970s: analysis of the distinctions between "high" and "low" culture. The first challenge in such research is to develop a consensus on subdivisions and terminology. Reviewing the history of debates on the definition of culture itself, it is not surprising to discover that there is yet little agreement on how culture should be subdivided or how the various subcultures are to be studied or by what criteria they are to be evaluated—if they are to be evaluated at all.

Milton Yinger (1960) proposed a distinction between subculture and contra-culture. A subculture is a group defined by a set of relatively consistent and stable behaviors that differ from those displayed by members of the larger society. Subcultures may be created by ethnic minority status, religious differences, linguistic differences, occupational ties, or economic class. The subculture retains a distinct identity within a dominant culture, but does not perceive itself to be in conflict with that culture. A contraculture, on the other hand, is a group that defines itself in terms of its conflict with the larger society. It is, in Yinger's view, a social psychological concept that can be understood best by reference to the dominant culture and the clash of values.

Herbert Gans (1974), noting that critiques of popular culture have been present in some form or another for at least two centuries and that these critiques have been overwhelmingly negative, undertook an objective assessment of the nature of popular culture. Gans argued that the concept of popular culture is too broad, and proposed five taste cultures or publics that represented different forms of popular culture:

High culture: Creators, their critics, and their patrons

Upper-middle culture: Professionals, executives, and well-educated individuals not involved in creativity and not interested in radical innovation

Lower-middle culture: Lower-middle and lower socioeconomic classes; conservative tastes and values; rely heavily on television for entertainment

Lower culture: Hostile to art and culture, prefers stereotypes in entertainment

Quasi-folk culture: Strongly rural and/or immigrant based; strong family and church orientations

Gans acknowledged that some researchers also refer to youth and ethnic cultures but suggested that these are temporary offshoots of the five major taste cultures. These five cultures are shaped by many influences, but socioeconomic status is the strongest influence. The balance of Gans's work concerned the various subcultural tastes and the factors influencing the dynamics of each taste culture. Other authors that have followed a similar research design include Ray Browne (1980), who used a classification scheme similar to Gans's (elite, popular, mass, and folk), and Edward Shils (1959), who proposed a deliberately more provocative scheme (superior culture, mediocre culture, and brutal culture).

Those authors presented alternative designs for classifying subcultures. Other scholars have focused on the different components of culture, rather than different social groups. For example, Ernst Gombrich (1969) described culture as a wheel with eight spokes, representing religion, government, morality, laws, customs, science, art, and technology. These radiate away from a central hub Gombrich labeled "the indescribable essence of culture." Begin at any point on the circle and, although you will proceed in different directions depending on your starting point, you ultimately arrive at the same point—the essence of culture. John Meisel (1979) has developed a more traditional and less picturesque structural classification of cultural components: anthropological issues, political issues, aesthetic or intellectual issues, and leisure issues.

The most interesting and intensely debated topics in the modern study of culture, however, are not typologies or classification schemes, but normative judgments about the significance and value of various forms of popular culture. Although this body of literature is large and continues to grow, the numerous perspectives may be generally categorized as being either optimistic or pessimistic. The optimistic view typically holds that (1) the quality of popular culture has many fine examples of artistic merit; (2) it is not damaging efforts to increase the level of education, taste, and moral development in society and, in fact, may actually help these goals; (3) the common man has as much right to freedom of choice in entertainment as does his elite counterpart; and (4) popular culture is the source of vitality and innovation in art.

The pessimistic view, in contrast, holds that (1) mass culture is degrading and has no artistic merit, (2) it is shaped largely by commercial interests whose only motivation is profit, (3) it acts as a barrier to proper intellectual and moral development and thus should be strictly controlled by government, and (4) it tends to destroy the dignity of minorities and women by dealing in stereotypes. Many other issues, including drug abuse, illiteracy, feminism, pornography, and violence are often introduced into these debates as well. Regrettably, many of the arguments on both sides are driven by anecdotal information and subjective impressions rather than careful, replicated, and independent research. There continues to be a very great need for a balance in research into culture, whether the particular design is based on the humanistic or the social science paradigms.

Bernard Rosenberg and David White (1957, 1971) provide two dated but still-useful and readable collections illustrating both the optimistic and pessimistic sides of the popular culture debate. As leisure and recreation continue to grow as important expressions of our culture and as leisure activities, especially creative artistic activities, help to shape the future of our culture, the study of culture and cultural phenomena will be important to RECREATION and leisure scholars.

REFERENCES

Adelung, Johann C. 1781. *Versuch einer Geschichte der Cultur des Menschlichen Ge-schlechts*. Leipzig: Verlegts Johann Gatlob Immanuel Breikopf. An early example of a "universal history" concerned with the development of cultures around the world.

Arnold, Matthew. 1869. *Culture and Anarchy*. London: T. Nelson. A philosophically oriented book interpreting culture as the pursuit of perfection and ennoblement.

Browne, Ray (ed.). 1980. *Rituals and Ceremonies in Popular Culture*. Bowling Green, OH: Bowling Green State University Press. A sociological analysis of popular culture, comparing tastes and behaviors of different social groups.

Eliot, T. S. 1948. *Notes Towards the Definition of Culture*. New York: Faber and Faber. A personal search for an understanding of the meaning of culture and its role in civilized society.

Gans, Herbert J. 1974. *Popular Culture and High Culture*. New York: Basic Books. An important analysis of popular culture, with a particular emphasis on analyzing and interpreting tastes and lifestyles.

Gombrich, Ernst. 1969. *In Search of Cultural History*. Oxford: Clarendon. Offers conceptual definition of culture plus an overview of themes and methods in cultural history.

Herder, Johann G. 1887. *Ideen zur Philosophie der Menschleit*, Vols. 13, 14 of *Samtliche Werke*, ed. B. Suphan. Berlin: Auflua-Verlag. Another influential "universal history."

Klemm, Gustav. 1843. *Allgemeine Cultur-geschichte der Menschheit*, 10 vols. Leipzig: Arnoldo Scha Buchhandlung. An important early cultural history of the world; an influence on Tylor's work.

Kroeber, Alfred. 1944. *Configurations of Culture Growth*. Berkeley: University of California Press. An example of a "middle ground" research design, attempting to combine the best of both historical and social scientific research paradigms in the study of culture.

Kroeber, Alfred, and Kluckhohn, Clyde. 1952. *Culture*. New York: Vintage Books. This book provides a critical review of concepts and definitions of culture, with a special reference on English-language and German-language usages. This is a particularly good reference for an overview of the evolution of the concept of culture.

Malinowski, Bronislaw. 1944. *A Scientific Theory of Culture*. Chapel Hill: The University of North Carolina Press. Presents the author's arguments for believing that scientifically verifiable laws governing the development of culture are possible.

Meisel, John. 1979. "Social Research and the Politics of Culture." In *Social Research and Cultural Policy*, ed. Jiri Zuzanek, 3–14. Waterloo, Ont.: Otium. An overview of research and policy issues in popular culture, particularly from a Canadian perspective.

Pieper, Josef. 1952. *Leisure: The Basis of Culture*. New York: Pantheon Books. An essay examining leisure and culture from a Catholic theological perspective.

Radcliffe-Brown, Alfred. 1940. "On Social Structure." *Journal of the Royal Anthropological Institute of Great Britain and Ireland* 70:1–12. A functional analysis of culture as a form of social structure; developed in response to some of the weaknesses associated with earlier, historical cultural studies.

Rosenberg, Bernard, and White, David. (eds.). 1957. *Mass Culture*. Glencoe, IL: The Free Press. An excellent collection of readings on popular culture.

Rosenberg, Bernard, and White, David (ed.). 1971. *Mass Culture Revisited*. New York: Van Nostrand Reinhold. A follow-up collection of popular culture essays, updating many of the views expressed in the editors' 1957 collection.

Shils, Edward. 1959. "Mass Society and Its Culture." In *Culture for the Millions*, ed. Jacob Norman, 1–27. New York: The American Academy of Arts and Sciences. A personal interpretation of "mass culture"; categorizes mass culture into "superior," "mediocre," and "brutal."

Tylor, Edward. 1871. *Primitive Society*. London: John Murray. An early and important ethnographic study that set a model for many subsequent cultural anthropologists and cultural historians.

Yinger, J. Milton. 1960. "Contraculture and Subculture." *American Sociological Review* 25:625–635. Defines and distinguishes between these two subclassifications of culture.

SOURCES OF ADDITIONAL INFORMATION

The relationship between recreation and leisure, on one hand, and culture, on the other, is so intimate that the development of a bibliography on culture is a daunting task. In addition to the sources provided in the references, some useful sources include: Eric Larrabee and Rolf Meyersohn, ed., *Mass Leisure* (Glencoe, Illinois: The Free Press, 1958); Max Kaplan, *Leisure in America* (New York: John Wiley, 1960); and Thomas Kando, *Leisure and Popular Culture in Transition* (Saint Louis: C. V. Mosby, 1975).

Three of the better sources for insights in the historical development of recreation and leisure in various cultures include: Michael Marrus, ed., *The Emergence of Leisure* (New York: Harper Torch Books, 1974); Byron Dare, George Welton, and William Coe, *Concepts of Leisure in Western Thought* (Dubuque, Iowa: Kendall Hunt,1987); and

Thomas Goodale and Geoffrey Godbey, *The Evolution of Leisure* (State College, PA: Venture Publishing, 1989).

A relatively new journal, *North American Culture,* a publication of the Society of the North American Culture Survey, also contains articles on aspects of recreation, leisure, tourism, and sport as cultural phenomena. Information can be obtained from the Society for the North American Culture Survey, Department of Geography, Oklahoma State University, Stillwater, OK 74074.

D

DEINSTITUTIONALIZATION. Part of the process of MAINSTREAMING; the shifting of disabled individuals from institutional residences to community-based residences.

For many centuries, people labeled as mentally ill, retarded, or disabled were often segregated from society by being housed in institutions. These institutions frequently contained hundreds of individuals in crowded, geographically isolated, and dehumanizing conditions (Salzberg and Langford, 1981). Beginning in the late 1950s, a social movement began in Scandinavia (Nirje, 1969, 1970) to provide typical living environments and experiences for mentally retarded individuals and greater ACCESSIBILITY to social services and recreational facilities. This movement spread to other countries and grew to cover the rights of all disabled people. Based on the ideology of NORMALIZATION, the main principle is that individuals who are disabled have the right to live in the least restrictive environment possible; this environment should offer age and culturally appropriate educational, residential, social, recreational, and vocational opportunities. A key strategy in realizing that ideal is mainstreaming. And one of the major components in mainstreaming is deinstitutionalization.

It should be emphasized that deinstitutionalization is not synonymous with mainstreaming. Deinstitutionalization refers to changing the residential location and environment of an individual. Mainstreaming includes this process, but also involves other educational, support, and ADVOCACY activities.

REFERENCES

Bullock, Charles C. 1979. "Mainstreaming—In Recreation Too!?" *Therapeutic Recreation* 13(4):5–10. Reviews development of mainstreaming and implications of PL 94–142 on recreation programs.
Nirje, Bengt. 1969. "The Normalization Principle and Its Human Management Implications." In *Changing Patterns in Residential Services for the Mentally Retarded*, ed. R. Kugel and W. Wolfensberger, 179–195. Washington, DC: President's Committee on Mental Retardation. An early and important statement about integration and normalization.
Nirje, Bengt. 1970. "The Normalization Principle: Implications and Comments." *Journal of Mental Subnormality* 16(3):62–70. A summary of some operational principles associated with normalization.
Salzberg, Charles, and Langford, Cynthia. 1981. "Community Integration of Mentally Retarded Adults through Leisure Activity." *Mental Retardation* June:127–131. Describes practice of mainstreaming in recreation programs.
Wolfensberger, Wolf. 1972. *Normalization: The Principle of Normalization in Human Services*. Toronto: National Institute on Mental Retardation. One of the most important statements about normalization and its applications.

SOURCES OF ADDITIONAL INFORMATION

A good introductory text to deinstitutionalization and other related concepts in Richard Kraus's *Therapeutic Recreation Service: Principles and Practices* (3rd edition, New York: Saunders, 1983). Gene Hayes examines some of the broader issues of deinstitutionalization and mainstreaming in "Philosophical Ramifications of Mainstreaming in Recreation" (*Therapeutic Recreation Journal* 12 no. 2:5–9, 1978). The entire 1979 fourth-quarter issue of the *Therapeutic Recreation Journal* is devoted to papers on mainstreaming and related concepts.

DELIVERY SYSTEM. The combination of public and quasi-public RECREATION and LEISURE service agencies that provide public open space, recreation facilities, and recreation programs.

The concept of the delivery system (or the leisure service delivery system) tends to be used most frequently in the context of professional practice and agency planning (Hjelte and Shivers, 1972). It also usually carries the connotation of municipal or community recreation services rather than state, provincial, or national facilities and services.

   The delivery system model is ultimately based on an "industrial" model of recreation services in which an agency takes basic inputs such as space, land, personnel, and unstructured blocks of time to produce intermediate outputs such as recreation programs, leagues, specialized facilities, schedules, and course offerings. The consumer then selects which of these services he desires for further "processing" to produce the final output of recreation—individual satisfaction, pleasure, or well-being. In this context, the delivery system includes the RESOURCES of the agency as well as the intermediate outputs the agency produces. It normally does not include the consumer per se. The delivery system exists to serve the consumer, but does not co-op the consumer into the system.

An alternative approach to the provision of leisure services is a FACILITATOR model, in which the agency assists the local community to produce its own services. In this model, which is related to the concept of COMMUNITY DEVELOPMENT, the distinction between the leisure service delivery system and the consumer becomes blurred. As a result authors who advocate a facilitation model (e.g., Murphy et al., 1973) tend to include the consumer as part of the delivery system.

When the phrase *leisure service delivery system* was first used in the early 1970s, many practitioners and researchers found the phrase to be needlessly contrived or artificial. Over time, however, *delivery system* has become a convenient shorthand expression to refer to the combination of municipal recreation and parks agencies, libraries, Ys, and other agencies that provide the myriad of modern leisure services to communities.

REFERENCES

Hjelte, George, and Shivers, Jay. 1972. *Public Administration of Recreational Services.* Philadelphia: Lea & Febiger. Provides a detailed discussion of the concept of a system and its relevance to recreation and park agencies.

Murphy, James, Williams, John, Niepoth, E. William, and Brown, Paul. 1973. *Leisure Service Delivery System: A Modern Perspective.* Philadelphia: Lea & Febiger. One of the first major discussions of the concept. These authors adopt a broader view of the delivery system than is suggested in this definition in that they include the consumer and his social and physical environment as part of the delivery system.

SOURCES OF ADDITIONAL INFORMATION

The literature on delivery systems is basically the literature of public recreation, leisure, and parks administration. Some of the standard references in this literature that explicitly refer to the concept of a delivery system for leisure services are H. Douglas Sessoms, Harold Meyer, and Charles Brightbill, *Leisure Service: The Organized Recreation and Park System* (Englewood Cliffs, NJ: Prentice Hall, 1975); Peter Graham and Lawrence Klar, Jr., *Planning and Delivery Leisure Services* (Dubuque, IA: William C. Brown, 1979); and Christopher Edginton and Charles Griffith, *The Recreation and Leisure Service Delivery System* (New York: Saunders College, 1983). An example of empirical research into the nature of delivery systems may be found in David Ng's "Leisure Service Delivery Systems: An Ontario Small Municipality Perspective" (*Recreation Research Review* 13 no. 3:15–21, 1987).

DEMAND. The schedule of consumption levels of a leisure commodity, by an individual or group, that is expected at different prices. 2. expected consumption levels, usually under specific conditions of price and supply.

Demand, as word, is used in at least five different ways by recreation and leisure scholars. The most traditional is the neoclassic definition (essentially definition 1): the schedule of quantities that will be consumed at various prices. Generally, higher prices are associated with lower consumption or participation rates; lower prices with higher consumption or participation.

The second way in which demand is used is to refer to current consumption, (essentially a version of definition 2). This usage relates known consumption to current price and supply levels. It is one of the most common uses of the term, but one of the least useful because it does not allow a researcher or planner to make any conclusions about expected levels of consumption or participation under different price or supply conditions.

The third definition refers to expected future consumption. This is usually based on some forecast of likely supply and price conditions (as specified in definition 2), and perhaps additional variables such as different age structures, economic changes, or promotional efforts. This usage of demand is most often associated with various forecasting exercises aimed at predicting future levels of participation as part of a planning exercise. Very often the word *demand* itself will be used as part of the project title, as in the *Canadian Outdoor Recreation Demand Study* (Parks Canada, 1977) or the National Academy of Sciences' (1975), *Assessing Demand for Outdoor Recreation*.

Demand is also used to refer to unmet need. This fourth use of the term is sometimes expressed as *latent demand*. Latent demand is the difference between the potential level of consumption and the observed level (Richardson and Crompton, 1988). Such differences exist because of a lack of supply or time, cost constraints, or other BARRIERS. If these barriers can be reduced or insufficient supply increased, participation normally rises to a higher level. Latent demand is also linked to the concepts of *option value* and *option demand*. Option value refers to the value of the opportunity to use a recreation resource at some point in the future, rather than its value for immediate use. For example, many Americans value the existence of the Grand Canyon because, like heaven, they hope to get there some day but have no immediate plans to do so. Option demand is a measure of the number of people who hold this desire. The issue of option value and demand is discussed in Richard Bishop (1982).

Finally, demand is used to describe the desire for an experience (Driver and Brown, 1975). In this sense, demand is more of a behavioral or social psychological concept than an economic or planning concept, as was the case for the first four definitions. When one hears of a certain group "demanding" services or resources, they are usually applying the term in this context.

Of the five definitions, the neoclassic definition is usually considered to be the most scientific and useful. A major reason is that this definition provides a foundation for developing several other concepts as well as for providing some of the best estimates for future use levels and resource valuations. As a schedule

of participation or consumption levels associated with different prices, demand
may be represented graphically.

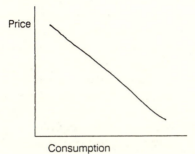

The usual form of this graph, as illustrated, is a negatively sloping line representing declining consumption with increasing prices. The slope of the line
reflects the degree of the relationship between price and consumption. This degree
of association is called "price elasticity." Elasticity is percentage change expected in consumption or participation given a 1 percent change in price. Some
commodities, such as gasoline, exhibit a relatively flat line. A 10 percent increase
in the price of gasoline, across the board, results in something less than a 10
percent drop in consumption of gasoline. There are few substitutes for gasoline,
at least in the short run, and gasoline is generally considered to be a necessity
for modern life.

In other cases, such as the demand for a specific brand of wine, the demand
curve will be much steeper. This steeper curve reflects the fact that for most
people wine is more of a luxury than gasoline. Furthermore, there are usually
many acceptable substitutes for any particular brand of wine. If the price of a
particular label and vintage rises by 10 percent but the prices of all competitors
stays the same, one might find that consumption of that particular label will
drop by more than 10 percent as people switch to alternatives. In general,
commodities that are considered necessities and that have few substitutes have
low price elasticities. Commodities that are considered to be luxuries or for
which there are many substitutes are highly price elastic. C. Price, J. B. Christensen, and S. K. Humphreys (1986) provide an example of a price elasticity
analysis of different types of recreation commodity. Among their findings were
the observations that the demand for specific recreation sites tends to be elastic
while the demand for recreation experiences, generally, are relatively inelastic.

Another type of elasticity that may be derived from the neoclassic demand
concept is income elasticity. In this case, the price of a commodity is replaced
in the analysis or on the demand graph by the consumers' incomes. Income
elasticity is the percentage change expected in consumption given a 1 percent
change in income of a potential purchaser (Thompson and Tinsley, 1978; Wagner
and Washington, 1982). The relationship between income and consumption is

normally positive. Higher incomes support higher levels of consumption. As with price elasticity, though, the degree of change varies with different commodities. Expenditures on food tend to rise slower than incomes. In fact, if one looks at the percentage of total income spent on food over a range of income levels, the usual pattern is one of declining percentage. Food has a low income elasticity. Expenditures on some forms of recreation also exhibit low income elasticities (Fisk, 1963). Participation in bowling or square dancing, for example, exhibit modest increases into upper-middle- and upper-income groups. In contrast, expenditures on electronic goods or attendance at opera increase dramatically with income. Many "high CULTURE" activities have a high income elasticity and are sometimes referred to as "superior" goods. The term *superior* is not intended to have any particular aesthetic or moral connotation. Rather, it simply refers to the fact that the consumption of these goods increases faster than incomes rise.

Whether a particular activity has low, average, or high income elasticity may also depend on the range of incomes examined. For example, participation in hunting (Parks Canada, 1977) has been seen to rise with increasing income up to the middle-income categories. As one moves into the upper-middle incomes, the rate of increase begins to slow. At the highest levels of income, hunting participation actually drops. At that level, hunting is an "inferior" good, because it displays an inverse relationship between consumption and income instead of the usual positive relationship.

Changes in income or price are not the only forces that affect demand. Alterations in social attitudes; tastes; the use of promotional techniques; long-term shifts in occupational structures, age distributions, or educational levels (Gum and Martin, 1977); total supply (Smith and Stewart, 1980); the introduction or loss of products or other recreational opportunities; the crowding of a facility (McConnell, 1977); the potential for SUBSTITUTION (Price, Christensen, and Humphreys, 1986); and many other conditions can influence the demand for any given recreation commodity. These types of force are known as demand shifters. The term comes from the effect of these variables on the graphical representation of a demand curve. Variables that increase the demand for a commodity at a given price shift the curve to the right on the graph. Conversely, the curve shifts to the left if certain variables cause demand to decrease at a given price.

Demand, particularly in the neoclassic sense, is a very useful and important concept in recreation and leisure studies. The ability to specify a quantitative relationship between expected levels of consumption and other variables such as price, supply, or demographic characteristics of potential users can allow recreation planners to make forecasts of the future need for facilities, resources, and services. Demand also provides the conceptual basis of the TRAVEL COST METHOD, one of the more important techniques used for deriving shadow prices of PUBLIC GOODS and sites.

REFERENCES

Bishop, Richard C. 1982. "Option Value: An Exposition and Extension." *Land Economics* 58:1–15. An excellent review of the principles of option value and of methods for estimating it.

Driver, Bev L., and Brown, Perry J. 1975. "A Social-Psychological Definition of Recreation Demand, with Implications for Recreation Resource Planning." In *Assessing Demand for Outdoor Recreation,* 1–88. Washington, DC: National Academy of Sciences. An extensive argument for considering the concept of demand as a social-psychological phenomenon instead of a purely economic concept.

Fisk, George. 1963. *Leisure Spending—Behavior.* Philadelphia: University of Pennsylvania Press. An early examination of income elasticity in recreation; concluded that the income elasticity was approximately unitary.

Gum, Russell L., and Martin, William E. 1977. "The Structure of Demand for Outdoor Recreation." *Land Economics* 53:43–55. An innovative analysis of the effects of demand shifters on the overall demand for specific types of recreation activity.

McConnell, Kenneth E. 1977. "Congestion and Willingness to Pay: A Study of Beach Use." *Land Economics* 53:185–195. A quantitative study of the effects of site crowding on neoclassical demand for beach recreation.

National Academy of Sciences. 1975. *Assessing Demand for Outdoor Recreation.* Washington, DC: National Academy of Sciences.

Parks Canada. 1977. *The Canadian Outdoor Recreation Demand Study.* Toronto: Ontario Research Council on Leisure. A three-volume technical report summarizing a multiyear project aimed at developing a battery of statistical tools for predicting outdoor recreation participation.

Price, C., Christensen, J. B., and Humphreys, S. K. 1986. "Elasticities of demand for recreation site and for recreation experience." *Environment and Planning A* 18:1259–1263. Illustrates concept of price elasticity by comparing slopes of demand curves for different recreation commodities.

Richardson, Sarah L., and Crompton, John L. 1988. "Latent Demand for Vacation Travel: A Cross-Cultural Analysis of French and English-Speaking Residents of Ontario and Quebec." *Leisure Sciences* 19: 17–27. Defines latent demand for vacation travel in terms of interest in travel versus actual travel behavior; applies a quantitative version of this definition to anglophone and francophone populations in two Canadian provinces.

Smith, Stephen L. J., and Stewart, Terry O. 1980. "Estimation of the Effects of Regional Variations of Supply on Participation in Cultural Activities." *Ontario Geographer* 15:3–16. Examines the effects of supply variations on the demand for cultural activities; concludes that supply effects are comparable in magnitude to many socioeconomic variables.

Thompson, C. Stassen, and Tinsley, A. W. 1978. "Income Expenditure Elasticities for Recreation." *Journal of Leisure Research* 10:265–270. Calculation of income elasticity for recreation using household budget data.

Wagner, Fritz, and Washington, Verel R. 1982. "An Analysis of Personal Consumption Expenditures as Related to Recreation 1946–1976." *Journal of Leisure Research* 14:37–46. An historically based analysis of income elasticities for recreation.

SOURCES OF ADDITIONAL INFORMATION

The literature on the various aspects of demand is quite large. One of the standard references, which has served as a "touchstone" for many demand analyses is Marion Clawson's and Jack Knetsch's *Economics of Outdoor Recreation* (Baltimore: Johns Hopkins Press, 1966). Another early study, that may be difficult to track down but that was an important scholarly source for many studies in the 1970s is Charles Cicchetti, Joseph Seneca, and Paul Davidson, *The Demand and Supply of Outdoor Recreation* (New Brunswick, NJ: Rutgers Bureau of Economic Research, 1971). A more recent book that provides a good review of demand analyses as well as other issues in recreation economics is Richard Walsh, *Recreation Economic Decisions: Comparing Benefits and Costs* (State College, PA: Venture, 1986).

A few useful articles, out of hundreds that have been published on demand, include Russell Gum and William Martin, "Problems and Solutions in Estimating Demand for and Value of Rural Outdoor Recreation" (*American Journal of Agricultural Economics* 57:558–566, 1975); Robert Kalter and L. E. Gosse, "Recreation Demand Functions and the Identification Problem" (*Journal of Leisure Research* 2:43–53; 1970); and Rod Ziemer, Wesley Musser, and Carter Hill, "Recreation Demand Equations: Functional Form and Consumer Surplus" (*American Journal of Agricultural Economics* 62:136–141; 1980).

The U.S. Forest Service's *Outdoor Recreation: Advances in Application of Economics* (general technical report WO-2, Washington, DC: Department of Agriculture, 1977) is an excellent collection of papers on demand concepts and applications as well as other economic issues. The proceedings of the National Outdoor Recreation Trends Symposia (1980 and 1985) also contain a number of empirically based demand studies. These proceedings have been published by the Department of Parks, Recreation, and Tourism Management, Clemson University, Clemson, South Carolina. The National Recreation and Park Association, has published the monograph *Demand for Recreation in America* (Alexandria, VA, 1984) as the first in a series called *Quest for Quality*. This particular monograph takes less of a neoclassic view of demand; rather, it generally considers demand to be a combination of observed consumption levels and the desire for certain types of experience.

Finally, all of these sources have additional reference lists or bibliographies that will help the reader to pursue more specialized topics as desired.

DEPRECIATIVE BEHAVIOR. Any action that is deemed inappropriate or unacceptable in a given recreation site or facility by the managers of that facility or by a significant number of other users.

Depreciative behaviors (Clark, Hendee, and Campbell, 1971) include overt criminal acts (such as thefts), acts that are violations of rules or policies specific to recreation facilities (such as taking flash photographs of paintings in a gallery), or that infringe on the rights or enjoyment of other users (such as failing to slow a motorboat to avoid upsetting a canoe with the motorboat's wake). This latter form of depreciative behavior often results in user CONFLICT. The U.S. Department of the Interior (1981) has identified research on depreciative behaviors to be one of the top ten research needs in the field. A major factor contributing to such a high ranking for this topic is the scarcity of scientific studies into the topic. Specific research needs include (1) more accurate base line studies to determine the actual magnitude, costs, and specific impacts or various forms of depreciative behavior; (2) the causes of that behavior; and (3) the effectiveness of various control and prevention strategies.

Most of the available literature is anecdotal or rhetorical although a number of empirical studies (primarily on littering) have been published. A useful overview of the literature may be found in Harriet Christensen (1986).

REFERENCES

Christensen, Harriet H. 1986. "Vandalism and Depreciative Behavior." In *A Literature Review: The President's Commission on Americans Outdoors*, Management-73–Management-87. Washington, DC: U.S. Government Printing Office. A brief and excellent survey of the limited research on the topic of depreciative behavior.
Clark, Roger N., Hendee, John C., and Campbell, Fred L. 1971. *Depreciative Behavior in Forest Campgrounds: An Exploratory Study*; research note PNW-161. Portland, OR: U.S. Department of Agriculture, Pacific Northwest Forest and Range Experiment Station. An early study of littering in national forests and its effect on users.
U.S. Department of the Interior. 1981. *A National Agenda for Recreation Research*. Washington, DC: U.S. Department of the Interior, National Park Service. Presents recommendations for research projects that should receive a high priority; developed in cooperation with the National Recreation and Park Association.

SOURCES OF ADDITIONAL INFORMATION

Some examples of empirical research into littering, perhaps the most common depreciative behavior studies by recreation researchers, include Robert L. Burgess, Roger Clark, and John Hendee, "An Experimental Analysis of Anti-litter Procedures" (*Journal of Applied Behavior Analysis* 4 no. 2:71–75, 1971); S. M. Reiter and W. Samuel, "Littering as a Function of Prior Litter and the Presence of Absence of Prohibitive Signs" (*Journal of Applied Social Psychology* 10:45–55, 1980); and Harriet H. Christensen and Roger N. Clark, "Increasing Public Involvement to Reduce Depreciative Behavior in Recreation Settings" (*Leisure Sciences* 5:359–379, 1983). An example of research into a form of depreciative behavior more serious than littering is D. R. Shaffer, M. Rogel, and C. Hendrick, "Intervention in the Library: The Effect of Increased Responsibility on Bystanders' Willingness to Prevent a Theft" (*Journal of Applied Social Psychology* 5:303–319, 1975).

DISPLACEMENT. A temporary or permanent change of behavior resulting from conflict or other adverse changes in a recreation facility or site.

The concept of displacement was developed in the context of studying the response of recreationists to problems of crowding in recreation ENVIRONMENTS (Nielsen and Endo, 1977). These researchers defined displacement in the literal sense of recreationists being displaced from their place of RECREATION because of crowding. The early conceptualization of displacement combined a "push" force (avoidance of a crowded environment) with a "pull" force (the seeking of a more attractive environment). Robert Becker (1981) challenged this notion in his study of boaters in Wisconsin and Minnesota by observing that displacement occurs simply as a strategy for escape from an unacceptable situation.

Richard Schreyer (1979) broadened the early conceptualization of displacement by redefining it to be a process involving a combination of an activity change, a change in the timing of participating, and/or a change in the location of participation in response to any threat to a user's satisfaction with an activity in a given location. To Schreyer, the displacement process does not occur simply as a function of crowding or other adverse condition, but as a result of the user's perception and interpretation of those conditions in light of specific recreation NEEDS. It is, therefore, a combination of attitude and behavior. Identical environmental problems can produce very different displacement processes (or no displacement at all) in different recreationists. Although Schreyer did not provide any empirical support for his broader conceptualization of displacement, Dorothy Anderson and Perry Brown (1984) did empirically test this conceptualization. The results of their work in the Boundary Waters Canoe Area Wilderness lend support to the idea that displacement is best interpreted as an attitude-behavior process, but that certain environmental cues (such as seeing wornout campsites) were predictably more likely to prompt displacement than certain other cues (such as simple crowding).

Available research on displacement confirms the common notion that certain people will temporarily or permanently leave a recreation environment when it degrades to a given level. More research is needed, however, to identify the actual causal linkages between various forms of degradation and the rates of displacement as well as to identify the interpersonal characteristics that distinguish between people who tend to be displaced easily and those who are more resistant to displacement.

REFERENCES

Anderson, Dorothy H., and Brown, Perry J. 1984. "The Displacement Process in Recreation." *Journal of Leisure Research* 16:61–73. A social-psychological examination of displacement using a Fishbein model of behavioral intentions.
Becker, Robert H. 1981. "Displacement of Recreational Users between the Lower St. Croix and Upper Mississippi Rivers." *Journal of Environmental Management* 13:259–267. Examines the relative role of "push" and "pull" forces in displacement.
Nielsen, J. M. and Endo, R. 1977. "Where Have All the Purists Gone? An Empirical Examination of the Displacement Hypothesis in Wilderness Recreation." *Western Sociological Review* 8:61–75. An early discussion of the displacement concept.
Schreyer, Richard. 1979. Succession and Displacement in River Recreation. Part 1, Problem Definition and Analysis. Unpublished report, Logan, UT, Utah State University, Department of Forestry and Outdoor Recreation. Proposes a more social psychological conceptualization of displacement, in contrast to the earlier notions of simply response to crowding.

SOURCES OF ADDITIONAL INFORMATION

Much of the research related to displacement is found in the context of research on crowding. A couple of examples of this type of research include J. L. Cohen, B. Sladen, and B. Bennett, ''The Effects of Situational Variables on Judgments of Crowding'' (*Sociometry* 38:273–281, 1975); E. Langer and S. Saegert, ''Crowding and Cognitive Control'' (*Journal of Personality and Social Psychology* 35:175–182, 1977); and D. Stokols, ''A Social Psychological Model of Human Crowding Phenomena'' (*American Institute of Planners Journal* 38:72–83, 1972). A useful background article on the relationship between attitudes and recreation behavior (including displacement) is M. P. Willis, W. D. Schonz, P. W. Dorfman, and A. I. Williams, ''Recreation Lifestyle Versus Activity Involvement Patterns: Beliefs as Correlates of Behavior'' (*Psychological Reports* 43:1219–1229, 1978). A general reference on user's perceptions of their environments, particularly other users, is Paul Bell, Jeffrey Fisher, and Ross Loomis, *Environmental Psychology* (Philadelphia: Saunders, 1978).

E

EMISSIVENESS. The trip-generation potential of an origin (usually estimated statistically).

The term *emissiveness* was coined by Frank Cesario (1971) to refer to a statistically derived coefficient used in recreation trip forecasting. It is a measure of the ability of an origin, such as a city, to generate recreation trips. In trip forecasting, it may be contrasted with the ATTRACTIVITY, a measure of the ability of a destination to attract travelers. Emissiveness can be conceptualized as a function of the social and economic characteristics of a destination, such as per capita income and especially total population size. In practice, however, emissiveness is usually estimated statistically from observed travel patterns, rather than by direct measurement from origin characteristics.

REFERENCES

Cesario, Frank J. 1971. Parameter Estimation in Trip Distribution Modeling. Unpublished Ph.D. dissertation, The Ohio State University, Department of Industrial Engineering. Describes the development of a generalized trip distribution model, with special attention to the statistical task of estimating model parameters.

SOURCES OF ADDITIONAL INFORMATION

Frank Cesario has summarized the issues of statistical estimation of emissiveness in "A Generalized Trip Distribution Model" (*Journal of Regional Science* 13:233–247, 1978). He further discusses the concept in "More on the Generalized Trip Distribution Model" (*Journal of Regional Science* 14:389–397, 1974). A less technical review of methods of travel forecasting may be found in Stephen Smith's *Recreation Geography* (London: Longman Group, 1983, Chapt. 6).

ENVIRONMENT. The totality of external things, conditions, and forces that affect a living organism or group of organisms.

The concept of environment as the surroundings of an entity is well established. The *Oxford English Dictionary* quotes Thomas Carlyle's use of the term with reference to the environment of a village as early as 1830. Modern definitions of the concept still conform largely to the notion of the surroundings of a plant, animal, or community. Some important differences begin to emerge, however, when the term is expressed as an operational definition.

Many ecologists, for example, tend to restrict their conception of environment to the abiotic or physical conditions that affect the identity, diversity, and population size of plants and animals. The interactions of plants and animals—biotic factors—are often not included as part of the environment proper. Other authors, however, include both biotic and abiotic elements in their conception of the environment. In both cases, an essential implicit characteristic of the environment is the idea of cause-and-effect relationships. Environmental factors are those that exert some influence over the life of organisms; if some object or condition (perhaps such as the color of the sky) does not exert any influence on an organism, it is not considered part of the environment.

Environment is also used in a broader context: the entire set of species, things, forces, and conditions that make up the natural world. This generic use of the term has been the basis for terms such as the environmental movement, environmentalists, and departments or ministries of the environment.

In the natural sciences, especially with respect to studies in CONSERVATION, environment is closely linked with other concepts and terms such as habitat and ecosystem. Paul Colinvaux (1973) provides an overview of the evolution of these terms. He notes that one of the earliest scientific insights into the natural environment was the recognition of the natural succession of plants and animals in specific locales, such as ponds or meadows (Shelford, 1911). Field ecologists eventually recognized that the species mix at any particular stage of succession was unique to that stage and the associated abiotic environment (Vestal, 1914). Special effort was made to identify index species that could be used to characterize specific stages in different environments. This line of research led to the tradition of species labels, such as the infamous "spruce-moose complex" joke of older ecologists, to label environments.

Ecologists then began to recognize the need for a generic label for the natural units characterized by some physical boundary and containing established associations of flora, fauna, and abiotic factors. Terms proposed during the 1920s and 1930s included holocene, naturcomplex, Räume, biogeocenoses, biotic distributions, and biochores (Whittaker, 1962). None of these were viewed as wholly satisfactory (or in some cases, pronounceable). In 1935, A. G. Tansley proposed ecosystem to refer to the whole complex of species inhabiting a given region plus the whole complex of physical factors (which Tansley called the "environment"). Ecosystem continues to be the preferred label of most ecologists for the system created by the interaction of species and their physical environment. Some authors, however, appear to use environment and ecosystem interchangeably (Cain, 1966).

Eugene Odum (1971) notes that authors who come from a Germanic or Slavic literary tradition use the terms biocoenosis, biocoenose, and biogeocoenosis, as equivalent to ecosystem. F. C. Ford-Robertson (1971) suggest using biocoenosis (or its variants) to refer to real biological units and ecosystem to refer to conceptual units.

The word *environment* is also used in other more specific contexts. Social scientists refer to the social or political environment, business leaders speak of the business environment, interior designers and architects address problems of office and residential environments, and public health and industrial safety experts are concerned with the environment of the workplace. The term has also served as a euphemism: a toilet bowl cleaner has been marketed as a cleanser for "environmental surfaces," and garbage collectors and street sweepers have been retitled "environmental managers" in some communities. Despite its use in euphemisms and political rhetoric, environment remains an important term and concept in recreation and leisure studies.

REFERENCES

Cain, Stanley A. 1966. "Biotype and Habitat." In *Future Environments of North America,* ed. Fraser Darling and John Milton, 38–54. Garden City, NY: Natural History Press. A broad discussion of environment-related issues.

Colinvaux, Paul. 1973. *Introduction to Ecology.* New York: Wiley. A good overview of the methods, concepts, perspectives, and basic relationships in the study of ecology.

Ford-Robertson, F. C. 1971. *Terminology of Forest Science, Technology, Practice, and Products.* Washington, DC: Society of American Foresters. An extended examination of the lexicon of environmental and silvaculture and related industrial applications.

Odum, Eugene P. 1971. *Fundamentals of Ecology,* 3rd edition. Philadelphia: Saunders. Another good introduction to the study of ecology, with some attention paid to technical terminology.

Tansley, A. G. 1935. "The Use and Abuse of Vegetational Concepts and Terms." *Ecology* 16:284–307. The first use of "ecosystem" as a term.

Shelford, V. E. 1911. "Ecological Succession—II: Pond Fishes." *Biological Bulletin* 21:127–151. An example of an early study into the process of natural succession in ecosystems.

Vestal, A. G. 1914. "Internal Relations of Terrestrial Association." *American Naturalist* 48:413–445. An example of an early inquiry into identification of index species and species complexes associated with specific environments.

Whittaker, Robert H. 1962. "Classification of National Communities." *Botanical Review* 28:1–239. A lengthy review article on the methods and concepts of ecological classification.

SOURCES OF ADDITIONAL INFORMATION

Virtually all books on ecology and conservation will address environmental topics and concepts; a typical reference in this category is Raymond F. Dasmann, *Environmental Conservation* (4th edition, New York: Wiley, 1976). A classic example of the use of the term environment in a generic sense is Paul R. Ehrlich and Anne H. Ehrlich, *Population, Resources, Environment* (San Francisco: Freeman, 1970). The issue of human perception of the environment and its impact on human behavior is addressed in Donald K. Adams in his forward to Peter H. Klopfer, *Behavioral Aspects of Ecology* (Englewood Cliffs, NJ: Prentice Hall, 1963).

ENVIRONMENTAL EDUCATION. The process of helping individuals develop an understanding of environmental processes, problems, and problem solving.

Although some authors have argued that environmental education is an old tradition—Keith Wheeler (1975), for example, argued that its roots go back to the early days of the Industrial Revolution—the term and the concept did not appear formally until the 1960s. Growing out of the CONSERVATION movement and OUTDOOR EDUCATION, environmental education was developed as part of the overall strategy of environmental advocates in the 1960s.

During that decade, outdoor education—the precursor of environmental education—began to broaden its self-concept to the point where educators were involved in teaching not just environmental skills and values, but also general science, mathematics, art, languages, and social studies. The shift from the affective domain (values) to the cognitive domain (fact and processes) may have been spurred by public reaction to the Soviet launch of Sputnik, the first artificial satellite (Donaldson and Goering, 1970). The reaction of the American public as well as American politicians was an immediate outcry for greater attention to science and mathematics in the school curriculum.

Whether concern over the quality of science education in America's schools really was responsible for the change in outdoor education, it is clear that there was also a growing concern in the mid- and late 1960s for the quality of the biophysical ENVIRONMENT. The move of outdoor education away from narrowly conceived conservation concerns left room for other educators and activists to renew their commitment to a strengthened and updated form of conservation education—a form that became known as environmental education.

Thus although outdoor education and environmental education are still sometimes treated as synonyms, there are distinctions. Perhaps the most important is that outdoor education is used to teach topics across the entire curriculum, from the physical sciences to the humanities, while environmental education borrows from virtually the entire curriculum to reinforce the teaching of environmental facts, values, and problem solving. As the Environmental Education Act PL 91–516, U.S.C. 1531–1536) put it,

[The purpose of environmental education is to foster] greater understanding of society's environmental problems and also the processes of environmental problem-solving and decision-making. . . . [It involves] synthesis with ideas and materials from many other areas, such as the social sciences, the applied and theoretical natural sciences, the arts, and other areas of the humanities, all as appropriate and needed for the particular topic of inquiry.

Environmental educators generally view their role as one of FACILITATOR or of ADVOCACY, with a high level of commitment and political urgency (Schafer and Disinger, 1975). The issue of ultimate concern to most environmental educators is not the teaching of facts about the environment, but of instilling certain values, including a concern for the quality of human life and a belief that human survival depends on protecting the natural environment.

REFERENCES

Donaldson, George W., and Goering, Oswald H. 1970. *Outdoor Education: A Synthesis.* Las Cruces, NM: Educational Resources Information Center and Clearinghouse on Rural Education and Small Schools. A brief monograph examining the nature and background of outdoor education.
Schafer, Rudolph J. H., and Disinger, John F. (eds). 1975. *Environmental Education Perspectives and Prospectives.* Columbus, OH: ERIC Center for Science, Mathematics, and Environmental Education. Proceedings of a conference which advocated the goal of environmental education as developing proper social attitudes; sees educators as facilitators rather than traditional teachers.
Wheeler, Keith. 1975. *Insights into Environmental Education.* Edinburgh, Scotland: Oliver and Boyd. A readable introduction to the philosophy and principles of environmental education.

SOURCES OF ADDITIONAL INFORMATION

The literature on environmental education is predominantly curricular, motivational, or anecdotal, rather than empirical research. Typical collections of readings may be found in James Swan and William Stapp, eds., *Environmental Education: Strategies Toward a More Livable Future* (New York: Sage, 1974); Robert Saveland, ed., *Handbook of Environmental Education with International Case Studies* (New York: Wiley, 1976); and Tirlochan Bakshi and Zev Naveh, eds., *Environmental Education: Principles, Methods, and Applications* (New York: Plenum Press, 1978). Journals that contain articles on environmental education issues include *Journal of Environmental Education, Environment and Behavior, Journal of Experiential Education,* and *Journal of Outdoor Education.*

EQUITY. The assertion that individuals or groups should be treated with justice and fairness, including having appropriate access to goods and services offered by public agencies.

Equity is a value that virtually everyone professes in principle but disputes in practice. The disputes stem from a lack of agreement about how equity is to be operationally defined in different circumstances. As a general rule, most individuals in a democracy would agree with the ideal of similar treatment of individuals in similar circumstances. More difficult is whether individuals in dissimilar circumstances should receive similar or dissimilar treatment. This is an especially contentious issue in times of fiscal restraint in governmental budgets (Lucy and Mladenka, 1980).

In discussing the concept of equity, it is useful to recognize that the concept is actually used in three distinct but related realms: (1) as a moral precept, (2) as a principle in jurisprudence, and (3) as a decision-making tool in public policy (Merget, 1981).

In the moral realm, equity has been part of theories of justice since at least the time of Aristotle (Winthrop, 1978). (It should be noted that Aristotle was skeptical about theories purporting that the highest role of government was to ensure equity and justice.) Contemporary interest in equity as a moral issue was given new life by the work of John Rawls (1971) in his *Theory of Justice*. Rawls's speculations about the nature of equity and justice in modern society were based on three axioms:

1. Equal opportunity is the point of departure for social planning, not its goal.
2. Deviations from equal opportunity are not only acceptable but desirable as long as they benefit the least advantaged groups in society.
3. Society should provide all groups with a minimum level of service.

Rawls's work stimulated much commentary as well as further work by other authors. His thoughts may be viewed as providing part of the philosophical justification for contemporary affirmative action programs. Another, less obvious contribution of Rawls was his assertion that both the process used to reallocate public and private RESOURCES to further the goal of equity as well as the actual results of that reallocation are important.

Rawlsian theory has been criticized on several grounds. To many people, one of its most disturbing aspects is that it redefines civil rights in terms of groups rather than individuals. An individual may benefit from a social program only by virtue of being a member of a designated group that has suffered past injustice—but not by being an individual who has suffered. The result, of course, is that some individuals who have been the victims of discrimination cannot expect restitution or differential corrective resource allocation if they are a member of the "wrong" group. Conversely, other individuals who are members of a designated group may receive benefits regardless of whether they have personally been subjected to discrimination.

A more general criticism of Rawls is that his ideas do not provide politically or administratively practical guidelines for managers responsible for day-to-day delivery of services. Despite these criticisms, Rawls's ideas have exercised a strong influence on inquiry into the nature of equity in American and Canadian society.

A more recent example of the study of equity as a moral precept is the work of Lester Thurow (1980, 1985) who examined equity in light of his interpretation of the U.S. economy as a "zero-sum" society. Thurow suggests that all social progress comes at a cost to some group and cannot be achieved as a Pareto optimal allocation decision. Like Rawls, Thurow asserts arguments for affirmative action programs that could be based on race, income, class, and other social group definitions.

Attention to equity as a principle in the realm of jurisprudence stems from a series of court cases in the late 1960s and early 1970s. The basic effect of these decisions was to partially refine and strengthen the concept of equity as it applies to access to public services and as an integral aspect of due process.

One of the landmark decisions addressing equity as an issue in public service was *Hawkins v. Town of Shaw* (437 F.2d. 1268, 5th Cir. 1971). The municipal government of Shaw, Mississippi, was successfully sued for a more equitable allocation of municipal services. Evidence brought forward in *Shaw* revealed that 98 percent of all homes on unpaved streets were the residences of blacks. Nineteen percent of black homes were without sanitary sewers, compared to 1 percent of white homes. All of the modern street lamps were located in white neighborhoods. The court's decision established two points. The first was that minority citizens in a community should receive approximately the same quality and quantity of public services as the majority citizens. While there may be instances in which unequal distribution of services may legitimately exist, race is not one of them. The second point was that an inventory of public facilities— essentially an output measure—could be used as a measure of equity.

In another case, *Beal v. Lindsay* (468 F2d. 287, 2nd Cir. 1972), the borough of the Bronx was sued over the condition of a PARK serving a predominantly black and Puerto Rican neighborhood. The complainants noted that the park was more poorly staffed and maintained than other parks in other Bronx neighborhoods. The city countered by offering evidence that they were already spending a disproportionately large amount of money on the park. They further argued that the current condition of the park reflected locally high rates of vandalism. The city's defense was accepted by the court, which implied an acceptance of an input measure for assessing equity in municipal services.

Other lawsuits established further legal precedents or options for defining equity. These include *Serrano v. Priest* (483 P.2d. 1241, 1244, Cal. 1971), which confirmed the principle of fiscal neutrality (service must not be allocated on the basis of the taxes paid by a given neighborhood), and *Southern Burlington County NAACP v. Township of Mount Laurel* (67NJ 151, 336 A.2d. 713, 1975), which confirmed the relationship between equal protection and due process as legal principles and the goal of equity in the context of land use planning, zoning, and revenue sharing.

Taken in total, the corpus of legal decisions does not provide a comprehensive, clear, and consistent set of guidelines for describing and measuring equity in municipal services. This failure, however, is due principally to the complexity of the processes of public service provision and resource allocation. Inequitable decisions can occur at numerous points along the allocation process: setting taxation rates, allocating general tax revenues, variations in outcomes or social impacts of the services. It is not feasible to be able to specify a priori a workable and comprehensive set of decision-making or legal principles that will guarantee equity in all conceivable situations in all communities. At a minimum, however, court cases have identified some key questions that give shape to how equity can be interpreted and examined (Merget, 1981):

1. What is the proper range and mix of services that should be provided?
2. Disparity in which services indicated invidious discrimination?
3. How is one to describe and measure the quality and quantity of public services?
4. How are the various groups of citizens who benefit from and/or pay for services to be classified?
5. What are the range of permissible variations in inputs, outputs, and outcomes of services?
6. If some corrective allocation of resources is needed, how great is it and where should the resources come from?

Literature addressing the third realm of equity, as a decision-making tool in public policy, can be interpreted as attempts to restate, refine, and answer the six questions raised by the courts. One such line of work is illustrated by the approach that geographers have taken in their study of equity. Geographers typically focus on questions of ACCESSIBILITY as a key in operationalizing equity. Donald McAllister (1975, 1976) suggested that the central task in providing public services (he used recreation centers as an example) was to find the optimal balance between equity and efficiency—or more precisely, a balance among number, size, and spacing of facilities. Public policymakers can opt for one large central facility or some number of smaller facilities located throughout the community. McAllister defined this problem as one in which both efficiency (measured in terms of total use of facilities) and equity (measured in terms of having the maximum walking distance from any home to the nearest facility equal in all neighborhoods) were optimally balanced subject to budget constraints. A similar approach was adopted by Richard Morrill and John Symons (1977) and David Bigman and Charles ReVelle (1977). Although these contributions to defining equity are now more than a decade old, they continue to influence the use of recreation planning standards in many large urban areas.

Bryan Smale (1987) suggested that equity might be best conceived as balancing DEMAND and supply. Using data obtained from a household survey and facility inventory in Oakville, Ontario, Smale calculated both a demand "surface" and a supply "surface." Areas of divergence between these two surfaces represent supply-rich or supply-poor neighborhoods, or areas of inequity.

On a national scale, Harry Richardson (1979) also examined the trade-offs necessary between efficiency and equity. In this case, efficiency was conceived in terms of maximum national economic growth, while equity was couched in terms of equalizing regional growth rates and minimizing regional income disparities. Trade-offs between efficiency and equity are often inherent in the debate about the proper form and role of equity in public policy. Some authors have attempted to deny the need for trade-offs. Their dismissal of the dilemma is based on a strategy of redefining efficiency so that one speaks of "efficient" ways of achieving equity goals. As such, their "solution" tends to merely confuse the debate rather than truly offer a solution.

A very different approach to studying equity has been proposed by political scientists, Frank Levy, J. Arnold Meltsner, and Aaron Wildavsky (1974). They suggest that the best way of studying equity is to look at the results of public services—or their "outcomes" to use Levy et al.'s terminology. The outcome of recreation services could be measured several ways, such as total or percentage participation rates. This contrasts with input measures (e.g., dollars spent on recreation facilities by neighborhood) and output measures (e.g., hours of programing in each recreation center).

Still another approach to the development of indicators for studying equity is the work of Robert Lineberry (Lineberry and Welch, 1974; Lineberry, 1977). Lineberry and Welch note that there are major methodological problems in measuring the outputs of public services, as desired by some philosophers such as Rawls and some court decisions such as *Shaw*. What, for example, is the output of public open space? Lineberry and Welch suggest that a more practical approach to the study of equity is to identify substitute measures strongly associated with the quality of service outputs, such as:

1. Input quantity relative to potential demand (e.g., acres of parkland/capita).
2. Input quantity relative to expressed demand (e.g., acres of parkland/user).
3. Input quality (e.g., quality and type of facilities).
4. Service delivery quality from the perspective of the consumer (e.g., range of programs; crowdedness; accessibility; frequency of programing).
5. Community service facility conditions (e.g., age and state of repair of facilities).
6. Neighborhood conditions (e.g., participation levels; rates of vandalism; number of single-parent households).

While all measures are potentially useful, the authors conclude that for public policy decision making, "service delivery quality from the perspective of the consumer" is probably the preferred indicator type. In another study, Lineberry (1977) illustrates how those measures can actually be developed and used in assessing equity in municipalities. Using measures related to the range of services, crowdedness, and accessibility for recreation and cultural services, Lineberry empirically studied a wide range of urban neighborhoods. He observed some variations in the levels of service from the perspective of the consumer, but could not correlate these with race, income, or other socioeconomic variable. He described his finding as "unpatterned inequalities." This finding has been

challenged by F. N. Bolotin and D. L. Cingaranelli (1983) but has been supported in other empirical studies by Kenneth Mladenka (1985) and John Thomas
(1986).

Lineberry's approach, as well as that of other researchers who have followed
him, may be described as starting with the observation of a spatial pattern of
service and followed by an assessment of the pattern to determine whether it is
equitable. This approach has been criticized by Astrid Merget and Renee Berger
(1982) as focusing more on disparities than on equity. Or perhaps more clearly,
some authors feel that one should begin with a more developed notion of what
equity really means, derive an ideal pattern on the basis of that understanding,
and then compare the observed pattern with the ideal (Wicks and Crompton,
1986).

Wicks and Crompton note that before one can begin to develop an ideal pattern
based on some general notions of equity, it is necessary to understand the full
range of options available for defining equity. Many of these options have been
identified previously here. Wicks and Crompton, in reviewing the literature on
equity suggest that the various options can be grouped into four equity models:

1. EQUALITY. The provision of equal opportunity or equal accessibility. This is based
   on the Fourteenth Amendment (equal treatment under law) but has been criticized as
   ignoring differential needs.
2. NEED. The provision of resources in proportion to some measure of relative need.
   This requires the ability to objectively define need and implies acceptance of unequal
   delivery of services and redistributive role of service provisions.
3. MARKET. The provision of services in accordance to the amount a consumer is willing
   to pay for. Often used for services such as water, sewage, telephone, and electricity.
   Based on assumption that all individuals have adequate incomes to pay and that
   willingness to pay, rather than ability to pay, is the driving force for variations in
   resource consumption.
4. DEMAND. In the context of Wicks and Crompton, *demand* refers to nonmonetary
   expressions of interest or desire for services. This expression may be based in terms
   of historic rates of consumption or in terms of political pressure that may be brought
   to bear on public officials.

The authors then developed a series of alternative, hypothetical practices
reflecting the provision of public recreation and parks services under the various
models of equity. The hypothetical practices were then shown to a sample of
municipal parks and recreation directors as well as a sample of citizens to
determine their preferences for which practices were deemed to be most acceptable. Generally, models based on the Fourteenth Amendment's notion of
equality were preferred to provision on the basis of need, market, or demand.

Equity continues to be a difficult and contentious topic in recreation services
as in most other public sectors. It has also stimulated a large and growing body
of literature devoted to exploring moral issues, legal issues, and especially practical, empirical ways of defining and measuring equity in the provision of public

services. While many questions remain unresolved, the prospects for continuing progress are excellent.

REFERENCES

Bigman, David, and ReVelle, Charles. 1977. "The Theory of Welfare considerations in Public Location Problems." *Geographical Analysis* 10:229–240. Presents a theoretical strategy for siting public facilities on the basis of social welfare concerns.

Bolotin, F. N., and Cingaranelli, D. L. 1983. "Equity and Urban Policy: The Under-Class Hypothesis Revisited." *The Journal of Politics* 45:209–219. Empirical study of service delivery systems in terms of equity; finds some evidence of racially based patterns of inequity.

Levy, Frank S., Meltsner, J. Arnold, and Wildavsky, Aaron B. 1974. *Urban Outcomes.* Berkeley, University of California Press. Examines equity in context of schools, students, and libraries: recommends focusing on the results or outcomes of service rather than inputs or direct outputs.

Lineberry, Robert L. 1977. *Equality and Urban Policy.* Beverly Hills, CA: Sage. An empirical study of service patterns in several cities; concludes that occasional patterns of inequity cannot be attributed to race, income, or class effects.

Lineberry, Robert L., and Welch, Robert E. 1974. "Who Gets What: Measuring the Distribution of Urban Public Services." *Social Science Quarterly* 54:700–712. Discusses methodological difficulties in defining equity; summarizes six major approaches and makes recommendations about the preferred approach.

Lucy, William H., and Mladenka, Kenneth R. 1980. *Equity and Urban Service Distribution: Module 1,* 401–436. Washington, DC: U.S. Department of Housing and Urban Development, National Training and Development Service. Reviews concept of equity in urban services, especially as it may be interpreted in times of fiscal restrictions.

McAllister, Donald. 1975. "Planning an Urban Recreation System: A Systematic Approach." *Natural Resources Journal* 15:567–580. Suggests efficiency in urban services should be defined in terms of maximizing total use, and that equity can be defined in terms of equalizing maximum distance travelled by users.

McAllister, Donald. 1976. "Equity and Efficiency in Public Facility Location." *Geographical Analysis* 8:47–63. Examines sensitivity of both efficiency and equity, as defined in his 1975 paper, to alternative models of facility size and spacing.

Merget, Astrid E. 1981. "Achieving Equity in an Era of Fiscal Restraint." In *Cities under Stress,* ed., Robert W. Burchell and David Listokin, 401–436. Piscatawy, NJ: Center for Urban Policy Research. An excellent review of equity as a concept in philosophy, law, and public policy.

Merget, Astrid, and Berger, Renee. 1982. "Equity as a Decision Rule in Local Services." In *Analyzing Urban Service Delivery Service Distribution;* ed. Richard Rich, Lexington, MA: Heath. Includes a critique of contemporary research designs for studying equity in municipal services.

Mladenka, Kenneth R. 1985. "The Myth of the Machine and the Decline of Racial Politics: Distribution in Chicago." Paper presented at the Annual Meeting of the American Political Science Association, New Orleans. Empirical study of service delivery patterns in terms of equity; finds no racially based pattern of inequity.

Morrill, Richard, and Symons, John. 1977. "Efficiency and Equity Aspects of Optimum Location." *Geographical Analysis* 9:215–225. Conceives equity solely in terms of accessibility; discusses implications for locational strategies in public facility planning.

Rawls, John. 1971. *A Theory of Justice*. Cambridge, MA: Belknap Press. An important, wide-ranging, and provocative discussion of equity as a moral issue; it stimulated many other authors in the 1970s.

Richardson, Harry W. 1979. "Aggregate Efficiency and Interregional Equity." In *Spatial Inequalities and Regional Development*; ed. Henrick Folmer and Jan Oosterhaven, 161–183. London: Martinus Nijhoff. Examines trade-offs between maximizing total national growth and minimizing interregional incomes as a typical dilemma in equity.

Smale, Bryan J. A. 1987. Equipotentiality in Urban Recreation Opportunities. Unpublished Ph.D. dissertation, London, Ont. University of Western Ontario, Department of Geography.

Thomas, John Clayton. 1986. "The Personal Side of Street-Level Bureaucracy: Discrimination or Neutral Competence." *Urban Affairs Quarterly* 22(3):80–100. Examines patterns of one-to-one civil servant-citizen interactions; concludes that courtesy and cooperation in study settings were equitably distributed in various neighborhoods, without regard to race or class.

Thurow, Lester C. 1980. *The Zero-Sum Society: Directions and the Possibilities for Economic Change*. New York: Basic Books. An interpretation of the American economy that emphasizes the author's pessimistic views about the future.

Thurow, Lester C. 1985. *The Zero-Sum Solution: Building a World-Class American Economy*. New York: Simon & Schuster. An updated statement of his 1980 book, with an emphasis on policy recommendations to correct some of the problems he sees.

Wicks, Bruce, and Crompton, John L. 1986. "Citizen and Administer Perspectives of Equity in the Delivery of Park Services." *Leisure Sciences* 8:341–365. Summarizes different approaches to equity and reports on result of a survey of citizens and park administrators asked about their preferences for various measures.

Winthrop, Dalba. 1978. "Aristotle and Theories of Justice." *American Political Science Review* 72: 1201–1217. An historical review of early conceptions of equity in Aristotle's philosophy of justice; argues Aristotle was skeptical about all theories of justice in government.

SOURCES OF ADDITIONAL INFORMATION

Additional articles on equity in recreation services include John L. Crompton and Charles W. Lamb, "The Importance of the Equity Concept in the Allocation of Public Service" (*Journal of Macromarketing* 3:28–39, 1983); Bruce E. Wicks and John L. Crompton, "Implementing Equity in the Urban Recreation and Park Context" (*Trends* 25 no. 3: 34–39, 1988); Grant Cushman and Elery Hamilton-Smith, "Equity Issues in Urban Recreation Services," in David Mercer and Elery Hamilton-Smith, eds., *Recreation Planning and Social Change in Urban Australia* (Malvern, Australia: Scorrett, 1980, 167–178); and J. M. Kavanaugh, J. M. Marcus, and R. M. Gay, *Program Budgeting for Urban Recreation* (New York: Praeger, 1973). E. Savas provides a brief overview of various equity tools and discusses some general principles of equity for managers in "On

Equity in Providing Public Services" (*Management Sciences* 24: 800–808, 1978). A critical review article of research approaches used in the study of equity is found in Richard Rich, "Neglected Issues in the Study of Urban Service Distributions: A Research Agenda" (*Urban Studies* 16: 143–156, 1979).

ETHNICITY. See MULTICULTURALISM.

EXPECTANCY-VALENCE MODEL. A model describing the relationship between beliefs and attitudes; the model states that an individual's attitude toward an object is a direct function of his evaluation of each attribute of the object and the probability that the object possesses the attribute.

The expectancy-valence, or expectancy-value, model is based on a long-held view in psychology that because people learn, over time, to associate certain outcomes with different behaviors, behavior that produced desired outcomes is reinforced by those desired outcomes (Tolman, 1932). One result of this line of research was the development of the stimulus-response school of psychology, usually associated with B. F. Skinner. This research also led to the development of a series of models of human behavior and attitude formation.

One of the first of these models was an early version of the expectancy-valence model: the Subjective Expected Utility Model (SEU), developed by W. T. Edwards (1954). Edwards hypothesized that an individual would select the one alternative among all possible behaviors that he believed would most likely lead to a desirable outcome. This hypothesis was formalized as an equation:

$$SEU = \sum_{i=1}^{n} SP_i U_i$$

where SEU = probability of choosing any given behavior in a particular situation
       n   = all possible behaviors
      SP_i = probability that a given behavior will lead to outcome i
      U_i = desirability of outcome i
      (Note: the sum of SEUs for all possible behaviors in a particular situation is 1.00)

Edwards developed his model as an attempt to understand overt behavior. The SEU model is, therefore, essentially a causal model. In practice, however, researchers have found only a weak relationship between measures of perception or subjective values and behavior, due to the existence of BARRIERS and other variables missing in the SEU model. One class of variables that psychologists recognize as critical in the deeper understanding of human behavior is attitude. An attitude is, to most social scientists, a "relatively stable affective response to an object [that is] accompanied by a cognitive structure made up of beliefs about the potentialities of the object for attaining or blocking the realization of valued states"(Rosenberg, 1956:367).

In his work to develop a clearer understanding of how attitudes and beliefs are related, Morris Rosenberg developed an " instrumentality model." His model stated essentially that the more an "object" (which may include specific forms of human behavior) was *instrumental* in obtaining a desired outcome or in blocking an objectionable outcome, the more favorable an individual's attitude would be toward that object. Rosenberg also expressed his model in the form of a simple equation:

$$A_o = \sum_{i=1}^{n} I_i V_i$$

where A_o = attitude toward object o
      i   = attribute of object
      n   = number of attributes
      I_i = probability that o possesses a particular attribute
      V_i = value or instrumentality of attribute in obtaining a desired outcome
              or in blocking an objectionable outcome

Rosenberg's instrumentality model is clearly parallel to Edwards's SEU model. The basic difference is that Edwards attempted to predict behavior while Rosenberg attempted to explain how attitudes are developed or changed. In Rosenberg's view, attitudes exist because they are functional for individuals; that is, they help the individual to interpret information, pursue goals, and select different specific behaviors under varying conditions.

Martin Fishbein and Icek Ajzen (1975) built on Rosenberg's work, extended it to encompass the formation and evolution of beliefs, and examined how beliefs and attitudes shape behavior. As a result of their extensive work on the topic, the expectancy-valence model is now usually associated with Fishbein and Ajzen. The contemporary name for the model is intended to reflect its two components: (1) the degree an individual *expects* to find a particular attribute or benefit associated with some object or action and (2) the *valence* (a term borrowed from physics and chemistry that refers to "attractive power" of an atom in a chemical reaction) or value of the attribute.

Although none of the original work on expectancy-valence models was intended to be used in marketing research, the model has become very popular in that field. In fact, James Engel, Roger Blackwell, and David Kollat (1978) have estimated that more market research was published on expectancy-valence models (sometimes known in the marketing literature as Fishbein models) than on any other aspect of human behavior. The model has also played an important role in the development of the RECREATION OPPORTUNITY SPECTRUM. It has become one of the more important theoretical tools in both TOURISM and LEISURE studies and is likely to continue to stimulate research.

REFERENCES

Edwards, W. T. 1954. "The Theory of Decision-Making." *Psychological Bulletin* 51:380–417. Developed a causal model of human behavior that presaged the development of expectancy-valence models.

Engel, James F., Blackwell, Roger D., and Kollat, David T. 1978. *Consumer Behavior,*

3rd edition. Hinsdale, IL: Dryden Press. A very useful introduction to research and concepts on understanding consumer behavior; covers the use of expectancy-valence models in marketing.

Fishbein, Martin, and Ajzen, Icek. 1975. *Belief, Attitude, Intention, and Behavior: An Introduction to Theory and Research*. Reading, MA: Addison-Wesley. An excellent text on the most important theories related to attitudes and behavior.

Rosenberg, Morris D. 1956. "Cognitive Structure and Attitudinal Effect." *Journal of Abnormal and Social Psychology* 53:367–372. The first formal articulation of a basic expectancy-valence model for analyzing attitude formation.

Tolman, Edward C. 1932. *Purposive Behavior in Animals and Man*. New York: Appleton Century Crofts. An important early inquiry into the forces shaping behavior; helped provide the basis for subsequent research on stimulus-response theory as well as expectancy-valence models.

SOURCES OF ADDITIONAL INFORMATION

An example of the use of the model in tourism is Douglas R. Scott, Charles D. Schewe, and Donald G. Frederick, "A Multi-brand/Multi-attribute Model of Tourist State Choice" (*Journal of Travel Research* 17 no. 1:23–29, 1988). J. R. Cohen, M. Fishbein, and O. T. Ahtola discuss model application in "The Nature and Uses of Expectancy Value Models in Consumer Attitude Research" (*Journal of Marketing Research* 9:456–461, 1972). Simplified guidelines for using the model in tourism are provided by Stephen Smith, *Tourism Analysis* (London: Longman, 1989, Chapt. 4). The role of expectancy-valence models in the development of the Recreation Opportunity Spectrum is described briefly in B. L. Driver, Perry Brown, George Stankey, and Timothy Gregoire, "The ROS Planning System: Evolution, Basic Concepts, and Research Needs" (*Leisure Sciences* 9:201–212, 1987).

EXTERNALITIES. Direct costs or benefits generated by a producer's or consumer's actions but affecting a third party.

The notion of externalities (also known as spillovers, neighborhood effects, and social costs and benefits) is now generally understood by the public as a result of concern over pollution and the quality of the ENVIRONMENT. Such understanding, however, was too slow to develop even among economists. Adam Smith (1976), John Stuart Mill (1848), Maffeo Pantaleoni (1883), Emil Sax (1883), Ugo Mazzola (1890), Knut Wicksell (1896), and Erik Lindahl (1928) all addressed topics that a modern reader would see as related to the issue of externalities. These topics—the functions and failures of the free marketplace, effects of taxation on society, the role of legislation in the market, and the most efficient and fair methods of taxation in terms of general social welfare—very slowly moved economists toward recognizing the need for a more explicit discussion of externalities and PUBLIC GOODS.

It was not until 1920, with A. C. Pigou's *Economics of Welfare*, that an economist directly tackled theoretical problems of externalities arising from the production of commodities. Pigou based his discussion on a distinction between private net products (for which costs and benefits were adequately internalized in the market price) and social net products (for which costs and benefits were not adequately internalized). If production imposed a cost on parties other than the producer or consumer, the market price would be too low for a socially efficient allocation of resources. Pigou suggested that in these circumstances government should impose a tax on the producer to reflect the "misplaced" costs. If the production of a commodity creates benefits enjoyed by others than just the immediate producer or consumer, the level of production would be too low for a socially efficient allocation of resources. Pigou prescribed for this condition a system of "bounties" or subsidies to promote greater production.

Pigou, however, did not take his insights the additional step that would have formally linked externalities with a theory of public expenditures and public goods. Although Alfred Marshall (1925) was the next to draw attention to externalities, the full linkage between this concept and public expenditure policy required the cumulative contributions of Richard Musgrave's (1938) work on efficiency in the production of public goods, Howard Bowen's (1948) analysis of the demand for public goods (and his rediscovery of Lindahl's insights), and the work of Paul Samuelson (1954, 1955, 1958) on the nature of public expenditures, public goods, and GAME theoretic issues affecting individual expressions of willingness-to-pay (see DEMAND) for public goods.

The modern conceptualization of externalities is often expressed in terms of real-life illustrations. As one example, consider a promoter arranging a rock concert at a local stadium. The exchange between the promoter and the band is a Pareto optimal reallocation of RESOURCES, that is, both benefit from the reallocation. The band earns income by selling its services to the promoter who then earns income by selling tickets. Presumably, the concert goers are also satisfied with their part in the eventual exchange by obtaining a recreational experience with a value equal to or greater than the cost of their tickets. Neighbors in the area of the stadium, however, may experience externalities. If they like the music being played, they enjoy a benefit by virtue of hearing the concert free. If they dislike the music, the noise represents a cost to their quality of life. Congestion and litter represent additional costs for the neighbors that neither the promoter, band, nor concert goer absorb.

The proper response by government to externalities of production or consumption can be difficult to determine. In the concert example, if the most serious externality is the cost of cleaning up litter from neighboring streets the next day, one can make a reasonable estimate of the cost of cleanup and recover those costs by levying an appropriate tax on concert tickets. If the chief complaint is noise or the potential for violence, estimating the magnitude of the cost to society and finding an appropriate response is much more difficult.

The same basic problem of determining the magnitude of externalities and identifying the proper governmental response also occurs in the case of external benefits. The presence of a PARK in a neighborhood may increase neighboring land values, enhance the beauty of the community, and perhaps even make a marginal contribution to local air quality if the park is large enough. Improved fitness levels of park users may yield further externalities such as lower health care costs to society and increased productivity for the users' employers. In practice, though, these effects can be very difficult to objectively and accurately measure. Estimating the value of externalities of public parks and recreational facilities is fundamental to the justification of their provision by a public agency. If the benefits of recreational facilities are limited exclusively to those who directly use the facility, one can challenge the fairness of allocating public resources for exclusively private gain. Option values (see DEMAND) and the philosophical arguments behind the CONSERVATION movement represent approaches to assert the importance of externalities in recreational resources.

Although other issues besides externalities are important in determining whether or not a commodity should be publicly provided, an understanding of the nature of externalities and the problems associated with documenting their existence and measuring their magnitude is fundamental to policy analysis in recreation and leisure studies.

REFERENCES

Bowen, Howard. 1948. *Toward Social Economy*. New York: Rinehart. A theoretical inquiry into demand for and willingness to pay for public goods.

Lindahl, Erik. 1928. "Einige strittige Fragen de Steurertheorie." *Die Wirtschafttheorie der Gegenwart*. Hans Mayer, ed., vol. IV, 238–304, Vienna. Reprinted (1958) as "Some Controversial Questions in the Theory of Taxation" (trans. Elizabeth Henderson). In *Classics in the Theory of Public Finance*, Richard Musgrave and Alan Peacock, eds., 214–232. New York: Macmillan. Argues that many principles of economics can be used to guide the amount and distribution of taxes, including the valuation of public services.

Marshall, Alfred. 1925. *Principles of Economics*. London: Macmillan. One of the early, great introductory texts on modern economics; was also one of the first to refer to "external effects" of production processes.

Mazzola, Ugo. 1890. "I dati scientifici della finanza pubblica." Chapter IX, 159–183. Rome. Reprinted (1958) as "The Formation of the Prices of Public Goods" (trans. Elizabeth Henderson). In *Classics in the Theory of Public Finance*, Richard Musgrave and Alan Peacock, eds., 37–47. New York: Macmillan. Argues that the price of public goods should be structured to avoid pricing members of the public out of the opportunity to purchase goods; a major point is that the utility of public goods is approximately the same across the population and that the price should be the same to all consumers—not set differentially to reflect the differential value of the good to the individual.

Mill, John Stuart. 1848. *Principles of Political Economy*. Reprinted (1965). In *Reprints of Economic Classics*. New York: A. M. Kelley. An early inquiry into the proper role of government in economic policy and public services.

Musgrave, Richard. 1938. "The Voluntary Exchange Theory of Public Economy." *Quarterly Journal of Economics* 53:213–237. A rejection of the voluntary exchange theory (based on the belief that traditional pricing principles can be used to develop public finance policy) and presentation of a brief model based on social value scales.

Pantaleoni, Maffeo. 1883. "Contributo alla del riparto delle spese pubbliche." *Rassegna Italiana*, Oct. 15. Reprinted (1958) as "Contribution to the Theory of the Distribution of Public Expenditure" (trans. D. Bevan). In *Classics in the Theory of Public Finance*, Richard Musgrave and Alan Peacock (ed.), 16–27. New York: Macmillan. An essay on principles that should guide parliamentary decisions about public budgets.

Pigou, A. C. 1920. *The Economics of Welfare*. London: Macmillan. Introduces a useful, new perspective on government budgeting procedures by describing the difference between "internal" and "external" costs and benefits of production.

Samuelson, Paul A. 1954. "The Pure Theory of Public Expenditures." *Review of Economics and Statistics* 36:387–389. The first of three important articles on economic policy and allocation principles for public expenditures.

Samuelson, Paul A. 1955. "Diagrammatic Exposition of a Theory of Public Expenditure." *Review of Economics and Statistics* 37:350–356. Further elaboration of his ideas about the production of public goods and the allocation of public expenditures.

Samuelson, Paul A. 1958. "Aspects of Public Expenditure Theories." *Review of Economics and Statistics* 40:332–338. Still more reflections on the nature of public goods, theories of public goods, externalities, and public policies.

Sax, Emil. 1924. "Die Wertungstheorie der Steuer." *Zeitschrift für Volkswirtschaft und Sozialpolitik*. New Series IV. Vienna. Reprinted (1958) as "The Valuation Theory of Taxation" (trans. Elizabeth Henderson). In *Classics in the Theory of Public Finance*, Richard Musgrave and Alan Peacock, eds., 177–189. A restatement of an earlier argument (first presented by Sax in 1883) that theoretically links the share of taxes people pay to the value of the public goods they receive.

Smith, Adam. 1976. *An Inquiry into the Nature and Causes of the Wealth of Nations*. Oxford: Clarendon Press. A modern reprint of Smith's 1776 classic work on mercantilist economics; presents a strong argument for *laissez-faire* in economic policy.

Wicksell, Knut. 1896. "A New Principle of Just Taxation." Reprinted (1985). In *Classics in the Theory of Public Finance*, 72–118. New York: Macmillan. Rejects an argument made by some political philosophers that decisions on public finance required virtual unanimous support of all affected parties and argues that parliamentary majority is sufficient; critiques (as well) many earlier authors' views on taxation and public finance.

SOURCES OF ADDITIONAL INFORMATION

Although many recreation writers allude to the existence of external benefits as a justification for the provision of recreation facilities and services as a public good, relatively few empirical studies have been conducted. One major study looking at both positive and negative externalities, in terms of social, environmental, and economic impacts is Alister Mathieson and Geoffrey Wall, *Tourism: Economic, Physical, and Social Impacts* (London: Longman Group, 1983). Externalities of neighborhood parks are examined in Timothy D. Schroeder, "The Relationship of Local Public Park and Recreation Services to Residential Property Values" (*Journal of Leisure Research* 14:223–234, 1982); J. W. Kitchen and W. S. Hendon, "Land Values Adjacent to an Urban Neighborhood Park" (*Land Economics* 46:231–243, 1967); and J. C. Weicher and R. H. Zerbst, "The Externalities of Neighborhood Parks: An Empirical Example" (*Land Economics* 49:99–105, 1973).

More general discussions of externalities may be found in numerous texts and articles on public finance. See for example, Milton Friedman, *Capitalism and Freedom* (Chicago: University of Chicago Press, 1962, 22–36); Richard A. Musgrave, "Provision for Social Goods," in eds., J. Margolis and H. Guitton, *Public Economics* (London: Macmillan, 1969, 124–144); and Bruce F. Davie and Bruce F. Duncombe, *Public Finance* (New York: Holt, Rinehart, and Winston, 1972, 46–52). An informative, albeit dated, review article is E. J. Mishan's, "The Postwar Literature on Externalities: An Interpretive Essay" (*Journal of Economic Literature* 9:1–28, 1971).

F

FACILITATOR. One who works with a community group in a support capacity to help the group develop its own abilities so that they can successfully achieve their goals.

The role of facilitator (or enabler) emerged in the 1950s and 1960s as part of the COMMUNITY DEVELOPMENT movement (Ross, 1955; Biddle and Biddle, 1965). The role was conceived from the beginning as a support or educational function for local groups attempting to solve self-defined problems. The facilitator assists with the process of problem solving but does not select problems, specify goals, or take an active lead in actually solving substantive problems.

The concept has become a popular one as a "leadership" style for recreationists involved in MAINSTREAMING as well as in GENERAL RECREATION PROGRAMING (Carpenter and Howe, 1985). It does, however, have some critics. For example, many citizens hold the view that they pay taxes to municipalities so that recreation services can be provided directly to them. They have no interest or time in working with a facilitator so that they can learn how to provide recreation services for themselves.

The concept has also been watered down by being extended to contexts quite remote from community development and self-help. One increasingly common application is to label the moderator in a panel discussion as a facilitator. Workshop leaders and educators involved in self-directed learning projects are also sometimes called facilitators.

REFERENCES

Biddle, William W., and Biddle, Laureide J. 1965. *The Community Development Process: The Rediscovery of Local Initiative*. New York: Holt, Rinehart, and Winston. A community development text with a brief discussion of the concept of enabler and "field-worker" as community development agents.

Carpenter, Gaylene M., and Howe, Christine Z. 1985. *Programming Leisure Experiences*. Englewood Cliffs, NJ: Prentice Hall. A general recreation leadership text; considers the "facilitative approach" as one possible leadership style.

Ross, Murray G. 1955. *Community Organization: Theory and Principles*. New York: Harper. An early community development planning text.

SOURCES OF ADDITIONAL INFORMATION

Detailed, critical, and scholarly inquiries into the theory and principles of facilitation as a leadership style are very rare in recreation. Brief descriptions of this approach in general group processes relevant to recreation as well as other settings may be found in David Johnson and Frank Johnson, *Joining Together: Group Therapy and Group Skills* (2nd ed., Englewood Cliffs, NJ: Prentice Hall, 1982). Carol Ann Peterson and Scout Lee Gunn examine the role of facilitators in *Therapeutic Recreation Program Design: Principles and Procedures* (Englewood Cliffs, NJ: Prentice Hall, 1984).

FESTIVAL. A celebration of a theme or special event for a limited period of time, held annually or less frequently (including one-time only events), to which the public is invited.

The notion of a festival is historically linked with the HOLIDAY concept. Many holidays are marked by special festivals highlighting its particular theme. Festivals, however, are also held independently of official holidays. They may be celebrated at any level from small, local celebrations organized by a service club to major international events such as the Olympic Games or the World's Fair. Festivals are also known as special events or, in the case of more major festivals, hallmark events. They differ from other types of events and attractions in three ways (Smith, 1988):

1. They are held annually or less frequently, perhaps even one-time only.
2. They have predetermined opening and closing dates, delimiting a running time usually of no more than one year and frequently for only one day.
3. They do not own permanent facilities or structures.

These characteristics mean that a number of events that some may label as festivals are excluded from this categorization. Such events include regular concerts and theater presentations, special displays at galleries or theaters that own (or hold a long-term lease on) their property, regularly scheduled sporting events, and annual exhibitions tied to permanent sites such as state fairs.

Even with these exclusions, a wide variety of events may be considered to be festivals:

1. Hallmark events (e.g., a World's Fair).
2. Other major international events (e.g., the Gathering of the Clans).

3. Annual community festivals (e.g., Oktoberfest).

4. Historic milestones (e.g., bicentennials).

5. Local celebrations of national events or holidays (e.g., Labor Day).

6. Sports events (e.g., the Pan-American Games).

Donald Getz and Wendy Frisby (1988), in a survey of community-run festivals in Ontario, identified the following themes:

Theme	Percent of Provincial Festivals
Seasonal	27.3
Food	18.2
Ethnic	14.3
Historic	11.6
Music	8.0
Sports	3.0
Arts	1.9
Other	15.7

The interest of Getz and Frisby in community-run festivals was more than just simply cataloging their themes, however. Their basic interest was in developing guidelines for monitoring the effectiveness of festivals as a potential tool for COMMUNITY DEVELOPMENT. Festivals offer several practical benefits for community development including the creation of a body of experienced volunteers, promotion of a sense of community self-reliance, and enhancement of the LEISURE INFRASTRUCTURE for a community. Elsewhere, Getz (1984) introduced the notion of a "social MULTIPLIER" to describe the general, beneficial spin-offs of festivals and other forms of TOURISM development: development of local leadership abilities, enhancement of a sense of accountability, promotion of a spirit of public/ private sector cooperation, and reinvestment of proceeds of festivals into the community.

Other authors have adopted different perspectives in the study of festivals. Government agencies may see festivals primarily in terms of their potential as a tool for regional economic growth, usually as part of a larger tourism strategy (Tourism Canada, 1987). Such publications emphasize organizational and promotional skills for developing festivals, but pay little heed to the effectiveness or impacts of the festivals. The impact of festivals has been examined by Brent Ritchie and Donald Beliveau (1974), the Canada Council (1980), the Province of Saskatchewan (1985), and Clare Mitchell and Geoffrey Wall (1986), among others.

A still different perspective on festivals may be found in the work of cultural anthropologists. Here the focus of attention is on festivals as part of a local CULTURE (Wilson and Udall, 1982; Van Esterik, 1982). Related to this perspective is the interest of Dean MacCannell (1976) and Philip Pearce (1982) on linking festivals to some tourists' desire for AUTHENTICITY in their travel.

130

FESTIVAL

REFERENCES

Canada Council. 1980. *The Impact of Culture on Tourism in Canada: A Review of Travel and Festival Surveys*. Ottawa: Supply and Services. Provides guidelines for organizing festivals.

Getz, Donald. 1984. "Tourism, Community Organization, and the Social Multiplier." In *Leisure, Tourism, and Social Change,* ed. Jonathan Long and Richard Hecock. Edinburgh: Centre for Leisure Research, Dumferline College. Introduces the notion of a "social multiplier" as an indicator of social changes brought about by tourism and festival development.

Getz, Donald, and Frisby, Wendy. 1988. "Evaluating Management Effectiveness in Community-Run Festivals." *Journal of Travel Research* 27(1):22–27. Explores the nature and effectiveness of voluntary management in community-run festivals.

MacCannell, Dean. 1976. *The Tourist: A New Theory of the Leisure Class*. New York: Schocken Books. A social psychological examination of tourist behavior; relates desire for "authenticity" to interest in local festivals and events.

Mitchell, Clare, and Wall, Geoffrey, 1986. "Impacts of Cultural Festivals on Ontario Communities." *Recreation Research Review* 13(1):28–37. Examination of social and economic impacts of theatre "festivals" on three small towns.

Pearce, Philip. 1982. *The Social Psychology of Tourist Behavior*. Oxford: Pergamon Press. A general survey of motivations and consequences of tourists' behaviors; does include brief material on festivals as a form of tourism.

Province of Saskatchewan. 1985. *A Study to Determine the Impact of Events on Local Economies*. Regina, Sask.: Ministry of Tourism and Small Business. An economic impact study of local festivals on small and mid-size communities.

Ritchie, J. R. Brent, and Beliveau, Donald. 1974. "Hallmark Events: An Evaluation of a Strategic Response to Seasonality in the Travel Market." *Journal of Travel Research* 13(2):14–20. Examines the effectiveness of the Quebec Winter Carnival in extending the Quebec tourist season.

Smith, Stephen L. J. 1988. "Other Tourism Services: Examples of the Lesser-Documented Industries." In *Tourism in Canada: A Statistical Digest,* ed. Kathleen Campbell, Pierre Hubert and Robin Chadwick, 129–139. Ottawa: Supply and Services. An empirically based study of selected tourism services, one of which is festivals and local events.

Tourism Canada. 1987. *Planning Festivals and Events*. Ottawa: Supply and Services. A practical handbook designed for local festival organizers.

Van Esterik, P. 1982. "Celebrating Ethnicity: Ethnic Flavor in an Urban Festival." *Ethnic Groups* 4:207–227. A cultural anthropological study of festivals as a form of ethnicity.

Wilson, Joseph, and Udall, Lee. 1982. *Folk Festivals: A Handbook for Organization and Management*. Knoxville: The University of Tennessee Press. A practical guide to the administration, marketing, and operation of folk and craft festivals.

SOURCES OF ADDITIONAL INFORMATION

Authors who have written handbooks to guide local organizers in managing festivals include Richard Howell and Timothy Bemisdorfer, *South Carolina Tourism Development Handbook: A Primer for Local Communities* (Clemson, SC: Clemson University, Department of Recreation and Park Administration, 1981); Joseph Wilson and Lee Udall,

Folk Festivals: A Handbook for Organization and Management (Knoxville: The University of Tennessee Press, 1982); and Edward McWilliams and Allan Mills, *Evaluation of Festivals, Special Events, and Visitor Attractions* (College Station, TX: Texas A & M University, Department of Recreation and Parks, 1985).

Bruce Wicks and Carson Watt, *Texas Festivals and Events: Survey Results* (College Station, TX: Texas A & M University, Department of Recreation and Parks, 1984) examined the impacts and effectiveness of local festivals. Brent Ritchie also offered some general advice on measuring the impacts of festivals in "Assessing the Impact of Hallmark Events: Conceptual and Research Issues" (*Journal of Travel Research* 13 no. 2:2–11, 1984).

FLOW. The experience of total, intrinsically satisfying involvement in an activity in which an individual's skills are in balance with the challenges posed by the activity.

Flow was first proposed as a term for a type of positive transcendental state by Mihaly Csikszentmihalyi (1975) as a result of a series of in-depth interviews with chess players, rock climbers, dancers, and surgeons. As Csikszentmihalyi noted, the term is a "native category"—it was a word used repeatedly by his subjects to describe their experiences. Flow appears to be similar to other experiences labeled as "peak experiences" by Abraham Maslow (1962) or as an "origin state" by Richard DeCharms (1968). Csikszentmihalyi also suggested that it is essentially the same as some forms of religious experience and meditation. This connection, however, is less certain because the transcendental states achieved by meditation or religious ecstasy often come from relaxation, "letting go," or a form of temporary emotional surrender to another realm of consciousness. Flow, in contrast, is achieved by action and involves a sense of control.

Csikszentmihalyi identified six elements common in those experiences he identified as "flow" in his interviews:

1. A merging of action with awareness. The participant concentrates solely on performing the actions, not on consciously evaluating them or questioning why he is involved in the activity.

2. A centering of attention on a limited stimulus field. This typically takes the form of the participant losing track of time, and of focusing on the immediate surroundings: a chessboard, a rock face, a dance floor, or the surgical patient in the examples Csikszentmihalyi studied in his original work.

3. A loss of self-consciousness or a transcendence of individuality. Reports of participants engrossed in their activities often includes expressions of feeling at one with the world, or of being caught up in a larger and richer reality outside themselves. (It is this particular element of flow that has prompted some authors to link the flow experience with religion.)

4. A feeling of control over one's actions and ENVIRONMENT. This feeling of control does not necessarily manifest itself in the conscious experience of having to maintain and exercise control, but in the easy and confident exercise of control.

5. A perception of coherent or unambiguous DEMANDS, linking goals and means. It is not uncommon in ordinary life for an individual to experience contradictory demands or to feel pressure to do incompatible things. In a state of flow, all actions are perceived to be coherent and directed towards the fulfillment of a goal. There is a clear, pragmatic distinction between good and bad activities.

6. Flow is autotelic. In other words, flow is based on INTRINSIC MOTIVATION, "the purpose of the flow is to keep on flowing" (Csikszentmihalyi, 1975:47).

These six elements of flow are achieved when an individual becomes caught up in an activity that balances the skills ("action capabilities" in Csikszentmihalyi's original terminology) with the challenges ("action opportunities") inherent in the activity. Flow exists on a continuum, from microflow states associated with relatively less demanding tasks such as reading a good book to deep flow associated with highly challenging activities such as rock climbing. This continuum represents an important distinction between flow and Maslow's notion of peak experiences. Peak experiences are essentially a dichotomy: a person is either in one or not. Flow, on the other, may occur along a range of levels of involvement.

One problem with the original formulation of flow is that the model predicted the experience of flow for all activities in which the person's skills were balanced with the demands of an activity, even at the lowest levels of skill and challenge. In 1987, Csikszentmihalyi suggested a slightly modified flow model in which flow occurs under the combination of two conditions: (1) challenge and skill are in balance and (2) the activity requires above-average skills (for the individual) to meet above average challenges (again, defined from the perspective of the participant) (Csikszentmihalyi and Le Fevre, 1987). If the skills possessed by the participant are far above the challenge of the activity, the person feels boredom; if the challenges are too great, the person feels anxiety. And if both skills and challenges are very low, the individual moves into a state of apathy.

Flow is a positive, expansive feeling with a strong intrinsic motivational element. As such, it bears a marked similarity to the characteristics many authors have noted for LEISURE (Iso-Ahola, 1979). Indeed, Csikszentmihalyi observed that leisure activities such as GAMES and PLAY could provide intense flow experiences. More recent work by Csikszentmihalyi (Graef, Csikszentmihalyi, and McManama Gianinno, 1983) as well as by Diane Samdahl (1988) have successfully documented a direct relationship between intrinsic motivation (as an independent variable) and the experience of a specific component of flow in positive affect. Roger Mannell (1979) and Mannell and William Bradley (1986) also noted that an increase in PERCEIVED FREEDOM associated with game playing in a laboratory setting resulted in increases in a positive evaluation of the experience. While such work is suggestive of a close connection between leisure and flow, positive affect is not unique to flow.

Building on these limited studies, Mannell, Jiri Zuzanek, and Reed Larson (1988) next attempted to determine if higher levels of several components of flow occur in activities that are perceived as intrinsically motivated and freely chosen than in activities that are perceived as being constrained and extrinsically motivated. Their model involved measuring reported levels of psychological response to statements addressing psychological constricts of affect, potency, concentration, relaxation, and the balance of skill with challenge. These responses were studied in each of four contexts created by combining each of two conditions of freedom (constraint and freedom) with each of two conditions of motivation (extrinsic and intrinsic). This model was based on John Neulinger's (1981) paradigm of leisure/ nonleisure experiences: "pure job" (constrained and extrinsic), "pure work" (constrained and intrinsic), "leisure job" (free and extrinsic), and "pure leisure" (free and intrinsic). Mannell et al. hypothesized that the various components of flow would be experienced most strongly in pure leisure and least strongly in pure job. Pure work and leisure job would have intermediate levels.

Their results indicated that only the experience of relaxation corresponded with the hypothesized pattern. Affect, potency, concentration, and the feeling of a balance between skills and challenge were not highest in the state of pure leisure. The finding that relaxation is a strong correlate of pure leisure supports a finding by Susan Shaw (1984) that feeling relaxed was a good indicator of when people felt they were in a leisure state.

The failure to find the expected direct correlation between other components of flow and the "purity" of the leisure state may indicate that flow is not the best experimental model for studying leisure/nonleisure experiences. In other words, leisure and intense psychological involvement may not be necessarily related or even compatible. Work by Csikszentmihalyi and Le Fevre (1987) also tends to confirm this negative conclusion. In a study of positive psychological intensity and involvement in an activity (flow) by both clerical and managerial workers the authors found that flow was experienced most often in work settings and less in leisure settings.

The finding that work tends to provide more frequent flow experiences than leisure may have some interesting implications for understanding what Robert Stebbins (1982) has labeled "serious leisure" (see AMATEUR). For example, the most psychologically engrossing and rewarding leisure activities may necessarily involve some form of deep personal commitment to an activity or to other people. (This tentative observation should not be taken as an implicit criticism of the use of leisure for rest and relaxation). It also appears to suggest that some activities engaged in for extrinsic reasons may be the most intrinsically rewarding.

The relationship between components of flow and the nature of the leisure experience is far from being fully understood. Existing research has both confirmed some common notions about what people find important and satisfying in leisure and work and appears to lead to some apparent paradoxes (such as extrinsic motivation leading to intrinsic satisfaction). The concept of flow provides the leisure researcher with a provocative and testable model of human motivation and behavior and therefore promises to continue to be an important concept in future research.

REFERENCES

Csikszentmihalyi, Mihaly. 1975. *Beyond Boredom and Anxiety*. San Francisco: Jossey-Bass Publishers. The original formulation of the flow model.

Csikszentmihalyi, Mihaly, and Le Fevre, Judith. 1987. "Optimal Experience in Work and Leisure." Paper presented at the 5th Canadian Congress on Leisure Research, Halifax, N.S. Updates the original model of flow, including a prediction about the causes of apathy; noted that flow occurs more often in work than in leisure.

DeCharms, Richard. 1968. *Personal Causation*. New York: Academic Press. A theoretical examination of some basic behavioral issues in psychology. Describes an experiential state achieved by some individuals as "the origin state," that appears to resemble flow.

Graef, Ronald, Csikszentmihalyi, Mihaly, and McManama Gianinno, Susan. 1983. "Measuring Intrinsic Motivation in Everyday Life." *Leisure Studies* 2:155–168. Uses the experiential sampling method to study how often people describe their activities as being freely chosen and a sense of overall well-being.

Iso-Ahola, Seppo. 1979. "Some Social Psychological Determinants of Perceptions of Leisure: Preliminary Evidence." *Leisure Sciences* 2:305–314.

Mannell, Roger C. 1979. "A Conceptual and Experimental Basis for Research in the Psychology of Leisure." *Society and Leisure* 2:179–196. A state-of-the-art paper for the social psychological study of leisure; includes a brief discussion of the relevance of the flow concept to leisure.

Mannell, Roger C., and Bradley, William. 1986. "Does Greater Freedom Always Lead to Greater Leisure? Testing a Person x Environment Model of Freedom and Leisure." *Journal of Leisure Research* 18:215–230. A laboratory-based study of the effects of perceptions of freedom on self-reported feelings about leisure.

Mannell, Roger C., Zuzanek, Jiri, and Larson, Reed. 1988. "Leisure States and "Flow" Experiences: Testing Perceived Freedom and Intrinsic Motivation Hypotheses." *Journal of Leisure Research* 20:289–304. Examines relationship between components of flow and the experience of leisure; empirical findings provide only limited support for a direct relationship.

Maslow, Abraham. 1962. *Towards a Psychology of Being*. Princeton, NJ: Van Nostrand. Includes a description of a transcendental state, "peak experiences" that appears to resemble flow experiences in some aspects.

Neulinger, John. 1981. *Psychology of Leisure*, 2nd edition. Springfield, IL: Charles C. Thomas. A good overview of the psychology of leisure experiences; proposes a paradigm relating motivation and freedom to leisure experiences.

Samdahl, Diane. 1988. "A Symbolic Interactionist Model of Leisure: Theory and Empirical Support." *Leisure Sciences* 10:27–39. Used the experiential sampling method in asking respondents how "leisure like" various activities were.

Shaw, Susan M. 1984. "The Measurement of Leisure in Everyday Life." *Leisure Sciences* 7:1–24. Empirical examination of people's feelings about leisure and how they define the experience for themselves.

Stebbins, Robert A. 1982. "Serious Leisure: A Conceptual Statement." *Pacific Sociological Review* 25:251–272. Discusses amateurism in art and science, hobbies, and volunteerism as forms of "serious leisure."

SOURCES OF ADDITIONAL INFORMATION

One researcher who has paid special attention to the relationship between flow and leisure is Roger Mannell. In addition to the references in the definition, other works by Mannell on this topic include "Social Psychological Strategies and Techniques for Studying Leisure Experiences," in Seppo Iso-Ahola, ed., *Social Psychological Perspectives on Leisure and Recreation* (Springfield, IL: Charles C. Thomas, 1980, 62–88) and "A Psychology for Leisure Research" (*Leisure and Society* 7:13–21, 1984). Douglas Kleiber and Guy Dirkin applied aspects of the flow concept in their chapter, "Interpersonal Constraints on Leisure," in Michael Wade, ed., *Constraints on Leisure* (Springfield, IL: Charles C. Thomas, 1985, 17–42) as have Howard Tinsley and Diane Tinsley in "A Theory of the Attributes, Benefits, and Causes of Leisure Experience" (*Leisure Sciences,* 8:1–45, 1986). A text that examines the role of intrinsic motivation in leisure behavior is Edward Deci and Richard Ryan, *Intrinsic Motivation and Self-Determination in Human Behavior* (New York: Plenum Press, 1985).

FUN. Merriment, mirth, a spirit of light-hearted enjoyment and pleasure.

The concept of fun is an awkward one in recreation and leisure studies. On one hand, it connotes foolishness or even degeneracy. Sebastian de Grazia (1962: 320–321), one of the few authors who even addressed the concept, considered it disparagingly: "The pleasure in doing what one is unable to do during the work week—stay up late, sleep late, get drunk, fight, whirl away at one's own crazy speed, act the boss, give way to the Dionysian rhythm of the dance, spend like the sailor—this is called fun. Some would call it puerility." Tibor Scitovsky (1976) equates fun with cheap pleasure and thrills, and distinguishes it from "true joy" born of self-sacrifice, commitment, and effort. Such authors restrict the term to its earlier connotation of foolishness, practical joking, trickery, and dishonest behavior. Perhaps because of this still frequent connotation, most RECREATION and LEISURE authors avoid using the term at all.

Yet on the other hand, John Huizinga (1955) writes unabashedly of the fun of play, and the powerful, generative force represented by simple, childlike fun. Stephen Smith (1977), in an essay on *A Midsummer Night's Dream* as an accidental study of play, also argues for the significance of fun as a transcendent human experience. To Huizinga, Smith, and a few other authors, fun is fundamental (pun intended) to the understanding of leisure phenomena.

Fun may be considered to be an implicit aspect of other leisure phenomena or models such as FLOW and INTRINSIC MOTIVATION. As the scholars who have contributed to these other concepts would point out, though, fun is only incidental to the essence of these concepts. PLAY may be fun, but the real reason for playing, allegedly, is found in intrinsic motivation or OPTIMAL AROUSAL. Yet Huizinga (1955:3) argued that fun "resists all analysis, all logical interpretations. As a concept, it cannot be reduced to any other mental category." In the view of Huizinga or Smith, fun is essentially an element—an entity or experience that is truly basic and that needs no other explanation. It is real; it exists; it is sufficient in itself.

REFERENCES

de Grazia, Sebastian. 1962. *Of Time, Work, and Leisure*. New York: Twentieth Century Fund. An influential, elitist look at leisure and work.

Huizinga, Johan. 1955. *Homo Ludens*. Boston: Beacon Press. A classic examination of play as the basis of culture; argues that play and fun are essentially lighthearted and mirthful, yet basic to many forms of social and cultural life.

Scitovsky, Tibor. 1976. *The Jobless Economy*. New York: Oxford University Press. A personal look at the alleged displacement of joy and deeply satisfying experiences in life by ''cheap thrills'' and the desire for instant gratification.

Smith, Stephen. 1977. ''*A Midsummer Night's Dream:* Shakespeare, Play and Metaplay.'' *The Centennial Review* 21:194–209. The author interprets this Shakespearean comedy as an ''essay'' by Shakespeare on the nature of play.

SOURCES OF ADDITIONAL INFORMATION

As noted, fun is not a particularly common topic per se in the recreation and leisure studies literature. Some aspects of fun do appear in Roger Caillois, *Man, Play, and Games* (trans. Meyer Barash). (New York: The Free Press, 1961), especially in his discussion of the nature of PAIDIA. An oblique argument for the importance of fun (and play) in another aspect of leisure—the writing of poetry—is put forward by John Ciardi, ''Adam and Eve and the Third Son'' (*Saturday Review,* Aug. 29, 1964, 143ff). David Miller also refers to the importance of a spirit of fun in *Gods and Games: Towards a Theology of Play* (New York: Harper Colophon, 1973).

G

GAME. An activity designed to achieve a particular result using methods prescribed by specific rules, and where those methods are more limited than they would be in the absence of such rules, and where the sole purpose for accepting the rules is to voluntarily engage in the constrained activity.

Few words in recreation and leisure studies have the history and diversity of meanings as game. It is generally considered to have been derived from the Indo-European root word *ga,* "to rejoice." Modern speakers of English use *game* to refer to a wide variety of competitive recreational activities (whether based on physical skill, intellectual strategy, or chance) as well as the prize in a contest, correct rules of behavior, hypocritical behavior, a formal simulation of human behavior, a debate, a joke, an occupation, wildlife, or a metaphor for rational decision making under conditions of competitive uncertainty. "To be game" refers to the willingness to take part in some action, to suffer from a lame leg, or to the quality of having a wild or unpleasant odor or taste. Game can refer to the action of playing in a game or competing in a contest. Earlier generations also applied the word to lovemaking, skill in entertainment, an incubus or succubus, as well as an entertainer or minstrel. Game is thus used as a noun, adjective, and verb. It may imply a compliment, an insult, or an objective assessment of some phenomenon. It can be a metaphor or a measurable, demonstrable human action. Game is one of the most malleable, ambiguous, and difficult terms to define in the entire lexicon of leisure studies.

One of the first modern scholars to address the subject of games was Johan Huizinga, a Dutch historian who specialized in the Middle Ages. Huizinga, during the 1930s, was intrigued by the endurance of game playing and other play forms during the medieval period. Games and PLAY, generally considered trivial by contemporary authors, showed a remarkable vitality and acceptance during a time in which life was typically brutal, dangerous, and short. Huizinga investigated the possible reasons for this phenomenon, and eventually developed his thesis that play and games endured because they were the basis of CULTURE. He outlined this thesis in HOMO LUDENS (1955) and described the play basis of warfare, education, law and other "serious" aspects of culture.

One of the few contemporaries of Huizinga who was also interested in games was an American sociologist, George Mead (1934). Mead helped to formulate the notion that the study of games could yield insights into other forms of social development, especially in children. Games, were to Mead, paradigmatic of social situations—situations in which human beings follow rules and adopt roles as they associate with each other. Mead's work is considered to be the basis of modern role theory in sociology.

Jean Piaget (1928, 1932, 1951) also conducted an extensive study of games in childhood. His particular focus was on cognitive and moral development through childhood. Like Mead, Piaget examined the child's consciousness of rule following and role-playing. Piaget, however, went further. He described how the child's conception of rules and roles change with age. Very young children see game rules as something imposed on them, almost as a sacred obligation. As the child grows, he increasingly sees rules as socially defined and, to a degree, self-imposed.

Roger Caillois (1961), a French sociologist, was influenced by Huizinga's analysis of play and its relationship to culture and used some of Huizinga's concepts as the basis of his *Man, Play, and Games*. Caillois disagreed with Huizinga on several details, however. He believed that Huizinga's definition of game was too narrow in that he excluded profit-making activity. On the other hand, Caillois felt that Huizinga was too liberal in that Huizinga included secrecy and mystery as elements of game playing and that sacred mysteries, in particular, had no connection with games.

One of the Caillois's lasting contributions to the study of games was his matrix of game forms. He first classified games into four fundamental types: AGON (competition), ALEA (chance), MIMICRY (simulation), and ILINX (vertigo). Each game type contains a balance of two opposing qualities: PAIDIA (freedom, spontaneity) and LUDUS (organization, planning). The following table illustrates how some types of activity can be classified. Each column represents one of the four types of game; the rows represent different levels of ludus and paidia.

Caillois viewed his work as serving two functions. First, he asserted that his work was the first to set out a formal sociology of games. Second, Caillois suggested his work represented the first step toward building a sociology from the study of games. He offered, as a contribution to the goal of a game-based sociology, a model that related his basic game classification matrix to "serious" social institutions such as stock market speculation as well as deviant, corrupt, or violent social behaviors, such as forgery.

	AGON	ALEA	MIMICRY	ILINX
HIGH PAIDIA	Parent-child wrestling	Selection rhymes (e.g. "eenie-meenie")	Children's imitations	Whirling contests
MIXED PAIDIA AND LUDUS	Sandlot football	Casino slot machines	Improvisational theatre	Drinking contests
HIGH LUDUS	Major league baseball	State-supported lotteries	War gaming	Dancing contests

David Miller (1973), in reviewing Caillois's work, suggested that Caillois was too optimistic and ambitious in attempting to extend his work to both functions. In fact, his attempt was fundamentally impossible because it required that he adopt two conflicting positions: game playing as the basis of culture (a view similar to that of Huizinga) and culture as the basis of game playing. Although both positions are tenable hypotheses, Caillois failed to recognize the inherent conflict and, as a result, was unable to develop a convincing foundation for his sociology derived from games. Caillois did, however, successfully convince an international academic audience that one could write seriously about games, in contrast to Huizinga who wrote about games because he saw that they were serious.

A different approach to the subject of games in scholarly inquiry can be traced from Erving Goffman (1959, 1961, 1967) who built on the work of Mead. Goffman used the concept of a game as a metaphor for analyzing face-to-face interactions between individuals in social settings. Other authors independently adopted the game metaphor or adapted the work of Mead and Goffman. Norton Long (1958), for example, described the relationships of various social divisions in urban society (business, church, government, education, and so on) as a series of interacting games that were coordinated, with varying degrees of success, through the "political game." Peter Berger (1961) used the metaphor of game to criticize what he referred to as "social fictions." Much of ordinary life was, to Berger, a game in the sense that it was hypocritical, morally irresponsible, and "not real." SOCIALIZATION places people into artificial roles or games as a result of the overemphasis on economic and social COMPETITION. Game playing keeps people apart, hampers the development of trust and communication, and ultimately destroys the sense of community among groups of people.

Perhaps the most widely read author who popularized the game metaphor was Eric Berne (1964) who wrote *Games People Play*. To Berne, a game is a strategy of actions consciously chosen by one individual to achieve an ulterior motive. To play a game is to be deceitful. Berne's desire was to encourage people to live in a world "beyond games" (a title of one of his chapters). The point of this phrase was to describe the creation of a healthy and honest relationship among people who live, work, play, or otherwise come into contact with each other.

One of the more unusual uses of the game metaphor was proposed by Nigel Calder (1967) in *Eden Was No Garden*. Noting that English speakers use the same word to denote a play activity as well as wildlife, Calder suggested a new conception for the term *gamekeeper*. A gamekeeper, to Calder, was not only one who protects wildlife, but also one who promoted healthy games. The most important game to be promoted was the "ENVIRONMENT game," a joyful and nurturing attitude toward both natural and man-made environments.

The game metaphor was used in an especially provocative context by Thomas Szasz (1961) in his analysis of psychiatric medicine. Building on the conceptualizations of human behavior as role-playing and rule following as first developed by Mead and Piaget, Szasz argued that the phenomenon usually referred to as mental illness could be more usefully viewed as a type of game playing. In fact, according to Szasz, the very term *mental illness* is an illogical term. Illness refers to a physical or somatic condition, and it is erroneous to apply it to a mental condition. Forms of mental illness such as hysteria and psychosis, which do not have a neurological basis, are actually types of impersonation or game playing. People who exhibit these symptoms have been encouraged or forced to adopt the "mental illness game" as the only game they have success in. Mental illness was viewed by Szasz as a type of coercive game to obtain help and attention and as a game encouraged by physicians and psychiatrists who "need" patients to legitimize their profession.

Szasz also introduced the concept of metagames and styles of game playing. Every game has a set of rules that the players accept. Each game also has a set of metarules, that describe a metagame, a higher order game. Metarules, for example, dictate whether the competitors will adhere closely to the formal rules, or whether some minor infractions will be tolerated. The game may be tennis, but the metagame may be an intense competition between business rivals or a social period of aerobic exercise for two friends. Many individuals with various forms of mental illness adopt different metagames in their interpersonal relationships than do the people they come into contact with. These metagames are not always a conscious decision by the mentally ill individual, but are nevertheless adopted to fulfill some personal goal.

Sociologists, psychologists, and psychiatrists are not the only ones to study games. A large body of literature has been developed by anthropologists and folklorists with respect to the description of games in other cultures. This research, based primarily on field observation plus some secondary documents and artifacts, is concerned with identifying the nature, variety, and diffusion of games around the world. Although some research has confirmed that games and game playing are very widely spread, several cultures have been identified that do not appear to have games. These cultures, according to John Roberts and Brian Sutton-Smith (1966), tend to be limited to tropical regions with simple, subsistence economies; little technology; weak political organization; no class-based social stratification; and little stress in child socialization.

Mathematicians and economists have developed another large body of literature known as game theory. Game theory was first outlined by Johann von Neumann in the 1920s and more fully articulated in *Theory of Games and Economic Behavior* (von Neumann and Morgenstern, 1944). Game theory, in this context, refers to a deductive theory of rational behavior for two or more individuals acting in a situation where they are in competition. This competition can, of course, be some type of recreational activity such as a card game, but the theory was actually intended to apply to more "serious" forms of competition such as labor negotiations, pricing strategy for a retailer, or even war.

The simplest game situation in game theory is a two-person, zero-sum game. Two individuals are in direct competition; one's gain imposes an equal loss on the other. Von Neumann and Morgenstern proved that there always exists an optimal solution that each player should adopt. Generally, this solution is that combination of actions that will minimize the maximum loss the opponent can inflict on the other player. This is referred to as the minimax solution. More complex strategies can be derived for nonzero-sum games and for games with more than two players, including games in which different players can form coalitions.

Game theory is not intended to serve as a description of how people actually behave; rather, it is a model of optimal, rational behavior. It defines the best strategy of actions for any given player in a conflict situation when the preferences of other players are known and quantifiable. The theory thus is more about game playing than about games themselves. The emphasis is on the outcome of a game, and that outcome is maximization of utility or profit. Such an emphasis is fundamentally different from the emphasis placed on the study of games as recreational activities by most social scientists.

Game theory generated a great deal of interest initially among many researchers. By the 1960s, however, the enthusiasm was replaced by cynicism. The theory had failed to produce practical models that could be used to guide the resolution of many real life conflicts. It was a legitimately impressive mathematical achievement in terms of its internal logic, but its application fell far short of original expectations. The primary reason for this failure was that game theory is based on assumptions of full knowledge and rationality. Not only are such assumptions patently false in most real world situations, neither term was adequately defined by the developers of the theory to permit the complete specification of hypothetical situations in which the theory could be empirically tested and refined.

One positive result of the attention generated by game theorists was the widespread development of games as simulation techniques for various types of conflict studies. Military games date back to at least the 1700s, but the early promise of game theory inspired the application of gaming to new problems. One of the first new areas to explore the applications of games as simulations

were business schools. The initial management games were introduced in business programs in the 1950s as part of seminars offered to senior undergraduate
and graduate students. Early games were strictly pedagogical devices, intended
to help students synthesize lecture material. More sophisticated games were
eventually developed for application outside of the classroom to identify optimal
negotiating strategies in real business settings. The use of games as simulation
devices spread throughout other academic fields, especially political science and
planning, through the 1960s and 1970s. Although game simulations have had
relatively little success in analyzing and resolving real disputes, they continue
to be quite popular as teaching tools at all grade levels.

The study of games has also had some appeal to philosophers. Suits (1967),
for example, has developed a formal definition of game that was virtually an-
tithetical to the mathematicians' conception of a game as implied in game theory.
Although Suits focuses on game playing rather than games directly (like game
theorists), he describes the essence of game playing as voluntary inefficiency.
The point of playing a game is not to maximize utility or to minimize potential
losses, but to follow unnecessary rules to perform some action. Furthermore,
the purpose of this action is inextricably bound up with the rules associated with
the action.

To illustrate this point more clearly, we can consider one of Suits's own
examples: a footrace around a track. The point of the race might be described
as getting from the starting line to the finish line as quickly as possible. This
could be done by running a straight line across the infield or by riding a motorcycle. The rules of a footrace, though, prescribe inefficient behavior. The
runners must race on foot around a track. The only purpose of this rule is to
permit the running of the race around the track over a distance longer than is
necessary. Cheating by running across the infield or by using a motorcycle to
finish before the other runners would not only be a violation of the rules but,
would destroy the gamelike quality of the footrace.

Inefficiency and the inseparability of rules and ends, however, are not sufficient
to describe some behavior as a game. Many religious observances or moral
prescriptions exhibit forms of rules and behavior that are "inefficient." The
fastest way to get money might be to rob a bank, but morality and law prohibit
this as an acceptable action. The distinction between morality and game playing
was summarized by Suits in the following formula: rules in morality make the
action right; rules in game playing make the action. An essential feature of game
playing, therefore, is that the rules are not ultimately binding. We can rationally
and ethically choose to accept them or to reject them. Even more importantly,
the means for playing the game are also nonbinding. We ultimately remain free
to play a game or to not play.

Suits's definition of a game is based on these characteristics. He suggests,
"To play a game is to engage in an activity directed toward bringing about a
specific state of affairs, using only means permitted by specific rules, where the
means permitted by the rules are more limited in scope than they would be in

the absence of the rules, and where the sole purpose for accepting such limitation is to make possible such activity'' (Suits, 1967:148). This definition provides the basis for the definition of the concept of game given at the outset of this entry.

Aurel Kolnai (1966) has suggested that game playing is an example of a ''genuine paradox'' in that each player participates in a game in complete agreement with the other player, for the mutual pleasure of the game, but also with the mutual intention of ending the game by beating the other player. Suits (1969) counters that there is no paradox because the agreement between the players is that they will compete. The purpose of playing the game is not directly to win, which Kolnai assumes, but simply to play the game.

Research into games and the use of the game metaphor has declined from a peak in the late 1960s and the early 1970s. The cause of this decline are uncertain, but they likely include the unavoidable ambiguity in the word, the failure of game theory and the use of the game metaphor to yield new and demonstrably true insights into human behavior, and the use of the concept throughout the social sciences to denote too many unrelated phenomena.

REFERENCES

Berger, Peter. 1961. *The Precarious Vision*. Garden City, NJ: Doubleday. An early use of the game metaphor in social interactions.
Berne, Eric. 1964. *Games People Play*. New York: Grove Press. A widely read book that uses game as a metaphor for manipulative behavior.
Caillois, Roger. 1961. *Man, Play, and Games*. Glencoe, IL: The Free Press. One of the first and most important scholarly studies of games.
Calder, Nigel. 1967. *Eden Was No Garden*. New York: Holt, Rinehart, and Winston. Explores the relationship between games and environment.
Goffman, Erving. 1959. *The Presentation of Self in Everyday Life*. Garden City, NJ: Doubleday. Examines social interactions in terms of role playing and rule following.
Goffman, Erving. 1961. *Encounters*. Indianapolis: Bobbs-Merrill. Extends the inquiry begun in Goffman's 1959 book.
Goffman, Erving. 1967. *Interaction Ritual*. Garden City, NJ: Doubleday. Extends Goffman's 1959 and 1961 work.
Huizinga, Johan. 1955. *Homo Ludens*. Boston: Beacon Press. The classic study of play and games.
Kolnai, Aurel. 1966. ''Games and Aims.'' *Proceedings of the Aristotelian Society*, (New Series) 66:103–128. Suggests game playing is an example of a true paradox.
Long, Norton. 1958. ''The Local Community as an Ecology of Games.'' *American Journal of Sociology* 64:251–261. Describes a variety of occupations and social functions in terms of games.
Mead, George. 1934. *Mind, Self, and Society: From the Standpoint of a Social Behaviorist*. Chicago: University of Chicago Press. Examines social interactions in terms of game and drama metaphors.
Miller, David. 1973. *Gods and Games*. New York: Harper Colophon. A new theological study of games. Good review of the study of games in academia.

Piaget, Jean. 1928. *Judgement and Reasoning in the Child*, trans. M. Warder. London: Routledge and Kegan Paul. An exploration of childhood development, especially through play.

Piaget, Jean. 1932. *The Moral Judgement of the Child*, trans. M. Gabain. Glencoe, IL: The Free Press. Extends Piaget's 1928 work.

Piaget, Jean. 1951. *Play, Dreams, and Imitation in Childhood*, trans. C. Gattegno and F. Hodgson. London: William Heinemann. Examines fantasy, role-playing, and play in children from a developmental perspective.

Roberts, John, and Sutton-Smith, Brian. 1966. "Cross-Cultural Correlates of Games of Chance." *Behavior Science Notes* 3:131–144. Considers characteristics of different societies and their relationship to game playing.

Suits, Bernard. 1967. "What Is a Game?" *Philosophy of Science* 34(2):148–156. A philosophical definition of game playing.

Suits, Bernard. 1969. "Games and Paradox." *Philosophy of Science* 36(3):316–321. A response to Kolnai's article.

Szasz, Thomas. 1961. *The Myth of Mental Illness*. New York: Dell. Suggests that mental illness is a type of game playing.

Von Neumann, Johann, and Morgenstern, Oskar. 1944. *Theory of Games and Economic Behavior*. New York: Wiley. The classic mathematical study of game theory.

SOURCES OF ADDITIONAL INFORMATION

A useful collection of readings based on different social scientific and humanistic approaches to the study of play may be found in Elliott Avedon, and Brian Sutton-Smith, *The Study of Games* (New York: Wiley, 1971). The effect of technological change on game playing is assessed in Elliott Avedon "Games, Game-Playing, and Technology" (*Impact*, 32 no. 4:405–417, 1982. Additional information about Caillois's analysis of games is contained in his "Unity of Play, Diversity of Games" (*Diogenes*, 19:92–121, 1950). Two philosophical inquiries into the nature of games are Bernard Suits, "Can You Play a Game without Knowing It?" in R. Tursman, ed., *Studies in the Philosophy and History of Science* (Lawrence, KS: Coronado Press, 1970, 132–138), and by the same author, *The Grasshopper: Games, Life, and Utopia* (Toronto: University of Toronto Press, 1978).

GRAVITY MODEL. A trip forecasting or spatial interaction model based on an analogy with Newton's Law of Gravitation.

The gravity model, also known as a spatial interaction model or potential model, is probably the most historically important quantitative tool in travel forecasting. Although it is now rarely used in its original simplistic form, most contemporary travel forecasting models were derived from the gravity model. The basis for the model is ultimately the commonplace observation that, *ceteris paribus*, the number of people making a trip decreases as the distance of the trip increases: the so-called distance decay phenomenon. The gravity model is one of two general explanations for this observation; the other competing hypothesis being the INTERVENING OPPORTUNITY model.   The gravity model states that the interaction between two places is directly proportional to their population or social magnitude and inversely proportional to the distance between them. Mathematically:

$$I_{ij} = \frac{f(P_i,P_j)}{f(D_{ij})}$$

where I_{ij} = interaction between an origin i and a destination j such as the number of trips taken by residents of i to j

$P_{i,j}$ = the social magnitude of i and j, often defined in terms of their respective populations

D_{ij} = the distance between i and j

The notion that the form of Newton's Law of Gravitation could be applied to describe social flows and interactions dates from at least the mid-1800s. Henry Carey (1858/59) was probably the first to explicitly state the analogy, "Man, the molecule of society, is the subject of Social Science. . . . The great law of Molecular Gravitation [is] the indispensible condition of the existence of the being known as man. . . . The greater the number collected in a given space, the greater is the attractive force that there is exerted. . . . Gravitation is here, as everywhere, in the direct ratio of the mass, and the inverse one of distance" (quoted in McKean, 1870).

Carey's ideas, however, had little effect on other social scientists, for the gravity concept did not appear again in social science literature until 1885 when Ernest Ravenstein made an independent, partial restatement of the concept. Ravenstein was specifically interested in the forces that affected migration into cities. On the basis of data available to him, he concluded that as a general principle the volume of movement of people into cities varies inversely with the distance between the source of migration (smaller towns and rural areas) and the "center of absorption." Ravenstein's observations also had little effect on social scientists. Not until the mid-1920s did another researcher raise the notion of "social gravity." E. C. Young, also interested in migration patterns, "rediscovered" Ravenstein's general principle. Young (1924) hypothesized that the rate of migration from farms into cities was directly proportional to a "force of attraction," determined by population size and employment opportunities in cities, and inversely proportional to the square of the distance between a rural community and a city.

A few years later, William Reilly (1931) advanced his "Law of Retail Gravitation." This law, a unique conceptualization of the gravity concept, posited that the boundary of trade between neighboring, competing cities would be positioned such that the ratio between the population of each city and the square of its distance from the trade boundary would be equal for each city.

James Bossard (1932) shifted the focus from directly on travel patterns to another form of social interaction. He found that a partial gravity model was an accurate tool for explaining the pattern of marital partner selection in an urban area: the likelihood of an individual in one neighborhood of selecting a partner for marriage decreased with the square of the distance between the prospective partners' neighborhoods.

In 1941, John Stewart offered a virtual restatement of Carey's Newtonian analogy nearly a century earlier. Stewart was an astronomer working at Princeton University and thus had a good working knowledge of Newtonian physics. He noticed that the numbers of students attending Princeton from different states decreased with the distance of the state from Princeton. Upon a more careful analysis, he discovered that the number of students from any state could be predicted with reasonable accuracy if one knew the total student population at Princeton, the population of the state, and the distance between the two. The precise relationship mirrored Newton's Law of Gravitation. Stewart published a number of articles exploring the concept of "social gravitation," including a description of the concept of the "potential of population," a measure of the intensity of the possibility of interaction at any point in space.

George Zipf (1946) working at the same time as Stewart independently used Newton's law to model the movement of people (Zipf described his model as the "P_1P_2/D hypothesis"). Sociologists and geographers have subsequently used the gravity model to describe not only the movement of people but other forms of social interaction such as telephone calls, mail flows, financial flows, and newspaper circulation.

The gravity model was first applied to the study of recreational travel by L. J. Crampon (1966). Edward Ullman and Donald Volk (1962) did use the distance decay phenomenon as a key feature of their recreation trip forecasting model four years earlier, but did not explicitly link their work to gravity modeling.

When used in recreational trip forecasting, the basic gravity model is usually expressed in a form resembling:

$$T_{ij} = \frac{GP_iA_j}{D_{ij}^a}$$

where T_{ij} = number of trips from origin i to destination j
P_i = population of i
A_j = ATTRACTIVITY of j
D_{ij} = distance between i and j
a and G = statistically estimated coefficients

Through the close of the 1960s and into the 1970s, the gravity model became an increasingly important tool in the study of recreational travel. Carlton Van Doren (1967), for example, applied the gravity model to forecasting statewide recreational travel flows in Michigan. One of the problems Van Doren noted in his work was that the gravity model tended to overpredict very short trips and to underpredict very long trips—a finding substantiated by other researchers. A tentative solution to this problem was proposed by Roy Wolfe (1972). Wolfe suggested adding an "inertial" component to the gravity model. This would have the effect of reducing short trips, because some potential travelers would not overcome the "inertia" required to make even a short trip. On the other hand, the momentum generated by starting a trip (also a form of inertia) would help to "carry" more travelers a farther distance. Wolfe illustrated his approach with hypothetical data, but did not apply it to a real-world situation. Perhaps as a result, his inertial model has not been directly incorporated into published forecasting models. His model, however, stimulated other researchers to examine the same problem identified by Van Doren and to propose refinements in the basic gravity model to overcome the inaccuracies. These refinements have typically been in how the distance component is structured (e.g., Beaman, 1976).

Each component of the gravity model has been subject to modification and refinements. Frank Cesario (1976), for example, expanded the basic origin component into a measure of EMISSIVENESS. Hubertus van Lier (1978) demonstrated how population-specific measures of recreation site attractiveness can be defined. S. L. Edwards and S. J. Dennis (1976) have expanded the distance measure into a multivariate measure of travel costs.

Despite how the various components of the gravity model are defined, one inherent limitation in the traditional gravity model is that it is unconstrained— that is, there is no upper limit to the number of trips a model might forecast. This becomes a special problem for forecasting trips a decade or so into the future for an origin that is expecting significant growth in the number of quality of destinations. Under certain circumstances, a model can predict far more trips than the population could realistically take, given time and budget constraints in the population. In response to this limitation, researchers such as Frank Cesario and Jack Knetsch (1976) developed a form of the gravity model known as a "constrained gravity model." A constrained gravity model consists of two parts: a trip generation component that estimates the total number of trips a given origin is likely to produce and a trip distribution component that allocates the total trips among competing destinations. A typical trip generation component is some form of multiple regression equation relating expected trips (the dependent variable) to population, income, mobility, and other socioeconomic characteristics (the independent variables). Trip distribution is often handled through a form of probabilistic gravity model (Wennergren and Nielsen, 1968)–which produces predictions of market shares or trip probabilities on the basis of distance and site attractiveness.

The evolution of the gravity model is a good illustration of the cumulative nature of social science. Starting with a relatively simple descriptive tool that showed promise as a way of describing certain phenomena, subsequent generations of researchers have refined and strengthened the tool. Although the gravity model is not often used these days in its original form, it continues to provide a conceptual base for the development of increasingly sophisticated and effective travel forecasting tools.

REFERENCES

Beaman, Jay G. 1976. "Distance and the Reaction to Distance as a Function of Distance."
    In *Canadian Outdoor Recreation Demand Study, Vol. 2. The Technical Notes*,

387–398. Toronto: Ontario Research Council on Leisure. Examines a variety of
distance functions and their potential to correct for certain biases in gravity models.

Bossard, James H. S. 1932. "Residential Propinquity as a Factor in Marriage Selection."
American Journal of Sociology 38:219–244. An empirical study of the effect of
distance on the selection of spouses.

Carey, Henry C. 1858/59. *Principles of Social Science*. Philadelphia: J. B. Lippincott.
A very early general social science text; probably the first statement of the gravity
model.

Cesario, Frank J. 1976. "Estimating Park Attractiveness, Population Centre Emissiveness, and the Effect of Distance (Location) in Outdoor Recreation Travel." In
Canadian Outdoor Recreation Demand Study, Vol. 2., The Technical Reports,
99–132. Toronto: Ontario Research Council on Leisure. Introduces the concept
of emissivity in travel forecasting.

Cesario, Frank J., and Knetsch, Jack L. 1976. "A Recreation Site Demand and Benefit
Estimation Model." *Regional Studies* 10:97–104. Develops a constrained gravity
model.

Crampon, L. J. 1966. "A New Technique to Analyze Tourist Markets." *Journal of
Marketing* 30(Ap.):27–31. A simple description and application of the gravity
model—probably its first published application in recreation and tourism.

Edwards, S. L., and Dennis, S. J. 1976. "Long Distance Day Tripping in Great Britain."
Journal of Transport Economics and Planning 10:237–256. Defines the distance
component in a gravity model in terms of a multivariate travel cost index; develops
an estimate of the total travel volume for long-distance day trips in Great Britain.

McKean, Kate. 1870. *Manual of Social Science: Being a Condensation of the "Principles
of Social Science" of H. C. Carey*. Philadelphia: Henry Carey Baird. A condensed
edition of Cary's earlier volume.

Ravenstein, Ernest G. 1889. "The Laws of Migration." *Journal of the Royal Statistical
Society* 48:167–235. An empirical analysis of patterns of rural-urban migration;
describes a partial gravity model.

Reilly, William J. 1931. *The Law of Retail Gravitation*. New York: W. J. Reilly. A
marketing-oriented text describing the size and interfacing of competitive trade
areas around cities.

Stewart, John Q. 1941. "An Inverse Distance Variation for Certain Social Influences."
Science 93:89–90. One of the first modern formalizations of the gravity model.

Ullman, Edward L., and Volk, Donald J. 1962. "An Operational Model for Predicting
Reservoir Attendance and Benefits: Implications of a Location Approach to Water
Recreation." *Papers of the Michigan Academy of Science, Arts, and Letters*
47:473–484.

Van Doren, Carlton S. 1967. An Interaction Travel Model for Projecting Attendance of
Campers at Michigan State Parks: A Study in Recreational Geography. Unpub-
lished Ph.D. dissertation, Michigan State University, Department of Geography.
A detailed discussion of the development and calibration of gravity models.

Van Lier, Hubertus N. 1978. "Comments on the Article of F. J. Cesario: A New Method
for Analyzing Outdoor Recreation Trip Data." *Journal of Leisure Research*
10:150–152. Identifies some problems in a gravity model formulation proposed
by Cesario; proposes a refinement in the formulation of the attractiveness component.

Wennergren, E. Boyd, and Nielsen, Darwin B. 1968. *A Probabilistic Approach to Es-*

timating Demand for Outdoor Recreation, bulletin 478. Logan: Utah Agricultural Experiment Station. Describes a probabilistic gravity model for predicting boaters' travel, based on distance and reservoir size.

Wolfe, Roy I. 1972. "The Inertia Model." *Journal of Leisure Research* 4:73–76. A modification of the gravity model in which the traveler's response to distance is made a function of distance.

Young, E. C. 1924. *The Movement of Farm Populations*, bulletin 426. Ithaca, NY: Cornell Agricultural Experiment Station. An empirical analysis of rural-urban migration; describes some patterns similar to those found by Ravenstein.

Zipf, George K. 1946. "The P_1P_2/D Hypothesis: On the Intercity Movement of Persons." *American Sociological Review* 11:677–686. An influential early sociological application of the gravity model.

SOURCES OF ADDITIONAL INFORMATION

The literature on gravity modeling is substantial. It includes both applications of gravity models to forecasting problems as well as technical studies of various aspects, limitations, and possible refinements of the basic model. A general overview of gravity models in recreation may be found in Stephen Smith *Recreation Geography* (London: Longman, 1983); the same author provides guidelines on how to calibrate a basic gravity model for tourism forecasting in *Tourism Analysis* (London: Longman, 1989, Chapt. 5). A typical example of how gravity models are used in tourism forecasting in Garey Durden and Jonathan Silberman, "The Determinants of Florida Tourist Flows: A Gravity Model Approach" (*The Review of Regional Studies* 5 no. 3, 31–41, 1975). A more technical treatment of gravity modeling for recreational trip analysis, including the use of a constrained form, is Mike Baxter and Gordon Ewing, "Models of Recreational Trip Distribution" (*Regional Studies* 15:327–344, 1981). Gordon Ewing also has written on several travel forecasting issues in "Forecasting Recreation Trip Distribution Behavior," in Stanley Lieber and Daniel Fesenmaier, eds., *Recreation Planning and Management* (State College, PA: Venture, 1983, 120–140).

One modification not discussed in the preceding section is the development of cognitive gravity models. A useful introduction to this topic is Martin Cadwallader, "Towards a Cognitive Gravity Model: The Case of Consumer Spatial Behavior" (*Regional Studies* 15(275–284, 1981). The relationship between gravity models and intervening opportunity models is examined from a conceptual perspective in Atsuyuki Okabe, "A Theoretical Comparison of the Opportunity and Gravity Model" (*Regional Science and Urban Economics* 6:381–397, 1976). An empirical comparison of a gravity model-type distance decay function and the intervening opportunity model in the context of recreation may be found in Stephen Smith, "Intervening Opportunities and Travel to Urban Recreation Centers" (*Journal of Leisure Research* 12:296–308, 1980).

Two helpful monographs on gravity models generally are Kingsley Haynes and Stewart Fotheringham, *Gravity and Spatial Interaction Models* (Beverly Hills, CA: Sage, 1984) and Peter Taylor, *Distance Decay in Spatial Interactions* (Concepts and Techniques in Modern Geography no. 2, East Anglia, UK: GeoAbstracts, 1975).

H
_____

HEDONIC TRAVEL COST MODEL. A framework for determining the value of a recreation site on the basis of the utility or quality of the various attributes associated with the site.

The hedonic travel cost (HTC) model is a rather technical framework for estimating the VALUE of a recreation site (Brown and Mendelsohn, 1984). Although the model is not as familiar to recreation researchers as the TRAVEL COST METHOD (TCM), the CONTINGENT VALUATION METHOD, or the UNIT DAY VALUE METHOD, the hedonic travel cost model arguably has a longer tradition.

This model grew out of a technique known as hedonic price estimation. Hedonic price estimation developed during the Great Depression of the 1930s as a tool for monitoring the effects of federal policies on the recovery of the nation's economy. For standardized "raw" commodities (such as milk cows) or simple processed commodities (such as butter) the construction of price indexes, an important measure of economic growth, was fairly simple. Other commodities, however, presented a greater problem. Automobiles, for example, come in a variety of models, each with different options. With each new year, new models are released, sometimes with new options. Price changes year to year reflect both economic change as well as shifts due to evolution of the product. A. T. Court (1939) developed the hedonic price function as a tool to estimate the price (or value) associated with specific features of the various automobiles available on the market. The word *hedonic* is intended to emphasize that the price indexes reflect the contributions of the various features of an automobile (or any other complex product) to the overall happiness of the consumer.

Recreational sites also offer the consumer various bundles of features or attributes. The goal of the HTC model is to derive estimates of values associated with various specific attributes at alternative sites so that an overall assessment of the value of alternative destinations may be made. It is a common observation, for example, that recreationists will often travel farther to reach a site that offers some superior combination of attributes than a closer but inferior site. By regressing travel costs on the bundles of attributes at the alternative sites, it is possible to derive a measure consumers are willing to pay for quality. One can then derive a demand curve for various combinations of site attributes on the basis of actual travel patterns to different sites with different attributes or different qualities of attributes.

The hedonic travel cost model differs from the travel cost method in that the HTC model is based on the valuation of individual site attributes while the TCM is limited to the evaluation of an entire site.

Despite the relatively long tradition of hedonic price functions, the HTC model is still experimental. There are, in particular, some unanswered theoretical issues associated with the framework that must be resolved before the model can be reliably employed by policy analysts (Smith and Kaoru, 1987).

REFERENCES

Brown, Gardner, and Mendelsohn, Robert. 1984. "The Hedonic Travel Cost Method," *The Review of Economics and Statistics* 66:427–433. One of the first and best explanations of the model.

Court, A. T. 1939. "Hedonic Price Indexes." In *The Dynamics of Automobile Demand*, 99–117. Detroit: General Motors Corp. One of the original presentations of the general hedonic price concept. Includes a brief critique by a federal policy analyst who identifies several inherent problems.

Smith, V. Kerry, and Kaoru, Yoshiaki. 1987. "The Hedonic Travel Cost Model: A View from the Trenches." *Land Economics* 63:179–192. An assessment of some theoretical issues associated with the HTC framework; concludes that many issues are still unresolved.

SOURCES OF ADDITIONAL INFORMATION

A general reference on the development of hedonic models is James Brown and Harry Rosen, "On the Estimation of Structural Hedonic Models" (*Econometrica* 50:765–768, 1982). Of more direct application to recreation and leisure studies is Kenneth McConnell, "Values of Marine Recreational Fishing: Measurement and Impact of Measurement" (*American Journal of Agricultural Economics* 61:921–925, 1979). John Charbonneau and Michael Hay provide another illustration of hedonic modeling in "Determinants and Economic Values of Hunting and Fishing" (*Transaction of the 43rd North American Wildlife and Natural Resources Conference*, Washington, DC: Wildlife Management Institute, 1978, 391–403. Robert Mendelsohn provides an example of the hedonic travel cost framework in "An Application of the Hedonic Travel Cost Framework for Recreation Modelling to the Value of Deer" in Kerry Smith and Ann D. Witte, eds., *Advances in Applied Micro-Economics*. (Greenwich, CT: JAI Press, 1984).

HERITAGE. The objects and activities that provide a sense of identity and history to a group of people or a society.

The concept of heritage is ancient. From the earliest civilizations, people have passed certain objects, buildings, parcels of land, knowledge, and traditions from generation to generation. Even today, the legal notion of heritage often refers to the devolving of property rights from one individual to another through an inheritance (Fram and Weiler, 1981). In the context of recreation and leisure studies, heritage usually has a much broader social or cultural connotation. Rather than being limited to real property owned by just one individual or family, heritage in the larger social sense refers to property of "historical, architectural, archaeological, recreational, aesthetic, and scenic interest" to society, regardless of ownership (Government of Ontario, 1980). In practice, heritage to recreation and leisure agencies implies the protection of historic buildings, museums, galleries, artifacts, and historic districts in communities as part of a society's CULTURE. The literature on CONSERVATION and NATIONAL PARKS also contains the term *heritage*. Stuart Udall (1962:2) in his keynote address to the First World Conference on National Parks, for example, talked of the role of national parks in preserving the "natural treasures [that] are in reality a heritage of all mankind."

Through the 1970s and 1980s, the term *heritage* began to be applied increasingly to nonmaterial entities such as traditional ways of working, art and craft techniques, economic systems (especially folk or farmers' markets), HOLIDAYS, religion, and even language. Formal definitions of heritage also became more comprehensive to reflect this change. Two examples of these more comprehensive definitions (both quoted in the Ministry of Citizenship and Culture, 1987) include the Canadian Museums Association: "The tangible and intangible aspects of our natural and cultural past from prehistory to the present" and the United Nations Educational, Scientific, and Cultural Organization: "The products and witness of the different traditions and the spiritual achievement of the past . . . an essential element in the personality of the people of the world."

The growth in the recognition of the importance of heritage as a concept in recreation and leisure studies has roughly paralleled the increase in the appreciation of the importance of MULTICULTURALISM, and for many of the same reasons. RECREATION, LEISURE, and TOURISM are shaped by a society's heritage; these activities, in turn, are often pursued at heritage sites or are based on the use of heritage RESOURCES. A major dilemma facing the managers and protectors of heritage resources in simultaneously protecting those resources while permitting the public use that keeps them relevant and vital. As Lily Munroe, Ontario Minister of Citizenship and Culture observed, "Our slowly awakening concern for the conservation of both our natural resources and our human history [the two components of heritage] is linked to a reawakening to the ancient idea of *stewardship*—our personal and collective responsibilities for the continuity of life and of civilization. What we have received we hold in trust for future generations" (Ministry of Citizenship and Culture, 1987:6, emphasis in the original).

REFERENCES

Fram, Mark, and Weiler, John. 1981. *Continuity with Change*. Toronto: Historical Planning and Research Branch, Ministry of Culture and Recreation. A survey of heritage presentation methods and projects in Ontario.
Government of Ontario. 1980. *Ontario Heritage Act*. 1980 Ontario Statutes, Chapt. 337. Provides a legal definition of heritage and prescribes appropriate community mechanisms for protecting heritage sites; strong architectural and historic emphasis.
Ministry of Citizenship and Culture. 1987. "Giving Our Past a Future." Toronto: Ministry of Citizenship and Culture with the Ontario Heritage Foundation. A discussion paper prepared as part of the background for the Ontario Heritage Policy Review; includes extensive discussion on important themes and issues in heritage conservation.
Udall, Stuart. 1962. "Nature Islands for the World." In *First World Conference on National Parks*, ed. Alexander B. Adams. 1–10. Washington, DC: U.S. Government Printing Office. The opening keynote address, reflecting on the development of national parks worldwide.

SOURCES OF ADDITIONAL INFORMATION

Much of the literature on heritage is ephemeral, or at least very difficult to find. Good public libraries and university libraries will likely carry articles, pamphlets, and books on local, state, provincial, and national efforts to protect heritage sites and resources. *Canadian Heritage* magazine, published by the Heritage Canada Foundation (Ottawa, Ont.) contains numerous excellent articles and essays on the philosophy and practice of heritage conservation. Jacques Dalibard is the author of two essays in *Canadian Heritage* that discuss the concept of heritage and its relationship to culture and to tourism: "Building a Cultural Identity" (Dec. 1984/Jan. 1985) and "Has Cultural Tourism Become a Trivial Pursuit" (Feb./Mar. 1985).

The Nature Conservancy (Arlington, VA) has published a two-volume collection of profiles of national and state activities devoted to heritage conservation: *Preserving Our Natural Heritage* (Washington, DC: U.S. Government Printing Office, 1977).

HOLIDAY. A day or group of days designated to commemorate some theme or event; usually marked by TIME off work.

The derivation of *holiday* from *holy day* is an obvious bit of etymology. The elision of the two words, though, is more than just a simple linguistic evolution. It represents a long-term shift in how most English-speaking people view LEISURE.

The earliest holy days were probably seasonal FESTIVALS devoted to placating or beseeching spirits that controlled food sources used by primitive peoples (Granet, 1932, 1959; Frobenius, 1954). Because primitive peoples did not have a reliable calendar, the timing of these holy days was linked to natural phenomena such as game migrations or changes of the seasons. The first fixed holy day was probably the Jewish Sabbath, instituted in the thirteenth century B.C. While the reasons for selecting every seventh day as a holy day are speculative (unless one accepts a literal reading of Genesis), one should not overlook the advantages of having a small number of days specified between observances of successive holy days in the absence of a reliable calendar.

The development of a reliable calendar was one of the first inventions of any CULTURE in the ancient world. The development of calendars is an important technological breakthrough in the observance of holy days because they permit the fixing of precise dates for the observance of holy days. Another general pattern in most societies, including early civilizations, was that the number of holy days tends to increase over time. Eventually, with the downfall of the civilization or a major change in the government, the schedule of holy days is replaced by a new and much reduced set. The pattern then begins again with a slow increase in the number of holy days.

Robert Lee (1964), for example, noted that at the peak of the Hellenistic civilization, the Greeks had instituted more days for celebration than for work. Most of these were subsequently eliminated when Rome conquered Greece. However, by the time of the late Roman Empire in the fourth century A.D., the pendulum had swung back to the point where Rome observed 175 official holidays plus numerous other festivals called by the reigning emperor to celebrate special events.

In the latter part of the Roman Empire, early Christians began to develop their own calendar. One of the first steps in the very slow process of defining their church year was to reinterpret a number of major Roman holidays in a Christian light. The winter solstice feast of Saturnalia, for example, was transformed into the celebration of Christmas. After the fall of Rome in the fifth century, the church began to work more openly on calendrical reforms. A major step in these reforms was the dissociation of Easter from its origins with Passover. Eviatar Zerubavel (1982) suggested that this shift was part of a conscious strategy to provide the early Church with a sense of independence from its Jewish origins. The shift of the Sabbath to last from sundown Friday to sundown Saturday to be the first day of the week was another part of this strategy. The overall effect of the Christian calendrical reforms was to eliminate most pagan and Jewish holidays and to redefine remaining holidays in Christian terms to strengthen the sense of Christian uniqueness as well as to provide more days for work—a necessity for both spiritual purity and physical survival.

As life became more secure and the traditions of the Church grew, holy days were added to the year. Originally intended to promote the honoring of various saints and to help teach the illiterate faithful, these holy days became popular respites from long days of physical labor. They even provided temporary relief from local wars through truces set up to observe holy days and the sabbath (the *pax dei*).

The Protestant revolution against corrupt church practices pushed the pendulum back. Martin Luther banned all holy days from his revised church calendar and imposed a grim new tone for the observance of the sabbath. Sundays were for reflection, meditation, and prayer—not FUN. This grim Sunday philosophy dominated much of Western European and North American life until well into the nineteenth century. In fact, its influence continued into the mid-twentieth century in the form of Blue Laws (named for the color of the paper they were printed on) that banned most forms of recreation on Sundays. Laws restricting forms of recreation, including shopping, on Sunday may still be found in some places such as Ontario.

The mistrust of ordinary people enjoying themselves in their free time was consistent not only with the WORK ETHIC of most religious leaders until the mid-nineteenth century, but also of many industrialists and politicians. There was a widespread belief that if employees were allowed time for recreation, they would dissipate themselves in drink. Given the living conditions caused by the Industrial Revolution, such a suspicion was not unfounded. TIME off work for holidays thus not only meant lost productivity, but represented a time of grave temptation for sins against the virtues of diligence, thrift, and abstemiousness. This attitude toward leisure was most strongly personified in the fictional character of Ebenezer Scrooge, from Charles Dickens's *A Christmas Carol*. Although fictional, Scrooge had many kindred spirits among real people.

Between 1850 and 1900, the pendulum began a return swing. Some employers and political leaders began to believe that workers might be more productive and healthier in the long run if they had shorter working hours punctuated with occasional holidays. The issue was not one of enlightened leaders providing leisure for the SELF-ACTUALIZATION of the citizenry, but a strategy for increasing the morale, health, and productivity of workers. Some business leaders also began to recognize that leisure could mean increased consumption. If workers were well rested, healthy, and had a bit of spending money, a holiday could prompt increased purchases on consumer goods. This, too, would make holidays a good idea for business.

The trend that began in the second half of the nineteenth century became a way of life in the second half of the twentieth. Holidays, whether tied to religious or patriotic observances, provided well-earned (or at least much-desired) breaks from work. They were increasingly viewed as a right and as a necessary component of a well-balanced lifestyle. The notion of holidays as escape from work and school is also the origin of the use of the term *holidays* as a synonym for vacation. The holiday's theme is less important than the opportunity it provides for recreation and the consumption of material goods, especially food, drink, and entertainment. The decline of the importance of the theme of a holiday as part of its rationale perhaps reached its nadir with establishment of Ontario's August Civic Holiday—(the first Monday of August) designated as an official holiday for no other reason than to provide a day off work.

The evolution of the meaning of holidays has not always been viewed as positive. Modern holidays have been cited by some authors as symbols of what is wrong with our culture's notions of leisure. Johan Huizinga (1955), Josef

Pieper (1964), Sebastian de Grazia (1952), and Robert Lee (1964) have noted that the roots of holidays were in celebration and PLAY. These, in turn, are viewed by the authors as requiring a sense of transcendence above the ordinary world. Reducing holidays to time off of work devoted to material consumption is a form of spiritual and social decay. (It should be recalled, though, that the spiritually acceptable activities of meditation, reflection, and self-renewal advocated by Pieper, de Grazia, and Lee can too easily be translated into modern versions of Luther's grim Sunday philosophy.)

A more objective criticism of holidays is that the activities associated with them have become increasingly homogenized (Lee, 1964). Although official civic holidays celebrate a variety of themes, most are marked by a very narrow range of celebratory activities. Whether the holiday is Victoria Day, Memorial Day, Canada Day, the Fourth of July, the August Civic Holiday, or Labor Day, people go on picnics, play outdoor games, go swimming, or go camping. For cool-weather holidays such as Thanksgiving, Christmas, and New Year's, they host parties, eat and drink, watch football, and visit friends and relatives.

Greater variation may be found in the observance of unofficial holidays. This may be due to the role of these religious or ethnic holidays as symbols of membership in minority groups. Ironically, some holidays that have strong religious or ethnic orientations have become observed by the general public who eagerly participate in the unique activities associated with the day: St. Valentine's Day, Halloween, and St. Patrick's Day. Although the celebrations associated with these holidays are now virtually devoid of any religious content, they all have religious roots and are still marked by traditional activities that make them distinct from the official, homogenized holidays.

Celebrations of even homogenized holidays, however, can be modified by small groups of individuals to symbolize their group cohesiveness. Barbara Brown and Carol Werner (1985), for example, found that houses on cul-de-sac were more likely to be decorated and to have more elaborate decorations than houses on through streets. Furthermore, the residents of houses on cul-de-sac scored significantly higher on measures of neighborhood unity and territoriality than other residents. Many communities host local special observances of official holidays to promote community spirit.

Holidays are a familiar form of leisure. Their significance as an institutionalization of our beliefs and values is easily overlooked. However, recent debates about proposals such as (1) the shifting of traditional holidays from original dates to a specified Monday to permit the creation of three-day weekends, (2) renaming Dominion Day as Canada Day, (3) the recognition of Martin Luther King Day as an official holiday, and (4) the rights of employees and students to take off to observe significant religious holy days serve to remind us that the common phenomenon of a holiday still has its roots deep in our sense of personal well-being and group identity.

REFERENCES

Brown, Barbara B., and Werner, Carol M. 1985. "Social Cohesiveness, Territoriality, and Holiday Decorations: The Influence of the Cul-de-Sac." *Environment and*

Behavior 17:539–566. Examines communal displays of Halloween and Christmas decorations as evidence of neighborhood unity.

de Grazia, Sebastian. 1952. *Of Time, Work, and Leisure*. New York: The Twentieth Century Fund. An influential book on the nature of leisure; presents an "elitist" philosophy of leisure.

Frobenius, Leo. 1954. *Kulturgeschichte Afrikas, Prolegomena Zu Einer Historischen Gestaltehre*. Zurich: Phaidon. An inquiry into the relationship between culture and the environment; special attention is paid to the development of culture.

Granet, Marcel. 1932. *Festivals and Songs of Ancient China*. New York: E. P. Dutton. An ethnographic study of ancient Chinese traditions; describes links between folk festivals and early animistic beliefs.

Granet, Marcel. 1959. *Dances and Legends of Ancient China*. Paris: Universitaires de France. A continuation of the research first presented in his 1932 book.

Huizinga, Johan. 1955. *Homo Ludens*. Boston: Beacon Press. The classic study of play, games, and culture.

Lee, Robert. 1964. *Religion and Leisure in America*. Nashville, TN: Abingdon Press. An examination of the religious roots and meaning of leisure; includes a good discussion on holy days and holidays.

Pieper, Josef. 1964. *Leisure: The Basis of Culture*, trans. A. Dru. New York: Pantheon Books. A spiritually oriented examination of leisure and its role in culture.

Zerubavel, Eviatar. 1982. "Easter and Passover: On Calendars and Group Identity." *American Sociological Review* 47:284–289. Presents an argument that early Christian calendrical reforms of the scheduling of Easter were primarily motivated by the desire to emphasize the distinctiveness of Christianity from Judaism.

SOURCES OF ADDITIONAL INFORMATION

The subject of holidays and their relationship to aspects of leisure has been examined from a number of very different perspectives. One approach that emphasizes travel, tourism, and the escape associated with holidays and leisure experiences is Roger Mannell and Seppo Iso-Ahola, "Psychological Nature of Leisure and Tourism Experiences" (*Annals of Tourism Research* 14:314–331, 1987). Leah S. Marcus examines social and political attitudes toward holidays and festivals as revealed in literature in *The Politics of Mirth* (Chicago: The University of Chicago Press, 1987). Stephen Smith also touches on the origins of holidays and festivals in *"A Midsummer Night's Dream*: Shakespeare, Play, and Metaplay" (*The Centennial Review*, 21:105–117, 1977).

In a totally different vein, David Lester and Aaron Beck have studied the relationship between holidays and suicide rates in "Suicide and National Holidays" (*Psychological Reports* 36:52, 1975).

Three useful studies on the evolution of the sabbath are Roger Beckwith and Wilfrid Scott, *This Is the Day* (London: Marshall, Morgan, and Scott, 1978), which looks at the biblical doctrine regarding the sabbath and its changing interpretation in early Christianity; John Wigley, *The Rise and Fall of the Victorian Sunday* (Manchester, UK: Manchester University Press, 1980), which looks at the origins of the perverse reluctance to enjoy oneself on Sunday and the determination to prevent others from enjoying themselves; and Samuele Bacchiocchi, *From Sabbath to Sunday* (Rome: The Pontifical Gregorian University Press, 1977), a learned historical account of the rise of Sunday observance in early Christianity.

HOMO LUDENS. A Latin phrase meaning "Man the Player."

The name *Homo ludens* was first suggested by Johan Huizinga (1955), a Dutch medievalist, to emphasize the importance of PLAY in shaping human CULTURE. Although Huizinga's suggestion parallels the scientific term for human beings, *Homo sapiens,* the author emphasized in his writings that the play element in culture was to be studied historically, not scientifically, and that play should be understood as a cultural phenomenon not as a biological phenomenon.

Huizinga (1955: ix) notes in his preface to his book *Homo Ludens* that his interest in the importance of play appears as a subtheme in his writing as far back as 1903. Play occupied a special role in the Middle Ages. During a period in the history of Western civilization when life was especially hard, dangerous, and uncertain, a spirit of play permeated many aspects of life. Huizinga examined forms of medieval life in his [1924] 1965 work *The Waning of the Middle Ages,* considered by many scholars to be his most important book. Although the subject of play was not given particular explicit treatment in *Waning,* it presaged his fuller inquiry in *Homo Ludens.*

Homo Ludens is one of the classic texts for the study of play, LEISURE, and RECREATION.

REFERENCES

Huizinga, Johan. 1955. *Homo Ludens.* Boston: Beacon Press. One of the most provocative and literary works produced in the study of play, recreation and leisure; a combination of history, literary analysis, and cultural anthropology.
Huizinga, Johan. [1924] 1965. *The Waning of the Middle Ages.* Harmondsworth, UK: Penguin Books. A reprint of the 1924 original; a study of medieval life and art in fourteenth and fifteenth century France and the Netherlands; offers hints of Huizinga's growing interest in play as a vital element of culture.

SOURCES OF ADDITIONAL INFORMATION

Roger Caillois has built on some of Huizinga's ideas (although he also disagrees with some of Huizinga's conclusions) in *Man, Play, and Games* (Glencoe, IL: The Free Press, 1961).

HUMAN LIFE CYCLE. A conceptual set of stages of personal development over an individual's life; usually tied to chronological age and characterized by relatively distinct sets of psychological concerns, physical needs, social roles, and activities.

Jacques, a character in Shakespeare's *As You Like It,* observed,

> And one man in his TIME plays many parts,
> His acts being seven ages. At first, the infant, . . .
> And then the whining school-boy, . . .
> . . . And then the lover, . . .
> . . . Then a soldier, . . .

... And then the justice, ...
... The sixth age shifts ...
Into the lean and slipper'd pantaloon, ...
... Last scene of all,
That ends this strange eventful history,
Is second childishness, and mere oblivion,
Sans teeth, sans eyes, sans taste, sans everything. (II:vii, 129–166)

The idea that human beings experience a predictable sequence of life stages or life experiences is a familiar one. As a concept in the social sciences, models of the human life cycle stem at least from work by both Sigmund Freud and Carl Jung (summarized in Erikson, 1982). Their models were based on their perceptions of regular patterns of psychosexual and psychosocial development. Another early model of human life stages was proposed by Charlotte Buhler (1968) and her associates in the 1930s. Working with detailed life histories of 400 individuals, Buhler and her team empirically identified five phases of development. The phases were defined in terms of organic development (especially the development and eventual decline of reproductive ability), changes in external circumstances such as family structure, and the individual's psychological reaction to external conditions as well as internal organic development.

Most advocates of the concept of the human life cycle emphasize at least two important properties of the complete cycle. First, each stage is characterized by a set of NEEDS and activities that are goal directed. The specific goals tend to change from stage to stage, but always can be interpreted as aspects of the drive for SELF-ACTUALIZATION. Second, the stages are separated from each other by relatively abrupt or distinct transitional phases or "crises" (Sheehy, 1976).

Within recreation and leisure studies, the concept of the human life cycle occurs in two general contexts. The first is as an organizing paradigm for analyzing patterns and variations in leisure participation (especially as a SOCIALIZATION phenomenon). Rhona Rapoport and Robert Rapoport (1975), for example, defined a series of life stages in terms of work, LEISURE, and family roles. They then identified specific developmental tasks that produced interests in certain types of activity or ACTIVITY CLUSTER. Peter Witt and Thomas Goodale (1981) used the concept to guide their inquiry into the complex nature of BARRIERS to leisure participation, noting that different stages emphasized or perceived different types of barrier.

The second use of the concept of family life cycles is in RECREATION PROGRAMMING and LEISURE EDUCATION. By understanding the specific needs and VALUES of any given stage, recreation programmers can select activities and approaches that will most benefit their clients. Patricia Farrell and Herberta Lundegren (1983) and Gaylene Carpenter and Christine Howe (1985) have provided illustrations of linking the needs and goals specific to each stage with the planning of leisure activities for individuals in each stage. For example, Farrell and Lundegren note that preschoolers (one of their stages) have a short attention span (5 to 10 minutes) and need activities that promote large muscle development.

In contrast, individuals in "later old age" (another stage) are concerned with health, alleviating boredom, and having emotional and economic security.

Many different models of the human life cycle have been proposed. Buhler's (1968:14) five stages were

1. A period of progressive growth without reproductive ability (zero to fifteen years).
2. A period of progressive growth with the onset of reproductive ability (fifteen to twenty-five years).
3. A period of reproductive ability and stationary growth (twenty-five to forty-five years).
4. A period of beginning decline and loss of reproductive ability (forty-five to sixty-five years).
5. A period of further decline (sixty-five to the end).

Erik Erikson (1963) defined eight stages characterized by a series of struggles created by conflicting concerns:

1. *Infancy*. Trust versus mistrust.
2. *Early childhood*. Autonomy versus doubt.
3. *Play age*. Initiative versus guilt.
4. *School age*. Industry versus inferiority.
5. *Adolescence*. Identity versus role confusion.
6. *Young adulthood*. Intimacy versus isolation.
7. *Maturity*. Growth versus stagnation.
8. *Old age*. Integrity versus despair.

Harold Meyer (1957) identified a simpler set of four stages specific to adults:

1. *Young adulthood*. Twenty to thirty-five.
2. *Middle years*. Thirty-five to fifty.
3. *Toward retirement*. Fifty to sixty-five.
4. *Retirement*. Sixty-five and older.

A dozen or more examples could be provided, each reflecting different values or beliefs of the authors proposing the models. John Kelly (1987) has grouped the various models of the human life cycle into five general models: (1) the family life cycle, emphasizing sociological insights into roles and role shifts (e.g. Rapoport and Rapoport, 1975); (2) the life span, emphasizing psychological or behavioral issues closely associated with chronological age (e.g., Baltes and Schaie, 1973); (3) the life course, with a broader basis than just traditional family roles, and more emphasis on patterns of continuity and transition (e.g., Riley, 1979); (4) the crisis model, focusing on the transitions between stages rather than on the stages themselves (e.g., Sheehy, 1976); and (5) the developmental model (e.g., Erikson, 1963), focusing on psychosocial development and the conflicts inherent at various stages.

Regardless of the various assumptions and disciplinary orientations taken by the numerous social scientists who have developed models of the human life cycle, all share the belief that some understanding and order can be found in the "strange eventful history" of a human life.

REFERENCES

Baltes, Paul B., and Schaie, K. Warner. 1973. *Life-span Development Psychology*. New York: Academic Press. A behaviorally based examination of the human life cycle.
Buhler, Charlotte. 1968. "The General Structure of the Human Life Cycle." In *The Course of Human Life*, ed. C. Buhler and F. Massarik, 12–26. New York: Springer. An overview of both the concept of the human life cycle from a humanistic psychological perspective, with a description of the results of some early empirical evidence.
Carpenter, Gaylene M., and Howe, Christine, Z. 1985. *Programming Leisure Experiences: A Cyclical Approach*. Englewood Cliffs, NJ: Prentice Hall. An introductory test for leisure programming; much of the approach is based on the notion of the life cycle.
Erikson, Erik. 1963. *Childhood and Society*. New York: Norton. Includes a chapter on "the eight ages of man"; strong neo-Freudian approach.
Erikson, Erik. 1982. *The Life Cycle Completed*. New York: Norton. A brief monograph reviewing the life cycle, with a special emphasis on old age.
Farrell, Patricia, and Lundegren, Herberta. 1983. *The Process of Recreation Programming*, 2nd edition. New York: Wiley. Discusses both concepts and techniques of recreation programming, including the implications of the human life cycle.
Kelly, John R. 1987. *Freedom to Be: A New Sociology of Leisure*. New York: Macmillan. Offers an examination of the implications of eight different theoretical approaches to the study of leisure; Chapter 4, on developmental theory, includes a good discussion of the life cycle.
Meyer, Harold. 1957. "The Adult Cycle." *Annals of the American Academy of Political Science and Sociology* 313:58–67. Presents a simplistic model of four stages of changes in adult roles and needs.
Rapoport, Rhona, and Rapoport, Robert. 1975. *Leisure and the Family Life Cycle*. Boston: Routledge and Kegan Paul. One of the first comprehensive studies of the human life cycle and leisure.
Riley, Matilda. 1979. *Aging from Birth to Death: Interdisciplinary Perspectives*. Boulder, CO: Westview Press. Emphasizes continuity between life stages more than the changes.
Sheehy, Gail. 1976. *Passages: Predictable Crises of Adult Life*. New York: Dutton. A popular look at a series of crises or transitions between major adult life roles.
Witt, Peter, and Goodale, Thomas. 1981. "The Relationships between Barriers to Leisure Enjoyment and Family Stages," *Leisure Sciences* 4:29–50. Examines changes in perceptions of barriers to leisure over the course of life.

SOURCES OF ADDITIONAL INFORMATION

A somewhat dated but still useful collection of readings on the life cycle, from the perspective of humanistic psychology, in Charlotte Buhler and Fred Massarik, eds., *The*

Course of Human Life (New York: Springer, 1968). Another collection, this one focusing on the issue of crises associated with transitions between stages, is Nancy Datan and Leon Ginsberg, eds., *Life-Span Developmental Psychology* (New York: Academic Press, 1975). John Kelly takes another look at the life cycle in his *Leisure Identities and Interactions* (London: George Allen & Unwin, 1983, Chapt. 3).

Specific models of life cycles discussed in-depth include the biological model of James Feibleman, *The Stages of Human Life* (The Hague: Martinus Nijhoff, 1975); Daniel Levinson's study of male development in *The Seasons of a Man's Life* (New York: Alfred A. Knopf, 1978); and the sociological work of George Kaluger and Meriem Fair Kaluger, *Human Development: The Span of Life* (3rd ed., St. Louis: Times Mirror/Mosby College, 1974).

I

ILINX. 1. The search for pleasurable disorder, dizziness, or vertigo in play. 2. Games that provide these types of qualities.

Roger Caillois (1961) proposed the use of *ilinx* as a term referring to one of four basic types of GAME. The term *ilinx* comes from the Greek word for "whirlpool." As a game type, it is to be distinguished from AGON (games of skill), ALEA (games of chance), and MIMICRY (games of imitation). The condition of ilinx may be a physical one obtained through a variety of whirling, dancing, tumbling, spinning, or falling games. Rides at theme PARKS can also satisfy the search for ilinx. Caillois suggests that there is an ilinix of a moral order: a drive for disorder or destruction that can be obtained through drinking or drug use, vandalism, rioting, and other forms of destructive or self-destructive behavior.

Some leisure scholars may challenge whether many ilinx activities should be classified as games because they are not subject to rules or limitations in time and place. In fact, the pleasure in ilinx can come through a refusal to acknowledge limits or rules on appropriate behavior, including the constrained behavior inherent in games.

REFERENCES

Caillois, R. 1961. *Man, Play, and Games*. New York: The Free Press. An important study of the sociology of games. Chapter 2 describes in detail Caillois's classification of games.

SOURCES OF ADDITIONAL INFORMATION

Some of Roger Caillois's ideas about play and games were first explored in his *Man and the Sacred* (New York: The Free Press, 1959). A classic study of play and games, which also greatly influenced Caillois, is Johan Huizinga, *Homo Ludens* (Boston: Beacon Press, 1955). Another, philosophically directed study of games and the spirit of game playing is David Miller, *Gods and Games* (New York, Harper Colophon, 1973).

IMPACT. Any verifiable change in the well-being of humans (or the ecosystem on which human survival depends) resulting from some human action.

The word *impact* is usually considered to be synonymous with effect or consequence. It is used in a wide variety of contexts including the effects of THERAPEUTIC RECREATION programs, the evaluation of education programs, and the consequences of policy changes on citizens and the effects of TOURISM development. In recreation and leisure studies, however, impact is most closely associated with environmental, economic, and social changes resulting from some form of development or growth. Lord Ashby (1976:3) noted that the idea of predicting and planning for environmental and social impacts may be viewed as beginning with Noah and his ark. The phrase, *environmental impact*, however, is more directly attributed to the National Environmental Policy Act (NEPA), which became law on January 1, 1970. Section 101 of this law stated, "The Congress, recognizing the profound impact of man's activity on the interrelationships of all components of the natural ENVIRONMENT . . . declares it is the continuing policy of the Federal Government to use all practicable means and measures . . . to create and maintain conditions under which man and nature can exist in productive harmony, and fulfill the social, economic, and other requirements of present and future generations of Americans." This law, which applies to all federal agencies and federal programs and laws, went on (in Section 102) to require "in every recommendation or report on proposals for legislation and other major Federal actions significantly affecting the quality of the human environment, a detailed statement by the responsible official on the environmental impact of the proposed action."

As a result of NEPA, the production of environmental impact statements and the production of books and reports on the methodologies appropriate for environmental impact statements became a growth industry in the 1970s. As a rule, this literature does not address the matter of defining impact as a concept, but rather focuses on how impacts are to be measured and evaluated (Munn, 1975; Erickson, 1979). R. E. Munn, for example, in his overview text, examined methods for (1) identifying specific significant impacts, (2) predicting future impacts, (3) interpreting the meaning or implications of these impacts for policy and planning purposes, (4) communicating the results of impact assessment studies, and (5) inspection of various projects likely to produce impacts. Although Munn also describes fourteen separate impact categories, he gave no definition of the concept of impact.

Paul Erickson (1979:120) noted that government agencies tend to use impact in a quasi-legal sense of "significant negative effects of project activity"; he suggested, however, that it is more appropriate for most purposes to consider impact to be synonymous with effect.

While the literature is largely devoid of explicit definitions of impact, it is replete with classification systems for impacts and indicators of impacts. A report from the Organization for Economic Cooperation and Development (OECD, 1980) on tourism and the environment advises consideration of impacts in the context of pollution, loss of natural landscapes, destruction of flora and fauna, degradation of HERITAGE sites, congestion, social CONFLICTS, and RESOURCE competition. Rostum Sethna (1980) identified seven aspects of tourism impacts: financial, moral, religious, social, physical, human, and cultural. Robert Johnston (1975) proposed that researchers should organize their work around four impact dimensions: (1) gross versus net effects, (2) direct versus indirect effects, (3) concentrated versus dispersed effects, and (4) the degree of importance of various impacts.

In their review of tourism impacts, Alistar Mathieson and Geoffrey Wall (1982) described several difficulties routinely encountered by anyone conducting research on impacts. Although their work focused on the environmental, economic, and social impacts of tourism development, these difficulties have relevance to impact studies in other areas of recreation and leisure studies.

The first difficulty is that of obtaining reliable baseline information against which to assess the degree of impacts. This becomes a special problem if one is attempting to evaluate the nature and degree of impacts of impacts after a project has been completed. Although one can more easily obtain contemporary baseline information for proposed projects, one is confronted by another problem: society and the environment are never static. Any baseline information represents a snapshot of one point in TIME, which may quickly become out of date. It is difficult to disentangle changes from some arbitrary baseline due to a project development from changes attributable to preexisting processes (natural or social) that are independent of the project.

Not only are society and nature dynamic, they are complex and have many interconnections. Some impacts can be readily documented, but a full and complete assessment of all impacts may be very difficult, if not impossible, to trace through all the interlinkages in any ecosystem or economy. Another aspect of this complexity is the fact that there often are spatial and temporal discontinuities between cause and effect. Impacts of a project may show up only well after a project has been initiated or at a distant location. Discovering and documenting the hidden linkages can be troublesome.

Finally, there are many choices to make among alternative evaluation procedures and alternative impact indicators. The issue is not just a matter of deciding which indicators to use, but of deciding how to interpret them. Evaluating whether social impacts, in particular, are "good" or "bad," involves value judgments that cannot always be resolved through research. One must consider not only what impacts are produced, but which groups in society bear which impacts (see EQUITY).

The study of impacts has become an important and popular topic in the field of recreation and leisure studies since the early 1970s. It represents, in effect, an attempt to instill a ''social conscience'' into project planning and development activities and to ensure that benefits and costs, particularly EXTERNALITIES, are fairly and equitably considered. Despite some early serious criticisms and abuses in impact assessment studies (Jain, Urban, and Stacey, 1977; Erickson, 1979), impact assessments are generally recognized as helping to provide fuller disclosure of all the consequences of proposed projects.

REFERENCES

Erickson, Paul. 1979. *Environmental Impact Assessment: Principles and Applications.* New York: Academic Press. A good, technical survey of the practices of environmental impact assessment.

Jain, R. K., Urban, L. V., and Stacey, G. S. 1977. *Environmental Impact Assessment: A New Dimension in Decision Making.* New York: Van Nostrand Reinhold. An excellent discussion of environmental impact assessment methods; from an engineering perspective; includes a discussion of early problems with some methods and assessment designs.

Johnston, Robert A. 1975. ''Assessing Social and Economic Impacts.'' In *Environmental Impact Assessment,* ed. Patrick Heffernan and Ruthann Corwin, 113–158. San Francisco: Freeman, Cooper. A popularly written survey of issues and techniques involved in social and economic impact assessment statements.

Lord Ashby. 1976. ''Background to Environmental Impact Assessment.'' In *Environmental Impact Assessment,* ed. T. O'Riordan and R. D. Hey, 3–15. Farnborough, UK: Saxon House. A brief historical overview of the development of impact assessments; special attention is given to the U.S. and British experience.

Mathieson, Alistar, and Wall, Geoffrey. 1985. *Tourism: Economic, Physical, and Social Impacts.* London: Longman. An excellent description of the entire range of impacts generated by tourism; based on extensive survey of the literature.

Munn, R. E. (ed). 1975. *Environmental Impact Assessment: Principles and Procedures.* Toronto: Scientific Committee on Problems of the Environment. A useful summary of the basic principles and methods associated with impact assessment.

OECD. 1980. *The Impact of Tourism on the Environment.* Paris: Organization for Economic Cooperation and Development. A brief and descriptive general survey of physical environmental impacts of tourism.

Sethna, Rostum J. 1980. ''Social Impact of Tourism in Selected Caribbean Countries.'' In *Tourism Planning and Development Issues,* ed. Donald Hawkins, Elwood Shafer, and James Rovelstad, 239–249. Washington, DC: George Washington University Press. Measures social impacts of tourism using attitudinal scales rather than objective measures.

SOURCES OF ADDITIONAL INFORMATION

The literature on environmental impact assessment is vast; literally tens of thousands of impact statements have been prepared by consultants, public agencies, and environmental groups. A few useful overviews of the impact assessment literature include Michael Carley and Ellan Derow, *Social Impact Assessment: A Cross-Disciplinary Guide to the*

Literature (London: Policy Studies Institute, 1980); T. O'Riordan and R. D. Hey, *Environmental Impact Assessment* (Farnborough, UK: Saxon House, 1976); and Ronald Barbaro and Frank Cross, Jr., *Primer on Environmental Impact Statements* (Westport, CT: Technomic, 1973).

Three specific impact assessment techniques that have become classics and that explicitly include references to recreation include L. Leopold, F. E. Clarke, B. B. Henshaw, and J. R. Balsley, *A Procedure for Evaluating Environmental Impact* (Geological Survey circular 645, Washington, DC: U.S. Government Printing Office, 1971); Ian McHarg, *Design with Nature* (Garden City, NY: Natural History Press, 1969); and N. Dee, J. Baker, N. L. Drobny, and K. Duke, *Environmental Evaluation System for Water Resource Planning* (Bureau of Reclamation, Washington, DC: U.S. Government Printing Office, 1972). A review of these and other assessment methods may be found in Robert Nichols and Eric Hyman, *A Review and Analysis of Fifteen Methodologies for Environmental Assessment* (Chapel Hill: University of North Carolina Center for Urban and Regional Studies, 1980).

A brief but good literature survey on recreation impacts is David Cole, "Resource Impacts Caused by Recreation," in *President's Commission on Americans Outdoors: A Literature Review* (Washington, D.C.: U.S. Government Printing Office, 1986, Management-1–Management-12).

INSTRUMENTALITY MODEL. See EXPECTANCY-VALENCE MODEL.

INTEGRATION. See MAINSTREAMING.

INTERPRETATION. The process of educating individuals about the natural and cultural HERITAGE of a society or region through the use of objects, personal experience, and a variety of printed, audio, and visual aids.

Interpretation, as a concept in recreation and leisure studies, is more than just the presentation of facts about nature or history. Ideally, its aim is to convey a sense of the deeper meaning of those facts and to instill or foster the love of learning and personal exploration. It is similar to OUTDOOR EDUCATION, and ENVIRONMENTAL EDUCATION but differs in a couple of important aspects. Unlike environmental education (and traditional outdoor education) interpretation is not limited just to the natural environment, but also includes CULTURE—the social, economic, political, technological, and artistic heritage of a society. And in contrast to both outdoor and environmental education, which are often linked to a formal curriculum, interpretation attempts to serve the general public in a LEISURE setting independent of a more structured learning experience.

Some interpreters trace the roots of their work back to the Greek scholar, Thales (640–546 B.C.) who wrote on the hydrologic cycle and on astronomy and to the Roman scholars Horace (65–8 B.C.) and Quintilian (40–118 A.D.) who emphasized the merits of learning by doing (Weaver, 1976). More recent and direct American precedents for interpretation can be found in the history of educational programs and services offered by botanical gardens, arboretums, zoos, and museums that date from the earliest years of the nineteenth century (the Philadelphia Botanical Society was established in 1806, for example). As innovative as these early programs and facilities were, they tended to emphasize the presentation of scientific facts more than the meaning or social significance of those facts to the general public.

A more successful form of interpretation, at least in terms of stimulating participants through a mixture of education, experience, and enjoyment, were nature field trips. One of the first of these in the United States were pleasure expeditions organized by Enos Mills in 1889. Mills and his customers toured the region that was to become Rocky Mountain NATIONAL PARK. As a guide, Mills was interested not just in making money but in helping his customers to understand the ENVIRONMENT they visited. He was also committed to developing and expanding the vocation of "guide" (as he described himself and other early interpreters). He wrote articles for the January 1916 issue of *Country Life in America* and the January 6, 1917 issue of *The Saturday Evening Post* urging the National Park Service to place qualified guides in all of their parks to help visitors experience and understand the PARK they were visiting. After initial resistance to these suggestions, the Park Service hired two scientifically qualified ornithologists to offer nature education programs in Yosemite National Park in the summer of 1920. The experiment was considered successful by the service, and they expanded the program initially to Yellowstone in 1921 and then slowly to other parks.

The term *interpretation* as well as the first formal statement of the philosophy and principles of interpretation is usually credited to Freeman Tilden (1957). Tilden's book *Interpreting Our Heritage* is still considered to be the standard text on the subject. By the time Tilden wrote, the practice of interpretation was reasonably well established, albeit conducted with little consistency or professional standards. Tilden helped to codify the best practices of interpretation and laid out a half dozen principles for interpreters:

1. Interpretation should relate the lesson or the object being discussed to something within the experience of the viewer.

2. Interpretation is not just information; it is revelation based on information.

3. Interpretation is a learnable art form.

4. The aim of interpretation is to stimulate and provoke curiosity and the desire to learn—not just to present facts.

5. Interpretation should emphasize the larger context, the whole, and not just the part.

6. Separate interpretive programs should be developed for children and for adults.

Tilden also noted that there was resistance to the use of the term *interpretation* for the form of education he was promoting. There were two main objections. First, interpretation had other connotations and thus should not be extended to this form of education. Second, some felt the word was a bit pretentious as a label for what they felt was a rather ordinary form of communication. *Interpreting*

Our Heritage provided arguments against these objections and, within a few years, the term was widely accepted.

Tilden's definition of interpretation provided the basis for the definition given above. He defined interpretation to be "an educational activity which aims to reveal meanings and relationships through the use of original objects, by firsthand experience, and by illustrative media, rather than simply to communicate factual information" (Tilden, 1957:8). Since Tilden's formulation, other authors have proposed other definitions. The differences are basically in selection of words rather than in any difference of opinion about the meaning of the term. For example, Harold Wallin (1965:1) defined interpretation as "the helping of the visitor to feel something that the interpreter feels—a sensitivity to the beauty, complexity, variety, and interrelatedness of the environment; a sense of wonder; a desire to know. It should help the visitor develop a feeling of being at home in the environment. It should help the visitor develop perception." Or as R. Yorke Edwards (1965:11) summarized it: "an information service, . . . a guiding service, . . . an educational service, . . . an entertainment service, . . . a propaganda service, . . . an inspirational service."

Interpretation is now considered by many recreation professionals to be not a luxury service provided by a park or heritage agency but an integral part of such agencies' mandates. Grant Sharpe (1976) believes that interpretation fulfills three objectives. First, it can help an agency explain the significance of the site or collection it operates. Interpretive programs enable visitors to develop a fuller appreciation of what they are viewing or experiencing. Second, interpretation can help managers meet administrative objectives such as protection of fragile environments through visitor information. Visitors tend to be more willing to accept restrictions on their actions if they understand the reasons for the restrictions. Finally, effective interpretive programs can increase overall public understanding and support for the agency. This latter function can be especially important in times of budget restraints. And it implies that interpretation should not be just limited to on-site visitors but should be incorporated into out-reach and public relations messages.

REFERENCES

Edwards, R. Yorke. 1965. "Park Interpretation." *Park News* 1(1):11–16. A discussion of the nature of park interpretation and its role in park management.
Sharpe, Grant W. 1976. "An Overview of Interpretation." In *Interpreting the Environment,* ed. Grant Sharpe, 3–22. New York: Wiley. A brief discussion of the definition, nature, objectives, and history of interpretation.
Tilden, Freeman. 1957. *Interpreting Our Heritage.* Chapel Hill: University of North Carolina Press. The first formal statement of the philosophy, principles, and practice of interpretation.
Wallin, Harold E. 1965. *Interpretation: A Manual and Survey on Establishing a Naturalist Program,* Management Aids bulletin 22. Arlington, VA: American Institute of

Park Executives, National Recreation and Park Association. A practical manual
on interpretive techniques.

Weaver, Howard E. 1976. "Origins of Interpretation." In *Interpreting the Environment,*
ed. Grant Sharpe, 23–42. New York: Wiley. An historical survey of the development of interpretation; special attention is paid to the National Park Service.

SOURCES OF ADDITIONAL INFORMATION

Grant Sharpe's collection of readings *Interpreting the Environment* (New York: Wiley,
1976) contains twenty-seven independently authored chapters on a wide range of interpretation topics. A dated but still useful reference on understanding the importance of
interpretation in park management is David Fischer, "The Role of Interpretation" (*Park
Practice Guidelines* 5:89–92, 1966). The *Journal of Environmental Education* contains
numerous articles on interpretation and outdoor education topics.

INTERVENING OPPORTUNITY MODEL. A model relating the distance
traveled by individuals for a given purpose to the accumulated number of opportunities between the origin and the ultimate destination.

A common observation in the study of human mobility is that the number of
people making a trip to any given destination tends to decrease as the distance
to that destination increases. This phenomenon, known as distance decay, is
often attributed to the "friction of distance" or the cost and effort of travel as
traditionally described in the GRAVITY MODEL. An alternative explanation about
how distance functions to retard travel was first proposed by Samuel Stouffer
(1940). Stouffer's hypothesis was based on the fact that most trips are made for
a given purpose—to reach a particular type of opportunity for some action,
service, or resource. He proposed that "the number of people going a given
distance is directly proportional to the number of opportunities at that distance
and inversely proportional to the number of intervening opportunities" (Stouffer,
1940:846). Mathematically:

$$\frac{\Delta y}{\Delta s} = \frac{a\Delta x}{x\Delta s}$$

where Δy = number of people traveling to a circular band surrounding an origin
      Δs = width of the band
      Δx = number of opportunities located within the band
      x = number of intervening opportunities
      a = statistically estimated coefficient

The intervening opportunity model has been applied in a recreation setting by
Stephen Smith (1980) in a study of attendance at Dallas, Texas, recreation
centers. Smith compared a traditional gravity model formulation of distance
decay with an intervening opportunity model and observed that the latter was
better in describing travel flows in this particular intraurban situation. Specifically, Smith plotted the decrease in the number of people traveling increasing
distances to visit recreation centers. When distance was measured in miles, each

neighborhood studied displayed a unique and irregular distance decay curve. In contrast, when distance was defined in terms of the numbers of intervening recreation centers a given user passed, the pattern was similar among all neighborhoods studied regardless of their socioeconomic makeup. Furthermore, the mathematical function used to describe the distance decay model using intervening opportunities was significantly more accurate than when distance was defined in terms of miles traveled.

The intervening opportunity model is most relevant in describing travel patterns where there are numerous destinations offering relatively comparable recreation opportunities. Recreation centers and public access reservoirs are two common examples. The gravity model, in contrast, is more useful for describing trips to relatively unique or noncompetitive destinations, such as NATIONAL PARKS and national historic sites.

REFERENCES

Smith, Stephen L. J. 1980. "Intervening Opportunities and Travel to Urban Recreation Centers." *Journal of Leisure Research* 12:296–308. Describes the intervening opportunity model and cites empirical evidence of its greater applicability in urban settings than the gravity model.
Stouffer, Samuel A. 1940. "Intervening Opportunities: A Theory Relating Mobility and Distance." *American Sociological Review* 5:845–867. The original formulation of the intervening opportunity model.

SOURCES OF ADDITIONAL INFORMATION

Despite its potential usefulness in modeling certain types of recreational travel flow, the intervening opportunity model has not been extensively used in published literature as it might be. A technical examination of some issues associated with intervening opportunities and their effect on travel patterns and modeling in a recreation context may be found in Jay G. Beaman and Stephen Smith, "The Definition and Evaluation of a Class of Alternative-Site Functions," in *Canadian Outdoor Recreation Demand Study, Vol. 2. The Technical Notes* (Toronto: Ontario Research Council on Leisure, 1976, 333–348).

Two comparisons of intervening opportunity and gravity models are Dale W. Dison and Carl W. Hale, "Gravity versus Intervening Opportunity Models in Explanation of Spatial Trade Flows" (*Growth and Change* (Oct.): 15–22, 1977) and Atsuyuki Okabe, "A Theoretical Comparison of the Opportunity and Gravity Models" (*Regional Science and Urban Economics* 6:381–397, 1976).

INTRINSIC MOTIVATION. 1. The internally generated intention to act. 2. The presumed cause of behavior that does not have any other apparent motive.

Precedents for the concept of intrinsic motivation, one of the key concepts of contemporary RECREATION and LEISURE studies, go back at least to the work of William James in the 1890s. James (1900), working in the early years of modern psychology, was interested in the nature of free will and human motivation. He observed that curiosity and the desire to learn—essentially internal mental forces—were sufficient in themselves to cause an individual to act. This same observation was repeated more formally by Robert Woodworth (1918) who was perhaps the first scholar to outline a theory of what would become known as intrinsic motivation. Twenty years later, Gordon Allport (1937) described a concept he called "functional autonomy" that bore many features similar to intrinsic motivation.

Despite these tentative explorations into the nature of intrinsic motives, the concept received little attention or support from most psychologists through the first half of the twentieth century. A major barrier to its widespread acceptance appears to have been the powerful intellectual appeal of the "drive" or instinct theories of Edward Thorndike (1913), and especially Sigmund Freud (1915). These theories attributed much of human behavior to the operation of inherent drives or instincts. Freud, for example, proposed that human behavior was shaped by instinctive drives for sex and aggression. Other authors proposed different sets of instincts, but all agreed that inherent drives existed and could be invoked to explain most aspects of human behavior. One particularly influential theory in psychology was that of Clark Hull (1943). He posited the existence of four drives: hunger, thirst, sex, and pain avoidance. A major aspect of Hull's theory that evoked substantial interest from psychologists was his description of how reinforcement mechanisms (extrinsic rewards) worked to reinforce or modify behavior (Pavlov's earlier work with conditioning dogs to salivate at the sound of a ringing bell is a well-known example). Numerous experiments on animals through the 1940s provided some support for Hull's theory, but they also produced some results that were contrary to Hull's predictions. Of particular importance were experiments by Daniel Berlyne (1950), Harry Harlow (1950), and W. L. Welker (1956) on both rats and nonhuman primates that demonstrated that these mammals would willingly engage in certain behaviors with no external stimulus or reward. Rats, for example, would willingly explore a maze even if there was no food reward at the end. Chimpanzees would spend time solving relatively complicated mechanical puzzles apparently for no other reward than the opportunity to solve the puzzles. In describing these phenomena Harlow was the first to use the term *intrinsic motivation* in print.

Still other research in the 1950s, such as the work by Donald Hebb (1955) on OPTIMAL AROUSAL and Robert White's (1959) proposition and description of an "effectance motive"—the presumed innate drive of an individual to be effective in his environment, to be competent, and to be self-determining—contributed further insights into the subtleties of human motivation. Much of this work was brought together by Edward Deci in a series of articles developing the concept of intrinsic motivation more fully. Deci's (1975) work eventually led to the publication of a standard reference in the field, *Intrinsic Motivation*. Although the concept is now considered to be fundamental to contemporary understanding of recreation and leisure, Deci, ironically, never used the terms recreation or leisure in his text. The linkage between these phenomena and the concept of intrinsic motivation was first made by John Neulinger (1974).

Neulinger proposed a model of leisure in which motivation (intrinsic, extrinsic, or mixed) was combined with PERCEIVED FREEDOM (or perceived constraint) to create six different psychological experiences. Intrinsic motivation combined with the perception of freedom produces the experience of "pure leisure," for example; intrinsic motivation and perceived constraint, on the other hand, create the experience of "pure work"; while extrinsic motivation and perceived constraint produce "pure job."

Coincidentally with the work of Deci and Neulinger, Mihaly Csikszentmihalyi (1975) explored intrinsic motivation from a different perspective. Csikszentmihalyi was intrigued by the phenomenon of individuals becoming totally engrossed in work or leisure activities. He coined the term FLOW to describe this experience and noted that flow was a special manifestation of intrinsic motivation.

Researchers in recreation and leisure now use the concept as a basic part of most psychological paradigms used to model leisure. The interest in the concept, however, goes beyond its use in models of leisure experiences. Research has been conducted on the relative importance of intrinsic and extrinsic motives in various forms of recreation and especially VOLUNTEERISM. Of particular interest is the question of the effects of the provision of rewards (as a form of extrinsic motivation) on self-perceptions that one is intrinsically motivated. Lynn Barnett (1980) reviewed this work and concluded that the perception of intrinsic motivation is a fragile experience. It can be destroyed by the linking of material rewards to the level of performance of a previously intrinsically motivated activity. This conclusion, however, has been challenged by at least one researcher, Jone Pearce (1983) in her work on the motives of volunteers.

The literature on intrinsic motivation is substantial, but despite its widespread acceptance and intuitive appeal in recreation and leisure studies there are several nagging problems with the concept. First, the term is properly used to refer to a type of drive that creates behavior. It is, therefore, an antecedent to behavior. Some authors, however, (such as Csikszentmihalyi) also use the term to refer to the results of leisure or to the experience of leisure itself. Such usage, in effect, confuses cause and effect. Second, the relationship between intrinsic motivation and other theories of motivation, including SELF-ACTUALIZATION, have not been fully clarified. Finally, the term is close to a tautology. The evidence for the existence of intrinsic motives is negative evidence. We say that someone is intrinsically motivated when we are unable to determine what his motives are. Intrinsic motivation is the default explanation for otherwise unexplainable human behavior. Self-reports of the experience of intrinsic motivation are not necessarily reliable because respondents who use the term have obviously been taught to think of it as an explanation. The same individuals, if questioned about their motives for actions fifty years ago, might well have been prompted by the theories of Freud and Hull to suggest instinct as an explanation for behavior.

Whether intrinsic motivation turns out to be a valid explanation for certain aspects of human behavior, or simply a metaphor for some other process, it has been an important concept in allowing researchers to advance our understanding of leisure.

REFERENCES

Allport, Gordon W. 1937. *Personality: A Psychological Interpretation*. New York: Holt. The author outlined a preliminary theory of human motivations that presaged the notion of intrinsic motivation.

Barnett, Lynn A. 1980. "The Social Psychology of Children's Play The Effects of Extrinsic Rewards on Free Play and Intrinsic Motivation." In *Social Psychological Perspectives on Leisure and Recreation,* ed. Seppo Iso-Ahola, 138–170. Springfield, IL: Charles C. Thomas. A review of the concept of intrinsic motivation, with particular attention paid to its relationship with extrinsic motivation.

Berlyne, Daniel E. 1950. "Novelty and Curiosity as Determinants of Exploratory Behavior." *British Journal of Psychology* 41:68–80. Presents the results of early experiments with rats; found evidence of nonextrinsically motivated behavior.

Csikszentmihalyi, Mihaly. 1975. *Beyond Boredom and Anxiety*. San Francisco: Jossey-Bass. The original formulation of the flow concept.

Deci, Edward L. 1975. *Intrinsic Motivation*. New York: Plenum Press. The first and still a standard reference on the concept.

Freud, Sigmund. 1915. "Instincts and Their Vicissitudes," *Collected Papers,* Vol 4. London: Hogarth. Outlines his theory that people are driven by sex and aggression instincts.

Harlow, Harry F. 1950. "Learning and Satiation of Response in Intrinsically Motivated Complex Puzzle Performance by Monkeys." *Journal of Comparative and Physiological Psychology* 43:289–294. Describes evidence for the existence of intrinsic motivation in primate behavior; perhaps the first appearance of the term in print.

Hebb, Donald O. 1955. "Drives and the C.N.S. (Conceptual Nervous System)." *Psychological Review* 62:243–254. An examination of the concept of optimal arousal and its relationship to human motivation.

Hull, Clark L. 1943. *Principles of Behavior: An Introduction to Behavior Theory*. New York: Appleton Century Crofts. An influential book that presented an instinct model of human behavior.

James, William. 1900. *Psychology*. New York: H. Holt. A classic text from the beginning of psychology as a social science.

Neulinger, John. 1974. *The Psychology of Leisure*. Springfield, IL: Charles C. Thomas. The first explicit linkage between a model of leisure and the notion of intrinsic motivation; still considered to be a major reference for insights into the psychology of leisure.

Pearce, Jone L. 1983. "Job Attitude and Motivation Differences between Volunteers and Employees from Comparable Organizations." *Journal of Applied Psychology* 68: 646–652. Tested the effects of the provision of extrinsic rewards on perceptions of intrinsic motivation in firefighters; found no impact.

Thorndike, Edward L. 1913. *The Psychology of Learning*. New York: Teacher's College, Columbia University. Another instinct model of human behavior.

Welker, W. L. 1956. "Some Determinants of Play and Exploration in Chimpanzees."

Journal of Comparative and Physiological Psychology 49:84–89. Presents evidence of the role of intrinsic motivation in primate behavior.

White, Robert W. 1959. "Motivation Reconsidered: The Concept of Competence." *Psychological Review* 66:297–333. An important statement of the idea of competence as a motivating force in human behavior; argues that the desire to be competent is a major force in shaping and motivating human actions.

Woodworth, Robert S. 1918. *Dynamic Psychology*. New York: Columbia University Press. Still another instinct model of human behavior.

SOURCES OF ADDITIONAL INFORMATION

An excellent, updated review of the literature and issues associated with the concept is provided by Edward Deci and Richard Ryan, *Intrinsic Motivation and Self-Determination in Human Behavior* (New York: Plenum Press, 1985); unlike Deci's earlier volume, this monograph includes a discussion of leisure and sport. John Neulinger provides a measurement system for intrinsic motivation and leisure research in *What Am I Doing? The WAID* (Dolgeville, NY: The Leisure Institute, 1986).

A general overview of intrinsic motivation in leisure is found in Seppo Iso-Ahola, *The Social Psychology of Leisure and Recreation* (Dubuque, IA: William C. Brown, 1980). Ronald Graef, Mihaly Csikszentmihalyi, and Susan McManama Gianinno examine the frequency of the perception of intrinsic motivation and the correlation between this perception and a sense of psychological well-being in "Measuring Intrinsic Motivation in Everyday Life" (*Leisure Studies* 1:155–168, 1983).

L
_____

LEAST EFFORT PRINCIPLE. A hypothesis that humans exert effort to accomplish goals or to solve problems in such a way that the average rate of probable work is minimized.

The notion that people usually try to avoid unnecessary work is a very old one, both in folk beliefs as well as in scholarly studies. This notion is closely related to Maupertius's (mid-eighteenth century) "principle of least action" and Occam's (mid-fourteenth century) "law of parsimony." The Least Effort Principle, in a formal sense, was proposed by George Zipf (1949) in his book *Human Behavior and the Principle of Least Effort*. His goal in developing this principle was to offer a single unifying principle that could help systematize all human behavior and the evolution of CULTURE in a mathematical form.

Zipf's idea of minimizing average probable work refers to his assertion that individuals or groups will seek to find the optimum balance between minimal work now and minimal work in the future. As common experience confirms, avoiding effort in the short run can result in the need for even greater effort later. Zipf's principle states that people will, within the limits of their knowledge and foresight, attempt to minimize *total* work. It should be emphasized, however, that his principle does not imply that foresight will always be accurate, nor does it give any guidelines about how people should rationally discount future work and future benefits derived from that work with respect to the "present value" of that future work and benefits.

The fundamental basis behind Zipf's principle is the dynamic balance between two forces that Zipf calls the force of unification and the force of diversification. Zipf introduces these forces using the example of human vocabulary. Speakers, Zipf contends, would prefer to use as few words as possible, having each word carry as much meaning as possible. The long-term result of this trend would be to simplify or unify vocabulary so that a very few words carry many connotations. In contrast, listeners would prefer to have each word carry a distinct, precise, and unambiguous meaning. The result of this preference would be diversification or the growth of a large number of words, each with a unique meaning.

The result of the interplay of these two forces is a general mathematical function that predicts, in the case of vocabulary, a regular relationship between the frequency different words are used and their "rank." This relationship is known variously as Zipf's 'law,' the Bradford-Zipf distribution linking Zipf's observations with those of S. C. Bradford (1934) who discovered a simplified version of the mathematical function a decade before Zipf, and the rank-size rule. Again, Zipf introduces this relationship using a vocabulary example, in this case, James Joyce's novel *Ulysses*. He noted that *Ulysses* is 260,430 words long and is composed of 29,899 different words. Plotting the rank (r) of each word (where $r = 1$ for the most frequently used word) against its frequency of use (f), on double-log paper produces a nearly straight line descending from the upper left-hand corner to the lower right-hand corner, with a slope of -1. This implies that:

$r \times f = C$
where $C = $ a constant

Using selected data from *Ulysses,* one can observe

Word	Rank	Frequency	C
	(r)	(f)	(r × f)
I	10	2,653	26,530
All	20	1,311	26,220
Bloom	30	926	27,780
But	40	717	26,680
When	50	556	27,800

This stable relationship is found in other novels and lengthy poems in English and other languages, both ancient and modern. The significance of the relationship is not just that it works for summarizing vocabulary patterns in an empirically testable mathematical function, but that the same function applies in a wide variety of human and social situations. Zipf provided examples of the validity of his law from economics, politics, geography, and society. He suggested, in fact, that the rise of a LEISURE CLASS was predictable from the Principle of Least Effort. Other authors have found Zipf's law closely predicts patterns of scientific bibliographic citations (Brookes, 1968) and SPORT participation (Loy and Rudman, 1984). John Loy and William Rudman examined the number of different sports people reported participating in, and found that the overall distribution of SPORT participation across a sample of North Americans closely matched the pattern predicted by Zipf's law.

The Principle of Least Effort and its corollary, the Bradford-Zipf distribution (Zipf's law or rank-size rule) offers an empirically useful tool for predicting and summarizing certain quantitative patterns relevant to recreation and leisure studies. Just why this empirical regularity exists—its theoretical foundation—is still not well understood. Zipf himself noted that his observations should be treated with caution and subject to further testing and refinement. That advice—and the invitation to further explore theoretical and empirical issues associated with the Principle of Least Effort—are still valid.

REFERENCES

Bradford, S. C. 1934. "Sources of Information on Specific Subjects." *Engineering* 137:85–86.
Brookes, B. C. 1968. "The Derivation and Application of the Bradford-Zipf Distribution." *Journal of Documentation* 24:247–259. Discusses quantitative aspects of Bradford-Zipf distribution and illustrates it with data from research on vitamins.
Loy, John W., and Rudman, William J. 1984. "An Analysis of Patterns of Sport Involvement Using Zipf's Law." *North American Culture* 1:35–46. An empirical examination of validity of the Bradford-Zipf distribution to sport participation.
Zipf, George K. 1949. *Human Behavior and the Principle of Least Effort.* Cambridge, MA: Addison-Wesley. The original formulation of the least effort principle; includes numerous empirical illustrations of Zipf's law or the Bradford-Zipf distribution.

SOURCES OF ADDITIONAL INFORMATION

Walter Isard provides a brief discussion of the rank-size rule in population distributions in *Location and Space-Economy* (New York: Wiley, 1956, 55–60). Brian Berry and Walter Garrison provide a more extended discussion of this rule and some underlying theoretical issues in "Alternate Explanations of Urban Rank-Size Relationships" (*Annals of the Association of American Geographers,* 48:83–91, 1958). A more recent discussion of Zipf's law is B. Roehner and K. E. Weise, "A Dynamic Generalization of Zipf's Rank-Size Rule" (*Environment and Planning* 14:1449–1467, 1982).

LEAST RESTRICTIVE ENVIRONMENT. See DEINSTITUTIONALIZATION; MAINSTREAMING; and THERAPEUTIC RECREATION.

LEISURE. TIME free from obligations such as work, personal maintenance, housekeeping, parenting, and other nondiscretionary commitments.

It has been written that the ancient Athenians were the first to discover leisure (Kando, 1975:23). Whether or not the Hellenic civilization was the first to formalize the concept of leisure, the writings of the Greek philosophers, especially Aristotle, are the earliest addressing the subject of leisure (*schole,* in Greek). Leisure, to Aristotle, was one of the three goals of human life: theoretical wisdom, happiness, and leisure. Leisure was more than just a prerequisite to achieve the other two objectives, "it represented the satisfaction of truly disinterested interest, the achievement of understanding which is man's highest goal'' (Craven 1937:402). Leisure to the ancient Greeks was an ideal state of being, a lofty lifestyle composed of the proper activities made possible by the refinement of the mind and by the existence of a large slave class.

The ancient Romans differed from the Greeks in many ways. Their conceptualization of leisure was one of these. To the Romans leisure was time off work. As such and if properly managed, it could be used to combat boredom, to renew energy for work or warfare, and to win political support from the masses through provision of free entertainment. During the Roman Empire, especially in the reigns of Caligula and Nero, leisure was also filled with special events that helped to fan religious bigotry and persecution.

The two conceptualizations of leisure exemplified by Greece and Rome—the Greek emphasis on the humanistic characteristics of leisure as a lifestyle with an undercurrent of elitism and the Roman emphasis on the quantitative characteristics of leisure with an undercurrent of manipulation of the masses—still dominate modern thinking about leisure.

Even though Rome fell in the fifth century, many Roman ideas and institutions were perpetuated by the Catholic Church. One of these was their fundamental conceptualization of leisure as time free from work obligations. Although the early Church abhorred the excesses and cruelty of the Roman Empire—many of which occurred during leisure—it was the excesses and cruelty the Church sought to avoid and to condemn, and not the basic conceptualization of leisure. Life was to be spent in hard work for physical survival and in atonement for sin. Periods of leisure were permissible, but were for rest and recuperation. The precedent for this was, of course, the belief that God labored for six days and rested on the seventh. From the beginning of the Church, leisure was closely tied to designated blocks of time, particularly the Sabbath and a few special holy days (although attendance at Mass on Sundays and holy days of obligation were mandatory for Christians, they were expected to view the Mass as a communal celebration and not as an odious responsibility).

The pattern of manual work interspersed with religious obligations and time for rest was most formally structured in early religious orders such as the Benedictines. Benedict divided the day his followers lived into time for secular work, time for religious work and worship, and time for leisure, which included time for sleep and eating.

With time, the holy days became HOLIDAYS, growing in both number and the emphasis on enjoyment. Through the Middle Ages and into the early Renaissance life became easier for many Europeans with more time and money available for art, music, poetry, romance, and eating and drinking well. This improvement in lifestyles was enjoyed not only by lay people, but also by the clergy. Eventually the excesses of some of the clergy and religious orders became so offensive that religious reformers began to call for revolution—a revolution that became known as the Protestant Reformation. A major change brought about by the Reformation was a return to a harsh, ascetic lifestyle in which leisure and pursuits were severely curtailed. As with the early Church after the fall of Rome, the New Protestant sects condemned the excesses they perceived, but did not change the conceptualization of leisure. It remained a block of time that could be used or misused. The renewal of the belief that man should spend most of his days in manual labor and seek identity in labor, with only a minimal amount of leisure for rest, is usually known as the Protestant WORK ETHIC. In fact, it had its roots in the daily schedules of early Catholic religious orders centuries before.

The Protestant work ethic continued in force in Europe for generations, and was brought to the New World by the first colonists. In the New World the work ethic was reinforced by the practical necessity of hard work if the colonists were to survive. Both religious dogma as well as practical need thus kept leisure defined in terms of work and subservient to the greater value of work. Many of Benjamin Franklin's aphorisms in *Poor Richard's Almanack* were popularizations of the basic tenets of the work ethic. These values also helped to drive the Industrial Revolution, until the excesses and abuses associated with the workplace (as opposed to the excesses of leisure, for the first time) began to generate growing concern among social critics, politicians, and philosophers. It was this setting in which nineteenth-century reformers such as Robert Owen and John Stuart Mill began to press for change. These authors, however, were more concerned with broad political and social reform rather than the specific role of leisure in society.

The beginnings of modern leisure scholarship ("modern" in the sense of being post-Industrial Revolution) include Paul Lafargue's (1883) *La droite à la paresse* (*The Right to be Lazy*), which emphasized the importance of leisure, and Thorstein Veblen's (1899) *The Theory of the Leisure Class,* which was an attack on the excesses of the idle rich although not necessarily on the merits of leisure itself (see LEISURE CLASS). Despite their different positions and interests, both continued to see leisure in terms of time free from obligations.

It was not until the 1920s that authors began to examine seriously a different conceptualization of leisure. The shift began gradually by the turning of attention away from time alone to the nature and role of activities engaged in during free time (Strumilin, 1925; May and Petgen, 1928; Lynd and Lynd, 1929, 1937; Lundberg, 1934). After World War II, social scientists, predominantly sociologists shifted their attention even more decisively to leisure activities and their role in shaping a person's identity and degree of SOCIALIZATION. One of the most important works of this period was David Riesman's (1950) *The Lonely Crowd.* Riesman suggested that Western man has experienced only two revolutions in social character over the last 500 years. The first was during the Renaissance when the force of tradition, especially epitomized by the Church, was replaced by a growing respect for the authority of one's own conscience and intellect. This was a shift from "tradition-directedness" to "inner-directedness" (in Riesman's lexicon). The second revolution came in the wake of World War II when a booming consumer economy, the emergence of the mass media, the availability of mass leisure began to replace "inner-directedness" by "other-directedness." Here the authority of the self began to be replaced by a growing concern for comparing oneself to others, especially in terms of consumption and social status. This theme was also pursued by Robert Havighurst and Kenneth Feigenbaum (1959) and Harold Wilensky (1964).

The scope of sociological inquiries into leisure broadened through the 1960s and 1970s, extending into the relationship between work and leisure roles (Riesman, 1964; Parker, 1971), leisure and the family (Scheuch, 1960; Anderson, 1961), and the role of leisure in forming community values and shaping CULTURE (Pieper, 1948; and de Grazia, 1962). Social psychologists also increased their interest in understanding the motivations and consequences of leisure behavior (Neulinger, 1974; Iso-Ahola, 1980; Mannell, 1984). In most of this work, the authors' conceptualizations of leisure emphasized the subjective, humanistic, or psychological aspects of leisure. This orientation is very similar to the Hellenic philosophy of leisure as a matter of lifestyle and proper activity. Although a few authors such as Henry Fairchild (1944), Charles Brightbill (1961), and Stanley Parker (1971) still considered leisure to be a matter of time, the humanistic conceptualization dominated leisure studies from the 1940s until the current time. A brief description of views of three authors in this group will help to illustrate this perspective.

Joffre Dumazdier (1968) viewed leisure as a restricted set of activities that required two preconditions and four concurrent characteristics. The first precondition was that a society had to be sufficiently advanced so that the majority of its activities were no longer governed by tradition or common ritual obligations. Most activities were the personal responsibility of the individual. This change, recalling Riesman (1950), is generally considered to have occurred for most Western societies during the Renaissance. The second precondition is that the scheduling of the activities by which an individual earns his living (his job) are essentially arbitrary rather than natural. This change is usually associated with the shift from a primary economic base (agriculture, fishing, hunting) to a secondary economic base (manufacturing). Thus Dumazdier believed that leisure only exists for industrial or postindustrial societies. Although Dumazdier denied that the ancient Greeks had leisure in his sense of the term, his conceptualization of leisure is similar to the Hellenic conception.

The first of the four characteristics leisure activities must meet, is that the activities are the result of PERCEIVED FREEDOM. Specific forms of leisure may be subject to social restrictions, obligations, and norms, but they are free of "primary obligations" such as commitments to work, school, and religious observances. Next, leisure must be "disinterested," a term also used by Craven (1937) to characterize Aristotle's view of leisure. In other words, leisure precludes the pursuit of any activity for economic or social gain (see also AMATEUR). Third, leisure is pleasure seeking. It is not synonymous with pleasure or happiness; these can be obtained a variety of ways. But an essential goal of leisure is that it is FUN. Any activity that is not fun cannot be leisure. Finally, and closely related to the first three characteristics, leisure fulfills three basic human needs: (1) rest, (2) entertainment, and (3) self-transcendence. Any activity that fails to fulfill those three needs is a "seriously defective" form of leisure (Dumazdier, 1968:251).

John Neulinger's (1974) concept of leisure goes further than Dumazdier in making leisure a psychological condition. Neulinger proposed a model of leisure based on two dimensions: perceived freedom and motivation. Perceived freedom is classified into two levels: "freedom" and "constraint"; motivation is classified into three: "intrinsic," "mixed," and "extrinsic." These are then combined into six "states of mind."

Combination	State of Mind	Example
Freedom + INTRINSIC MOTIVATION	Pure leisure	Listening to music
Freedom + Mixed motivation	Leisure-work	Antique furniture refinishing
Freedom + Extrinsic motivation	Leisure-job	Playing tennis for the exercise
Constraint + Intrinsic motivation	Pure work	Finding pleasure in lawn work
Constraint + Mixed motivation	Work-leisure	Teaching as a profession
Constraint + Extrinsic motivation	Pure-job	Assembly line labor

Neulinger's model distinguishes between leisure and nonleisure largely on the basis of the perception of freedom. The emphasis on perception is important. Social norms, the way individuals were raised as children, economic and RESOURCE limitations, and other variables all serve to limit the true freedom of choice of any individual. But if these forces are accepted and internalized, the perception of freedom may prevail.

Sebastian de Grazia (1952) in his book *Of Time, Work, and Leisure* goes still further in pushing for a subjective view of leisure. De Grazia noted that the Industrial Revolution not only involved a revolution in production processes, but in how most people viewed time. In de Grazia's view, clock time became a virtual tyrant at the same time people were rejecting political tyrants. To achieve leisure, de Grazia called for a shift in VALUES and lifestyles so that we (1) rely less on the consumption of commodities for recreation, (2) slow down the pace of life and work, and (3) develop better tastes and preferences. Despite the sincerity of his advice, de Grazia had no illusions about the fact that few people would likely accept it. He noted, "It [leisure] is an ideal, a state of being, a condition of man, which few desire and fewer achieve" (1952:5).

In all of these definitions, there is still a distinction between leisure and nonleisure, and that distinction contains some element of time. Even for the most "antitime" author, de Grazia, there is the implicit recognition that leisure does occur during real free time. The difference between the humanistic view of leisure and the quantitative view is essentially whether one wishes to impose certain additional preconditions or psychological requirements on the basic ingredient of time. However desirable these preconditions might be in terms of promoting a high quality of life or a superior form of leisure experience, the fundamental and enduring feature of leisure is that it is a period of time free of primary obligations.

A problem with the humanistic view of leisure is that the additional preconditions or psychological requirements can be very value laden. While there may be some educational value in examining and debating different personal definitions, perceptions, and matters of taste (which many of the preconditions appear to resemble), they have limited value for research, policy analysis, and management purposes.

This is not to suggest that the quantitative conceptualization of leisure as free time is without its problems. This approach tends to beg the question of how "work" and "obligations" are to be defined. Although the notion of a job or of work is not too difficult to define operationally, there is a continuum from formal work commitments through a broad gray area until we get to unambiguously free time. For example, is time spent commuting to work to be classified as part of one's obligations or as free time? If the commuting is done behind the wheel of a car on a crowded interstate, there is little doubt about it not being leisure. But what if the time is spent in the first class section of a commercial airliner on the way to a conference in Hawaii?

Parker (1971) has attempted to summarize this continuum as a six-point scale. The first three points are directly related to work, the last three to nonwork:

1. Work or employment.
2. Work obligations such as commuting or training.
3. "Leisure in work" or intrinsically satisfying work.
4. Meeting of psychological needs such as sleep or eating.
5. Nonwork obligations such as time with the children.
6. Leisure or free time.

The problems of defining free time are usually associated with attempting to determine the limits or boundary of the concept of free time—boundaries that are inherently indistinct, like those of fog. But just because the boundary of fog is impossible to define precisely, this cannot be taken as an argument against either the reality of the fog or its essential features. The definition of leisure should focus on its essential feature not its indistinct edges. That essential feature is free time.

The matter of selecting the "correct" definition of leisure is more than just a quodlibet. Research on leisure often must begin with a clear understanding of how the phenomenon is to be defined or measured. And as Peter Witt and Gary Ellis (1985) noted, the choice of a definition of leisure can influence how leisure service agencies are operated. The choice of a humanistic definition leads to greater attention being paid to the role of LEISURE EDUCATION, COMMUNITY DEVELOPMENT, MAINSTREAMING, and ADAPTIVE PROGRAMMING, among other concerns, in the agency. The choice of a quantitative definition, on the other hand, implies greater concern over ACCESSIBILITY, BARRIERS, CARRYING CAPACITY, DEMAND, and STANDARDS, among other issues.

It is unlikely that all researchers, leisure service professionals, and philosophers will ever agree on which definition of leisure is best. At a minimum, however, one should be aware of the variety of definitions proposed as well as their respective strengths, weaknesses, and implications.

REFERENCES

Anderson, Nels. 1961. *Work and Leisure*. New York: Free Press. A scholarly examination of the relationship between work and leisure; adopts a sociological perspective in studying these two phenomena.

Brightbill, Charles K. 1961. *Man and Leisure: A Philosophy of Recreation*. Englewood Cliffs, NJ: Prentice Hall. Brightbill was an early and influential leisure educator; he presented a definition of leisure based on free time.

Craven, Ida. 1937. "Leisure." In *Encyclopedia of the Social Sciences*, Vol. 9, 402–405. New York: Macmillan. A dated but excellent summary of the concept of leisure and of the major contemporary research emphasis in leisure studies.

de Grazia, Sebastian. 1962. *Of Time, Work, and Leisure*. New York: Twentieth Century Fund. Lengthy cultural and historical survey of leisure; proposes an elitist view of leisure.

Dumazdier, Joffre. 1968. "Leisure." In *International Encyclopedia of the Social Sciences*, Vol. 9, 248–254. New York: Macmillan. A definitional essay on the nature of leisure; emphasizes leisure as an activity; gives particular attention to the sociology of leisure as opposed to other social science perspectives.

Fairchild, Henry. 1944. *Dictionary of Sociology*. New York: Philosophical Library. An example of the free time conceptualization of leisure.

Havighurst, Robert J., and Feigenbaum, Kenneth. 1959. "Leisure and Lifestyle." *American Journal of Sociology* 64:396–404. A sociological inquiry into mass leisure and its part in American lifestyles.

Iso-Ahola, Seppo. 1980. *The Social Psychology of Leisure and Recreation*. Dubuque, IA: William C. Brown. A comprehensive inquiry into leisure as a social psychological phenomenon; emphasizes leisure as a human experience.

Kando, Thomas. 1975. *Leisure and Popular Culture in Transition*. St. Louis, Missouri: C. V. Mosby. An introductory text on recreation, leisure, and culture.

Lafargue, Paul. 1883. *Le droit à la paresse*. Chicago: Kerr. One of the earliest post-industrial revolution studies on the importance of leisure.

Lundberg, George A. 1934. *Leisure: A Suburban Study*. New York: Columbia University Press. A dated but important early study on leisure in American society during the Great Depression.

Lynd, Robert A., and Lynd, Helen M. 1929. *Middletown: A Study in Contemporary American Culture*. New York: Harcourt. An important early study on popular culture in "mainstream" America.

Lynd, Robert A., and Lynd, Helen M. 1937. *Middletown in Transition: A Study in Cultural Conflicts.* New York: Harcourt, Brace. A follow-up to their earlier study; examines the impact of social changes, especially the Depression, on social structures and values.

Mannell, Roger. 1984. "A Psychology for Leisure Research." *Leisure and Society* 7:13–21. Views leisure as a state of mind combining a sense of freedom and intrinsic motivation.

May, H. L., and Petgen, D. 1928. *Leisure and Its Uses.* New York: A. S. Barnes. An early sociological inquiry into the roles leisure played in the first decades of the twentieth century.

Neulinger, John. 1974. *The Psychology of Leisure: Research Approaches to the Study of Leisure.* Springfield, IL: Charles C. Thomas. A research-oriented examination of the nature of leisure; proposes a model of leisure based on a combination of perceived freedom and motivation.

Parker, Stanley. 1971. *The Future of Work and Leisure.* New York: Praeger. Contains a model of leisure based on two dimensions: time and motivation.

Pieper, Josef. 1948. *Leisure: The Basis of Culture.* New York: Pantheon Books. A philosophically oriented examination of leisure as a major force in the development of culture.

Riesman, David. 1950. *The Lonely Crowd: A Study of the Changing American Character.* New Haven, CT: Yale University Press. An important study of the rise of mass culture and consumerism in American society.

Riesman, David. 1964. *Abundance for What? And Other Essays.* Garden City, NY: Doubleday. A collection of sociological essays on work, leisure, and social values.

Scheuch, Erwin K. 1960. "Family Cohesion in Leisure Time." *Sociological Review* 8:37–61. A study of the strength of family ties and their correlation with leisure participation patterns.

Strumilin, Stanislav G. 1925. *Problem ekonomiki truda (Problems of Labor Economy).* Moscow: Izdatel'stvo "Voprosy Truda." One of the earliest time-budget studies; included an analysis of leisure time.

Veblen, Thorstein. 1899. *The Theory of the Leisure Class.* New York: New American Library. A critical analysis of the leisure patterns of the upper classes in late nineteenth-century America.

Wilensky, Harold L. 1964. "Mass Society and Mass Culture: Interdependence or Independence?" *American Sociological Review* 29:173–197. A major study examining leisure and work values in American culture and life.

Witt, Peter, and Ellis, Gary. 1985. "Perceived Freedom in Leisure: Implications for Research and Practice." *World Leisure and Recreation* 27(4):20–24. Examines several different definitions of leisure; promotes a humanistic definition and discusses implications of that definition.

SOURCES OF ADDITIONAL INFORMATION

There are numerous books and articles on leisure. Some journals that are especially useful include the *Journal of Leisure Research, Leisure Sciences, Leisure Studies,* and *Society and Leisure.* Several useful texts that help to introduce the reader to basic conceptual issues in the study of leisure are James Murphy, *Concepts of Leisure* (2nd edition, Englewood Cliffs, NJ: Prentice Hall, 1981); Byron Dare, George Welton, and William

Coe, *Concepts of Leisure in Western Thought* (Dubuque, IA: Kendall/Hunt, 1987); and Thomas Goodale and Peter Witt, eds., *Recreation and Leisure: Issues in an Era of Change* (State College, PA: Venture, 1985); and Alan Graefe and Stan Parker, eds., *Recreation and Leisure: An Introductory Handbook* (State College, PA: Venture, 1987). These books also have excellent reference lists and bibliographies which will help the reader further explore many topics.

LEISURE CLASS. A group of individuals in society who refrain from paid labor by virtue of personal wealth; often implies lavish and wasteful lifestyles emphasizing CONSPICUOUS CONSUMPTION.

The term *leisure class* was given widespread circulation by Thorstein Veblen (1899) in his book *The Theory of the Leisure Class*. His book is a caustic attack on the lifestyles and VALUES of the nouveau riche, particularly those he observed in the latter half of the nineteenth century in the United States. These included the Vanderbilts, the Goulds, and the Harrimans, among other famous names. To Veblen, the leisure class was synonymous with the upper class. He used anecdotal evidence to build a case that this group attempted to attain status through conspicuous consumption, wasteful display, and expensive and often self-destructive vices. They existed, Veblen believed, solely at the expense of the working class.

Despite its fame, Veblen's analysis contained several errors that have become increasingly obvious over time. He refused to acknowledge the existence of the working upper class. Wealth, he believed, only came through exploitation of the working poor and through financial manipulation; he did not or could not recognize that wealth could be obtained through honest, productive work. A related weakness in his analysis is that he neatly categorized everyone in society into either "the kept classes" or "the underlying population." No middle class and no transcendence of one's economic class through hard work was recognized.

Another shortcoming in Veblen's analysis was that, while he rightly ridiculed the sillier excesses of the late nineteenth-century upper class, he failed to take their status and social position seriously. This is not a criticism of Veblen's lack of respect, but of his failing to recognize that many members of his leisure class actually manipulated substantial political and (in some cases) military power. Veblen saw the group as shallow, foolish, and despicable. He did not see that they also constituted a power elite. His so-called leisure class was often quite busy with the work of political and economic intrigue.

A different perspective on the notion of the leisure class was provided by Ida Craven (1937). Craven noted with thinly veiled criticism that Veblen had made the notion of LEISURE vaguely disreputable. "It is indeed a rather bitter paradox that leisure has come to have a connotation of loose relaxation and that the term leisure class carried an accent of opprobrium." Craven then goes on to argue that other societies would have considered the scholar, priest, or artist to be a member of a leisure class—a productive and creative leisure class contributing to the good of society. Even in North American society, leisure classes—even if one limits the term as Veblen does to the richest classes—often help support the arts, research, and charities through donations of money and service on boards and foundations.

Veblen's terminology has become part of the standard lexicon of virtually every educated North American. Although many of his ideas about the leisure class were simplistic and sometimes unfair he did not call into question the fundamental value of leisure per se. And his attempts at social analysis of the role of leisure continue to provoke reflection and a spirit of inquiry into our social structure and lifestyles.

REFERENCES

Craven, Ida. 1937. "Leisure." In *Encyclopedia of the Social Sciences,* Vol. 9, ed. Edwin R. A. Seligman, 402–405. New York: Macmillan. An early reflective, scholarly essay on the nature of leisure; pays special attention to the nature of leisure classes.
Veblen, Thorstein. 1899. *The Theory of the Leisure Class.* New York: Macmillan. A classic attack on the idle rich and the misuse of wealth.

SOURCES OF ADDITIONAL INFORMATION

A very different perspective on the characteristics of the leisure class is Staffan Linder's, *The Harried Leisure Class* (New York: Columbia University Press, 1970). Other studies that have examined issues related to the leisure class and conspicuous consumption (as well as Veblen's cognate terms, conspicuous leisure, conspicuous waste, predatory culture, and so forth) are David Riesman, *The Lonely Crowd* (New Haven, CT: Yale University Press, 1950); C. A. R. Crosland, *The Future of Socialism* (London: Cape, 1956); John Kenneth Galbraith, *The Affluent Society* (Boston: Houghton Mifflin, 1984); and Tibor Scitovsky, *The Joyless Economy: An Inquiry into Human Satisfaction* (New York: Oxford University Press, 1976).

LEISURE EDUCATION. A process of using any of a wide variety of educational or counseling techniques to enhance an individual's life through LEISURE.

The notion that an important goal of education is to prepare the individual to handle leisure is well established, although not always implemented. Jean Mundy and Linda Odum (1979:18) observed that as far back as 1868 Harry Barnard, the first U.S. Commissioner of Education, called for a form of leisure education in his 1868 *Biennial Report of the United States Commission on Education*: "The science of education includes the science of RECREATION and elaborate arrangements for the education of the community must be regarded not only as incomplete but radically unsound in which suitable provisions for physical training and recreation are not included."

Other authors cited by Mundy and Odum as precursors of the contemporary leisure education movement include John Dewey (1916), C. D. Burns (1932), Anna May Jones (1946), and Charles Brightbill (1966) as well as the entire January 1960, issue of the *Journal of Education.*

Most of the early authors viewed education for leisure as the preparation of individuals for the enjoyment of a productive and wholesome free time. Beginning in the 1960s, however, some authors broadened the concept of leisure education from simply a part of the complete school curriculum to an obligation of many social service agencies (Kraus, 1964) and from promoting activity skills alone to clarifying values and articulating personal philosophies (Lieberman and Simon, 1965).

While this broader view of leisure education is still generally accepted as valid, in the 1970s and 1980s another concept was developed and promoted that has created confusion about the content of leisure education. This newer concept is leisure counseling. Leisure counseling is variously considered to be either a specific strategy that leisure educators may employ in certain circumstances (Chinn and Joswiak, 1981) or as a more inclusive concept in which leisure education is a specific strategy (Allen and Hamilton, 1980).

There is still no consensus as to the proper denotation of either leisure education and leisure counseling as words, but there does appear to be some agreement among most authors as to the types of activity that may be included under at least one of the terms. Chester McDowell's (1977) list of activities is still one of the best. He suggested that leisure counseling included four activities.

1. Providing information about where one could find resources, facilities, or programs to allow an individual to pursue his specific interests.

2. Providing or advising about how to obtain skills necessary to engage in certain activities.

3. Assisting an individual to clarify his interests, values, and preferred lifestyle, including the selection of leisure activities that would be rewarding.

4. Providing some form of remedial or THERAPEUTIC RECREATION treatment to help an individual overcome psychological or emotional problems associated with his use of leisure time.

Other authors recognize the same set of activities, but group them differently. Karen Chinn and Kenneth Joswiak (1981) suggested the first three of these are actually leisure education, while the fourth is more properly considered leisure counseling. R. Stracke (1977) suggested that the first two activities should be labeled recreation counseling and thus made distinct from leisure counseling, which is associated with other activities. Lawrence Allen and Edward Hamilton (1980) saw the third activity (interest and values clarification) as being leisure education while the other activities are leisure counseling. They further suggested that the term *leisure counseling* should be applied to the use of leisure activities as a tool for the treatment of other emotional or psychological problems which would be a fifth item in McDowell's list.

A different approach to leisure education and leisure counseling has been proposed by Howard Tinsley and Diane Tinsley (1984). They developed a four-way classification based on two dimensions. The first dimension is the relative emphasis placed on using certain educational/counseling techniques to promote personal growth versus providing assistance in selecting activities. The other dimension reflects the relative emphasis on providing information versus counseling:

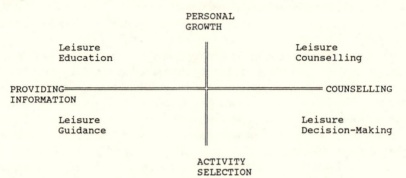

```
                              PERSONAL
                              GROWTH

        Leisure                  ‖               Leisure
        Education                ‖               Counselling
                                 ‖
PROVIDING════════════════════════╬═══════════════════ COUNSELLING
INFORMATION                      ‖
        Leisure                  ‖               Leisure
        Guidance                 ‖               Decision-Making
                                 ‖

                              ACTIVITY
                              SELECTION
```

Leisure education, to Tinsley and Tinsley, is characterized by an emphasis on making information available to individuals to help them achieve personal growth and SELF-ACTUALIZATION, whereas leisure counseling involves the use, obviously, of counseling tools. Leisure counseling also implies a set of professional values and a professional education identical to that acquired by other types of psychological counselors. The fundamental goal is the same for education and counseling: personal growth. The difference is in the techniques—predominantly cognitive approaches in the case of education versus affective and self-help strategies in the case of counseling.

Tinsley and Tinsley suggest two other terms: leisure guidance and leisure decision making. The first of these involves providing the client with factual information to assist in selecting an activity. Leisure decision making is also aimed at helping the client select activities or to develop a leisure lifestyle, but the emphasis is on the psychological issues and deeper symbolic meaning of activities than is the case for leisure guidance.

Despite the lack of agreement on terminology, there appears to be a growing consensus among leisure educators/counselors on some important issues. First, anyone engaged in activities that involve psychological counseling techniques must be trained professionally and must adhere to accepted professional standards of ethical behavior governing psychological counseling. Next, the proper techniques must be selected to help the individual to meet his goals, whether those are simple information-gathering or more complex needs. Finally, leisure educators/counselors agree with Chinn and Joswiak (1981:7) who summarized the goals of leisure education as: "What the field seeks to accomplish is important: the enhancement of the quality of life."

REFERENCES

Allen, Lawrence R., and Hamilton, Edward J. 1980. "Leisure Counselling: A Continuum of Services." *Therapeutic Recreation Journal* 14(1):17–22. A restatement and slight expansion of Chester McDowell's 1977 conceptualization of leisure counseling.

Brightbill, Charles K. 1966. *Educating for Leisure-Centered Living.* Harrisburg, PA: Stackpole. An influential statement on the importance of and techniques for leisure education.

Burns, Charles D. 1932. *Leisure in the Modern World.* New York: Century. A Depression-era text on the role of leisure in contemporary life.

Chinn, Karen A., and Joswiak, Kenneth F. 1981. "Leisure Education and Leisure Counseling." *Therapeutic Recreation Journal* 15(4):4–7. An introduction to an issue of *Therapeutic Recreation Journal* focussing on leisure education; reviews problems of terminology.

Dewey, John. 1916. *Democracy and Education.* New York: Macmillan. A classic work on the philosophy of public education; includes a call for education for leisure.

Jones, Anna May. 1946. *Leisure Time Education.* New York: Harper. A handbook prepared for leisure education in the New York City schools.

Kraus, Richard G. 1964. *Recreation and the Schools.* New York: Macmillan. Not only discussed the role of recreation in public schools but argued other community agencies should become involved in promoting leisure education.

Lieberman, P., and Simon, S.B. 1965. "A School's Responsibility: Worthy Use of Leisure Time." *The Clearing House* (Aug.):502–505. A brief essay advancing the idea that education for leisure should involve values and lifestyle clarification.

McDowell, Chester. 1977. "Integrating Theory and Practice in Leisure Counseling." *Journal of Physical Education and Recreation* 48(2):51–54. A description of various counseling strategies for leisure.

Mundy, Jean, and Odum, Linda. 1979. *Leisure Education: Theory and Practice,* New York: Wiley. An introductory text on the concepts and techniques of leisure education; Chapter 2—devoted to the history of the concept—is marred by a confusion about how centuries are numbered. For example, John Dewey is placed in the eighteenth century because he lived in the 1800s (which is the nineteenth century).

Stracke, Richard. 1977. "An Overview of Leisure Counseling." In *Leisure Counseling: An Aspect of Leisure Education,* ed. Arlin Epperson, Peter Witt, and Gerald Hitzhusen, 21–44. Springfield, IL: Charles C. Thomas. A useful collecting of readings on leisure counseling; offers a distinction between recreation counseling and leisure counseling.

Tinsley, Howard, and Tinsley, Diane. 1984. "Leisure Counseling Models." In *Leisure Counseling: Concepts and Applications,* ed. E. Thomas Dowd, 80–96. Springfield, IL: Charles C. Thomas. An extensive survey of various leisure counseling models presented in the literature; places a strong emphasis on the psychological basis for leisure counseling.

SOURCES OF ADDITIONAL INFORMATION

A number of useful primers or guidebooks on leisure education have been written. These include Steven Brannan, Karen Chinn, and Peter Verhoven, *What is Leisure Education? A Primer for Persons Working with Handicapped Children and Youth* (Washington, DC: Hawkins & Associates, 1981); Kenneth Joswiak, *Leisure Counseling Program Materials for the Developmentally Disabled* (Washington, DC: Hawkins & Associates, 1979); Larry

Loesch and Paul Wheeler, *Principles of Leisure Counseling* (Minneapolis: Educational Media, 1982); and Bob Ballantyne, *Leisure Lifestyles* (Toronto: Ontario Ministry of Tourism and Recreation, 1987). Another useful book, actually a collection of readings rather than a handbook, is Arlin Epperson, Peter Witt, and Gerald Hitzhusen, eds., *Leisure Counselling: An Aspect of Leisure Education* (Springfield, IL: Charles C. Thomas, 1977).

Some specific models for leisure education/counseling have been proposed by Scout Lee Gunn in "A Systems Approach to Leisure Counseling" (*Journal of Physical Education and Recreation* 48 no. 4:32–35, 1977) and by M. Magulski, V. H. Faull, and B. Rutkowski in "The Milwaukee Leisure Counseling Model" (*Journal of Physical Education and Recreation,* 48 no. 4:49–50, 1977). A more extensive discussion of the "Milwaukee model" is found in R. P. Overs, S. Taylor, and C. Adkins, *Advocational Counseling in Milwaukee* (Milwaukee: Curative Workshop of Milwaukee, 1973). Finally, a synthesis of numerous ideas and developments in the field is presented in Howard E. A. Tinsley and Diane J. Tinsley, "A Holistic Model of Leisure Counseling" (*Journal of Leisure Research* 14:100–116, 1982).

LEISURE INFRASTRUCTURE. The entire collection of recreation and leisure opportunities available in a community.

Leisure infrastructure is a relatively new concept, first proposed by Ronald Johnson and Robert Payne (1988). It is related to the concept of the DELIVERY SYSTEM, but is broader in its scope. While the leisure services delivery system refers to public and quasi-public agencies, the leisure infrastructure of a community is the combination of management setting (i.e., public agencies, commercial firms serving the general public, and private operations whose services or facilities are limited to members) and recreation opportunities (high CULTURE, popular culture, sport, social activities, and nature-based activities). This combination of three management settings and five types of opportunity or ACTIVITY CLUSTER provides a total of fifteen separate categories of leisure settings, such as "private natural" or "public high culture."

A leisure infrastructure index may be calculated by inventorying the total number of facilities or programs in each of the fifteen categories of leisure settings.

A leisure infrastructure index may be calculated for: (1) any given leisure setting out of the fifteen defined; (2) an entire management environment; or (3) an entire opportunity set. Tables 1 and 2 illustrate each of these indexes. The data in Table 1 are a hypothetical inventory of recreation facilities for a community of 12,500 people.

The leisure infrastructure index is conceptually similar to the notion of recreation STANDARDS, the use of some form of per capita measure as a guideline for determining the adequacy of existing recreation and leisure opportunities. The major difference, of course, is that the index is a measure of the existing supply rather than a guideline. The infrastructure index may also be defined for a particular management environment, an opportunity setting, or as a general aggregate figure for the entire community (a measure that is of questionable

Table 1
Inventory*

	Opportunity					
Management	Natural	Social	Sport	Pop Culture	Hi Culture	Total
Private	3	22	4	I	0	30
Commercial	0	I	2	20	6	29
Public	7	19	16	21	5	68
Total	10	42	22	42	11	127

*Dividing each inventory number by the town's population in 1000s, 12.5, produces the indexes contained in Table 2.

usefulness given the extreme diversity of the different types of recreation facility represented by the fifteen separate categories).

REFERENCE

Johnson, Ronald, and Payne, Robert. 1988. Leisure Infrastructure in Small Ontario Communities, unpublished manuscript. Introduces concept of infrastructure and

Table 2
Infrastructure Index

	Opportunity					
Management	Natural	Social	Sport	Pop Culture	Hi Culture	Total
Private	0.24	1.76	0.32	0.08	0.00	2.40
Commercial	0.00	0.08	0.16	1.60	0.48	2.32
Public	0.56	1.52	1.28	1.68	0.40	5.44
Total	0.80	3.36	1.76	3.36	0.88	10.16

illustrates its use through a comparison of the infrastructure of sixteen small municipalities.

SOURCES OF ADDITIONAL INFORMATION

The specific concept of leisure infrastructure is so new that relatively little has yet been written on it. It is, however, closely related to the concepts of DELIVERY SYSTEMS and STANDARDS. The references and sources of additional information associated with those concepts will be of relevance to this term.

LEISURE LIFESTYLE. See THERAPEUTIC RECREATION.

LIMITS OF ACCEPTABLE CHANGE. A planning procedure designed to identify appropriate resource and social environmental conditions in a given recreation area (usually a WILDERNESS) and to guide the development of management techniques to achieve and protect those conditions.

Social scientists studying wilderness management issues became keenly aware, by the early 1970s, of certain inherent limitations in the concept of CARRYING CAPACITY. David Lime (1970) and Sidney Frissell and George Stankey (1972), for example, had begun to argue for increased attention to the management of the IMPACT of recreational use in wilderness than on simply estimating maximum levels of user density. The basis for their arguments included the failure of researchers to show reliable, empirical connections between user density and user satisfactions in a variety of resource ENVIRONMENTS. These authors, as well as others, had also accepted the realities that any use of a wilderness area caused some environmental change and the political, social, and legal traditions of the United States mandated human access and use of most wilderness areas.

The awareness eventually forced a change in the conception of wilderness management away from the more naive goals of measuring and implementing maximum acceptable levels of user densities to a more sophisticated and indirect approach. This new approach emphasized identification of the objectives of a specific wilderness area and the development of management techniques to achieve those objectives.

The evolution of the limits of acceptable change (LAC) process from the carrying capacity concept was helped along by the work of Victor Godin and Raymond Leonard (1977) on design capacity in wilderness areas and by the work of Sidney Frissell et al. (1980) on estimation of the effects of alternative use levels on recreation environments. The development of LAC also paralleled the growth of the management-by-objectives approach to planning (Hendee, Stankey, and Lucas, 1978).

A manager must undertake four basic tasks in following the LAC process. The first is to identify acceptable social and resource characteristics of the wilderness site being managed. This is followed by comparing existing conditions with those desired. The manager then identifies a series of possible actions that will achieve the desired conditions. Finally, an environmental monitoring procedure is developed to measure the effectiveness of the management actions undertaken. These four tasks are broken down further into nine specific steps.

A key element in the application of the LAC process is the definition of a series of opportunity classes. These classes describe the different conditions that the manager expects to encounter (or to restore) in the recreation area. Opportunity classes are usually designated in accordance with the divisions of the RECREATION OPPORTUNITY SPECTRUM.

LAC differs from the earlier conceptions of carrying capacity by focusing on the management of wilderness conditions as experienced by visitors rather than on directly limiting the number of visitors to some preconceived maximum. LAC was originally developed for wilderness management, but it has the potential for being applied to other types of recreation environments.

REFERENCES

Frissell, Sidney S., Lee, Robert G., Stankey, George H., and Zube, Evin H. 1980. "A Framework for Estimating the Consequences of Alternative Carrying Capacity Levels in Yosemite Valley." *Landscape Planning* 7:151–170. Describes methods for estimating the effects on the natural environment of different levels of visitor use.

Frissell, Sidney S., and Stankey, George H. 1972. "Wilderness Environmental Quality: Search for Social and Ecological Harmony." *Proceedings of the Society of American Foresters,* 170–183. A precursor of the development of LAC to help to sharpen the focus on user management in wilderness areas.

Godin, Victor B., and Leonard, Raymond E. 1977. "Design Capacity for Backcountry Recreation Management Planning." *Journal of Soil and Water Conservation* 32:161–164. Describes an approach to environmental planning that emphasizes design for users rather than use limitations.

Hendee, John C., Stankey, George H., and Lucas, Robert C. 1978. *Wilderness Management,* miscellaneous publication 1365. Washington, DC: U.S. Department of Agriculture, Forest Service.

Lime, David W. 1970. "Research for Determining Use Capacities of the Boundary Waters Canoe Area." *Naturalist* 21:8–13. Lays the foundation for the eventual development of the LAC process by focusing on the users' experiences as a measure of capacity.

SOURCES OF ADDITIONAL INFORMATION

A useful introduction to the LAC process may be found in George H. Stankey, David N. Cole, Robert C. Lucas, Margaret E. Petersen, and Sidney S. Frissell, *The Limits of Acceptable Change (LAC System for Wilderness Planning)* (general technical report INT-176, Ogden, UT: U.S. Department of Agriculture, U.S. Forest Service, 1985). Some studies that illustrate the use of LAC concepts may be found in Roger N. Clark and George H. Stankey, "Determining the Acceptability of Recreational Impacts: An Application of the Outdoor Recreation Opportunity Spectrum," in R. Ittner, D. R. Potter, J. K. Agee, and S. Anschell, eds., *Recreational Impact on Wildlands* (report R-7-001,

Portland, OR: U.S. Department of Agriculture, U.S. Forest Service, 1979); David N. Cole, "Managing Ecological Impacts at Wilderness Campsites: An Evaluation of Techniques" (*Journal of Forestry* 79: 86–89, 1981); Sidney S. Frissell, "Judging Recreation Impacts on Wilderness Campsites" (*Journal of Forestry* 76: 481–483, 1982); and David J. Parsons and Susan A. MacLeod, "Measuring Impacts of Wilderness Use" (*Parks* 5:8–12, 1980). Background material on LAC may be found in Robert G. Lee, "Alone with Others: The Paradox of Privacy in Wilderness" (*Leisure Sciences* 1:3–20, 1972); Richard Schreyer and Joseph W. Roggenbuck, "The Influence of Experience Expectations on Crowding Perceptions and Social-Psychological Carrying Capacities" (*Leisure Sciences,* 1:373–394, 1978); Randel F. Washburne, "Wilderness Recreational Carrying Capacity: Are Numbers Necessary?" (*Journal of Forestry* 80:726–728, 1982); and Randel F. Washburne and David N. Cole, *Problems and Practices in Wilderness Management: A Survey of Managers* (Research paper INT-304, Ogden, UT: U.S. Department of Agriculture, U.S. Forest Service, 1987).

LOCUS OF CONTROL. See PERCEIVED FREEDOM.

LUDUS. The quality of effort and challenge in a GAME.

Ludus is a term proposed by Roger Caillois (1961) to describe the quality of effort and challenge in GAME playing. It is the spirit that presumably motivates individuals who play games to create rules to make the game more difficult and less boring. It has the effect of controlling and directing its polar quality PAIDIA to add depth and pleasure to play forms. Caillois suggests that ludus is also the force behind the development of hobbies. He describes ludus as the primitive desire to find pleasure in arbitrary, repetitive effort, in the overcoming of needless but recurring obstacles.

Together, ludus and paidia define the extremes of a spectrum of a fundamental game quality. Specific games can be first classified as one of four game types: AGON, ALEA, ILINX, or MIMICRY; within each classification, games may be placed somewhere along the ludus/paidia continuum.

REFERENCES

Caillois, R. 1961. *Man, Play and Games.* New York: The Free Press. An important study of the sociology of games. Chapter 2 describes in detail Caillois's classification of games.

SOURCES OF ADDITIONAL INFORMATION

Some of Roger Caillois's ideas about play and games were first explored in his *Man and the Sacred* (New York: The Free Press, 1959). A classic study of play and games, which also greatly influenced Caillois, is Johan Huizinga, *Homo Ludens* (Boston: Beacon Press, 1955). Another, philosophically directed study of games and the spirit of game playing is David Miller, *Gods and Games* (New York: Harper Colophon, 1973).

M

MAINSTREAMING. The integration of disabled persons into RECREATION PROGRAMS serving either the general public or age-sex cohorts of nondisabled individuals.

Mainstreaming, also known as integration, is based on the ideology of NOR-MALIZATION and represents the goal of the DEINSTITUTIONALIZATION process. For much of the nineteenth and twentieth centuries, individuals who were classified as mentally ill or retarded were kept separate from society in residential institutions, often housing hundreds of individuals (Salzberg and Langford, 1981). In the late 1950s, a movement began in Scandinavia to urge governments to remove these individuals from what was seen as dehumanizing institutions and to help them move back into society, with appropriate outpatient support or other social services. (Nirje, 1969). This movement spread and grew, resulting in, first, increased citizen ADVOCACY on the part of the disabled and then civil litigation (Bullock, 1979; Wolfensberger, 1972), particularly with respect to educational services. The movement supporting greater rights of disabled individuals grew strong enough and broad enough so that in the 1970s two major pieces of legislation were passed by the U.S. Congress: PL 93–112 (the Rehabilitation Act) and PL 94–142 (the Education for All Handicapped Children Act). While PL 94–142 addressed education specifically, RECREATION and LEISURE services were described as a ''necessary but related service'' and thus were explicitly covered in PL 94–142. PL 93–112 contained a broadly applicable ''Nondiscrimination Clause,'' Section 504, that specified; ''No otherwise qualified handicapped individual . . . shall, solely by reason of his handicap, be excluded from participation or be denied the benefits of, or be subjected to discrimination under any program or activity receiving Federal financial assistance.''

In practice, the concept of mainstreaming implies more than just removal of regulations or other policies that bar disabled individuals from participating. It also implies modifying facilities, resources, programs, and activities wherever possible to allow the maximum participation possible. This involves ACTIVITY ANALYSIS and ADAPTIVE PROGRAMMING in the case of recreation programs, as well as the analysis of ACCESSIBILITY and BARRIERS of facilities and programs. Mainstreaming also implies helping the public, service managers, and other participants understand and accept the rights of the disabled participants. Finally, mainstreaming requires working with disabled individuals to help prepare them for integration. As Jay Shivers and Hollis Fait (1975) have noted, some disabled individuals are not psychologically ready for mainstreaming. A period of counseling and education—ideally, LEISURE EDUCATION (Kay and Kendrigan, 1980)—will help prepare the individual for successful integration.

Mainstreaming is not simply a goal that is either achieved or not achieved. Because participation in recreation is largely intrinsically satisfying, participation in recreation is both a goal and a process (to gain greater life satisfaction). Mainstreaming, too, is both a goal and a process. As a process, the ideal is to develop the least restrictive environment in which individuals live, work, and play. This environment provides the minimum of physical, attitudinal, and social barriers and restrictions. Different disabilities will necessitate different types of environment and support, ranging on a continuum from relatively structured programs with a high degree of user support and human management to full integration in ''normal'' or traditional, unstructured activities with no need for guidance and support. At any point along the continuum, however, it is imperative that the individual be in an environment that maximizes his full potential with the least possible amount of barriers and restrictions.

REFERENCES

Bullock, Charles C. 1979. ''Mainstreaming—In Recreation Too!?'' *Therapeutic Recreation Journal* 13(4):5–10. Reviews development of mainstreaming and implications of PL 94–142 on recreation programs.

Kay, Darla, and Kendrigan, Keven. 1980. ''Education for Leisure—A Critical Step to Normalization.'' *Parks and Recreation* (Apr.): 55. Discusses role of leisure education as an aid in mainstreaming.

Nirje, Bengt. 1969. ''The Normalization Principle and Its Human Management Implications.'' In *Changing Patterns in Residential Services for the Mentally Retarded,* ed. R. Kugel and W. Wolfensberger, 179–195. Washington, DC: President's Committee on Mental Retardation. An early and important statement about integration and normalization.

Salzberg, Charles, and Langford, Cynthia. 1981. ''Community Integration of Mentally Retarded Adults through Leisure Activity.'' *Mental Retardation* (June):127–131. Review of principles and practices of mainstreaming in community recreation programs.

Shivers, Jay S., and Fait, Hollis F. 1975. *Therapeutic and Adapted Recreational Services.*

Philadelphia: Lea & Febiger. Good introductory text on therapeutic recreation and related topics.

Wolfensberger, Wolf. 1972. *Normalization: The Principle of Normalization in Human Services*. Toronto: National Institute on Mental Retardation. One of the most important statements about normalization and its implications.

SOURCES OF ADDITIONAL INFORMATION

A good introductory text to mainstreaming and other related concepts is Richard Kraus's *Therapeutic Recreation Service: Principles and Practices* (3rd edition, New York: Saunders, 1983). Bengt Nirje, one of the leaders in the early normalization and deinstitutionalization movement has written further on normalization in "The Normalization Principle: Implications and Comments" (*Journal of Mental Subnormality* 16:62–70, 1970). Gene Hayes examines some of the value implications of mainstreaming in "Philosophical Ramifications of Mainstreaming in Recreation" (*Therapeutic Recreation Journal* 12 no. 2:5–9, 1978). The entire 1979 fourth-quarter issue of the *Therapeutic Recreation Journal* was devoted to papers on mainstreaming.

A recent text, *Special Recreation: Opportunities for Persons with Disabilities,* (New York: CBS College, 1987) by Dan W. Kennedy, David R. Austin, and Ralph W. Smith, does an excellent job of discussing mainstreaming in recreation service provision. Patrick West examines issues of mainstreaming in "Social Stigma and Community Recreation Participation by the Mentally and Physically Handicapped" *Therapeutic Recreation Journal* 18 no. 1:40–49, 1984). See also Diana Richardson, Billie Wilson, Laura Wetherald, and Jay Peters, "Mainstreaming Initiative: An Innovative Approach to Recreation and Leisure Services in a Community Setting" (*Therapeutic Recreation Journal* 21 no. 2:9–19, 1987).

MERIT GOODS. See PUBLIC GOODS.

MIMICRY. 1. The spirit of imitation, illusion, or make-believe in GAMES. 2. The playful act of imitation or make-believe.

Mimicry was proposed by Roger Caillois (1961) as one of four basic types of GAME. Mimicry or games of illusion were set in contrast to AGON (games of skill), ALEA (games of chance), and ILINX (games based on vertigo or dizziness).

The FUN in mimicry lies in passing for another, but as a game form, it is not intended to really deceive other players or spectators. Mimicry in LEISURE and games requires the willing suspension of disbelief. "Serious" mimicry, such as that of a spy, illegal immigrant, or informer, seeks to deceive and is not a game.

Although Caillois considers mimicry to be a fundamental type of game, it does not usually involve rule following. This feature probably would cause most scholars to not include acts of mimicry among true game forms. It should, perhaps, be considered a form of illusory PLAY involving incessant and unique invention.

REFERENCES

Caillois, R. 1961. *Man, Play, and Games*. New York: The Free Press. An important
    study of the sociology of games. Chapter 2 describes in detail Caillois's classi-
    fication of games.

SOURCES OF ADDITIONAL INFORMATION

Some of Roger Caillois's ideas about play and games were first explored in his *Man and
the Sacred* (New York: The Free Press, 1959). A classic study of play and games, which
also greatly influenced Caillois, is Johan Huizinga, *Homo Ludens* (Boston: Beacon Press,
1955). Another, philosophically directed study of games and the spirit of game playing
is David Miller, *Gods and Games* (New York: Harper Colophon, 1973).

MULTICULTURALISM. A doctrine that holds that the integration of ethnic
minorities into the dominant society should include formal policies protecting
and promoting the maintenance of the cultural identity of ethnic minorities while
guaranteeing their rights to enter fully into the political, social, and economic
life of society.

Multiculturalism is one of three doctrines describing possible relationships between a dominant CULTURE and its ethnic minorities (Hughes and Kallen, 1974:
184–185). The first of these is majority group conformity, in which the immigrant
abandons his ancestral culture and merges totally with the culture of the mainstream. This model has traditionally been followed by many European and Asian
countries. The second doctrine is the "melting pot." Many different immigrants
bring elements of their HERITAGE with them to a new country, forming an
amalgamation with earlier immigrants (or their descendants) to create a new
and continually evolving society. This is the model usually espoused for the
United States. Multiculturalism, also known as pluralism or the mosaic model,
implies a varying degree of acculturation and assimilation by ethnic minorities
into different aspects of society. Many elements of their heritage are retained
and even protected by governmental policy, while political and economic rights
as citizens are also guaranteed. This doctrine provides the model guiding social
development in Canada and may become the de facto model for the United
States.

   One of the first formal articulations of the principles of multiculturalism as a
policy doctrine was a statement by Canadian Prime Minister Pierre Trudeau
before the House of Commons in 1971. Trudeau identified four objectives his
government would pursue in a multicultural program:

1. Ethnic minorities would be given public assistance to retain significant aspects of their
   heritage.

2. Ethnic minorities would also be given governmental assistance in overcoming BARRIERS
   to their full participation in society.

3. The government would sponsor special events and programs to promote interethnic contacts.

4. The government would provide assistance to new immigrants to learn one of the two official languages, English or French.

While there is widespread (although not unanimous) support for the general goals of multiculturalism in Canada, its implementation has been criticized on several points. As early as 1965, prior to Trudeau's pronouncements, John Porter (1965) described Canada as a vertical mosaic, composed of many different cultural groups but with the English and French on top. Other cultural groups were lower in the political and economic power hierarchy, given support by the two dominant cultures only for "song and dance programs." Similar criticisms have been made by Donald Loree (1978) and by Lance Roberts and Rodney Clifton (1982). They have argued that multiculturalism merely preserves the appearance of tolerance by promoting symbolic ethnicity but without promoting cultural growth and the attainment of true economic and political power at a national level by ethnic minorities.

Another common observation of multiculturalism, at least as practiced in Canada, is that individual ethnic groups become competitors for scarce public dollars, seeking only to promote their own FESTIVALS and events rather than getting involved in joint programs that would benefit many groups or that would promote greater tolerance and understanding among all ethnic groups.

There is also a basic methodological problem associated with implementing multicultural policies and studying multicultural and ethnic issues. Ethnicity, as a concept, is difficult to define. Wsevolod Isajiw (1974) found that of sixty-five studies addressing ethnic issues, only thirteen attempted even a cursory definition of the concept. Concluding that there is a need for a workable definition, Isajiw (1974: 124) proposed defining an ethnic group as "an involuntary group of people who share the same culture or descendants of such people who identify themselves and/or are identified by others as belonging to the same involuntary group."

Tom Smith (1980) identified three other approaches for defining ethnicity: (1) the natal approach, (2) the behavioral approach, and (3) the subjective approach. With the natal approach, ethnicity is defined in terms of the birthplace of the individual or his parents. The behavioral approach, in contrast, defines ethnicity in terms of participation in ethnic organizations or the use of a minority (or unofficial) language with family and friends. Finally, the subjective approach sees ethnicity in terms of a subjective sense of identity with the nationalistic origins of one's ancestors. While each of these approaches seems reasonable in the abstract, they can lead to contradictory conclusions. Consider an individual who is the son or daughter of Irish and German parents, is married to an individual from a Caribbean nation and is active, through the spouse, in Caribbean cultural agencies, and who immigrated from the United States to Canada, and retains U.S. citizenship. The person may be considered by the various definitions to be

Irish or German (natal approach), Caribbean (behavioral approach), or American (subjective approach). The debate in the late 1980s over whether certain individuals should be called "black" or "Afro-American" further illustrated the difficulties of defining and labeling ethnicity.

The issue of multiculturalism and ethnicity is important in recreation and leisure studies because ethnicity is often expressed through leisure and SPORT phenomena generally (Allison, 1982; Klobus-Edwards, 1981; Stamps and Stamps, 1985; Richardson and Crompton, 1988) and has particular significance for seniors and their leisure patterns (McCue, 1986). Isajiw (1977) discussed the relationship between the expression of ethnicity through various forms of activities and the sense of one's self and pursuit of SELF-ACTUALIZATION.

A further aspect of the significance of ethnicity to recreation and leisure services is the fact that recreation and leisure provide for highly visible or overt and usually nonthreatening expressions of one's culture. Ethnic celebrations, festivities, sporting events, and cultural activities (song, dance, visual arts) are among the more easily maintained expressions of ethnicity. One may feel socially pressured into adopting American- or Canadian-style dress and social manners in work and school settings, but still feel free to express one's heritage through selected leisure activities and observance of ethnic HOLIDAYS.

Few people will publicly oppose the principles of tolerance, democracy, and EQUITY for all cultural groups. Putting those principles into practice through multiculturalism or the "melting pot" models, however, often leads to significant political debates and problems. Recreation and leisure professionals will increasingly find themselves on the "cutting edge" of both improved multicultural understanding and ethnic CONFLICTS. This challenge will continue to grow as both the United States and Canada experience ever greater numbers of visible ethnic minorities. Some special problems recreation and leisure services leaders will be facing are (1) the potential need for provision of services in heritage languages, (2) the demand for specialized or modified public leisure services to serve the unique needs or interests of one ethnic group, and (3) the political and administrative dilemma of whether leisure services should be provided through parallel structures designed to help serve and promote individual cultural identities or through integrated structures that promote greater intercultural contact but do not enhance or promote one specific culture.

REFERENCES

Allison, Maria T. 1982. "Sport, Ethnicity, and Assimilation." *Quest* 34:165–175. Examines whether sport participation helps ethnic minorities merge into mainstream society as the "melting pot" model predicts; concludes that most ethnic groups modify sport to fit their culture rather than vice versa.

Hughes, David, and Kallen, Evelyn. 1974. *The Anatomy of Racism: Canadian Dimensions*. Montreal: Harvest House. A broad inquiry into the nature of ethnicity and race relations in Canada; includes a discussion of various models of interethnic relations.

Isajiw, Wsevolod. 1974. "Definitions of Ethnicity." *Ethnicity* 1:26–34. Examines a large number of ethnic studies to determine how ethnicity, as a concept, is defined; concludes most authors avoid the topic.

Isajiw, Wsevolod. 1977. *Identities: The Impact of Ethnicity on Canadian Society*. Toronto: Peter Martin Associates. Examines the role of ethnicity in shaping the individual's sense of identity and its impact on participation in social institutions.

Klobus-Edwards, Patricia. 1981. "Race, Residence, and Leisure Style: Some Policy Implications." *Leisure Sciences* 4:95–112. Examines the issue of whether leisure differences are due to intercultural differences or barriers; conclusion is that intercultural differences (ethnicity) may be the most important in explaining differences in participation.

Loree, Donald J. 1978. "Multiculturalism in a Bicultural Province." *Multiculturalism* 2(2):18–32. Criticizes multiculturalism as a policy on the grounds that it has failed to truly promote cultures other than English and French in Canada.

McCue, Wilson. 1986. "Involving Ethnic Older Adults in Community Recreation Programs." *Recreation Canada* 44(3):15–25. Describes some of the specific challenges facing older adults who are members of ethnic minorities.

Porter, John. 1965. *The Vertical Mosaic*. Toronto: University of Toronto Press. Coins the concept, "vertical mosaic" as a metaphor for English and French-dominated multicultural society.

Richardson, Sarah L., and Crompton, John. 1988. "Vacation Patterns of French and English Canadians." *Annals of Tourism Research* 15:430–435. A brief empirical look at the relative proclivity for travel of the two major cultural-linguistic populations in Canada; possible explanations for the differences are given.

Roberts, Lance W., and Clifton, Rodney A. 1982. "Exploring the Ideology of Canadian Multiculturalism." *Canadian Public Policy* 8:88–94. A policy critique of multiculturalism and its effectiveness in promoting cultural minorities.

Smith, Tom. 1980. "Ethnic Measurement and Identification." *Ethnicity* 7:78–95. Examines various methods for defining and measuring ethnicity of individuals.

Stamps, Spurgeon M., and Stamps, Miriam B. 1985. "Race, Class, and Leisure Activities of Urban Residents." *Journal of Leisure Research* 17:40–56. An inquiry into the relative importance of race and social class as predictors of leisure participation.

SOURCES OF ADDITIONAL INFORMATION

The literature on race and ethnic relations is very large. A few studies of special relevance to the concept of multiculturalism in leisure include Maria Allison, "On the Ethnicity of Ethnic Minorities in Sport" (*Quest* 31 no. 1,1979)); Neil Cheek, Don Field, and Rabel Burdge, *Leisure and Recreation Places* (Ann Arbor, MI: Ann Arbor Science, 1976, 113–129); Jarmila Horna, "Leisure Re-Socialization among Immigrants in Canada" (*Society and Leisure* 3 no. 1:96–106, 1980); and an entire issue of *Recreation Canada* (44 no. 3, 1986).

MULTIPLE USE. The principle of managing a land or water area in such a way as to provide the highest sustainable yield possible from a harmonious, coordinated mix of different RESOURCE uses.

Multiple use, in a literal sense, has been around for thousands of years. M. R. Carroll (1978) noted that a single forest could provide Neolithic man with shelter, wildlife, fuel, livestock protection, and grazing land. Multiple use as a modern concept, however, is more than just the simultaneous use of some parcel of land for different purposes. It is a management concept or principle growing out of the CONSERVATION movement. The concept is often associated first with the work of John Wesley Powell on rangeland management and Gifford Pinchot on forest management. In their use of the concept, multiple use became part of the strategy to meet the famous goal articulated by Secretary of Agriculture James Wilson in 1905: "the greatest good of the greatest number in the long run."

As a guiding principle for land managing agencies, one of the first official definitions of the concept comes from Section 4(a) of Public Law 86–517 (the 1960 Multiple Use-Sustained Yield Act):

"Multiple use" means: The management of all the various renewable surface resources of the national forests so that they are utilized in the combination that will best meet the needs of the American people; making the most judicious use of the land for some or all of these resources or related services over areas large enough to provide sufficient latitude for periodic adjustments in use to conform to changing needs and conditions; that some land will be used for less than all of the resources; and harmonious and coordinated management of the various resources, each with the other, without the impairment of the productivity of the land, with consideration being given to the relative values of the various resources, and not necessarily the combination of uses that will give the greatest dollar return or the greatest unit output.

That definition, because it was addressed to the national forests, does not give a complete indication of how multiple use is pursued by different agencies. The concept is interpreted in two different ways (Shanklin, 1962). First, multiple use may imply integrating all compatible uses so that the total utility of the products exceeds the total otherwise possible from a single use. This implies that no single dominant or best use is recognized. National forests are typically managed this way. In contrast, multiple use may mean recognizing a dominant use of a resource but also accommodating secondary uses that are socially desirable and are compatible with the dominant use. This type of management exemplifies the NATIONAL PARKS whose dominant purpose, as stated in the 1916 act that created the National Park Service, is "to conserve the scenery . . . and to provide for the enjoyment of the same."

Besides these conflicting connotations of the concept, another issue can complicate the understanding of the phrase *multiple use*: that issue is the areal definition of the land or water resource. First, multiple use may be directed toward the management of large complex ENVIRONMENTS under the control of one agency. The large areas may have a number of different land and water units with different resource potentials. This pattern typically results in a mosaic of different uses in different areas. Alternatively, the concept may be used for the management of relatively uniform tracts of land or water by providing for sequential or rotated uses throughout the year. Finally, multiple use may be a principle for the management of uniform tracts in such a way as to permit simultaneous but different resource uses. This latter situation can especially lead to CONFLICT among various users.

Multiple use can also be used as more than just a management principle. The term is sometimes imbued with broader social or political connotations, implying that a publicly owned resource should be managed in such a way as to provide a broad range of benefits including aesthetic, cultural, and environmental as well as economic returns.

REFERENCES

Carroll, M. R. 1978. *Multiple Use of Woodlands*. Cambridge, UK: University of Cambridge, Department of Land Economy. A British interpretation of the multiple use concept; provides a very brief summary of the history of the concept as it developed in the United States.
PL 86-517. 1960. *The 1960 Multiple Use—Sustained Yield Act*. Washington, D.C.: U.S. Government Printing Office. One of the first legal definitions of the concept of multiple use.
Shanklin, John. 1962. *Multiple Use of Land and Water Areas,* ORRRC Study report 17. Washington, DC: U.S. Government Printing Office. An excellent survey of the various legislative and administrative meanings of the concept; includes a useful collection of solicited statements from major federal land managing agencies on their interpretation of multiple use.

SOURCES OF ADDITIONAL INFORMATION

Warren A. Starr surveys some of the complexities of the concept as a managerial principle in "Multiple Use Management" (*Natural Resources Journal,* 1:288–301, 1961). J. S. Rowe and R. J. McCormack discuss some of the different interpretations of multiple use in "Forestry and Multiple Land Use," in *Proceedings of the 8th Commonwealth Forestry Conference* (New Delhi, India, 1968). A brief case study of how multiple use has been applied as a management system in a recreation context may be found in *American Outdoors: The Legacy, The Challenge* (Washington, DC: Island Press, 1987, 413–420).

MULTIPLIER. A quantitative estimate of the IMPACT of an external source of income or investment on income, sales, or employment in a regional economy.

The concept of multiplier is usually associated with TOURISM development, but it has been applied to other aspects of recreation and leisure investment such as assessing the impact of government spending on the arts (Todd, 1981). A simple example can illustrate the concept. A TOURIST stays at a resort for a week. During that time, he spends money on accommodation, transportation, food, attractions, and souvenirs. This spending results in a *direct* increase in the income of local merchants and tourism operators. They, in turn, spend some of the money they receive on wages and on replenishing their inventory. To the extent these second-round expenditures go to local employees, wholesalers, manufacturers, and service businesses, the tourist's original expenditures result in an additional indirect increase in their incomes. As the incomes of these individuals rise, they increase their spending on other goods and services, thus producing an induced increase in overall regional income. The total impact of this ripple of an initial injection of spending through direct, indirect, and induced effects is summarized as the multiplier. The ripple dampens and eventually disappears as money "leaks" from the regional economy through savings deposits, taxes, and expenditures to import goods and services. Generally, the multiplier is greater in larger and more self-contained economies because leakages are smaller in such economies.

Although the multiplier represents a real and very important economic phenomenon (it was a key concept in the Keynesian strategy developed for lifting the United States out of the Great Depression, for example), it is viewed with cynicism by some people. One basic reason for this cynicism is that the reporting of many multipliers in the tourism and recreation literature is based on dubious procedures. The accurate calculation of a multiplier requires substantial technical expertise and highly detailed and reliable data sources. Because these are not always easy to obtain, many consultants who cite multipliers in their reports to their clients often just guess at the correct value. Their estimates may be based on reported values drawn from other reports or simply crude and inaccurate guesses.

Other criticisms of multipliers have been made by John Bryden (1973). He observed, for example, that multipliers ignore the opportunity costs of RESOURCES used for tourism; that is, it is implicitly assumed that the allocation of resources to support tourism development does not force regions to forego other types of economic development. A more serious criticism, at least in Bryden's view, is that multipliers are often used to make inferences about the magnitude of potential benefits to be derived by a region from promoting tourism development. While multipliers do, in fact, do this, they are an incomplete measure of benefits. Furthermore, in terms of the conventions of benefit-cost analysis, the benefits estimated by multipliers are not attributable totally to increased productivity but also due to simple transfers of wealth (a form of benefit that is supposed to be excluded from benefit-cost analysis). Furthermore, the multiplier concept fails to provide any estimate of the costs of tourism development, including the opportunity costs just noted.

A final problem associated with cynicism and confusion associated with multipliers is that several different multipliers exist and there are several different ways an individual multiplier may be calculated. The distinctions between types of multiplier (and methods of estimation) are not always made clear by the individuals who report them (Archer, 1977). Brian Archer notes that there are four basic types of multiplier:

1. *The income multiplier.* This measures the impact of an exogenous expenditure or investment on local direct, indirect, and induced incomes. *Income* may be defined to refer solely to the disposable income of local residents, or it may include total income

(thus picking up that portion of income that ultimately goes to government in the form of taxes) as well as income that leaves the region when it goes to absentee businesses and property owners.

2. *The sales or transactions multiplier*. This measures the increase in business revenues due to exogenous expenditures or investment.

3. *The output multiplier*. This measures both increases in business revenues as well as changes in the value of their inventories. To further confuse the matter, the term *output multiplier* is also sometimes used to refer to the sales multiplier.

4. *The employment multiplier*. This measures the increase in the number of jobs associated with an expenditure or investment. It is defined in one of two ways: (a) as the ratio between the sum of direct, indirect, and induced job creation to direct job creation or (b) as the number of jobs created per unit of exogenous income.

Although the concept of multipliers began to receive serious attention in the recreation and leisure studies field only in the late 1960s, the concept dates back to the 1880s. The following brief history is drawn heavily from an excellent summary of the evolution of the concept of multipliers by A. Lloyd Wright (1956).

The first published reference to a concept that can be linked to our modern notion of a multiplier appears in a study by Walter Bagehot (1882:126–127) addressing a theory related to effective DEMAND and the effects of depressions on demand: "Under a system in which everyone is dependent upon the labour of everyone else, the loss of one spreads and multiplies through all. . . . And the entire effect of a depression in any single large trade requires considerable time before it can be produced. It has to be propagated and to be returned through a variety of industries before it is complete.''

Nicholas Johannsen (1925:5), examining the nature of economic depressions, spoke of a "multiplying principle" and introduced the concept of leakages of income through savings and imports. Johannsen ignored, however, the fact that effect of an economic stimulus rippling through a regional economy followed a geometric series producing a sequence of dampened effects at subsequent rounds of expenditures.

A. C. Pigou (1929) recognized the geometric series form of an economic stimulus, but failed to recognize the impact of leakages from a regional economy. He attributed the dampening effect of a stimulus over time to presumed inflationary price increases. The following year, Lyndhurst Giblin (1930) independently combined both the notion of a geometric series shaping successive economic impacts and the concept of a leakage to provide a method of analysis that closely resembles the current notion of a multiplier. Ironically, though, Giblin did not apply his method to assessing the impact of exogenous sources of income on an economy but to the study of the impact of diminishing exports. Then, in 1931, R. F. Kahn (1931) published the first formal statement of a theory of the economic multiplier. Originally, Kahn used the term *ratio* to refer to the economic index we know as the multiplier. John Maynard Keynes (1933) appears to be one of the first to use the specific term *the multiplier* in its full modern sense but Wright (1956) perceives in Keynes's usage evidence that the term was already in common use among professional economists by 1933. The concept became widely accepted and used by economists and policy analysts from the mid-1930s onward.

REFERENCES

Archer, Brian. 1977. *Tourism Multipliers: The State of the Art*, Bangor Occasional Papers in Economics No. 11. Bangor, Wales: University of Wales Press. An excellent monograph on the development, use, and abuse of multipliers in tourism.

Bagehot, Walter. 1882. *Lombard Street: A Description of the Money Market*. London: H. S. King. One of the earliest known discussions of an aspect of the multiplier concept; uses the word *multiplies* in terms of the diffusion of an economic impact.

Bryden, John M. 1973. *Tourism and Development: A Case Study in the Commonwealth Caribbean*. London: Cambridge University Press. A detailed analysis of the economic impacts of tourism development in former British colonies in the Caribbean; includes a very critical analysis of the misuse of multipliers in tourism consulting studies.

Giblin, Lyndhurst F. 1930. *Australia 1930*. Melbourne: University Press. An obscure work in which the method of calculating a multiplier was first developed; curiously, however, Giblin appeared to ignore the significance of his contribution, focusing instead on an analysis of the impacts of falling exports on Australia's economy.

Johannsen, Nicholas. 1925. *Business Depressions: Their Cause*. New York: Macmillan. Presented a model of the formulation and spread of economic depression that included a component very similar to the economic multiplier.

Kahn, R. F. 1931. "The Relation of Home Investment to Unemployment." *Economic Journal* 41:173–198. The first formal and complete articulation of the concept; ironically, Kahn does not use the term *multiplier* but refers to a "ratio."

Keynes, John Maynard. 1933. *The Means to Prosperity*. London: Macmillan. Includes a discussion of the concept of the multiplier as part of a recommended strategy for ending the Great Depression.

Pigou, A. C. 1929. "The Monetary Theory of the Trade Cycle." *Economic Journal* 34:183–194. An important partial development of the multiplier concept; focuses on how government spending can be used to reduce unemployment.

Todd, John. 1981. *Multiplier Analysis for Use by Art Galleries*. Toronto: Elenchus/ Econanalysis Consulting Services.

Wright, A. Lloyd. 1956. "The Genesis of the Multiplier Theory." *Oxford Economic Papers* 8:181–193. A well-documented history of the development of the concept; focuses especially on the contribution of R. F. Kahn.

SOURCES OF ADDITIONAL INFORMATION

W. E. Armstrong, S. Daniel, and A. A. Francis provide an illustration of how input-output analysis may be used to calculate a tourism "output" multiplier in "A Structural Analysis of the Barbados Economy, 1968, with an Application to the Tourist Industry" (*Social and Economic Studies* 23:493–520, 1974). Income and employment multipliers are developed in M. Brownrigg and M. A. Grief's, "Differential Multipliers for Tourism"

(*Scottish Journal of Political Economy* 22:261–275, 1975). J. M. Bryden and M. Faber provide an extensive critique of an infamous and now hard-to-find report, known as the "Zinder Report," that estimated extremely high multipliers for tourism in the Caribbean in "Multiplying the Tourist Multiplier" (*Social and Economic Studies* 20:61–82, 1971). William Strang used an input-output model to estimate the importance of outdoor recreation and tourism in a regional economy (including the development of an output multiplier) in *Recreation and the Local Economy: An Input-Output Model of a Recreation-Oriented Economy* (Sea Grant technical report 4, Madison: University of Wisconsin, 1970). Daniel Chappelle provides a useful overview on the use and interpretation of multipliers in recreation policy and planning analysis in "Strategies for Developing Multipliers Useful in Assessing Economic Impacts of Recreation and Tourism," in Dennis Propst, compiler, *Assessing the Economic Impacts of Recreation and Tourism* (Asheville, NC: Southeastern Forest Experiment Station, 1985).

N

NATIONAL PARK. An officially designated area established by a national government in which natural resources are protected by statutory power, which is of substantial size, which receives adequate administrative attention to ensure the continued protection of the resource base and in which some forms of REC-REATION or TOURISM are permitted.

The first national park, bearing the title, was Yellowstone National Park created in the United States in 1872. As Jean-Paul Harroy (1974) noted, Yellowstone was established to fulfill three objectives: (1) to prevent exploitation of wildlife, areas of natural beauty, and the ENVIRONMENT; (2) to enable visitors to derive enjoyment from their visit to the protected area; and (3) to promote scientific study of the natural RESOURCES and ecosystem included within the national park. With some relatively minor variations, these three themes have defined the general concept of a national park for the last eleven decades, including those such as the Great Smokies National Park that are also designated as BIOSPHERE RESERVES.

Although the creation of Yellowstone National Park served as a model for national park creation in many other countries, economic, political, and social difference among nations led to a wide variety of areas labeled as national parks in different countries. By 1959, the International Union for the Conservation of Nature and Natural Resources (IUCN) and the United Nations recognized the need for a more-or-less official definition for a national park. The first such attempt was released on February 15, 1961, by the United Nations (Harroy, 1968). In essence, the term *national park* was to be used for those formally designated areas possessing certain criteria established by the 1933 London Convention on the preservation of African fauna and flora or the 1942 Washington

Convention on the protection of flora, fauna, and landscape in American countries. This definition was refined and restated at the tenth General Assembly of the IUCN held in 1969 in New Delhi, India:

A national park is a relatively large area: (1) where one or several ecosystems are not materially altered by human exploitation and occupation, where plant and animal species, geomorphological sites and habitats of special scientific, educative and recreative interest or which contains a natural landscape of great beauty; and (2) where the highest competent authority of a country has taken steps to prevent or eliminate as soon as possible exploitation or occupation in the whole area and to enforce effectively the respect of ecological, geomorphological or aesthetic features which have led to its establishment; and (3) where visitors are allowed to enter, under special conditions, for inspirational, educative, cultural and recreational purposes.

This resolution also included several recommendations for certain areas that should not be designated as national parks, such as:

1. Nature reserves where access is limited to those with special permission.
2. Privately owned reserves, or reserves operated by state, provincial, or other lower-order governmental authorities.
3. Special reserves as defined in the African Convention on the Conservation of Nature and Natural Resource.
4. Inhabited and exploited areas that may have protected status, but in which recreation and tourism development take precedence over the CONSERVATION of ecosystems (IUCN:1975).

While these criteria establish the concept of a national park under more or less "ideal" conditions, certain political and social realities still present difficulties. For example, in Great Britain as in much of Western Europe one cannot find ecosystems that have not been modified by human occupation. In other countries, such as Australia, the highest central government does not have (or does not exercise) the authority to reserve land as national parks—although secondary levels of government (states or provinces) may exercise that power under agreement or concession of the senior level of government. To accommodate some of these circumstances, the secretariat of the IUCN, in its preface to the *1975 United Nations List of National Parks and Equivalent Reserves*, suggested the following definition. A national park is "an area of national territory for which the central Government authority has ordered the following requirements to be fulfilled: (a) status of general protection; (b) size in excess of a certain minimum; (c) protected status adequately maintained; and in which the central authority permits or actually encourages tourism."

REFERENCES

Harroy, Jean-Paul. 1968. "The Development of the National Park Movement." In *The Canadian National Parks: Today and Tomorrow,* ed. J. G. Nelson and R. C.

Scace, 18–34. Calgary, Alta: University of Calgary Press. A useful history of the development of national parks, with particular attention given to international trends and the broader historical context of the development of national parks.

Harroy, Jean-Paul. 1974. "A Century in the Growth of the 'National Park' Concept throughout the World." In *Second World Conference on National Parks,* ed. Hugh Elliot, 24–31. Morges, Switzerland: International Union for Conservation of Nature and Natural Resources. Another brief overview of the history of national parks; focuses on developments in the 1960s.

IUCN. 1975. *1975 United Nations List of National Parks and Equivalent Reserves.* Morges, Switzerland: International Union for Conservation of Nature and Natural Resources. Contains, in addition to an inventory of national parks, state and provincial parks, nature reserves, and other areas, a discussion of the concept of a national park.

SOURCES OF ADDITIONAL INFORMATION

The National Park Service of the United States and the Canadian Parks Service have numerous excellent publications on the nature, history, policies, and resources of the various properties under their jurisdiction. Two useful international collections of readings include the proceedings of the *First World Conference on National Parks,* edited by Alexander Adams (Washington, DC: National Park Service, 1962) and the proceedings of the *Second World Conference on National Parks,* edited by Hugh Elliott (Morges, Switzerland: IUCN, 1974). See also Raymond Dasmann, *Classification and Use of Protected Natural and Cultural Areas* (Morges, Switzerland: IUCN, 1973). A dated but articulate discussion of the concept of national parks in Freeman Tilden, *The National Parks: What They Mean to You and Me* (New York: Knopf, 1959).

NEED. The requirement for an activity, service, opportunity, or RESOURCE to achieve some desired goal or state.

The concept of need is as difficult in recreation and leisure studies as it is in other realms of thought. One superficial indication of its complexity is the fact that the *Oxford English Dictionary* (2d edition, 1989) devotes six columns, the equivalent of two full pages, to the term. The *OED* definitions include (1) violence or compulsion, (2) the condition of being in want, and (3) the quality of being a necessity. In the context of RECREATION and LEISURE studies, need tends to be used in the latter context and is discussed from two points of view: (1) a political or planning perspective and (2) a psychological or behavioral perspective.

A useful summary of the political or planning perspective was written by David Mercer (1973). Mercer based his analysis on the work by Jonathan Bradshaw (1972) on social needs. Translating Bradshaw's ideas into a recreation setting, Mercer observed that one of the most useful ways of conceptualizing need was that of comparative need. Comparative need is the degree of discrepancy between the existing supply of resources and the DEMAND for those resources. A traditional method for estimating demand is to use STANDARDS: a guideline specifying the number of acres of open space (or other measure of recreation supply) for a given number of people. While standards have been long used by the recreation profession, they have some significant limitations. One major limitation is that they are based on the assumption that all neighborhoods or regions have the same types and levels of interest in any specified activity. This assumption is not supported by empirical evidence.

Recognizing this problem, researchers have developed more sophisticated methods to estimate demand. For example, Michael Rogers (1974), in a technical manual developed for the Bureau of Outdoor Recreation, described how planners could use community and on-site surveys to project future demand. These estimates were then compared to current or projected supply inventories to determine where shortfalls would occur. Shortfalls were interpreted as needs and would receive special attention from the bureau in its efforts to help communities achieve greater EQUITY in the allocation of recreation resources.

A conceptually similar, but methodologically different, approach was used by Ed Staley (1968) in the city of Los Angeles. He developed two indexes for every neighborhood in Los Angeles: (1) a RESOURCE index reflecting the combined private and public supply of recreation resources available to local residents and (2) a need index based on youth population density, median income, juvenile delinquency rates, and other social variables. The difference between the resource index and the need index provided a measure of comparative need that could be used by the city in allocating resources.

A second category of social needs identified by Mercer is normative need. These are sets of statements about needs that are presumed to be objective and scientific assessments of human needs. There is substantial empirical proof of the needs for food, water, and oxygen, for example. Some authors have argued that recreation, parks, and leisure are similar "normative" needs (Dubos, 1970). Mercer quotes an example of an assertion of this type: "it seems likely that we are genetically programmed to a natural habitat of clean air and varied green landscape like any other mammal. To be relaxed and feel happy usually means simply allowing our bodies to react as evolution has equipped us to do for 100 million years" (Iltis, Loucks, and Andrews, 1970, quoted in Mercer).

Similar assertions are often made for other forms of leisure including physical recreation, artistic expression, and social interaction. These assertions are made to motivate people into getting involved who might otherwise not see the need to participate or to persuade those with budgetary power to allocate greater funding for activities. Although the rhetoric associated with normative needs is often impassioned, it is rarely backed up with rigorous evidence. It is doubtful that anyone has ever died from a lack of recreation or that any clinically verifiable illnesses have their cause in insufficient recreation. (One can cite tragic examples where a lack of leisure, in the form of sufficient rest, has contributed to the death of prisoners or internment camp detainees, but this is not the context in which recreation professionals argue the need for leisure.)

The third and fourth categories, felt need and expressed need, are closely related. Felt need is a subjective sense that one desires something. This may be motivated by a homeostatic need (one is thirsty and needs water) as well as by SOCIALIZATION (one's friends are taking midwinter breaks and thus one needs a break too). The issue here is not the origin or objective importance of the desire, but the fact that it is subjectively felt to be a need. When that subjective feeling results in action to satisfy it, it becomes an expressed need. Thus booking a midwinter break may be seen as evidence of the need for a break. Expressed needs may also be seen in political actions, such as petitions to a municipal recreation and parks department for new facilities or in the actions of a COMMUNITY DEVELOPMENT group to organize new leisure services.

The second perspective on needs in recreation and leisure is the psychological or behavioral perspective. The boundary between the first and second perspectives is often unclear, especially with respect to the notion of felt and expressed needs, because psychological research on needs often defines needs in terms of subjective feelings or overt behavior.

Peter Witt (1971), in an early study cited by many social psychologists as part of the history of research into recreation needs, conducted a factor analysis on reported participation in leisure activities by high-school students. Drawing on community surveys in three separate municipalities, Witt found four common factors, which he labeled "sports," "outdoors-nature," "adolescent-social," and "aesthetic-sophisticate." Witt's data came from a larger data set collected originally by Doyle Bishop (1970), who had found only three factors (for adults): "active-diversionary," "potency," and "status." Witt suggested that the difference between the two studies was evidence of differences in the needs met by leisure participation between adolescents and adults. Although the work of Doyle and Witt is now dated, their basic design—inferring needs from patterns of recreation behavior—continues to be employed by many recreation planners and policy analysts.

A more important line of work associated with this perspective stems from the work of Abraham Maslow (1968) and C. P. Alderfer (1972). Maslow hypothesized the existence of a hierarchical ordering of six basic human needs: physiological, security, social, esteem, autonomy, and SELF-ACTUALIZATION. Alderfer, an organizational psychologist, adapted Maslow's work by regrouping these needs into three general categories: existence, relatedness, and growth. Both Maslow and Alderfer have influenced other psychologists concerned with understanding needs. Richard Hackman and Greg Oldham (1975), for example, took Alderfer's notion of growth needs (comprising Maslow's needs for esteem, autonomy, and self-actualization) and designed a job diagnostic survey to measure the growth need fulfillment provided by different types of job. Manuel London, Rick Crandall, and Dale Fitzgibbons (1977) built on Hackman and Oldham and Alderfer by extending the earlier work to a study of needs fulfilled by various forms of leisure involvement.

In the same year, Howard Tinsley, Thomas Barrett, and Richard Kass (1977) further extended the work of Maslow, Alderfer, and Hackman and Oldham. Tinsley and his colleagues eventually identified forty-five separate needs they believed leisure satisfies. A theme running through all of this work is that need is essentially a psychological construct that can be identified through personality instruments or inferred from other measures of overt behavior.

This view has been challenged by Seppo Iso-Ahola (1980). He viewed the usual lists of needs developed by empiricists as superficial motivations, masking the true psychological forces that drive people to participate in recreation. Need, to Iso-Ahola, is a pyramid with increasingly deep levels of causality or explanation. The highest or most superficial level of need are the lists of motivations suggested by researchers such as Tinsley. These motivations are, in Iso-Ahola's view, shaped by deeper needs associated with perceived freedom and competence concerns. The desires of freedom and feelings of competence are, in turn, shaped by the need for OPTIMAL AROUSAL and incongruity. Finally, all these are based on early socialization experiences and biological dispositions. In response to the work of other authors, Iso-Ahola retorted that he cannot believe that people really walk around with forty-five different needs in their mind, assessing which ones they want to satisfy at any given moment. Such needs, he argued, are "nothing but cultural labels often used by others to describe their participation" and thus, ultimately, are just "culturally learned stereotypes" (Iso-Ahola 1980:247).

Although he wrote in 1973, Daniel Chappelle's essay on recreation needs provides some useful observations that help keep the discussion of recreation needs in perspective. Chappelle felt that a need may be either something essential for life or something that is just desirable. As noted earlier, there is no persuasive evidence that recreation is essential for life in the same way that food and water are. If, therefore, recreation and leisure needs are just desirables, then they are part of a very long list. Nonetheless, many recreation professionals appear to be (using a phrase Chappelle borrows from Eric Hoffer) "true believers"—so convinced that recreation and leisure are needs that they refuse to see evidence to the contrary. The significance of this belief is that it helps drive a logical process common in the recreation profession: (1) recreation is a need, (2) needs must be fully satisfied, (3) the marketplace is not fulfilling the needs of all people, (4) therefore the public sector must expand to meet the need. Chappelle reminded his readers, though, that the widely recognized needs for clothing, shelter, food, and medical care are still not met for all people. In that light, how can anyone credibly argue that government must meet all recreation needs?

In the final analysis, recreation and leisure, as many other social needs, are needs only to the extent that some individuals interpret them to be needs. They are, basically, VALUE judgments and a reflection of the beliefs a society or CULTURE holds.

REFERENCES

Alderfer, C. P. 1972. *Human Needs in Organization Settings*. New York: The Free Press.
    Proposes a categorization of needs met through work settings based on Maslow's earlier scholarship.
Bishop, Doyle. 1970. "Stability of the Factor Structure of Leisure Behavior: Analyses

of Four Communities." *Journal of Leisure Research* 2:160–170. An early example of factor analysis of leisure behavior; identified three dimensions summarizing adult behavioral patterns.

Bradshaw, Jonathan. 1972. "The Concept of Social Need." *New Society* 39:640–643. Introduces a typology of "social needs," including normative, comparative, felt, and expressed needs.

Chappelle, Daniel E. 1973. "The Need for Outdoor Recreation: An Economic Conundrum?" *Journal of Leisure Research* 5:47–53. An iconoclastic essay on recreation need written by an agricultural economist.

Dubos, Rene. 1970. "Will Man Adapt to the Megalopolis?" *The Ecologist* 1(4):12–15. A superficial essay suggesting the need for recreation, leisure, and open space, and arguing that the modern city runs the risk of failing to meet that need.

Hackman, J. Richard, and Oldham, Greg R. 1975. "Development of the Job Diagnostic Survey." *Journal of Applied Psychology* 60:139–170. Describes the development and properties of a psychological survey designed to assess various need satisfactions provided by jobs.

Iltis, Hugh, Loucks, Orie L., and Andrews, Peter. 1970. "Criteria for an Optimum Human Environment." *Ekistics* 29:449–452. A personal commentary by two botanists and an anthropologist about their belief that man has a genetic need for open space, especially the tropical savannah.

Iso-Ahola, Seppo E. 1980. *The Social Psychology of Leisure and Recreation*. Dubuque, IA: William C. Brown. Chapter 11, "Leisure Needs and Motives," is a good (albeit opinionated) review of the social psychological literature on needs; argues that needs should be studied as a series of "levels of causality."

London, Manuel, Crandall, Rick, and Fitzgibbons, Dale. 1977. "The Psychological Structure of Leisure: Activities, Needs, People." *Journal of Leisure Research* 9:252–263. Extends work of Hackman, Oldham, and Alderfer to the study of need satisfaction through leisure; infers need from statements on survey instruments.

Maslow, Abraham. 1968. *Towards a Psychology of Being*. New York: Van Nostrand. A restatement of earlier work on his model of hierarchical needs; the model is based largely on personal insight, interpretation, and anecdotal evidence rather than objective tests.

Mercer, David. 1973. "The Concept of Recreation Need." *Journal of Leisure Research* 5:37–50. Examines recreation need as an issue in planning and policy analysis.

Oxford English Dictionary, 2nd edition. 1989. J. A. Simpson and E. S. C. Weiner (preparers). Vol. 10, 287–289. An extended definition of "need," based on etymology and historical precedents.

Rogers, Michael P. 1974 *Assessing Public Recreation Needs,* Technical Assistance bulletin no. 1. Ann Arbor, MI: Lake Central Region, Bureau of Outdoor Recreation. A monograph that describes some key concepts associated with need, and outlines a possible research design for assessing need.

Staley, Edwin. 1968. *An Instrument for Determining Comparative Priority of Need for Neighborhood Recreation Services in the City of Los Angeles*. Los Angeles: Recreation and Youth Services Planning Council. A technical manual describing how secondary data sources can be used to generate estimates of comparative need for urban neighborhoods.

Tinsley, Howard E. A., Barrett, Thomas C., and Kass, Richard A. 1977. "Leisure Activities and Need Satisfaction." *Journal of Leisure Research* 9:110–120. Identifies forty-five separate needs met by leisure participation through an extensive literature review; reports on results of survey of adults who responded to relative importance of the forty-five needs.

Witt, Peter. 1971. "Factor Structure of Leisure Behavior for High School Age Youth in Three Communities." *Journal of Leisure Research* 3:213–220. An extension of work initiated by Doyle—based on same data set; infers need from observed participation patterns.

SOURCES OF ADDITIONAL INFORMATION

A speculative essay examining the biological basis of the desire for leisure is Stephen Smith, "On the Biological Basis of Pleasure: Some Implications for Leisure Policy," in Thomas Goodale and Peter Witt, eds., *Recreation and Leisure: Issues in an Era of Change* (rev. edition, State College, PA: Venture, 1985). Theories about the need (or desire) for play as a particular form of leisure are covered admirably in Michael Ellis, *Why People Play* (Englewood Cliffs, NJ: Prentice Hall, 1973). Richard Knopf examines the need for recreation and its implications for outdoor recreation in his "Recreational Needs and Behavior in Natural Settings," in I. Altman and J. F. Wohlwill, eds., *Behavior and the Natural Environment* (New York: Plenum Press, 1983, 205–240). The concept of needs is a fundamental issue in Peter Witt and Gary Ellis, "The Leisure Diagnostic Battery: Measuring Perceived Freedom in Leisure" (*Leisure and Society* 7:109–124, 1984). Rick Crandall examines a variety of motivations and needs in "Motivations for Leisure" (*Journal of Leisure Research* 12:45–54, 1980). Howard Tinsley and Richard Kass have extended their work (cited earlier) in "Leisure Activities and Need Satisfaction: A Replication" (*Journal of Leisure Research* 10:191–202, 1978) and in "The Latent Structure of the Need Satisfying Properties of Leisure Activities" (*Journal of Leisure Research* 11:278–291, 1979).

NONPARTICIPATION. The lack of participation in an activity or the lack of use of a facility by an individual who would otherwise be expected to use the service.

The concept of nonparticipation may seem to be quite simple: merely the absence of participation. Nonparticipation is, however, somewhat more complicated and more significant than this simplistic view. The success of recreation programs and services, whether in the private or public sector, depends on successfully attracting users. While only a relatively small percentage of any population will actually use a facility or will participate in a program, the reasons for nonparticipation and nonuse may be important to the manager, planner, or operator of a facility or program. Whether a manager can understand the reasons for nonparticipation and can take actions to correct them may ultimately determine the success or failure of his facility. Research into the phenomenon of nonparticipation is thus usually aimed at identifying, measuring, analyzing, and prescribing solutions to BARRIERS or CONSTRAINTS to participation.

Although no single, accepted classification system has been developed for barriers to participation, Geoffrey Godbey (1985) has proposed a model of nonparticipation in leisure services that summarizes the major reason, from the perspective of a leisure service organization:

I. Lack of information that service exists
II. Informed about existence of service, but
   A. Don't wish to participate
      1. Because of previous experience
         a. Which was negative due to resource problems
         b. Which was negative due to social problems
         c. Which was negative because of problems with the activity
      2. For other reasons
   B. Not eligible to participate
   C. Not appropriate to participate
   D. Wish to participate, but don't
      1. Due to reasons within control of agency
      2. Due to reasons outside of agency control

Other models may be developed that focus on barriers faced by the potential participant, such as Francis McGuire's (1984) analysis of expressed barriers by a group of adults aged forty-five and over. An analysis of thirty separate barriers revealed five major groupings that prevent participation: (1) external resource barriers, (2) TIME commitments or conflicts, (3) problems of social approval (SOCIALIZATION), (4) ability-related constraints, and (5) health and physical well-being limitations.

Edgar Jackson's (1983) work on identifying activity-specific barriers to participation confirms the implicit point made by the previous authors: nonparticipation is not an undifferentiated phenomena. In other words, different barriers affect different people and apply to different activities. Furthermore, apparently uniform barriers, such as cost are also more complex. Cost, as a barrier, affects activities differently depending on whether the operational definition of cost is transportation costs, admission charges, membership fees, or necessary investment in equipment. The issue is not just total dollar outlay, but a more complex evaluation based on perceived VALUE, durability of the product or service purchased, potential usefulness of the product for other activities, the availability of substitutable activities (see SUBSTITUTION), and other forces.

REFERENCES

Godbey, Geoffrey. 1985. "Nonuse of Public Leisure Services: A Model." *Journal of Park and Recreation Administration* 3:1–12. Presents a conceptual model classifying barriers to participation from perspective of an agency.
Jackson, Edgar L. 1983. "Activity-Specific Barriers to Recreation Participation." *Leisure Sciences* 6:47–60. Reviews literature on nonparticipation and examines variation in barriers by activity.
McGuire, Francis. 1984. "A Factor Analytic Study of Leisure Constraints in Advanced

Adulthood." *Leisure Sciences* 6:313–326. Analyzes the responses of a sample of adults, aged forty-five and over, to questions about perceived barriers.

SOURCES OF ADDITIONAL INFORMATION

A useful overview to issues of nonparticipation and nonuse may be found in the collection by Michael Wade, ed., *Constraints on Leisure* (Springfield IL: Charles C. Thomas, 1984). Edgar Jackson and Mark Searle have written several articles on this topic: "Recreation Non-participation and Barriers to Participation: Concepts and Models" (*Leisure and Society* 8:693–707, 1985); "Recreation Non-participation: Variables Related to the Desire for New Recreational Activities" (*Recreation Research Review* 10 no. 2:5–12, 1983); and "Socioeconomic Variations in Perceived Barriers to Recreation Participation among Would-be Participants" (*Leisure Sciences* 7:227–249, 1985). Gerald Romsa and Wayne Hoffman discuss the importance of research on nonparticipation and relate it to the so-called opportunity theory of recreation participation in "An Application of Nonparticipation Data in Recreation Research: Testing the Opportunity Theory" (*Journal of Leisure Research* 12:321–328, 1980). Additional references may be found in the BARRIER and CONSTRAINTS entries of this dictionary.

NORMALIZATION. The principle of establishing and maintaining patterns of personal behavior and living conditions for individuals classified as disabled to permit lives that are as socially normative as possible.

For centuries, disabled people were often kept separate from society by confining them to residential institutions. These institutions often housed hundreds of residents in crowded, dehumanizing conditions (Salzberg and Langford, 1981). In the late 1950s, concerned citizens began to seek alternative forms of care and support, particularly with reference to individuals classified as mentally retarded. The first major efforts were made in Scandinavia (Nirje, 1969, 1970), but, due to work by Wolf Wolfensberger (1972), others eventually spread to other Western countries and were broadened to reflect concern for other types of disability. An important aspect of this movement is the goal of increasing the ACCESSIBILITY of public services to disabled individuals.

Starting with ADVOCACY, the normalization movement led to civil litigation, and finally passage of legislation establishing specific rights of disabled individuals. Two major U.S. laws were PL 93–112 (The Rehabilitation Act) and PL 94–142 (The Education for All Handicapped Children Act). PL 93–112, in particular, had a major impact through Section 504, the so-called Nondiscrimination Clause that prohibited discrimination against any handicapped individuals in any program or facility receiving federal financial assistance. Both of these acts have been influential in establishing the mandate for DEINSTITUTIONALIZATION and MAINSTREAMING as strategies in the delivery of leisure services. The philosophical basis or ideology behind both concepts is normalization.

Essentially, the principle of normalization states that it is the right of every disabled individual to live in the least restrictive environment possible to have experiences that are as normative as the particular disability permits. The concept of "normative" here is a culturally bound one. A normative ENVIRONMENT will reflect contemporary social conditions in a community, and these may vary from community to community. Furthermore, the environmental conditions should be appropriate to the age and sex of the individual, while providing for mixing with individuals of other ages and the opposite sex. Bengt Nirje (1970) has identified a number of aspects of the environment that must be considered as part of adopting the normalization principle:

1. The individual should experience the normal rhythms of life on a daily, weekly, seasonal, annual, and HUMAN LIFE CYCLE basis (see TIME).

2. The individual's preferences, wishes, and desires in daily living should be respected as much as possible.

3. Contact with members of the opposite sex should be encouraged.

4. Reasonable economic integrity should be provided. This may include food and accommodation allowances, appropriate pocket money for discretionary spending, and equitable pay for employment, whether it is in a competitive environment, sheltered workshop, or institutional setting.

5. A normal living environment should be developed. This implies, among other things, residential densities in a home that are comparable to those in surrounding residences and a home that is not isolated from other residences on the basis that it houses disabled individuals.

6. Furnishings and decorations should be attractive and reflect contemporary standards in private residences. The residents should, if possible, be given some choice in the decoration of their accommodations.

In practice, the principle of normalization does not mean that every disabled individual is simply deinstitutionalized and placed in the community without support. Nor does it mean that persons who are disabled are made "normal." Instead, it involves providing opportunities to promote both physical and social integration in one's own community (see EQUITY). The degree of integration or mainstreaming possible for any particular individual must be based on the potential of the individual. Actual levels will typically fall on a continuum from full-time residence in an institution to full integration in the community. The principle of normalization emphasizes that each person has the right to as full and complete integration as possible.

REFERENCES

Nirje, Bengt. 1969. "The Normalization Principle and Its Human Management Implications." In *Changing Patterns in Residential Services for the Mentally Retarded*, ed. R. Kugel and W. Wolfensberger, 179–195. Washington, DC: President's Committee on Mental Retardation. An early and important statement on the principles and practices of normalization and integration.

Nirje, Bengt. 1970. "The Normalization Principle: Implications and Comments." *Journal of Mental Subnormality* 16(31):62–70. A summary of some operational principles associated with normalization.

Salzberg, Charles, and Langford, Cynthia. 1981. "Community Integration of Mentally
    Retarded Adults through Leisure Activity." *Mental Retardation* 19 (June):127–
    131. Describes the practice of mainstreaming in community recreation programs.
Wolfensberger, Wolf. 1972. *Normalization: The Principle of Normalization in Human
    Services*. Toronto: National Institute on Mental Retardation. One of the most
    important statements about normalization and its applications.

SOURCES OF ADDITIONAL INFORMATION

Charles Bullock examines the implications of normalization and mainstreaming in recreation in "Mainstreaming—In Recreation Too!?" (*Therapeutic Recreation Journal* 13
no. 4:5–10, 1979). Darla Kay and Keven Kendrigan argue for the role of leisure education
in normalization in "Education for Leisure—A Critical Step to Normalization" (*Parks
and Recreation*) 15, Apr.:55, 1980).

   In their book, *Problems, Issues, and Concepts in Therapeutic Recreation* (Englewood
Cliffs, NJ: Prentice Hall, 1985), Ronald P. Reynolds and Gerald S. O'Morrow devote
Chapter 7 to the discussion of normalization and its implications for day-to-day situations
encountered by recreation professionals. Another good source is Robert J. Flynn and
Kathleen E. Nitsch's *Normalization, Socialization, Interpretation, and Community Ser-
vices* (Baltimore: University Park Press, 1980).

O
___

OPTIMAL AROUSAL. A psychological construct referring to that level of mental stimulation at which physical performance, learning, or temporary feelings of well-being are maximized.

Optimal arousal is currently cited by many authors as the explanation for why people PLAY or engage in other forms of leisure activities. Although the concept became popular in the 1970s, its roots extend back into the early part of the twentieth century. A discussion of the origins of the concept may be found in Michael Ellis's (1973) *Why People Play,* on which portions of the following discussion are based.

Nineteenth-century theories of animal behavior were based on the belief that behavior was always directed at satisfying NEEDS. When all needs were met, animals (including humans) would rest. Quiescence—the lack of action—was seen as their preferred state. This belief, however, was contradicted by field observations of animals, especially of primates, engaged in activities with no discernible connection to need satisfaction. These activities included playfulness, exploration, and casual manipulation of objects in the natural environment. Early attempts to explain this phenomenon included William McDougall's (1923) belief in an investigatory reflex that compelled animals to explore unexpected changes in their ENVIRONMENT. These suggestions fell short of serving as explanations. They were, in fact, just explicit recognitions of the reality of enigmatic, nonutilitarian behavior. Appealing to the existence of an instinct as the explanation was a tacit admission that the explanation was unknown.

No significant advance in the understanding of nonutilitarian behavior was made until after World War II when three separate lines of research unexpectedly offered new insights. The first line of research, sometimes known as vigilance research, concerned the causes and rate of declining attention to a task. It had been observed during the war that individuals assigned to many simple but tedious tasks, such as monitoring a radar screen, began to lose their attention over time, despite their commitment to the task. The result of numerous studies on the phenomenon (summarized in Mackworth, 1970) was a complex theory involving issues of how one determined whether or not some significant event (such as the appearance of unidentified aircraft on a radar screen) had occurred, the probability of the event occurring, and the arousal level of the operator. With respect to this last point, it was discovered that an individual involved in a highly complex or demanding situation—such as an air traffic controller monitoring aircraft on a radar screen—were less likely to lose attention than someone involved in a less mentally or emotionally demanding task.

During the same period as this research was being conducted, other psychologists were studying the effects of sensory deprivation on humans. Through the use of specially designed test chambers, they deprived their subject of virtually all stimuli. The subjects found the experience to be highly disturbing. A number of subjects experienced hallucinations during the experiments; and some displayed behavioral disorders for several weeks after the experiment was over. This work, summarized by John Zubec (1969), also led to the conclusion that some level of stimulation or arousal was necessary for optimal human functioning.

The third line of research came from animal studies. Experiments with rats in mazes (which produced countless cartoons as well as some legitimate scientific findings) as well as with primates confirmed that higher vertebrates would seek out opportunities for exploratory or manipulative behavior even when not encouraged to do so through food rewards. D. E. Berlyne (1960), in his review and synthesis of hundreds of such studies, suggested that one single functional structure in the mammalian brain might be responsible for nonutilitarian behavior. The structure identified by Berlyne has become known as the reticulate arousal system (RAS). The RAS is a portion of the lower brain involved with transmitting signals from the body's sensory organs to the higher brain or cortex. As its name suggests, the RAS is responsible for arousing the cortex and is linked to certain stimulative processes such as awakening and sexual arousal. One of the significant findings of the research in the 1960s on the RAS (summarized in Hinde, 1966) was that the level of physical performance of an animal improved as the animal's level of arousal increased to some point, after which further increases in arousal led to declining performance. In other words, performance and arousal are related to each other through an inverted U-shaped function. This finding paralleled a much earlier discovery of a similar phenomenon by Robert Yerkes and Joseph Dodson (1908) on human learning and habituation (the so-called Yerkes-Dodson Law, as the inverted U-shaped function is sometimes known, has been important in helping researchers understand the effects of COMPETITION on SPORT performance).

Although these three lines of research have not been formally linked, Ellis

(1973) observed that all converged on a finding important in explaining non-utilitarian, exploratory, playlike behavior. Such behavior appears to be a strategy for animals to move their level of arousal to an optimum. Not just any form of behavior or stimulus seeking will work. The animal (or human) seeks those stimuli that are novel, complex, and present uncertain outcomes. The search for appropriate stimuli that will move the animal to a state of optimal arousal has been termed sensoristasis by Duane Schultz (1965) as a psychological analogy to Walter Cannon's (1932) homeostasis (the need to keep the condition of the body's tissues within a relatively narrow range of tolerable states).

Play is thus viewed (Ellis, 1973) as a strategy for seeking optimal arousal, particularly when an individual is in a suboptimal level of arousal. In fact, Ellis defined play as "that behavior that is motivated by the need to elevate the level of arousal to the optimal" and work as "the behavior emitted to reduce the level of stimulation" (1973:110). In some ways, optimal arousal is related to the experience of FLOW.

Although the available scientific and experiential evidence is persuasive that human beings operate best at some level of optimal arousal, there are still problems in using the concept as an explanation for play behavior. First, the observation that people use play to seek optimal arousal is perilously close to a tautology. The optimal level of arousal is, by definition, the level people seek; and play, by definition, has no other purpose than affecting arousal levels. The optimal level varies by activity, over time, and among individuals. It is not a precisely defined or easily measurable state, nor can its objective characteristics be reliably derived from theory or from other empirical data. The search for optimal arousal—or sensoristasis, to use Schultz's term—is thus not totally analogous to homeostasis. The homeostatic need for oxygen, for example, by any specific individual can be derived independently from data related to the individual's activities, metabolic rate, and certain other environmental factors.

A further problem is that play is seen as only raising arousal levels. The task of lowering arousal levels is consigned to work. Yet for many people, LEISURE activities are pursued for relaxation and rest. Whether play, TOURISM, or REC-REATION, these activities are desired to lower one's arousal level from the unacceptably high levels (i.e., stress) that work has placed them in.

The concept of optimal arousal has yielded some valuable insights into aspects of human behavior. It is, however, a very general concept that misses the essential element of FUN and does not yet provide a full explanation for why people engaged in leisure activities.

REFERENCES

Berlyne, D. E. 1960. *Conflict, Arousal, and Curiosity*. New York: McGraw-Hill. A major study into the origins of a wide variety of animal behaviors; provided the base for subsequent research into the role of the reticulate arousal system in animal and human behavior.

Cannon, Walter B. 1932. *The Wisdom of the Body*. New York: Norton. An examination of how the body senses need for food, water, oxygen, and other essentials; introduced the term homeostasis.

Ellis, Michael J. 1973. *Why People Play.* Englewood Cliffs, NJ: Prentice Hall. A good survey of various theories of the origin of play behavior; advocates the view that play is a form of arousal seeking.

Hinde, Robert A. 1966. *Animal Behavior: A Synthesis of Ethology and Comparative Psychology.* New York: McGraw-Hill. An excellent review and survey text on animal behavior.

Mackworth, Jane F. 1970. *Vigilance and Attention.* Baltimore: Penguin. An extensive survey of two decades of work on vigilance research; proposes a "signal detection" theory.

McDougall, William. 1923. *Outline of Psychology.* New York: Scribner. An early introductory text on psychology; proposes the existence of an instinct for curiosity.

Pavlov, Ivan P. 1927. *Conditioned Reflexes,* trans. G. V. Anrep. Oxford: Clarendon Press. Pavlov's classic work on animal reflexes; includes speculation that animal exploratory behavior is also a reflex.

Schultz, Duane P. 1965. *Sensory Restriction: Effects on Behavior.* New York: Academic Press. A review of the impacts of deprivation of sensory input on behavior.

Yerkes, Robert, and Dodson, Joseph. 1908. "The Relation of Strength of Stimulus to Rapidity of Habit-Formation." *Journal of Comparative Neurology and Psychology* 18:459–482. Observed an inverted-U function relating arousal level and rapidity of learning.

Zubec, John P. (ed). 1969. *Sensory Deprivation: Fifteen Years of Research.* New York: Appleton Century Crofts. A collection of essays and research articles on deprivation research.

SOURCES OF ADDITIONAL INFORMATION

A. Mehrabian examines the relationship between preferred environments and optimal arousal in "Characteristic Individual Reactions to Preferred and Unpreferred Environments" (*Journal of Personality* 46:717–731, 1978). The same topic is also considered in a broader social context by J. McVarish Hunt, *The Challenge of Incompetence and Poverty* (Champaign-Urbana: University of Illinois Press, 1969). D. E. Berlyne, one of the leading developers of the concept of optimal arousal, examines humor as a form of arousal in "Laughter, Humor, and Play" in G. L. Lindzey and E. Aronson, eds., *Handbook of Social Psychology* (New York: Addison-Wesley, 1968, 795–853). Optimal arousal and its effects on vacation preferences has been studied by Russell Wahlers and Michael Etzel, "Vacation Preference as a Manifestation of Optimal Stimulation and Lifestyle Experience" (*Journal of Leisure Research* 17:283–295, 1985).

OUTDOOR EDUCATION. The use of the outdoors as a setting for the teaching of skills, affective lessons, and cognitive lessons that include, but are not necessarily limited to, those directly associated with the natural ENVIRONMENT.

Although some authors (Smith, Carlson, Donaldson, and Masters, 1963) have interpreted writings from authors as far back as the English Romantic poet William Wordsworth (see, for example, Wordsworth's "The Tables Turned," 1982) as evidence of support for the principles of outdoor education, the concept of outdoor education actually dates from the 1930s. During the 1930s and 1940s, Lloyd Sharp and Julian Smith, working independently, developed the foundations for the outdoor education movement. Sharp was associated with the privately operated Life Camps, Inc., of New Jersey. Smith was closely involved with the Michigan public education system through the Kellogg Foundation. World War II temporarily interrupted their activities, but after the war, the concept of outdoor education enjoyed a period of rapid and dramatic growth.

In the first decades, outdoor education was concerned primarily with the teaching of skills such as woodlore, camping, hunting, fishing, archery, and canoeing through residential camping. Particular attention was also given to education in the affective domain—the inculcation of proper attitudes and values. These attitudes included both the values implicit in CONSERVATION as well as the ideals of democracy and fair play. Because much of the material covered in the education programs of outdoor camps presented in the context of conservation, the terms *conservation education* and *outdoor education* were often used synonymously. The emphasis on conservation was to continue as an important theme in many programs, and was eventually to become known as ENVIRON-MENTAL EDUCATION, a concept now closely related to but distinct from outdoor education.

The divergence in educational philosophies that led to the separation between outdoor education and environmental education began to appear in the late 1950s. George Donaldson and Oswald Goering (1970) have suggested the switch may have been due to the Soviet launching of *Sputnik,* the first artificial satellite. That launching caused, virtually overnight, a revolution in American education in which unprecedented importance was placed on mathematics and science. Whether the change was actually stimulated by *Sputnik* or was due to more subtle and long-term forces, the intellectual evolution of outdoor education can be appreciated by comparing three representative quotations. From the early 1950s: "the experience of living in the out-of-doors together as a regular part of the school program is not a fad, frill, or extra. . . . Here the students meet the more subtle problems involved in group living, the problems connected with the un-selfish and unbiased consideration of others, the problems involved in fears and prejudices" (Sharp, 1952:21). From the mid-1960s: With respect to outdoor education and teaching science, "we are trying to help pupils understand the methods of science and to use these methods, i.e. methods of discovery, inquiry, problem solving. We also want pupils to understand the meaning and use of scientific attitude, i.e., withholding judgement, using reliable sources of information, etc." (Blough, 1966). And finally, from the mid-1980s: "Outdoor education can be correlated with all subjects in the curriculum. The opportunities for studying science are unlimited but it should not dominate the outdoor education program. In this section are suggestions for enriching all areas of the curriculum through outdoor activity: . . . social studies . . . music . . . language arts . . . mathematics . . . science . . . health and physical education . . . art" (Rillo, 1985).

Despite the evolution from predominantly skills and affect learning related to conservation to cognitive learning in most disciplines, a basic principle stated by Sharp (1957:ix) continues to guide outdoor education: "That which can best be learned inside the classroom should be learned there. That which can best be learned in the out-of-doors through direct experience, dealing with native materials and life situations, should there be learned."

Outdoor education continues to be an important part of the recreation profession. It is still tied closely to residential camps, but is also conducted in school yards, city parks, on farms, at local conservation areas, and many other outdoor settings. Facilities such as Bradford Woods at Indiana University and the Outdoor Laboratory (actually a series of residential camps and continuing education programs) at Clemson University illustrate the important role outdoor education can and should play in university-level education and scholarship as well as in direct programming.

REFERENCES

Blough, Glenn O. 1966. "Science and Outdoor Education or 'Nobody Can Really Know How I Feel.' " *Journal of Outdoor Education* 1(1):8–9, 12–14. An anecdotal essay on the potential for teaching science through outdoor education.
Donaldson, George W., and Goering, Oswald H. 1970. *Outdoor Education: A Synthesis.* Las Cruces, NM: Educational Resources Information Center and Clearinghouse on Rural Education and Small Schools. A brief monograph examining the nature and background of outdoor education.
Rillo, Thomas J. 1985. *Outdoor Education: Beyond the Classroom Walls,* Fastback monograph 232. Bloomington, IN: Phi Delta Kappa. A brief monograph focusing on methods in outdoor education and curriculum development.
Sharp, L. B. 1952. "What is Outdoor Education?" *The School Executive* 71(Aug.):19–22. An essay defining outdoor education by one of the originators of the concept.
Sharp, L. B. 1957. "Introduction." In *Outdoor Education for American Youth,* ed. Julian W. Smith. Washington, DC: American Association of Health, Physical Education, and Recreation. Discussion of the setting, role, and techniques of outdoor education.
Smith, Julian W., Carlson, Reynold, E., Donaldson, George W., and Masters, Hugh B. 1963. *Outdoor Education.* Englewood Cliffs, NJ: Prentice Hall. A dated but excellent introductory text on the principles and practices of outdoor education.
Wordsworth, William. 1982. *The Poetical Works of Wordsworth.* Boston: Houghton Mifflin. "The Tables Turned" is on page 83; the poem was originally published in 1798.

SOURCES OF ADDITIONAL INFORMATION

The literature on outdoor education is rarely "social science"; instead it tends to emphasize guidelines and motivational essays for teachers. Articles related to outdoor education may be found in *Journal of Environmental Education, Journal of Experiential Education, Journal of Outdoor Education,* and *The Outdoor Communicator.*

A collection of early writings on outdoor education is Donald Hammerman and William

Hammerman, eds., *Outdoor Education: A Book of Readings* (2nd edition, Minneapolis: Burgess, 1973). Alexander Gabrielson and Charles Holtzer, *The Role of Outdoor Education* (New York: Centre for Applied Research in Education, 1965) discusses the practice of outdoor education and its place in the curriculum. Another text with the same basic orientation is John Hug and Phyllis Wilson, *Curriculum Enrichment Outdoors* (New York: Harper & Row, 1965). Two more recent texts are Phyllis Ford, *Principles and Practices of Outdoor/Environmental Education* (New York: Wiley, 1981); and Michael Link, *Outdoor Education: A Manual for Teaching in Nature's Classroom* (Englewood Cliffs, NJ: Prentice Hall, 1981).

P

PAIDIA. The quality of improvisation and joy in games.

Paidia, based on the Greek word for child, is a term coined by Roger Caillois (1961) to describe one of two polar qualities of GAMES. Its opposite is LUDUS. In its pure form, it is the spirit of FUN, freedom, exuberance, and spontaneity in PLAY. Paidia is a primitive quality that presages the existence and acceptance of rules. As a quality in real games, it is present only in some degree and is tempered by the balancing qualities of ludus.

Together, paidia and ludus define the extremes of a spectrum of a fundamental game quality. Specific games can be first classified as one of four game types: AGON, ALEA, ILINX, OR MIMICRY; with each classification, games may be placed somewhere along the paidia/ludus continuum.

REFERENCES

Caillois, R. 1961. *Man, Play and Games*. New York: The Free Press. An important study of the sociology of games. Chapter 2 describes in detail Caillois's classification of games.

SOURCES OF ADDITIONAL INFORMATION

Some of Roger Caillois's ideas about play and games were first explored in his *Man and the Sacred* (New York: The Free Press, 1959). A classic study of play and games, which also greatly influenced Caillois, is Johan Huizinga, *Homo Ludens* (Boston: Beacon Press, 1955). Another, philosophically directed study of games and the spirit of game playing is David Miller, *Gods and Games* (New York: Harper Colophon, 1973).

PARK. A designated area of land and/or water set aside for recreational, aesthetic, educational, or cultural uses.

The concept of a park is one of the oldest in the history of civilization. Eden, identified in the Bible as the first home of Adam and Eve, is a Hebraic term meaning "place of delight and pleasure." The Hebrews had another word, *gan,* that referred to an enclosure or fence. The combination of *gan* and *eden* has given us the English word *garden*, a term that is closely linked to that of park.

The word *park* itself has its etymological roots running deep in European linguistic history. According to Partridge (1966), the modern term *park* comes from the Middle English *parke,* which was adapted from the French *parc. Parc,* in turn, appears to have derived from the Latin *parricus* and the primitive Teutonic *parruk*, all of which meant "a small enclosure or pen." Old High German has a parallel term in *pfarrick,* as did the Anglo-Saxons in *pearruc.*

Some authors have argued that the concept of a park may be traced back to at least the Sumerian civilization. Charles Doell and Louis Twardzik (1973), based on the work of M. L. Gothian (1928), and Paul Wilkinson (1983) have suggested that the Sumerian King, Gudea (c. 2400 B.C.), established designated open spaces that served both for hunting as well as for public FESTIVALS. Their views, however, are not unchallenged. Jack Wright (1983) disputes the evidence for designated public open space in Sumeria. Furthermore, he quotes the work of Paul Zucker (1959:26) that no pre-Hellenic civilizations had the concept of a park: "The Indian, Mesopotamian, and Egyptian civilizations did not provide the political, governmental, social, and—most important—psychological conditions which would create the need for such gathering places."

Wright, as well as Doell, Twardzik, and Wilkinson do agree that the Greeks, by at least the fifth century B.C., had firmly established the concept of public open space, viz., the agora. The agora as a designated, functional open space for public gathering is, to most authors, the beginning of the concept of a public park. Doell and Twardzik also suggest that the classical Greeks helped to establish the idea of more natural, rural parks through the planting of groves of trees around graveyards that became, in time, the locations of SPORT events held to honor the deceased.

The Roman civilization adopted the concept of the agora from the Greeks. The agora became the Roman forum, which was more formally defined and visually limited than the more open and casual agora. The Romans also expanded and refined the concept of private gardens as they transformed rural homes and escapes of nobility to comfortable villas. Over time, the villas increased in size and local importance—and their gardens grew to include private hunting preserves as well as private pleasuring grounds for socializing.

Through the Middle Ages, nobility attempted to retain control over private hunting reserves, while urban centers continued to feature market squares that were feeble imitations of the Roman forum. As Europe entered the Renaissance, public open market spaces became increasingly used for active recreation and sporting events (Doell and Twardzik, 1973). Public squares also were pressed into service as training grounds for local militia.

An immediate precursor of contemporary public parks in the United States was the commercial park that appeared in England in the eighteenth century. These private parks and gardens were often established in connection with taverns, resorts, and teahouses. They often featured zoological displays, plantings, and sometimes special events such as balloon launchings. They slowly died out, however, as public attitudes toward appropriate recreational activities changed, and as the notion of public parks became more widely accepted. The English public park in the eighteenth and nineteenth centuries included ample area for active recreation, especially lawn bowling, as well as irregular or "natural" plantings and gardens.

The Industrial Revolution in England and the United States created a greater sense of urgency in the expansion of public parks. Ranging from the small sand gardens in Boston to the ambitious formal parks such as Central Park in New York, public parks were created to help citizens satisfy the perceived NEED for RECREATION, exercise, and open space.

Throughout the twentieth century, parks have increased in number and diversity. As LaGasse (1974) noted, they are now expected to serve three mandates: (1) CONSERVATION of natural resources, (2) the development and protection of an aesthetically pleasing ENVIRONMENT plus the provision of opportunities for passive recreation and rest, and (3) the provision of opportunities for active recreation, PLAY, and sport. Several systems have been proposed to classify the various types of park designed to meet these different needs. Marion Clawson (1959), for example, proposed classifying parks in (1) user-oriented parks (e.g., urban parks), (2) intermediate parks (e.g., state and provincial parks), and (3) resource-based parks (e.g., NATIONAL PARKS). Park planners, however, found many parks that could not be classified according to this simple system. In 1962, the Outdoor Recreation Resources Review Commission (ORRRC) proposed a more sophisticated system involving six classes of parks: (1) high-density recreational areas, (2) general outdoor recreational areas, (3) natural environmental areas, (4) unique natural areas, (5) primitive areas, and (6) historical and cultural sites. This system is similar to the zoning classification system used by the province of Ontario for its provincial parks, with the exchange of the "high-density recreational areas" for a classification based on provincial waterways and canals.

More recently, Seymour Gold (1980) proposed another system: (1) play lots, (2) vest-pocket parks, (3) neighborhood parks, (4) district parks, (5) large urban parks, (6) regional parks, and (7) special areas. A main difference between the ORRRC classification and Gold's was that the former emphasized the "what" of a resource (its physical characteristics) while Gold emphasized the "where" (its size and proximity to the potential user population). Furthermore, Gold's system tends to work best for urban parks while the ORRRC system is more easily adapted to rural parks.

Today, the total number of formal and informal park classifications may approach a hundred or more. They include designated areas ranging from traditional national parks with a strong preservation mandate through highly commercial and developed theme and water parks. Although they are not the only location where recreation may occur, parks are both the most traditional venues for recreation and social contact as well as the most contemporary and dynamic of leisure settings.

REFERENCES

Clawson, Marion. 1959. *Land for Americans: Trends, Prospects, and Problems*. Baltimore: Johns Hopkins University Press. The first of a series of influential policy background reports by Resources for the Future; introduced a three-part classification for public open space based on locational characteristics.

Doell, Charles E., and Twardzik, Louis F. 1973. *Elements of Parks and Recreation Administration*, Ch. 3, 28–60. Minneapolis: Burgess. A sweeping history of parks from the earliest times to modern America; based largely on secondary sources—with some debatable observations.

Gold, Seymour. 1980. *Recreation Planning and Design,* 2nd edition. New York: McGraw-Hill. Focuses on issues of park design, layout, and user management issues.

Gothian, M. L. 1928. *A History of Garden Art,* 2 vols. New York: Dutton. An extensive and detailed history of gardens from ancient times through early twentieth century; includes material relevant to the history of parks as areas for passive recreation.

LaGasse, B. A. 1974. *History of Parks and Recreation*. Arlington, VA: National Recreation and Parks Association. A good reference source for basic historical information on the recreation and parks movement.

Outdoor Recreation Resources Review Commission. 1962. *Outdoor Recreation for America*. Washington, DC: U.S. Government Printing Office. The summary report by the commission, based on the history-making twenty-seven-volume report that was the first comprehensive look at outdoor recreation in America.

Partridge, Eric. 1966. *Origins: A Short Etymological Dictionary of Modern English*. London: Routledge and Kegan Paul. A useful dictionary for tracing the historical development of many English words.

Wilkinson, Paul. 1983. *Urban Open Space Planning*. Toronto: York University, Faculty of Environmental Studies Publication. Contains a brief history of parks (based on secondary sources) along with more extensive material on park design and planning issues.

Wright, Jack R. 1983. *Urban Parks in Ontario. Part 1, Origins to 1860*. Toronto: Ministry of Tourism and Recreation. The first of a two-part history on Ontario urban parks; written largely from a landscape architectural viewpoint.

Zucker, Paul. 1959. *Town and Square*. New York: Columbia University Press. An architectural history of public urban open space.

SOURCES OF ADDITIONAL INFORMATION

The literature on parks is quite extensive, and covers a wide variety of perspectives. A few respected sources, old and new, that address parks include the following. For national parks, an excellent introduction is Freeman Tilden's, *The National Parks: What They*

Mean to You and Me (New York: Knopf, 1959). A Canadian perspective is provided by the aptly named, *Canadian Parks in Perspective* by Gordon Nelson (Montreal: Harvest House, 1969). International perspectives may be found in the proceedings of the *First World Conference on National Parks,* edited by Alexander B. Adams (Washington, DC: U.S. Government Printing Office, 1962) and the proceedings of the *Second World Conference on National Parks,* edited by Sir Hugh Elliott (Morges, Switzerland: International Union for the Conservation of Nature and Natural Resources, 1974).

In addition to the planning and design texts listed in the references, one might consult Albert Rutledge, *Anatomy of a Park* (New York: McGraw-Hill, 1971). A number of contemporary park issues are discussed in the context of national outdoor recreation planning in *Americans Outdoors: The Report of the President's Commission* (Washington, DC: Island Press, 1987).

Further material on urban parks may be found in G. Cranz, "Changing Roles of Urban Parks: From Pleasure to Open Space" (*Landscape* 22 no. 3:9–18, 1978). Richard Kraus also covers the history of urban parks and their relationship to the urban recreation movement in *Recreation and Leisure in Modern Society* (3rd edition, Chicago: Scott, Foresman, 1984).

A scholarly study of one aspect of the history of parks in L. M. Cantor and J. Hatherly's "Medieval Parks of England" (*Geography* 642: 71–85, 1979).

PERCEIVED FREEDOM. The psychological sense of having freedom of choice in deciding on a behavior or set of actions.

The notion of freedom as an inherent part of LEISURE is virtually as old as the concept itself. As a term, leisure stems from the Latin *licere,* "to be permitted." Many modern conceptions of leisure include the notion of freedom as a prerequisite for the experience of leisure. Max Kaplan (1960) included the concept of psychological freedom along with five other concepts such as playfulness and pleasure expectation as part of the leisure experience. Through the 1970s, authors began to place more and more emphasis on the importance of the perception of freedom as essential to leisure. Stanley Parker (1971), for example, spoke of a tension between constraint and freedom in discussing the bipolar qualities of work and leisure. Jack Kelly (1972) developed a leisure paradigm in which leisure was based on "freely chosen" experiences as opposed to "determined" experiences that characterized other forms of human activity such as work. And in 1974, John Neulinger defined "true leisure" as a combination of perceived freedom and INTRINSIC MOTIVATION alone.

Neulinger (1974:15) defined perceived freedom as the "state in which the person feels that what he is doing, he is doing by choice and because he wants to do it." The key issue here is the sense of choice. The notion of equating perceived freedom with the experience of choice is well established in psychological literature. Bernard Weiner (1974) noted that operational definitions of freedom—in psychological research (not political science or philosophy)—are usually operationalized in terms of attributional theory. In other words, the sense of being free is associated with the perception that control over one's actions can be attributed to oneself. Psychologists interested in perceived freedom also use the term "locus of control" to refer to the question of whether an individual feels he is in control of his own life or is subject to control by others (Rotter, 1966; DeCharms, 1968; Lefcourt, 1976).

The issue of locus of control can be applied to specific experiences or circumstances, but it is often applied to one's general attitudes about life. According to Neulinger, (1974: 16) those individuals who tend to feel that their actions are controlled by others will be "less prepared for a situation as leisure." This observation was supported by research by A. J. Brok (1973) who noted that individuals whose scores on "locus of control" instruments indicated that they were "externals"—i.e., they felt that others had more control over them and their actions than they did themselves—were less likely to find leisure activities meaningful, enjoyable, and refreshing.

Brok's research, however, was based on a small sample of black community-college students who also held full-time jobs. Douglas Kleiber (1979) attempted to replicate Brok's work with a larger and more representative sample. Kleiber's results were contrary to those of Brok. Specifically, Kleiber found that "internals" valued leisure less than "externals." Part of the reason for these contrary findings, Kleiber suggested, could be that his sample of "internals" may have had very strong WORK ETHIC and achievement orientations. They took pride and satisfaction in their work, and were uncomfortable with spending much time in leisure.

Kleiber and Rick Crandall (1981) next attempted to clarify further the reasons for Kleiber's earlier contrary findings. Using a "work ethic instrument," they attempted to control for varying levels of the work ethic in their sample, before analyzing the relationship between locus of control and attitudes toward leisure. Even with this control, however, they failed to support the hypothesized relationship.

Roger Mannell and William Bradley (1986) conducted a set of laboratory experiments to further investigate the relationship between perceived freedom, locus of control, and their experience of leisure—characterized by the degree of psychological involvement in a leisure activity, or FLOW. They found tentative evidence that the perception of freedom did have a positive relationship with psychological involvement in a leisure activity under certain environmental conditions (i.e., more highly structured settings). Mannell and Bradley also noted, that there are, in fact, two general hypotheses about the relationship between freedom and leisure. The first is that the greater the degree of freedom of choice in a specific setting, the more likely participants will experience "leisure." The second hypothesis is that the stronger the sense an individual has control over his life (generally perceives an internal locus of control), the more likely he is to experience "leisure" in a given situation. Mannell and Bradley interpreted their results as supporting the second type of hypothesis but not the first.

William Harper (1986), in his philosophical review of freedom and the experience of leisure, has argued that the perception of freedom is not necessarily an antecedent for leisure, but is the result of leisure. Freedom to Harper

(1986:127) is not the experience of the power to make choices but an "intensification of ordinary experience." Harper (1986:122–123) argued, "Freedom is undergone in the experience of leisure; it is lived through and is not some kind of apprehended point of departure or arrival . . . [it] is an experience of ongoing consent."

The view of freedom as choice was noted earlier; Harper's view of freedom is one of consent rather than choice. "If leisure is the experience of ongoing consent, then our leisure can indeed be compelling." In other words, it may be the one true mark of the leisure experience, in comparison to the nonleisure experience, that we do not choose leisure at all. Geoffrey Godbey (1981) has briefly noted this subtle difference between the altogether voluntary (choosing) and consent (cooperating) when he noted that while "it is often said that leisure is 'voluntary,' it might be more accurate to say that leisure is behavior which draws us to something' " (Godbey, 1981:10).

It is not an original thought to observe that it is difficult to define or measure freedom. This is not an argument against academic attempts to do so; rather, it should merely serve to remind that any discussion about the relationship between freedom and leisure are particularly fraught with semantic and measurement complexities.

REFERENCES

Brok, A. J. 1973. "Free Time and Internal-External Locus of Control: Is Socialization for Freedom Dignified?" Paper presented at the American Psychological Association Convention, Montreal.

DeCharms, Richard. 1968. *Personal Causation: The Internal Effective Determinants of Behavior*. New York: Academic Press. A theoretical examination of the locus of control and other behavior concepts in psychology.

Godbey, Geoffrey. 1981. *Leisure in Your Life, An Exploration*. Philadelphia: Saunders. A popularly written book on the importance of leisure to ordinary people.

Harper, William. 1986. "Freedom in the Experience of Leisure." *Leisure Sciences* 8:115–139. A philosophical examination of freedom and leisure; challenges the notion that freedom is an antecedent of leisure.

Kaplan, Max. 1960. *Leisure in America: A Social Inquiry*. New York: Wiley. A sociological examination of leisure in the United States; includes a brief discussion of the psychological characteristics of leisure.

Kelly, John R. 1972. "Work and Leisure: A Simplified Paradigm." *Journal of Leisure Research* 4:50–62. Presents a model of leisure in which perceived freedom is a key feature.

Kleiber, Douglas. 1979. "Fate Control and Leisure Attitudes." *Leisure Sciences* 2:239–248. A test of the relationship between perceived locus of control and attitudes toward leisure; results failed to support hypothesized relationship.

Kleiber, Douglas A., and Crandall, Rick. 1981. "Leisure and Work Ethics and Locus of Control." *Leisure Sciences* 4:477–485. A replication of Kleiber's 1979 work, with an attempt to control for "work ethic"; results were still ambiguous.

Lefcourt, Herbert M. 1976. *Locus of Control: Current Trends in Theory and Research.* New York: Wiley. A good, extensive discussion of the concept.

Mannell, Roger C., and Bradley, William. 1986. "Does Greater Freedom Always Lead to Greater Leisure? Testing a Person × Environment Model of Freedom and Leisure." *Journal of Leisure Research* 18: 215–230. The authors test the relationship between perceived freedom and the psychological involvement in a leisure activity in a laboratory setting; they find mixed results.

Neulinger, John. 1974. *The Psychology of Leisure.* Springfield, IL: Charles C. Thomas. Another paradigm of leisure in which perceived freedom is a central element.

Parker, Stanley. 1971. *The Future of Work and Leisure.* New York: Praeger. A sociological examination of leisure trends by a British academic; includes a "freedom-based" model of leisure.

Rotter, Julian B. 1966. "Generalized Expectancies for Internal Versus External Control of Reinforcement." *Psychological Monographs* 80:1–28. One of the early discussions of the concept of locus of control as a personality characteristic; includes an instrument for measuring locus of control.

Weiner, Bernard (compiler). 1974. *Achievement Motivation and Attribution Theory.* Morristown, NJ: General Learning Press. Discusses locus of control; noted that individuals with an internal locus of control enjoyed leisure activities and experiences more than those with an external locus of control.

SOURCES OF ADDITIONAL INFORMATION

Gary Ellis and Peter Witt identify some measurement techniques and issues in "The Measurement of Perceived Freedom in Leisure" (*Journal of Leisure Research* 16:110–123, 1984). Seppo Iso-Ahola has written several articles on perceived freedom; much of his work is summarized in his textbook, *The Social Psychology of Leisure and Recreation* (Dubuque, IA: William C. Brown, 1980). He also related perceived freedom to the concept of SUBSTITUTABILITY in "A Theory of Substitutability of Leisure Behavior" (*Leisure Sciences* 8:367–389, 1986).

PLAY. A pleasurable, intrinsically motivated, voluntary, and repetitive or patterned activity that is separate in time from other activities, and is governed by either implicit or explicit rules.

The term *play* like the closely related GAME and SPORT, is ambiguous. As a verb, it may refer to (1) participating in a game (2) performing on a musical instrument, (3) teasing, (4) the reflection of light off water, or (5) handling an object carelessly or absentmindedly. As a noun, it refers to (1) pleasurable, voluntary activities, (2) a set of actions completed as one step in a game; or (3) a dramatic production. Such ambiguity reflects the pervasiveness of play as a general concept in Western thought. As a form of RECREATION or LEISURE, it is probably universal among all human societies. It is also a characteristic of some higher mammalian, non-human species. Karl Groos (1901) was one of the first scholars to draw an explicit parallel between animal and human play as essentially the same non-purposeful, nonserious physical activity. Luther Gulick (1972), also writing around the turn of the century, identified seven key features of animal play, most of which pertain to human play, as well:

1. Play begins very early in the life of an individual.
2. The complexity of play forms appears to be directly related to the intelligence of the species.
3. Each species has distinctive play forms.
4. Play contributes to the long-term growth and physical coordination of the individual.
5. Individuals appear to play because they enjoy it.
6. Play usually involves a series of steps or regular sequence of specific actions.
7. Individuals appear to teach or influence other individuals in their play.

With respect to human play, intellectuals first examined play as a philosophical or religious topic; this perspective continued to be the dominant view until the twentieth century. An excellent brief history of this perspective is found in David Miller (1973). Portions of the following discussion are drawn from his scholarship.

One of the first Western philosophers to discuss play was Heraclitus (c. 535–470 B.C.) of Ephesus. D. Miller (1973:102) quotes an aphorism attributed to Heraclitus, "TIME is a child playing, moving counters on a game board." In attempting to unravel this bit of wordplay, D. Miller recalls a story told by Diogenes Laërtius about Heraclitus. When asked to accept a position of responsibility in his city-state's government, Heraclitus replied that it would be better for him to play knucklebones with the children of Ephesus. The context of this story was that Heraclitus considered the act of playing to be more virtuous than the act of governing. Frederick Nietzsche (1965), who was also interested in Heraclitus's enigma, recalled that the followers of Dionysus, active in sixth-century B.C. Ephesus, usually pictured their god as a child playing. If Heraclitus's use of the word *time* meant "eternity" (or, as D. Miller suggests, "the kingdom" as in "the kingdom of God"), Heraclitus could be viewed as suggesting play should be an ideal for the proper life. As the gods play, so should man. A basic point in Heraclitus's view was that there was no necessary dichotomy between play and the serious aspects of life.

This unity of play with certain serious aspects of life is also found in isolated texts of the Old Testament. The best known, of course, is the Garden of Eden, where Adam and Eve lived in a primal playground. Their sin drove them out of the garden and into a world of suffering, strife, death—and work. D. Miller (1973) also cites 2 Samuel 11:14, in which the sons of Abner are called on to join in "play" (i.e., a war). Again, the point here is that many early philosophers or religious thinkers saw no necessary dichotomy between play and seriousness. Although this dichotomy is now a normal way of thinking for us, most contemporary individuals still experience events that are simultaneously serious and playful. Sexual play is probably the most personal. Certain athletic events and the creation of art forms are other examples. Seriousness, in the context of play, does not imply grimness, imposed duty, or heaviness of spirit. It more properly means "importance" or "highly valued."

The dichotomy between play and seriousness probably began with Plato. In his *Sixth Letter,* Plato advises his pupils to "live the life of philosophy . . . in gentlemanly earnest, but with the playfulness that is the sister of solemnity" (quoted in D. Miller, 1973:105). Elsewhere, in *Laws,* in the middle of a discussion of play Plato urges, "every man and woman should walk seriously" (quoted in D. Miller, 1973:106). Plato values play, but sees it subordinate to the weighty matters of philosophy.

Aristotle, Plato's student, pushed the point further. In *Ethics,* Aristotle commanded, "Play so that you may be serious" and judged that, "serious things are intrinsically better than funny or amusing things" (quoted in D. Miller, 1973:107). Again, play was second fiddle to philosophy.

Early Catholic theologians opened wide the crack between play and seriousness. Living in a period in which human survival as well as the survival of the Catholic faith was perilous, play and frivolity were seen as threats to their very existence. Saint Ambrose often quoted Luke 6:25, "Alas for you who laugh now, for you shall mourn and weep." In one of Saint Chrysostom's sermons, he writes, "This world is not a theatre in which we can laugh; and we are not assembled together in order to burst into peals of laughter, but to weep for our sins. But some of you still want to say, 'I would prefer God to give me the chance to go on laughing and joking.' Is there anything more childish than thinking in this way? It is not God who gives us the chance to play, but the devil" (quoted in Rahner, 1967:98). The examples could be repeated hundreds of times, but the message is consistent: the Church was against play. The forcefulness and frequency of the warnings, however, suggests that the laity generally refused to live their lives with the level of seriousness and grimness the theologians felt appropriate.

Play continued in official bad graces during the Middle Ages, the Renaissance, the Reformation, and the so-called Age of Enlightenment. However, despite periodic attempts by the Church or state to crack down on people enjoying themselves, play also continued as a vital part of the lives of nonreligious and nonacademic people. Johan Huizinga (1955), for example, was inspired to write *Homo Ludens* by his observations of the persistence of play forms throughout the difficult times of the Middle Ages. A spirit of play infused social events, literature, art, music, and even serious matters such as law and war well into the Renaissance and even later.

In the nineteenth century, partially in response to the rise of extreme forms of rationalism—exemplified by the philosophy of Descartes in the seventeenth century—some philosophers began to explore new realms of thinking and experience. They were, in particular, interested in questions of aesthetics. One of the leaders of this movement was Johan Christoph Friedrich von Schiller (1954), who considered the implications of placing aesthetics, rather than pure reason, at the center of one's philosophical system. Noting that the poiesis (the art of creation of an art form) gave meaning and significance to the art form, Schiller wondered whether a better understanding of the driving power behind poiesis could provide insights into the search for meaning and significance in human life. The search for this answer led Schiller to rediscover play.

According to D. Miller (1973), Schiller believed that human life was difficult because man was called on to imitate divine ideals of Law, Charity, Duty, Mercy, Love, and so on. However, imitation in life is never as good, complete, or satisfying as the real thing. Thus MIMICRY as a serious activity is bound to frustrate. But mimicry as a play form could be successful. Through play, man could reach his ideals; seriousness and nonseriousness could be reconciled; the act of being and the meaning of being become one (Schiller, 1954). Nietzsche furthered Schiller's ideas by explicitly tying them to human consciousness. Nietzsche invoked the myths of Apollo and Dionysus to represent the conflicting philosophies of rationality and feeling (Smith, 1978). Through play, these philosophies could be reconciled, made one. As Nietzsche (1965:65) put it, "I know of no other manner of dealing with great tasks than as play; this, as a sign of greatness, is an essential pre-requisite." Nietzsche brought philosophers full circle to Heraclitus (D. Miller, 1973:115).

In the twentieth century, some philosophers are still interested in play, and tend to treat it sympathetically (Suits, 1978). However, most of the work on play in this century is no longer found in the humanities but in the social sciences. This shift is more than just a shift in disciplinary perspective. It represents a change in the nature of the questions scholars identify as important. Whereas philosophers and theologians ask, "Is play good?" social scientists ask, "What is play good for."

A dozen or more separate theories have been proposed to explain what play is good for. Gene Bammel and Lei Lane Burrus-Bammel (1982) provide a useful overview of these theories. They group the earliest explanations as "biological theories." Biological theories include the surplus energy theory [play is a safety valve for pent-up energy (Spencer, 1896)], the relaxation theory [play helps people recover from fatigue (Patrick, 1916)], the preexercise theory [play prepares children for adult roles (Groos, 1901)], and the recapitulation theory [children's play represents the inheritance of physical skills we received from our animal ancestors, e.g., tree climbing from monkeys (Gulick, 1902)].

These theories were eventually replaced by a set that Bammel and Burrus-Bammel label "environmental theories." Here the emphasis is on the role of external causes in shaping the desire to play, rather than on instinctual or biological causes. Two main theories from this set are Clark Hull's (1984) stimulus-response hypothesis and Sigmund Freud's (1955) psychoanalytic model. Hull believed that children were taught to play through a complex series of rewards given for participation in play: attention, praise, recognition, status, and so on.

Freud, on the other hand, felt that children naturally turned to play to relieve emotional problems and to release frustration resulting from pent-up, immature sexual urges.

A third set of theories is grouped by Bammel and Burrus-Bammel into a group called cognitive theories. The common theme here is that play is seen as a function of information-processing. Jean Piaget (1962) developed an influential model of play as a part of this larger model of childhood development. The child begins at birth in the "sensory-motor stage," and then progresses through three other stages of development. Each stage has a distinctive set of play forms that helps the child's cognitive growth:

Cognitive Stage	Play Forms	Approximate Age
Sensory-motor	Kinetic skill and physical activity	Birth to two years
Preoperational	Symbolic play	Two to seven years
Concrete operational	Games with rules	Seven to eleven years
Mature cognition	Creative and fantasy play	Eleven years and up

Another influential cognitive theory is that play is the seeking of OPTIMAL AROUSAL. This work began with psychologists such as Ivan Pavlov (1927) and D. E. Berlyne (1960) and has more recently been advocated by Michael Ellis (1973).

Most of the works of the authors cited above do not focus directly on play definitions. They examine, instead, its merits or purposes. Numerous definitions, however, may be found in the literature. A typical definition is that of John Loy, Barry McPherson, and Gerry Kenyon (1978:5), "Play is an activity that is free, separate, uncertain, unproductive, governed by rules, and characterized by make-believe." This definition contains many of the same qualities Huizinga used in defining his conception of play: play is a voluntary action; it is (implicitly) fun; it has rules; it is confined to particular times and places; it is distinct from ordinary life. Brian Vandenburg (1982) agrees with the emphasis on the lack of productivity and the absence of an extrinsic goal. The essence of play, to him, is that the means dominate the ends. Bammel and Burrus-Bammel (1982:42) also describe play as an end in itself, self-contained, with the only reward the immediate satisfaction of participation.

Numerous other authors, of course, focused on the contributions of play to life. Certainly the social scientists cited previously (e.g., Ellis and Piaget) saw play serving important functions. Brian Sutton-Smith (1967) saw play as a force for SOCIALIZATION, while Jerome Bruner (1975) felt that play promoted creativity and originality.

Mihaly Csikszentmihalyi (1979) noted the apparent paradox between definitions of play that emphasize its autotelic (INTRINSIC MOTIVATION) quality, and the definitions that emphasize the benefits play provides. He was not the first author to observe the paradox. Groos (1901) also saw it, and suggested that the resolution lay in the fact that while the consequences of play are real and beneficial, the content and context of play were unreal. Groos's explanation has long been accepted by other authors. Stephen Miller (1973:26), for example, reiterated that play offered a safe, protected environment for experimentation—"buffered learning" in his jargon.

Csikszentmihalyi, however, challenged this view. Based on his interviews with numerous vocational and avocational groups as part of his research into FLOW, he concluded Groos's solution is too simplistic. Rock climbers, for example (one of the groups Csikszentmihalyi studied), view their activity as play, but are also keenly aware that their play—its context and content—is very real and potentially fatal. They perceive the risk but value it as part of their experience. Stock market investors play the market much as professional gamblers play their games for real financial payoffs. Elsewhere, Csikszentmihalyi (1975) cited reports by some workers that they considered their jobs as a suspension of reality, allowing them to escape problems at home or as interruptions from their real lives with family and friends. This type of interruption or suspension of reality has traditionally been assigned as a role of play, yet here it is an aspect of work.

The solution of the paradox, in Csikszentmihalyi's view, is that the different authors have fundamentally noncomparable perspectives on play. Social scientists interested in the result of play emphasize the action of play; others who emphasize the subjective qualities of play focus on the experience of play—on playfulness. "Play ultimately is a state of subjective experience. Play can only exist where there is awareness of alternatives: of two sets of goals and rules, one operating here and now, one that applies outside the given activity. . . . We play when we know we are playing" (Csikszentmihalyi, 1975:19–20). This view is a virtual extension of Huizinga's views about play and GAMES. Play is not defined by the content of the activity but by the experience of the player. "An activity is not play because it suspends or evades the rules of reality, but because the player freely accepts the goals and rules that constrain his or her actions, knowing full well that he or she need not do so" (Csikszentmihalyi, 1975:20).

REFERENCES

Bammel, Gene, and Burrus-Bammel, Lei Lane. 1982. *Leisure and Human Behavior*. Dubuque, IA: William C. Brown. An introductory text of the social psychology of leisure; includes a useful summary of theories of play.

Berlyne, D. E. 1960. *Conflict, Arousal, and Curiosity*. New York: McGraw-Hill. A major study into the origins of a wide variety of animal behavior; provided the base for subsequent research into the reticulate arousal system and the concept of optimal arousal.

Bruner, Jerome S. 1975. "Play is Serious Business." *Psychology Today*, Jan., 81–83. A popularly written article noting the benefits of play, particularly its contributions to creativity.

Csikszentmihalyi, Mihaly. 1975. *Beyond Boredom and Anxiety*. San Francisco: Jossey-Bass. Introduces the concept of flow as a subjective state in which the challenge of a task and the individual's skills are in balance, resulting in a pleasurable feeling; notes flow is attained by play or work.

Csikszentmihalyi, Mihaly. 1979. "Some Paradoxes in the Definition of Play." In *Play as Context: Proceedings of the Annual Meeting of the Association for the Anthropological Study of Play*, ed. Alyce Taylor Cheska, 14–25. West Point, NY: Leisure Press. Identifies a problem in various definitions of play—some authors see play as offering benefits, others that play is intrinsically motivated; proposes a possible resolution.

Ellis, Michael J. 1973. *Why People Play*. Englewood Cliffs, NJ: Prentice Hall. An excellent review of theories of play; presents an argument for defining play in terms of optimal arousal theory.

Freud, Sigmund. 1955. "Beyond the Pleasure Principle." In *The Standard Edition of the Complete Psychological Works of S. Freud, 1920–1922*, Vol. 18, ed. and trans. James Strachey, 7–66. London: Hogarth and the Institute of Psychoanalysis. Presents a theory for the occurrence of play based on psychoanalytic principals: play as a form of catharsis.

Groos, Karl. 1901. *The Play of Man*, trans. E. L. Baldwein. New York: Appleton. An early inquiry into the nature of play, with special attention given to comparisons between the play of animals and of humans.

Gulick, Luther H. 1902. "Interest in Relation to Muscular Exercise." *American Physical Education Review* 7:52–65. Argued that popularity of various play forms is linked to the history of the human race.

Gulick, Luther H. 1972. *A Philosophy of Play*. Washington, DC: McGrath. A reprint of another early study on the nature of play that compares human and animal play forms.

Huizinga, Johan. 1955. *Homo Ludens: A Study of the Play Element in Culture*. Boston: Beacon Press. One of the classic cultural studies of the nature of play.

Hull, Clark L. 1984. "S-R Analyses of Cognitive Processes." In *Mechanisms of Adaptive Behavior: Clark Hull's Theoretical Papers*, ed. Abram Amsel and Michael Rashotte, 34–44. New York: Columbia University Press. A collection of papers on stimulus-response (S-R) theories of behavior; interprets play as just one version of S-R behavior.

Loy, John W., McPherson, Barry D., and Kenyon, Gerry. 1978. *Sport and Social Systems: A Guide to the Analysis, Problems, and Literature*. Reading, MA: Addison-Wesley. A comprehensive look at the sociology of sport; includes a discussion of play and games as part of the background material.

Miller, David L. 1973. *Gods and Games: Toward a Theology of Play*. New York: Harper Colophon. Explores the theological and philosophical significance of play; especially good historical overviews of the development of the play concept.

Miller, Stephen. 1973. "Ends, Means, and Galumphing: Some Leitmotifs of Play." *American Anthropologist* 75:87–98. Considers two questions: (1) Is play a single, coherent category of play? and (2) What is the evolutionary basis of play?

Nietzsche, Friedrich. 1965. *Ecce Homo*, no. 10. In *The Philosophy of Nietzsche*, ed. Geoffrey Clive. New York: New American Library, Mentor Books. One of Nietzsche's essays on the nature of the human experience; includes a discussion

of the role of play in synthesizing the "Apollonian" and "Dionysian" personalities.

Patrick, George T. W. 1916. *The Psychology of Relaxation*. Boston: Houghton Mifflin. Viewed play as a restorative action; also suggests play is instinctive.

Pavlov, Ivan P. 1927. *Conditioned Reflexes*, trans. G. V. Anrep. Oxford: Clarendon Press. Pavlov's classic work on animal reflexes; includes speculation that animal exploratory behavior is also a reflex.

Piaget, Jean. 1962. *Play, Dreams, and Imitation in Childhood*, trans. C. Gattegno and F. N. Hodgson. New York: Norton. Presents Piaget's cognitive developmental theory linking play forms of intellectual growth in children; has played a major role in the shaping of preschool curricula in the United States and other countries.

Rahner, Hugo. 1967. *Man at Play*. New York: Herder and Herder. A scholarly study on philosophical aspects of human play; includes extensive discussion of religious attitudes toward play.

Schiller, Johann Christoph Fredrich von. 1954. *On the Aesthetic Education of Man*, trans. R. Snell. London: Routledge and Kegan Paul. An important but difficult work on the role of aesthetics in human life; links appreciation of the play spirit with artistic creativity and appreciation.

Smith, Stephen L. J. 1978. "Image and Intuition in Leisure Studies." *Recreation Research Review* 6(1):15–22. Introduces the archetypes of Apollonian and Dionysian personalities and discusses their relationship to leisure.

Spenser, Herbert. 1896. *Principles of Psychology*, Vol. 2, Pt. 2, 3rd edition. New York: Appleton. Reports a common nineteenth-century idea: children and animals play to relieve excess energy; some of his ideas presaged optimal arousal theory.

Suits, Bernard. 1978. *The Grasshopper: Games, Life, and Utopia*. Toronto: University of Toronto Press. A retelling of the fable of the ant and the grasshopper, in the style of a Platonic dialogue, with the grasshopper arguing for the importance of play and games in life.

Sutton-Smith, Brian. 1967. "The Role of Play in Cognitive Development," *Young Children* 22:361–370. Discusses ideas about the role of play in childhood growth.

Vandenberg, Brian. 1982. "Play: A Concept in Need of a Definition?" In *The Play of Children: Current Theory and Research*, ed. Debra J. Pepler and Kenneth H. Rubin, 15–20. New York: Karger. Discussion of problems of defining play; suggests reasons for difficulties stem from the epistemologies used to study play.

SOURCES OF ADDITIONAL INFORMATION

The literature on play, as one would expect, is quite large and written from a number of different perspectives. One useful general source of material that is predominantly sociological/anthropological in bent are the proceedings of the annual meetings of the Association for the Anthropological Study of Play. H. B. Schwartzman has also written from an anthropological perspective in *Transformations: The Anthropology of Children's Play* (New York: Plenum, 1978).

Some psychologically oriented references include Jerome Burner, Alison Jolly, and Kathy Sylva, eds., *Play: Its Role in Development and Evolution* (New York: Basic Books, 1976); Lynn Barnett, "Young Children's Resolution of Distress through Play" (*Journal of Child Psychology and Psychiatry* 25:477–483, 1984); L. Barnett and B. Storm, "Play, Pleasure, and Pain: The Reduction of Anxiety through Play" (*Leisure Sciences* 4:161–

175, 1981); and the dated but still-relevant Gregory Bateson, "A Theory of Play and Fantasy" (*Psychiatric Research Reports* 2:39–51, 1955).

The symbolic meaning of play is examined in a collection of readings by I. Bretherton, *Symbolic Play: The Development of Social Understanding* (New York: Academic Press, 1984). Some biological issues are studied in P. K. Smith, "Does Play Matter? Functional and Evolutionary Aspects of Animal and Human Play" (*Behavioral and Brain Sciences* 5:139–184, 1982). The play of animals is covered in R. Fagen, *Animal Play Behavior* (London: Oxford University Press, 1981).

A useful review article on theories of play is Lynn Barnett, "Theorizing about Play: Critique and Direction" (*Leisure Sciences* 1:113–130, 1978). This article has a good bibliography for still more references.

PRODUCT LIFE CYCLE. A hypothetical model describing the expected changes in unit sales, market share, or other competitive measures of some RECREATION commodity from its introduction to its removal from the market or leisure service program.

The product life cycle became a popular model in recreation and leisure studies during the 1980s for describing the public acceptance of some recreation or TOURISM commodity. The original articulation of the concept, however, dates from at least 1950. Joel Dean (1950) is usually credited with introducing the concept in the business literature as a guide for pricing new products. William Cox, Jr. (1967) further elaborated the concept and extended it to broader marketing issues. Since then the concept has enjoyed substantial popularity in the business literature.

The classic model of the product life cycle is roughly a bell-shaped curve, with the vertical axis representing unit sales and the horizontal axis representing time. The curve is subdivided into a number of segments. The left-hand tail is associated with the introduction of the product. This period is characterized by very low but increasing sales immediately after release of the product. The curve then increases its slope, reflecting rapidly growing sales in the take-off stage of product life. As the curve begins to flatten out, with sales rising but at a decreasing rate, the market is said to become mature. Near the peak of the curve, the slope is nearly flat, representing high but stable sales or saturation. This is then followed by a negatively sloping line, representing declining sales. Once decline has set in, the producer must prepare to remove the commodity from the market or program or initiate some marketing effort to bring about rejuvenation.

A number of variations on the basic model have been used in the recreation and tourism literature. John Crompton, Ian Reid, and Muzaffer Uysal (1987) used a measure of market share for municipal recreation services, while Richard Butler (1980) used raw numbers of TOURISTS arriving in a tourist area or REGION.

Research on the product life cycle includes its application to various types of service, such as Crompton and Sharon Bonk's (1978) analysis of public library services and Butler's (1980) modeling of the tourist area cycle of evolution. Crompton, Reid, and Uysal (1987) exemplify another common line of research:

the empirical validation of the concept (in their case, in a municipal recreation setting). Geoffrey Wall (1982) explored some of the theoretical implications of the concept and has observed a possible contradiction with the notion of CARRYING CAPACITY. The concept is rarely used as an empirical forecasting tool, although Michael Haywood (1986) did describe some methodological and conceptual issues that have to be resolved for the use of the life cycle in forecasting.

Although the concept's name implies the existence of basically one traditional cycle (the bell-shaped curve described previously), Cornelius Kluyer (1977) identified fifteen distinct shapes for different types of product. Crompton, Reid, and Uysal (1987) found that different municipal recreation and parks departments displayed six of these fifteen curves. Given the lack of consistency in the selection of measurement of a product's public acceptance as well as the empirical evidence that a large number of fundamentally different types of curve appear to exist, the concept may have relatively little long-term value as a coherent theory. Its most enduring contribution may have been to help focus attention on the fact that researchers, planners, and marketing analysts need to have a historical or evolutionary perspective in studying the public DEMAND for any commodity.

REFERENCES

Butler, Richard W. 1980. "The Concept of a Tourism Area Cycle of Evolution: Implications for Management of Resources." *The Canadian Geographer* 24:5–16.

Crompton, John L., and Bonk, Sharon. 1978. "An Empirical Investigation of the Appropriateness of the Product Life-Cycle to Municipal Library Services." *Journal of the Academy of Marketing Science* 6:77–90. An example of how the concept may be applied to the public consumption of a nonmarket good.

Crompton, John L., Reid, Ian S., and Uysal, Muzaffer. 1987. "Empirical Identification of Product Life-Cycle Patterns in the Delivery of Municipal Park and Recreation Services." *Journal of Park and Recreation Administration* 5:17–34. A good review of the concept; finds evidence for six distinct product life cycles in municipal leisure services.

Cox, Jr., William. 1967. "Product Life Cycles as Marketing Models." *Journal of Business* 40:374–384. One of the first discussions of the product life cycle as a marketing tool.

Dean, Joel. 1950. "Pricing Policies for New Products." *Harvard Business Review* 28(Nov.–Dec.):45–54. Probably the first major statement of the concept; presented in the context of pricing strategies.

Haywood, K. Michael. 1986. "Can the Tourist-Area Life Cycle Be Made Operational?" *Tourism Management* 7:154–167. Reviews methodological, conceptual, and measurement issues of the concept, with particular attention to its application in tourism.

Kluyver, Cornelius. 1977. "Innovation and Industrial Product Life Cycles." *California Management Review* 20(Fall):21–33. Empirically identifies fifteen types of product life cycle.

Wall, Geoffrey. 1982. "Cycles and Capacity: Incipient Theory or Conceptual Contradiction?" *Tourism Management* 3:188–192. Argues that the product life cycle and the notion of carrying capacity are in contradiction with each other.

SOURCES OF ADDITIONAL INFORMATION
Gerald V. Hovinen explored evidence for the existence of a product life cycle in "A Tourist Cycle in Lancaster County, Pennsylvania" (*Canadian Geographer* 25:283–286, 1981) as did Klaus Meyer-Arendt in "The Grand Isle, Louisiana Resort Cycle" (*Annals of Tourism Research* 12:449–465, 1985). An excellent, general review of the concept is David Rink and John Swan, "Product Life Cycle Research: A Literature Review" (*Journal of Business Research* Sept.:219–245, 1979). A "devil's advocate" perspective is presented by Nariman Dhalla and Sonia Yuspeh, "Forget the Product Life Cycle Concept!" (*Harvard Business Review* 54 Jan.–Feb.:102–112, 1976).

PSYCHOCENTRIC. A category of TOURISTS characterized by a strong preference for the familiar and commonplace in TOURISM destinations.

Psychocentric tourists were first described by that name by Stanley Plog (1974) as part of a study into the motivation and barriers that affected the DEMAND for airline travel. Plog suggested that tourists could be placed on a spectrum ranging from ALLOCENTRICS to psychocentrics, with intermediate groups known as near-allocentric, mid-centric, and near-psychocentric.

The primary characteristics of psychocentrics include

1. A preference for familiar, well-developed tourist destinations.
2. Desire for relaxation, shopping, sunbathing in vacations.
3. Special concern for family-type restaurants, full-service hotels or resorts.
4. Prefer associating with people with backgrounds similar to themselves.
5. Seek complete tour packaging, including scheduling of activities and social events.

Plog further elaborates his allocentric/psychocentric model by suggesting that tourism destinations begin by being discovered by allocentrics. Their enthusiasm for a new destination slowly builds the destination's reputation, so that they become increasingly fashionable destinations. This leads, then, to an expansion of the tourism infrastructure and services at that destination, accompanied by a growth in the number of near-allocentrics that are attracted. As the destination matures, with increasing commercialization and mass marketing, the area draws more mid-centrics and some near-psychocentrics. The allocentrics, who discovered the destination, have lost interest or been repelled by the changing nature of the destination and have moved on to other areas. The process of evolution continues until the destination area appeals only to the most conservative and cautious tourists, the psychocentrics.

Plog further suggests that the number of tourists belonging to each category on the allocentric/psychocentric spectrum approximates a normal distribution. Only a small percentage of tourists are either allocentrics or psychocentrics, while a greater number are near-allocentrics and near-psychocentrics. The largest number are the mid-centrics. This aspect of Plog's model resembles Everett Rogers's (1962) model of product adoption (a version of the PRODUCT LIFE

CYCLE). Rogers's model is also approximately a normal curve with a small number of " innovators" and "laggards" on the extreme ends. "Early adopters," "early majority," and "late majority" make up the central part of the curve. One of the differences between Plog's curve and Rogers's curve is that Plog's model is explicitly based on personality and psychological traits while Rogers's model is based only on the timing of product adoption. Conceptually, though, Rogers's adoption groups are shaped by psychological differences and, as noted, Plog's psychological groupings imply the relative order of adoption of destinations as tourism products. Both models, therefore, may be viewed as different aspects of a more general model of commodity adoption and diffusion.

REFERENCES

Plog, Stanley C. 1974. "Why Destination Areas Rise and Fall in Popularity." *Cornell Hotel and Restaurant Administration Quarterly* 14(4):13–16. The original reference for the concept of psychocentrics.

Rogers, Everett M. 1962. *Diffusion and Innovation.* New York: Free Press of Glencoe. Presents a model of consumers based on a continuum running from innovators to laggards.

SOURCES OF ADDITIONAL INFORMATION

Robert McIntosh and Charles Goeldner provide a good discussion of the concept in *Tourism: Principle, Practices, Philosophies* (New York: Wiley, 1986, 135–141). Stephen Smith describes an empirical test of Plog's model in "A Test of Plog's Allocentric/ Psychocentric Model: Evidence from Seven Nations" (*Journal of Travel Research,* 24 no. 4: 40–42, 1990).

PUBLIC GOODS. That group of commodities that (1) may be equally and jointly consumed by any number of individuals without adversely affecting each other's consumption and (2) cannot be withheld from any potential consumer in the relevant market.

Goods (and services) may be classified as either private or public. Private goods are those that can be consumed by only one individual or group at a time and which can be withheld from people who do not wish to pay for them. Most marketplace goods, whether food, shelter, transportation, clothing, amusements, or utilities are private goods. A unit of any one of these can be consumed by only one person or group at a time, and/or can be withheld from people who are not willing to pay for consumption.

Public goods (also known as social goods or collective consumption goods), on the other hand, are characterized by joint consumption and nonexclusivity. Traditional examples of public goods include public open space, national defense, and lighthouses. Once these are provided, all members of the relevant community, REGION, or nation is equally served by them.

Public goods may or may not have EXTERNALITIES, and may or may not be merit goods. Merit goods are those goods that are produced and allocated by the public sector because of a political judgment that all people should have access to them for reasons of EQUITY. Not all public goods are necessarily merit goods, and not all merit goods are necessarily public goods. This distinction is sometimes muddied because both public goods and merit goods are offered by the public sector.

Modern theories of public goods date from Paul Samuelson's (1964) landmark study, "Pure Theory of Public Expenditures." Samuelson was interested in the problem of how an economy should optimally allocate resources for the production of a mix of public and private goods. He viewed the search for this optimal allocation—the "bliss point" in his terminology—as an extension of Pareto optimality. (Pareto optimality is a guideline or principle for RESOURCE allocation: resources should be allocated in such a way that all involved parties are made better off, and no one is made worse off.)

Samuelson's early work on public goods and expenditures is still recognized as an elegant and significant contribution to the study of public finance. It is also viewed by some authors as having very restricted practical application due to the fact that public goods probably do not exist (Lancaster, 1976). While some goods, such as our examples of public open space, national defense, and lighthouses approximate the definition of a public good, they fall short of complete adherence to the definition. For example, public open space could technically be fenced off so that access was possible only through an admission gate at which a fee was collected. National defense, in the abstract sense, may come close to being a pure public good, but actual military bases and installations are not. The presence of a military base in a community may significantly increase the risk of attack at that community in the event of war. Very strong defensive weapons surrounding Washington, D.C., for example, may cause an attacking force to select an alternative target. In such a case, national defense systems do not equally protect all regions of the country.

The service offered by lighthouses comes close to the criteria inherent in pure public goods, but lighthouse protection is of relevance to only a very small group of individuals. Some economists suggest, therefore, that services such as lighthouses may be more accurately described as "clublike" services than public services (Buchanan, 1965).

Although most scholars admit that few, if any, goods fully meet the strict criteria associated with the definition of a public good, they also recognize that some goods—including many in RECREATION, LEISURE, and CULTURE—approximate public goods. These goods are termed, therefore, "impure public" or mixed goods.

Whether one is studying pure or impure public goods, important questions to be answered include

1. How is the DEMAND for public goods to be determined?
2. How is the VALUE of public goods to be estimated?

3. What mix and what quantity of public goods would be produced?

4. How are public goods to be produced and who is going to pay for them?

These questions are also central to the study of the production and allocation of private goods, of course. The search for answers has attracted the attention of scholars since the time of Adam Smith in the eighteenth century and are likely to continue to intrigue policy analysts and managers into the twenty-first century.

REFERENCES

Buchanan, James M. 1965. "An Economic Theory of Clubs." *Economica* 32:1–14. Describes a theory of resource allocation in the context of limited publicness of goods.

Lancaster, Kelvin. 1976. "The Pure Theory of Impure Public Goods." In *Public and Urban Economics,* ed. Ronald E. Grieson, 127–140. Lexington, MA.: D. C. Heath. Reviews Paul Samuelson's contributions and explores the difficulties created by the possibility that pure public goods do not exist in fact.

Samuelson, Paul A. 1964. "Pure Theory of Public Expenditures." *Review of Economics and Statistics* 36:387–389. A classic theoretical exposition of the theory of production and allocation of public goods.

SOURCES OF ADDITIONAL INFORMATION

Very few recreation and leisure scholars have made important contributions to the literature on public goods, despite the importance of the concept in the field. Interestingly, several economists who have contributed to the literature on public goods use recreation examples. See, for example, James M. Buchanan, *The Demand and Supply of Public Goods* (Chicago: Rand McNally, 1976). Two recent general papers on public goods include Chapter 3 in A. R. Prest and N. A. Barr, *Public Finance in Theory and Practice* (London: Weidenfeld and Nicholson, 1985) and Richard A. Musgrave, "Samuelson on Public Goods," in E. C. Brown and R. Solow, eds., *Paul Samuelson and Modern Economic Theory* (New York: McGraw-Hill, 1983).

Some useful early theoretical papers include Charles Tiebout, "The Pure Theory of Local Expenditure" (*Journal of Political Economy* 64:416–424, 1956) and Alan Williams, "The Optimal Provision of Public Goods in a System of Local Government" (*Journal of Political Economy* 74:18–33, 1966). Keimei Kaizuka examined the distinction between public goods as final consumer products and public goods as intermediate goods used in the production of final private goods in "Public Goods and Decentralization of Production" (*Review of Economics and Statistics* 47:118–120, 1965).

R

RECREATION. A pleasurable activity, which may be relatively sedentary, largely pursued for INTRINSIC MOTIVATION during LEISURE.

The derivation of recreation from "re-creation" (as renewal or refreshment) is obvious and came originally from the Latin *recreare,* which also means "renewal." By the fifteenth century, the English term had begun to be used in the context of pleasurable, leisurely activity. From the *Oxford English Dictionary:* (1989) "To take his recreation he entryd in to his gardyn." The distinction between one's experience of an activity and one's engagement in the activity is subtle and is often blurred. The definition given above is an example. It mentions both the pleasurable, intrinsically satisfying experience of an activity as well as participation. Performance of an activity does not *ipso facto* cause the activity to be recreation. A game of chess played by a computer or a rubber tube being carried down a river without a rider are not recreation. The activity must be experienced by a human being for it to be recreation. On the other hand, feelings of refreshment or renewal are not recreation, either. Many activities—both recreation and nonrecreation—can give rise to these experiences.

Most authors emphasize activity, with reference to the nature of the experience, as the core feature of recreation. B. L. Driver and Ross Tocher (1970), however, have argued that activities are not recreation. They favor a behavioral or experiential definition—the essence of recreation is an experience, not an activity. Their view has formed part of the logical base of the RECREATION OPPORTUNITY SPECTRUM (ROS). ROS has been widely accepted by many resource-managing agencies as a managerial framework for providing diverse recreation opportunities. The definition of recreation as experience, however, has created some difficulties in the application of ROS. B. L. Driver, Perry Brown, George Stankey, and Timothy Gregoire (1987), in their review of ROS, noted that many experiences—such as kinship, exercise, and tranquillity—are provided by many different types of activity in many different settings. Because of this, these forms of "recreation" (i.e., these experiences) cannot be accommodated within ROS. One solution to the problem identified by Driver et al. would be to consider these experiences as NEED satisfaction or benefits provided by participation in recreation, rather than as recreation per se.

A more important debate about the connotations of the term concern whether or not recreation can occur during time spent in obligatory or extrinsically motivated activities, such as time on the job. Jay Shivers (1981) divided authors who propose definitions of recreation into traditionalists and progressives, depending on how they view the possibility of recreation occurring during work. Charles Brightbill (1960) as well as the author of this dictionary are examples of those who believe the term recreation should be limited to leisure activities. Martin Neumeyer and Esther Neumeyer (1958) and Shivers (1981) believe that recreation and work are not mutually exclusive. It is not likely that the two camps differ in their perception of reality. Both recognize that workers can find enjoyment in their work, and that they punctuate work time with moments of relaxation and even playful activity. The issue is perhaps one of a semantic decision as to whether these moments of relaxation and enjoyment during work are sufficiently similar to leisure activities (in terms of the experience) that they should receive the same label. Existing psychological tools assessing the nature of subjective human experiences are not sufficiently refined to permit an unambiguous answer. Mihaly Csikszentmihalyi (1975) has done extensive work on the experience of FLOW, and has evidence that the subjective experience he labeled as flow can occur in either work or leisure; but he also noted that flow is not synonymous with recreation or leisure.

Despite such debates there is general agreement on some of the basic elements of recreation. These are summarized by Neumeyer and Neumeyer (1958): (1) recreation is an individual or collective activity that can occur during leisure, (2) it must have some element of intrinsic value (although the authors argue it may also have extrinsic value, a view not necessarily shared by others), (3) the chief motive is the satisfaction of participating in the activity, and (4) social stimulation and cultural influences shape specific forms of recreation. Many of these features are quite similar to the features of PLAY. Indeed, Shivers (1981) argued that play and recreation are synonymous: "the same feelings are evoked in child play as in what adults call their play, the only difference being that adults have dignified their play by calling it recreation." Again, however, there is no unanimous agreement with that observation. Luther Gulick, for example, clearly stated the difference he saw between play and recreation. Although his views are now two generations old, they are held at least implicitly by many people. "There is a real difference between play and recreation. . . . [Recreation] means relaxation in contrast to the child's [play] outlet of energy " (quoted in Shivers, 1981:138).

A particular theme in recreation research is the development of classification schemes for recreation activities. These schemes are used to help develop a better theoretical understanding of the nature of recreation as well as to guide REC-REATION PROGRAMMING and management activities. One common method for developing a classification scheme is to analyze existing participation patterns to form ACTIVITY CLUSTERS. An early example of this approach was Charles Proctor (1962) who developed a classification system for the Outdoor Recreation Resources Review Commission (ORRRC). Based on his analysis of the activities of 3600 Americans, he identified four clusters: water recreation, passive recreation, backwoods recreation, and active recreation. Michael Chubb and Holly Chubb (1981) suggested types of activity on the basis of their appeal to different personality types: perfectionists, gentle individuals, domineering individuals, creative individuals, angry individuals, aggressive individuals, gregarious individuals, individuals who crave adulation, highly intelligent individuals, and insecure individuals. The Canadian Park Service (1980) identified twenty-seven activities that they classified into four groups of "appropriate activities": social, recreational, educational, and water related. Because each classification scheme is developed using different assumptions and for different purposes, no one scheme will ever be developed that will be universally acceptable or useful.

In his review of recreation classifications and definitions, Shivers (1981) noted that most authors impose some restrictive limits on their views of recreation. He summarized these as "five concepts": (1) when (during leisure time), (2) why (intrinsically satisfying), (3) how (freely chosen), (4) what (physical activity), and (5) context (socially acceptable). Shivers then challenged each restriction or concept. He argued, for example, that (1) recreation can occur during work or obligatory time spent with family; (2) that some forms of recreation, e.g., certain hobbies, can be extrinsically rewarding; (3) that recreation activities, especially in the context of THERAPEUTIC RECREATION, may be prescribed rather than freely chosen; (4) that sedentary activities such as reading or watching television are also recreation; and (5) the criterion of social acceptability or legality is needlessly restrictive and presents occasional paradoxes: sexual activity may be recreation if it is with a spouse but is not recreation if it is with a prostitute.

Another important theme in the recreation literature concerns the benefits participants derive from recreation. Charles Bucher, Jay Shivers, and Richard Bucher (1984) have discussed these benefits in the context of five philosophies: conservatism, liberalism, humanism, existentialism, and pragmatism. The conservative philosophy emphasizes the role of recreation in perpetuating CULTURE, HERITAGE, and as a force in SOCIALIZATION. This philosophy, however, does not place much value on innovation or activities that may be considered socially unacceptable. Liberalism is the opposite of conservatism. The followers of this philosophy emphasize freedom, self-expression, and creativity. Recreation as a strategy for SELF-ACTUALIZATION is especially prized. Liberalism, however, fails to place any emphasis on the richness of past human experiences, on the promotion of a sense of group or cultural identity, and largely ignores social VALUE of activities. Humanists tend to focus on the potential for recreation to contribute to physical and cognitive growth through play, games, sport, and related activities. The spiritual aspects of recreation as well as the significance of emotions and transcendent experiences through leisure are frequently ignored. The existentialist view of recreation highlights the subjective qualities of recreation, viewing recreation largely as a matter of personal experience that gives meaning to life. The fifth philosophy, pragmatism, emphasizes the need to develop skills, remove BARRIERS, and to work toward specified outcomes resulting from recreation participation. Therapeutic recreation programs often can be interpreted as being examples of the pragmatic philosophy.

Many authors identify special categories or types of recreation: commercial recreation, physical recreation, outdoor recreation, and so on. These various types are based on groupings of specific activities or particular contexts in which recreation occurs. One particularly important type of recreation is community recreation. Community recreation is the set of recreation activities and services sponsored or managed by public or nonprofit agencies for the general public residing in a defined, local community.

Finally, the term recreation is also used to refer, not directly to pleasurable intrinsically motivated activities occurring during leisure time, but to the study of such activities and to the professional preparation of individuals to work in any wide variety of recreation organizations. Thus one can have a dictionary of recreation concepts without defining a single recreation activity.

REFERENCES

Brightbill, Charles K. 1960. *The Challenge of Leisure*. Englewood Cliffs, NJ: Prentice Hall. A classic text in recreation; proposes a conservative definition of recreation as leisure time activity.

Butcher, Charles A., Shivers, Jay S., and Bucher, Richard D. 1984. *Recreation for Today's Society*. Englewood Cliffs, NJ: Prentice Hall. An introductory textbook on recreation; emphasis is on organized recreation, and recreation as a form of human behavior.

Canadian Park Service. 1980. Approved Activities. Unpublished mimeograph. An internal document identifying twenty-seven activities that park managers may promote within their national park in Canada.

Chubb, Michael, and Chubb, Holly. 1981. *One Third of Our Time?: An Introduction to Recreation Behavior and Resources*. New York: Wiley. A comprehensive look at recreation and its related resources, institutions, and concepts.

Csikszentmihalyi, Mihaly. 1975. *Beyond Boredom and Anxiety*. San Francisco: Jossey-Bass. The original statement of the concept of flow; includes anecdotal descriptions.

Driver, B. L.; Brown, Perry J.; Stankey, George H.; and Gregoire, Timothy G. 1987. "The ROS Planning System: Evolution, Basic Concepts, and Research Needed." *Leisure Sciences* 9:201–212. Describes the historical development of the Recreation Opportunity Spectrum and its role in federal recreation management.

Driver, B. L., and Tocher, S. Ross. 1970. "Toward a Behavioral Interpretation of Recreational Engagements with Implications for Planning." In *Elements of Outdoor Recreation*, ed. B. L. Driver, 9–31. Presents a conceptual framework for recreation planning based on a behavioral model of recreation.

Neumeyer, Martin H., and Neumeyer, Esther S. 1958. *Leisure and Recreation*, 3rd edition. New York: Ronald Press. A dated but still useful sociological inquiry in aspects of recreation as a form of social behavior.

Oxford English Dictionary, 2d edition. 1989. J. A. Simpson and E. S. C. Weiner (preparers). Vol. 13, 372–373. An extended definition of "recreation", based on etymology and historical precedents.

Proctor, Charles. 1962. "Appendix A." In *National Recreation Survey, ORRRC Study*, report 19. Washington, DC: U.S. Government Printing Office. Analysis of an early, major national survey of recreation patterns.

Shivers, Jay S. 1981. *Leisure and Recreation Concepts*. Boston: Allyn & Bacon. Examines five common concepts or perspectives adopted by most authors; presents a liberal definition of recreation that conceives recreation occurring in many nontraditional or nonconventional settings.

SOURCES OF ADDITIONAL INFORMATION

Any introductory textbook in recreation will include a discussion on the nature of the concept. A few sources the author has found useful, beyond those cited in the references, include the following: Richard Kraus, *Recreation and Leisure in Modern Society* (3rd edition, Chicago: Scott, Foresman, 1984); Allen Sapora and Elmer Mitchell, *The Theory of Play and Recreation* (New York: Ronald Press, 1961); Thomas Goodale and Peter Witt, eds., *Recreation and Leisure: Issues in an Era of Change* (rev. edition, State College, PA: Venture, 1985); and Alan Graefe and Stan Parker, eds., *Recreation and Leisure: An Introductory Handbook* (State College, PA: Venture, 1987).

A good, popularly written overview of important issues in outdoor recreation is *Americans Outdoors: The Legacy, the Challenge* (Washington, DC: Island Press, 1987). This particular report is the official report on the President's Commission on Americans Outdoors.

Some excellent books that focus on managerial issues in recreation include Charles Doell and Louis Twardzik, *Elements of Park and Recreation Administration* (4th edition, Minneapolis: Burgess, 1979); Geoffrey Godbey, *Recreation, Park and Leisure Services: Foundations, Organization, Administration* (Philadelphia: Saunders, 1976); and Douglas Sessoms, Harold Meyer, and Charles Brightbill, *Leisure Services: The Organized Recreation and Park System* (5th edition, Englewood Cliffs, NJ: Prentice Hall, 1975).

An ambitious collection of readings that cover many of the major topical areas in recreation research and scholarship is Edgar Jackson and Tim Burton, eds., *Understanding Leisure and Recreation: Mapping the Past, Charting the Future* (State College, PA: Venture, 1989).

RECREATION BUSINESS DISTRICT. A specialized retail district found in towns and cities that attract significant numbers of TOURISTS typified by a high concentration of souvenir shops, attractions, restaurants, and snack food stands.

The term *recreation business district* (RBD) was first proposed by Charles Stansfield and John Rickert (1970) to describe a long-recognized phenomenon in resort towns: the concentration of TOURISM-related businesses in a relatively limited section of each town. The term is a deliberate parallel to "central business district"—the core of commercial and retail establishments located in the heart of each city. Unlike the central business district and other secondary retail districts whose location is based on the interplay of centrality, land costs, ACCESSIBILITY, and economic rents, the recreation business district's location is usually determined by the presence of a natural or historic feature such as a beach, a major waterfall (e.g., Niagara Falls, Ontario), the entrance to a NATIONAL PARK (e.g., Gatlinburg, Tennessee), or a historic district (e.g., Williamsburg, Virginia). Exceptions may be found, however, such as the "strip" in Las Vegas, which is not tied to any particular natural feature, but rather a conscious design to limit casino development to certain areas of the city.

Most recreation business districts are designed to service pedestrians although, again, exceptions such as the Las Vegas strip may be found. The RBD is typically separated, geographically and functionally, from other retail districts, often experiences substantial seasonal variations in business levels, and has a SERVICE AREA that extends far beyond the limits of the city.

REFERENCES

Stansfield, Charles, A., and Rickert, John A. 1970. "The Recreational Business District," *Journal of Leisure Research* 2:213–225. Introduces the term and describes the formation of the RBD in three resort communities.

SOURCES OF ADDITIONAL INFORMATION

V. Taylor describes the delineation of the RBD of an African city in "The Recreational Business District: A Component of the East London Urban Morphology" (*South African Geographer* 5:139–144, 1975).

RECREATION OPPORTUNITY SPECTRUM. A RESOURCE-based managerial framework designed to help ensure the provision of a diversity of recreation opportunities.

Recreation planners and managers, from at least the time of Frederick Law Olmsted in the late nineteenth century (Stevenson, 1977), have recognized the need to provide a variety of recreation settings to accommodate the DEMAND for diverse activities. The point was vividly made by J. V. K. Wagar (1951) in his call for the nation to provide "complete recreation land systems . . . from the flower pot at the window to the wilderness." Roderick Nash (1967), in his discussion of the concept of WILDERNESS, suggested that wilderness could be best understood by considering it as part of a continuum of diverse ENVIRONMENTS ranging from "pure wilderness" to "total civilization." George Stankey (1977) also noted the existence of a spectrum of recreation activity preferences and its association with continua of different preferred environments, levels of development, and requirements for space. The work of these and other authors— a brief history of which is provided in B. L. Driver, Perry Brown, George Stankey, and Timothy Gregoire (1987)—eventually led to the formal development of a spectrum of recreation opportunities as a management tool. According to Robert Manning (1986), the work on the Recreation Opportunity Spectrum (ROS) was conducted by two groups working independently (although not in ignorance of each other's ideas): Roger Clark and George Stankey (1979) and Brown, Driver, and associates (Driver and Brown, 1978). The first group emphasized the practical issues of managing recreation settings to meet diverse visitor NEEDS while the second focused on developing a descriptive model for defining more precisely different opportunity classes or environments.

Part of the driving force behind the development of the ROS was the passage of several public laws mandating more effective and efficient ways of integrating recreation in MULTIPLE USE land management planning: the 1974 Renewable Resources Planning Act, the 1976 Federal Land Policy and Management Act, and the 1976 National Forest Management Act.

The ROS is built from three elements: activities, settings, and experiences. Experiences, which the developers of ROS consider to be synonymous with recreation (Driver and Tocher, 1970) are the products of participation in a given activity in a given setting. The objectives of recreationists are to have satisfying experiences; the objectives of managers are to provide opportunities for those experiences. From the perspective of ROS, these objectives are compatible and comparable. Demand (created by the recreationist) and supply (provided by the manager) are easily measured and reconciled because both represent essentially the same combination of activities, settings, and experiences. ROS provides a common metric or language for balancing the desires of recreationists and managers.

The combination of activities, settings, and opportunities for experiences that constitute the ROS are arranged along a continuum, usually divided into six classes: primitive, semiprimitive nonmotorized, semiprimitive motorized, roaded natural, rural, and urban. Each class may be broken down into subclasses as desired. A brief profile of each class follows.

Class	Description
Primitive	Fairly large, essentially unmodified natural environments; very low levels of use and user interaction; no motorized use; management essentially avoids imposing human restrictions and controls (other than to protect primitive environmental quality)
Semiprimitive: nonmotorized	Moderate to fairly large natural areas; low but nonmotorized observable levels of use; managed with some minimal on-site restrictions; no motorized use

Semiprimitive: motorized	Same as above, but with motorized use motorized permitted
Roaded natural	Natural-appearing areas with moderate evidence of human use; low to moderate user interaction; management and resource interaction; management and resource utilization is obvious, but consistent with natural environment; some built facilities to support conventional motorized use
Rural	Substantially human-modified environment; management objectives include maintenance of soil and ground cover; moderate to high levels of use and user interaction; moderate facility development supporting general and specialized activities; parking facilities are provided
Urban	Substantially developed environment, although the background may appear natural; vegetation is intensively managed and many include exotic species; large numbers of users and high user interaction; facilities available for high density and specialized uses; mass transit available

The ROS is currently used by the Forest Service and the Bureau of Land Management to help establish managerial guidelines, management standards, and policies for regional site planning and administration. ROS can also be used to help guide trade-offs between recreation opportunities when required by environmental restrictions or other management needs; to monitor user satisfaction levels; and to guide project planning. All these applications are based on fourteen tenets identified in Driver et al. (1987). Some of the more important of these are

1. Recreation is an experience, not just an activity.

2. Recreationists seek and managers provide opportunities for recreation; an opportunity is the provision of a setting, the potential to engage in an activity, and the possibility of achieving a desired experience.

3. Settings may be characterized as physical (emphasizing the resource base and the LEISURE INFRASTRUCTURE), social (emphasizing users and their interactions), and managerial (emphasizing regulations, personnel, moveable facilities and equipment associated with management of a site).

4. Opportunities to realize different experiences varies by setting along the spectrum. The same activity in different settings produces different experiences.

5. The experiences ROS is designed to support are the desired experiences of ''experienced'' recreationists. It is assumed these individuals will seek the same experience in any given combination of an activity and setting (e.g., cross-country skiing in a primitive area) regardless of the specific site.

6. Users are rational with respect to behaviors. In particular, their behavior conforms to the EXPECTANCY-VALENCE MODEL.

7. Only those experiences that are closely associated with specific sites and/or activities have relevance to ROS. Experiences that may be achieved in a wide variety of settings or activities (e.g., feelings of kinship or tranquility, cannot be efficiently provided for through ROS).

8. ROS is intended to provide guidelines or suggestions for management and planning— not to specify precise actions.

The Recreation Opportunity Spectrum is still being developed and refined. Among the issues that have yet to be resolved include: Does ROS have potential application to nationwide or systemwide planning issues? To what extent is the assumption that recreationists adhere to the expectancy-valence model accurate? What are the implications if the model is not an accurate predictor of recreation behavior? What are the implications of the assumption that managers should strive to satisfy experienced users? Are the needs of novices being ignored? Are sites being managed in such a way that the satisfaction or even the personal safety of inexperienced users is being jeopardized? Does ROS have any relevance to managing urban recreation systems? The diversity of urban recreation environments ranges from large, natural areas in major city parks through a wide variety of developed neighborhood parks to large domed stadia and other specialized built facilities. This diversity far exceeds the diversity represented by the primitive, semiprimitive nonmotorized, semiprimitive motorized, and roaded natural settings combined.

Despite some of these concerns and unanswered questions, the Recreation Opportunity Spectrum is an important contribution to the outdoor recreation management literature and a useful supplement to other related concepts such as CARRYING CAPACITY.

REFERENCES

Clark, Roger N., and Stankey, George H. 1979. *The Recreation Opportunity Spectrum: A Framework of Planning, Management, and Research,* general technical report PNW-98. Portland, OR: Pacific Northwest Forest Experiment Station, U.S.D.A. Forest Service. A good description of the ROS; written from a strongly applied and managerial perspective.

Driver, B. L., and Brown, Perry J. 1978. "The Opportunity Spectrum Concept and Behavioral Information in Outdoor Recreation Resource Supply Inventories: A Rationale." In *Integrated Inventories and Renewable Natural Resources: Proceedings of the Workshop,* ed. H. Gyde Lund. general technical report RM-55, 24–31. Fort Collins, CO: Rocky Mountain Forest and Range Experiment Station, U.S.D.A. Forest Service. Provides a descriptive overview of the opportunity classes and behavioral assumptions behind ROS.

Driver, B. L., Brown, Perry, J., Stankey, George H., and Gregoire, Timothy G. 1987. "The ROS Planning System: Evolution, Basic Concepts, and Research Needs." *Leisure Sciences* 9:201–212. Describes the history of the development of ROS, with particular attention given to the basic assumptions behind the method.

Driver, B. L., and Tocher, S. Ross. 1970. "Toward a Behavioral Interpretation of

Recreational Engagements, with Implications for Planning.'' In *Elements of Out-door Recreation Planning,* ed. B. L. Driver, 9–13. Ann Arbor: University of Michigan Press. Presents an argument for defining recreation in terms of experience rather than activity.

Manning, Robert E. 1986. *Studies in Outdoor Recreation.* Corvallis: Oregon State University Press. A book focusing on user-satisfaction issues in outdoor recreation; Chapter 7 is devoted to ROS.

Nash, Roderick. 1967. *Wilderness and the American Mind.* New Haven, CT: Yale University Press. An excellent review of the history and concept of wilderness in the American culture.

Stankey, George H. 1977. ''Some Social Concepts for Outdoor Recreation Planning.'' In *Outdoor Recreation: Advances in Application of Economics,* general technical report WO-2, 154–161. Washington, DC: U.S.D.A. Forest Service. A discussion of some major social concepts and tenets relevant to resource management, including the notion of several different types of recreation continuum.

Stevenson, Elizabeth. 1977. *Park Maker: A Life of Frederick Law Olmsted.* New York: Macmillan. A favorable biography of the famous nineteenth-century park planner.

Wagar, J. V. K. 1951. ''Some Major Principles in Recreation Land Use Planning.'' *Journal of Forestry* 49:431–434. An early essay on guidelines for recreation planning; refers to need for planning for diversity.

SOURCES OF ADDITIONAL INFORMATION

Many reports concerning ROS are ''fugitive'' government documents and difficult to obtain, even with complete references. A few items that are easier to find and still related to ROS include: Perry Brown and G. E. Haas, ''Wilderness Recreation Experiences: The Rawah Case'' (*Journal of Leisure Research* 12:229–241, 1980); Roger Clark, ''Promises and Pitfalls of the ROS in Resource Management'' (*Australian Parks and Recreation* May:9–13, 1982); Bev Driver and Richard Knopf, ''Personality, Outdoor Recreation, and Expected Consequences'' (*Environment and Behavior* 9:169–193, 1977); B. L. Driver and Donald H. Rosenthal, *Measuring and Improving the Effectiveness of Public Outdoor Recreation Programs* (Washington, DC: George Washington University Press, 1982); and J. W. Roggenbuck, ''Wilderness User Preferences: Eastern and Western Areas'' *Proceedings of Wilderness Management Symposium* (Knoxville: University of Tennessee Press, 1980, 105–146).

RECREATION PROGRAMMING. The process of planning, delivery, and management of RECREATION and LEISURE services for a constituency.

Recreation programming is a key concept in the recreation and leisure services profession and in the DELIVERY SYSTEM. Douglas Sessoms (1984:262) described it as ''the heart of the organized recreation and park service''; Christine Howe and Gaylene Carpenter (1985:vii) observed that it is ''one of the areas that is truly unique to the body of knowledge in park, recreation, and leisure services.'' While the social scientific study of leisure now places little attention on programming itself, the concept continues to be important to practitioners involved in public and private organizations, and is a fundamental part of the curriculum in professional development programs.

Although the core of the concept—the provision of recreation opportunities and services—has remained essentially unchanged since the beginning of public recreation services, the scope of recreation programming has expanded. In 1970, for example, Thomas Yukic identified only two basic strategies or services provided by recreation programming: (1) the operation of organized programs or activities, which are heavily dependent on leaders, and (2) the provision of facilities and areas for independent and unstructured use. Sessoms (1984) presents a more contemporary and broader view. He sees programming as providing services in five areas: (1) schedules, which would likely include Yukic's notion of organized programs; (2) facilities and areas; (3) information about recreation opportunities and RESOURCES in a community; (4) education, including LEISURE EDUCATION; and (5) technical assistance, including assistance for COMMUNITY DEVELOPMENT efforts in recreation.

The expansion of the concept of programming into nontraditional service has inevitably raised a number of challenges or problems for recreation programmers. Sessoms (1984) summarized these as priorities, roles, relationships, and charges or fees. With respect to priorities, one major debate is over the principle of universality. Should recreation services be made available to all individuals equally or should certain individuals or groups be given higher priority, presumably on the basis of greater NEED. This issue is, of course, a question of how to achieve EQUITY in the provision of leisure services.

The issue of roles refers to whether recreation and parks departments should limit themselves to traditional recreation activities or should begin to provide other forms of service such as day care or nutrition assistance. The distinction between the proper roles of different types of social service agencies can be difficult. Do leisure education and OUTDOOR EDUCATION, for example, belong under the aegis of a recreation department or under a school board? This type of question also illustrates the problem of determining the proper relationships among various public agencies, and among public, private nonprofit, and commercial recreation organizations. Finally, the providers of public recreation programming services must struggle with the proper use and level of fees and charges for their services.

Most authors of recreation programming books emphasize a common set of principles, although the application of these principles to specific situations is sometimes debated. The principles include

1. Public participation in planning and decision making for recreation programming to the extent possible.

2. Guide the development of recreation programs through careful assessment of community needs and the articulation of clear program objectives.

3. Ensure ACCESSIBILITY to programs through removal of BARRIERS and MAINSTREAMING; provide different programs as appropriate to different social groups and to individuals in different stages of the HUMAN LIFE CYCLE.

4. Respond to a diversity of needs and DEMANDS, including recognition of the MULTI-CULTURALISM of most American communities.

5. Effective programming is based on effective leadership, well-maintained facilities, adequate resources, and responsiveness to social change.

A variety of practical guidebooks or manuals are available to assist with recreation programming. Howe and Carpenter (1985) note that most are based on some variation of a five-part cyclical process: (1) needs assessment, (2) program planning, (3) program implementation, (4) program evaluation, and (5) program revision. This ongoing approach to programming helps to ensure that programs remain fresh and responsive to participants' needs and interests. It allows programmers and managers to monitor the evolution of their programs through the PRODUCT LIFE CYCLE and to make changes to revitalize the program once it passes the point of maturity and begins to decline in popularity or usefulness.

Although the basic steps of recreation programming are generally standard, Sessoms (1984) notes that there are two fundamentally different philosophies toward the process of programming. The first approach tends to be reactive, in which programmers attempt to respond to expressed needs of the public as they design and implement programs. The second approach tends to be proactive, in which programmers determine what constitutes appropriate service and make professional judgments about public needs. The former approach is the most responsive and democratic approach, but it can lead to a preoccupation with ADVOCACY, planning, education, and public participation with a concomitant loss of attention to implementation and facility maintenance. Special interest groups can also exert disproportionate pressure as they attempt to ensure their own preferences are met, sometimes to the exclusion of other, less well organized groups. The latter approach is administratively efficient, and allows professional recreationists to balance competing claims by different groups as well as to avoid committing resources to passing fads. On the other hand, the proactive approach can easily become authoritarian and out of touch with true community goals and preferences.

As a result of the strengths and weaknesses of both traditional philosophies, Sessoms believes that a hybrid approach is developing. This hybrid approach recognizes that recreation services should be provided by many different groups and in many different settings. Examples of the hybrid approach include co-operative ventures between municipal recreation departments and shopping mall managers to provide community center services and public recreation activities (such as indoor walking trails) at shopping malls.

Recreation programming is sometimes stereotyped by individuals outside of the recreation and leisure field as simply leading children in games or arts and crafts. In fact, recreation programming involves all aspects of management and marketing from need assessment through product development to evaluation.

The degree to which our profession meets its social mandate to serve the public is determined largely by the quality of recreation programming.

REFERENCES

Howe, Christine Z., and Carpenter, Gaylene. 1985. *Programming Leisure Experiences*. Englewood Cliffs, NJ: Prentice Hall. A practically oriented text that emphasizes a cyclical approach to programming.
Sessoms, H. Douglas. 1984. *Leisure Services,* 6th edition. Englewood Cliffs, NJ: Prentice Hall. An excellent introduction of the professional side of recreation and leisure studies; includes a descriptive chapter on the theory and principles of recreation programming.
Yukic, Thomas S. 1970. *Fundamentals of Recreation,* 2nd edition. New York: Harper & Row. A now-dated introduction to organized recreation services and community recreation administration.

SOURCES OF ADDITIONAL INFORMATION

In addition to a number of handbooks and manuals published by various professional associations and state/provincial agencies (most of which can be difficult to obtain if one is not a member of the association or a resident of the state or province), a number of books on programming are available. Some of the better, more comprehensive texts include Pat Farrell and Herberta Lundgren, *The Process of Recreation Programming* (New York: Wiley, 1983); Geoffrey Godbey, *Recreation, Park and Leisure Services* (Philadelphia: Saunders, 1978); Christopher Edginton, David Compton, and Carole Hanson, *Recreation and Leisure Programming* (Philadelphia: Saunders, 1980); and Howard Danforth, *Creative Leadership in Recreation* (Boston: Allyn & Bacon, 1970).

REGION. An area of defined extent and character that is distinct from surrounding areas.

The earliest use of region in the English language reflected its Latin origin, *regere,* "to rule." Regions were the realms of some ruler. In recreation and leisure studies, the term is not usually associated with governance but rather with research and planning in TOURISM and outdoor RECREATION.

One of the first explicit discussions of the importance of the spatial perspective in recreation was Roy Wolfe's (1964) review of the twenty-seven-volume final report of the Outdoor Recreation Resources Review Commission (ORRRC). As part of his review, Wolfe developed a schematic showing how various components of outdoor recreation (such as social trends, demographics, DEMAND, ACCESSIBILITY, RESOURCES) related to each other. He reported that in his initial attempts to develop the schematic, he tried putting "people," the most important component in the recreation system, in a central position. Such a strategy, however, did not work. It was not until he placed mobility (or "spatiality") at the center could he develop a clear and meaningful schematic. The significance of the central position for mobility is that, in the context of outdoor recreation and many other forms of recreation, the people are in one location, the resources in another. Normally, it is the people who must move. Recreation cannot occur until people and resources get together. This basic fact, often overlooked by other social scientists, speaks eloquently to the geographer of a fundamental spatial quality to many forms of recreation and, especially, of tourism. The connection between the importance of the spatial aspects of recreation and leisure and the concept of regions is relatively simple: areas in which users or resources are concentrated represent regions. Regions are an operational definition of "here" and "there."

Three types of regions are normally used in recreation and leisure studies. A priori regions are those that are defined by someone else and accepted by the researcher or planner for a particular project; such definitions are usually based on arbitrary or subjective perceptions as to the extent or character of the region. Political units, such as countries, states, and provinces are the most common type of a priori region. Other a priori regions include popular notions of certain places, such as the Sunbelt or the Upper Mississippi (Becker, 1979).

The second type of region is the homogeneous region. Homogeneous regions are defined on the basis of objective, internal similarities that provide a basis for imputing both a common identity to the places included in the region and boundaries that distinguish the region from surrounding areas. Joseph Fridgen, Ed Udd, and Cynthia Deale (1983) provide an illustration of homogeneous regions in tourism. Using the responses of a survey of automobile tourists to Michigan, they defined a series of multicounty regions that present more or less uniform images or experiences to the tourists.

The third type of region is the functional region. Unlike homogeneous regions, which are defined on the basis of an internal unity, functional regions are defined on the basis of a high degree of internal interaction. Stephen Smith (1983), for example, defined a series of functional travel regions in North America through an analysis of interstate and interprovincial travel flows. The resulting regions were large, multistate/province agglomerations in which both origins and destinations were combined. He noted, as one instance, the existence of a function travel region extending from Michigan and Ohio to Florida, centered on Interstate 75. The unifying force in the region was not any similarity of climate, social structure, or economy but rather a stable and consistent pattern of vacation travel north and south within the region.

Clare Gunn (1982) has argued for the existence of a special type of region— a tourism region. Gunn's tourism region is essentially a form of a homogeneous region. The special qualities of a tourism region include (1) its location at some distance away from the residences of potential visitors, (2) the perception of travelers as a potential destination, (3) an adequate degree of accessibility to potential visitors, (4) sufficient economic and social infrastructure to support tourism development, and (5) sufficient size that it contains two or more destination communities.

Regions provide social scientists with a tool to accomplish three important tasks. First, they help name a part of the world. Names simplify the process of communication. If you want to talk about something, it helps to have a label for that thing. Names can also assist with the marketing of areas for recreation and tourism. Second, regions help to simplify and order knowledge. No one can have all the facts about every spot on earth at his fingertips. Being able to speak of the Southwest or of the Great Lakes provides a form of intellectual shorthand that summarizes important information about the region, and communicates it effectively. This use of regions does not imply that there are no internal differences within the regions. Rather, it simply means that for certain purposes more is gained by creating a spatial stereotype that is lost by ignoring minor local variations. Finally, researchers use regions to make inductive generalizations, to form testable hypotheses, and to make predictions. The development of certain weather regions allows meteorologists to identify areas that face a high risk from tornadoes or hurricanes. Gunn's tourism regions are basically a prediction that any region that meets the five characteristics he identifies has the potential to be developed as a popular and successful tourism destination.

It should be noted, however, that regions do not have an intrinsic existence. They are defined by someone for some purpose. As a result, they are only a tool—but they can be an important tool in understanding certain aspects of recreation and leisure phenomena.

REFERENCES

Becker, Robert H. 1979. "Travel Compatibility on the Upper Mississippi River." *Journal of Travel Research* 17(1):33–36. An examination of tourists' conflicts in an a priori region.
Fridgen, Joseph, Udd, Ed, and Deale, Cynthia. 1983. "Cognitive Maps of Tourism Regions in Michigan." *Proceedings of the Applied Geography Conference* 6: 262–272. Describes a survey-based procedure for defining tourism regions.
Gunn, Clare. 1982. *A Proposed Methodology for Identifying Areas of Tourism Development Potential in Canada*. Report for the Canadian Government Office of Tourism. A consulting report that outlines and applies a restrictive concept for a tourism region.
Smith, Stephen L. J. 1983. "Identification of Functional Tourism Regions in North America." *Journal of Travel Research* 22(4):13–21. Describes the concept and development of a tourism-based functional region, utilizing interstate and interprovincial travel flows.
Wolfe, Roy I. 1964. "Perspective on Outdoor Recreation: A Bibliographic Survey." *Geographical Review* 54:203–238. An important and influential review of the nature of outdoor recreation and of the status of research on outdoor recreation up to the release of the ORRRC reports.

SOURCES OF ADDITIONAL INFORMATION

Stephen Smith discusses the logic, uses, and techniques of regionalization in tourism in Chapters 7 and 8 of *Tourism Analysis* (London: Longman, 1989). Clare Gunn provides extensive discussion of regions and regional issues in *Tourism Planning* (2nd edition, New York: Taylor and Francis, 1988).

Some more specific examples of regional research include K. R. Davis and B. W. Taylor III, "A Goal Programming Model for Allocating State Promotional Effort to Regional Markets in Accordance with Tourism Potential" (*Journal of Travel Research* 15 no.1:24–30, 1980) and Jonathan Goodrich, "Differences in Perceived Similarity of Tourism Regions: A Spatial Analysis" (*Journal of Travel Research* 15 no.1:10–13, 1977).

A nontourism example of the significance of regions in recreation is Douglas Dudycha, Stephen Smith, Terry Stewart, and Barry McPherson, *The Canadian Atlas of Recreation and Exercise* (Waterloo, Ont.: Department of Geography, University of Waterloo, 1983).

RESOURCE. Any commodity or amenity that contributes to the satisfaction of a human desire, DEMAND or NEED.

Resources are a familiar concept in recreation and leisure studies and in society generally. They include the usual tangible examples of soil and water as well as intangible amenities such as scenery. Personnel, budgets, and even information are resources. The most common use of the term in recreation, however, is probably in the context of natural resources: water, soil, vegetation, wildlife, open space, and so on.

Concern over the availability and quality of natural resources is long-standing. Eighteenth- and nineteenth-century political economists such as Adam Smith, Thomas Malthus, David Ricardo, and John Stuart Mill extensively discussed the relationship between resource availability and social well-being. Although many of their early ideas have proved to be too simplistic (Malthus's doctrines about resource scarcity limiting population growth are now cited more frequently for their errors than their basic content), most people—specialists and general citizens alike—recognize the importance of resources to the quality of human life. A quote by Meyer Kestnbaum (1955:6), the chairman of an advisory committee for President Dwight Eisenhower, is as appropriate today as it was a generation ago: "Natural resources are the foundation of the material prosperity of the Nation—both present and future. Their wise use is therefore the concern not only of all the people but of all levels of government." More recently, the authors of *Americans Outdoors: The Legacy, the Challenge* succinctly observed, "Outdoor recreation depends on healthy resources" (President's Commission, 1987:125).

Research, planning documents, and policy analyses about resources in recreation and in other fields reflect an important fact about the nature of resources. They are not simply "things," but ultimately social concepts. This observation was articulated early by Erich Zimmerman in 1933, in the first edition of his *World Resources and Industries*. In the second edition, Zimmerman (1951:814–815) elaborated on this observation in a well-known quotation: "Resources are highly dynamic functional concepts; they *are not, they become,* they evolve out of the triune interaction of nature, man, and CULTURE, in which nature sets outer limits, but man and culture are largely responsible for the portion of physical totality that is made available for human use" (emphasis in the original). Thus an object is not inherently a resource, but becomes one when society defines it as a resource because the object is seen as useful. WILDERNESS, for example, was long viewed as a threat or wasteland. It became perceived only as a resource by society in the twentieth century as attitudes toward a diminishing wilderness changed. Or to use a nonrecreation example: plutonium, a key element in the construction of breeder reactors and fusion bombs, is viewed as a valuable resource by some and as a highly toxic and dangerous substance with disturbing political and philosophical symbolism by others.

Not only are resources essentially social concepts, the literature on resources often has a "strong undercurrent of philosophical naturalism" (Barnett and Morris, 1963:22) despite its manifest concern with the practical and scientific problems of protection, development, and use. Barnett and Morris recalled the work of G. P. Adams (1948:69): "In the development of Greek thought, nature has a meaning, one intimately associated with the idea of birth, growth, and life. It is this idea of birth and coming to life which is caught by the Latin *natura,* as derived as it is from the stem which signifies "to be born." Nature is the mother of all things." Accepting Adams's notion that "nature" is a particularly potent and quasi-religious concept, Chandler and Morris (1963:22) then asked, "If, now, one can successively identify "nature" with "natural resources," natural resources with "CONSERVATION," and conservation with "economic policy," what are the consequences for conservation doctrine and economic policy?" The answer is the long history of heated debates within the conservation movement about the relative merits of wise use versus a preservationist ethic and even the alleged existence of legal rights of natural objects.

Natural resources are, as Kestnbaum noted, the foundation of the material well-being of a society. An early understanding of the social and political nature of resources is the foundation for a sound theoretical and practical knowledge of the role of resources in recreation and leisure and of the reasons for the complexity and passion often surrounding debates on resource policy.

REFERENCES

Adams, G. P. 1948. *Man and Metaphysics.* New York: Columbia University Press. A scholarly review of major philosophical ideas, particularly with respect to metaphysics; includes a good discussion of the origins of beliefs about nature as a semireligious concept.

Barnett, Harold, and Morris, Chandler. 1963. *Scarcity and Growth.* Baltimore: Johns Hopkins University Press. A dated but still-useful text on issues of resource scarcity and the implications for social and economic development; includes a brief history of eighteenth- and nineteenth-century views on resource scarcity.

Kestnbaum, Meyer. 1955. *Study Committee report on Natural Resources and Conservation.* Washington, DC: U.S. Government Printing Office. A position paper prepared for the U.S. Commission on Intergovernmental Relations advocating more aggressive and effective conservation measures.

President's Commission. 1987. *Americans Outdoors: The Legacy, the Challenge.* Washington, DC: Island Press. The official report of the commission; primarily descriptive and simple discussions of the important policy issues; includes numerous case studies on development and protection of outdoor recreation resources.

Zimmerman, Erich. 1933. *World Resources and Industries*. New York: Harper. An early and important statement about the nature and use of resources.

Zimmerman, Erich. 1951. *World Resources and Industries,* 2nd edition. New York: Harper. The second edition of this book on resources and resource use; advocates a social and functional interpretation of resources.

SOURCES OF ADDITIONAL INFORMATION

Most of the contemporary literature on resources concerns their protection, development, and use rather than the nature of the concept per se. In addition to the texts cited in the definition, a useful reference is S. V. Ciriacy-Wantrup, *Resource Conservation* (3rd edition, Berkeley: University of California, Division of Agricultural Sciences, 1968). A more recent book that includes a discussion of the nature of resources as well as a readable overview of key resource analytical issues is Bruce Mitchell's *Geography and Resource Analysis* (London: Longman, 1979). The scholar or student interested in pursuing resource-related topics should also be aware of Resources for the Future, a research-oriented, independent agency that has an extensive publications list on a wide variety of resource topics, including many recreation issues. Their address is Resources for the Future, 1616 P Street NW, Washington, DC 20036.

S

SEASONALITY. The tendency for TOURIST visitation or RECREATION use to concentrate in one period of the year.

Marc Boyer (1972:112) has written that TOURISM was "born seasonal" and that seasonality is the source of its "original sin." Despite such a suggestion of the profound importance of seasonality as an issue in tourism, John Allcock (1989) notes that relatively little research has been done on the topic. Most work on seasonality, in fact, has been produced only since 1980. An excellent review of this work is found in Allcock (and on which some of the current discussion is based).

At first glance, the concept of seasonality appears simple and readily explainable: most people take vacations in the summer because the weather is good and the children are out of school. It is hardly surprising, therefore, that popular vacation destinations experience a surge in tourism during the summer. However, destinations such as Florida or Hawaii may experience forms of seasonality that are unrelated to their own seasonal changes, but rather are dependent on seasons in more distant and northerly origins (Stynes and Pigozzi, 1983). Furthermore, like HOLIDAYS, tourist seasons are ultimately cultural inventions constructed out of society's perceptions of TIME. Many traditional tropical societies divide the year into only two seasons ("low sun" and "high sun," or wet and dry seasons), while Hindus divide the year into six parts. The Catholic Church's calendar has three seasons: Christmas, Easter, and "ordinary time." Some seasons are based on climatic trends, while others are based on astronomical events or cultural traditions. Tourism seasons, too, are culturally defined in ways that may or may not have much to do with weather. George Young (1973), for example, described how the tourism season in the early Mediterranean resorts were determined in large part by the social and parliamentary calendars in England. In North America, the traditional summer holiday period has its roots in the fact that the summer was the busiest time on the farm and that children were needed at home for agricultural work. The farm calendar no longer shapes most modern lives; summer is now seen as a special time for PLAY and relaxation rather than for long hours of work—but with the same result: children should not have to go to school in summer.

Certain forms of tourism in destination regions are closely tied to natural phenomena: outdoor swimming requires warm weather; skiing requires snow; fall color tours require the availability of autumn colors that are, in turn, triggered by shortening hours of daylight. However, whether public open-air bathing, snow skiing, or fall color tours are seen as appropriate vacation activities, depends on the CULTURE of the tourists and the destination region.

Although religious pilgrimages are not particularly common in the United States or Canada, they are significant forms of tourism in other countries. And pilgrimages may often be tied to religious holidays, such as Easter for Christians (which is a moveable feast) or the Islamic holy month of *Dhu'l-Hijja,* which is the preferred month for visiting Mecca (and is also a "moveable season" in terms of the Western Gregorian calendar).

A reason for travel more common in North America than pilgrimages are conferences. Allcock (1989) cities work by G. C. Fighiera suggesting that political, academic, and business calendars create "convention seasons." Furthermore, these seasons appear to be specific to particular countries or regions and are not necessarily tied to our conventional four climatic seasons of spring, summer, fall, and winter.

The phenomenon of seasonality is of interest to tourism researchers, not as merely a scholarly question concerning the causes of seasonal variations in tourist volumes, but as a practical problem requiring managerial and marketing attention. As Robert Manning and Lawrence Powers (1984:25) put it:

This peaking phenomenon, as it is often called, results in a number of significant management problems. . . . Facilities . . . must be able to handle peak loads [but] go largely unused at other times, resulting in considerable inefficiency in resource use and loss of potential profit. . . . Peak loads may exceed the social CARRYING CAPACITY of recreation areas . . . concentrated visitor use may even unnecessarily tax ecological carrying capacity . . . peaking of recreation use presents substantial administrative problems, particularly with respect to personnel scheduling.

Much of the published literature on seasonality is thus aimed at exploring ways to ameliorate the problems caused by seasonality. Manning and Powers discuss the potential of pricing strategies to even out use. Many communities attempt to develop special events and FESTIVALS in the shoulder or off-seasons to increase use during slack times. Both the Canadian and U.S. NATIONAL PARK Services also attempt to respond to problems of seasonality by encouraging visitors to visit less-frequented sites within PARKS, to switch vacations to less-visited parks. In some extreme cases, such as with the serious overcrowding in the Great Smokies National Park, there is discrete talk of "demarketing"—of attempting to persuade visitors to *not* attend through subtle messages and management techniques.

Seasonality continues to be an important concept in recreation and especially tourism. More research in needed on all aspects of seasonality, ranging from further clarification of its causes in specific situations, to the development of managerial and marketing techniques to cope with the problems it raises. Special attention is needed to develop improved methods for assessing the impacts of seasonality on hosts and guests, and on developing more refined measures for estimating the actual magnitude and trends in seasonality at specific sites.

REFERENCES

Allcock, John. 1989. "Seasonality," in *Tourism Marketing and Management Handbook,* ed. Stephen F. Witt and Luiz Moutinho, 387–392. Hemel Hempstead, UK: Prentice Hall International. An excellent, brief overview of the literature on seasonality.

Boyer, Marc. 1972. *Le Tourisme.* Paris: Editions du Seuil. A general review of tourism that gives particular attention to the importance of seasonality.

Manning, Robert, and Powers, Lawrence A. 1984. "Peak and Off-Peak Use: Redistributing the Outdoor Recreation/Tourism Load." *Journal of Travel Research* 23(2):25–31. A discussion of the implications of seasonality in outdoor recreation; reports on preferred methods for redistributing use—differential fees appear to be the most realistic.

Stynes, Barbara W., and Pigozzi, Bruce W. 1983. "A Tool for Investigating Tourism-Related Seasonal Employment." *Journal of Travel Research* 21(3):19–24. An illustration of the use of harmonic analysis to model seasonality patterns.

Young, George. 1973. *Tourism: Blessing or Blight?* Harmondsworth, UK: Penguin Books. A critical examination of tourism, which includes a brief review of the causes of shifts in tourism seasons.

SOURCES OF ADDITIONAL INFORMATION

Raphael Baron, *Seasonality in Tourism: A Guide to the Analysis of Seasonality and Trends for Policy Making* (London: Economist Intelligence Unit, 1976) is a dated but still excellent reference to the topic. Alan Jefferson and Leonard Lickorish discuss some practical things tourism marketers can do to meet the challenges of seasonality in *Marketing Tourism* (London: Longman Group, 1988, Chapt. 20). Alistair Mathieson and Geoffrey Wall consider some of the impacts of seasonality at various places in *Tourism: Economic, Physical, and Social Impacts* (London: Longman, 1982). R. Hartmann provides a useful conceptual, sociologically oriented review of seasonality in "Tourism, Seasonality, and Social Change" (*Leisure Studies* 5:25–33, 1986). Several different measures of estimating the magnitude of seasonality are compared in C. M. S. Sutcliffe and M. T. Sinclair, "The Measurement of Seasonality within the Tourist Industry: An Application to Tourist Arrivals in Spain" (*Applied Economics* 12:429–441, 1980).

SELF-ACTUALIZATION. A psychological episode in which the individual feels happiest, most complete, psychologically integrated, and closer to the core of his identity and being.

The term *self-actualization* was first used by Kurt Goldstein (1971) in the 1930s as part of his "organismic theory." Organismic theory hypothesizes that human beings are subject to one main drive—the drive to fully realize our inherent abilities. Goldstein called the goal of this drive, "self-actualization." The concept was adopted by Carl Rogers (1961) as part of his humanistic psychological theories and his therapy programs. The term is probably most closely associated, however, with Abraham Maslow (1954). All three authors used the term in essentially the same way, and all shared certain assumptions. Among these is their belief that human beings are innately good and predisposed toward growth and happiness. They acknowledge, though, that such a predisposition is fragile. SOCIALIZATION and other external pressures, especially during childhood, can distort or even destroy it. This belief is in direct contrast to Freudian psychology, which posits the existence of destructive needs and to Christianity, which teaches the existence of "original sin," a guilt or inherent evilness shared by mankind.

Maslow placed self-actualization high in a hierarchy of human NEED. At the lowest level were physiological needs such as food, air, water, and sex. Next was the need for safety, then the need for love, the need for esteem, the need for self-actualization, the need for knowledge, and finally the need for aesthetics. Lower level needs were seen as "prepotent" to high level needs. In other words, the need for love "waits" until physiological and safety needs are met. Once they are, the individual feels motivated to find love. When the need for love is met, he turns to the next higher need, esteem. The two highest needs, knowledge and aesthetics, are not explicitly tied into the potency hierarchy; Maslow felt that these highest needs overlapped with each other and were partially met through fulfillment of other needs.

In the original formulation, Maslow believed that very few people ever became self-actualized. His examples included Beethoven, Lincoln, Einstein, and Eleanor Roosevelt. (Maslow reported first attempting to find self-actualizing behaviors among university undergraduates, but found them too immature and generally devoid of the discipline that self-actualizing requires).

Later research, however, caused Maslow to modify his view of self-actualization (Maslow, 1968). This shift was due in particular to his study of "peak experiences" (Maslow, 1970), or episodes that Mihaly Csikszentmihalyi (1975) called FLOW. Such episodes, Maslow believed, were identical to the experience of self-actualization. "This makes it possible for us to redefine the experience of self-actualization in such a way as to purge it of its static and typological shortcomings, and to make it less of a kind of all-or-nothing pantheon into which some rare people enter at age 60. . . . Such states or episodes can, in theory, come at any time in life to any person" (Maslow, 1968:75).

Maslow still believed that there are people who do enter a "pantheon" of self-actualization—people to whom peak experiences come frequently. These individuals are characterized by the following traits (Maslow, 1968:26):

1. Superior perception of reality.
2. Greater levels of acceptance of self, others, and nature.
3. More spontaneity in life.
4. More problem-centered interest (particularly social problems).
5. Strong feelings of independence, accompanied by a greater need for privacy.
6. Increased levels of personal autonomy and less susceptibility to the forces of socialization.
7. Richer emotional reactions to life's events.
8. More frequent peak experiences.
9. Strong sense of identity and belonging with other people.
10. Better interpersonal relations.
11. Strong democratic ideals.
12. More creative (not just artistically).
13. Greater patience and good sense of humor.

While a popular concept in recreation and leisure studies, the term *self-actualization* is often used ambiguously. Many writers still cite Maslow's original hierarchy in which self-actualization was one of the highest and thus more irrelevant needs to the majority of people. On the other hand, the concept is also often implicitly interpreted as Goldstein and Rogers used it—as a general driving force for greater self-esteem and for the realization of one's inherent abilities. In addition to the fuzziness of the concept, it has another potential weakness. While Maslow, Rogers, and Goldstein believed the concept was universal among humans, it may be culturally specific. For example, the notion that people have a need and an implicit right to develop themselves as individuals would likely be interpreted as "deranged" thinking in a strongly Marxist society such as Albania or a fundamentalist society such as Iran. Self-actualization—in the sense of a feeling of independence, freedom from social pressures, and a frequent desire for privacy—may not exist as a meaningful concept in some modern countries such as Japan, where the patterns of socialization, education, and identity formation are quite different than in North America.

The concept appears to be most frequently used as a general, "philosophical," and untested explanation of what people seek from a recreation experience (see, for example, Edginton and Williams, 1978). It has generated relatively little empirical research and has even more rarely been tested as an explanatory behavioral model by leisure researchers. One of the few examples is Alan Mills's (1985) test of "Maslow's theory" (his need hierarchy) in the context of outdoor recreation. The results of Mills's test suggest that the hierarchy, as popularly understood, may be simplistic.

REFERENCES

Csikszentmihalyi, Mihaly. 1975. *Beyond Boredom and Anxiety*. San Francisco: Jossey-Bass. Defines and illustrates the concept of flow, a psychological experience closely related to Maslow's notion of peak experiences.

Edginton, Christopher, and Williams, John. 1978. *Productive Management of Leisure Service Organizations*. New York: Wiley. An example of the uncritical application of Maslow's ideas to recreation and leisure studies.

Goldstein, Kurt. 1971. *Selected Papers/Ausgewahlte Schriften*, ed. Aron Gurwitsch. The Hague: M. Nijhoff. A collection of Goldstein's key addresses, essays, and lectures.

Maslow, Abraham H. 1954. *Motivation and Personality*. New York: Harper & Row. The original articulation of the "need hierarchy" and the role of self-actualization within it.

Maslow, Abraham H. 1968. *Toward a Psychology of Being*. New York: Van Nostrand. An updated restatement of self-actualization; presents a more "generous" definition of the concept.

Maslow, Abraham H. 1970. *Religions, Values, and Peak Experiences*. 1970. New York: Viking. An examination of the origins of the religious and mystical experiences and of the importance of transcendence in a healthy personality.

Mills, Alan S. 1985. Participation Motivations for Outdoor Recreation: "A Test of Maslow's Theory." *Journal of Leisure Research* 17:184–199. An examination of the accuracy of Maslow's hierarchy of needs as a model for recreation motivations; the author concludes that the hierarchy is inadequate as a model of recreation motivations.

Rogers, Carl. 1961. *On Becoming a Person*. Boston: Houghton Mifflin. Personal reflections by Rogers on psychotherapy and the nature of the human personality.

SOURCES OF ADDITIONAL INFORMATION

An excellent examination of various views related to self-actualization and other concepts such as mental health and normality is Richard Coan's *Hero, Artist, Sage, or Saint* (New York: Columbia University Press, 1977). Seppo Iso-Ahola briefly discusses self-actualization in the context of leisure in *The Social Psychology of Leisure and Recreation* (Dubuque, IA: William C. Brown, 1980); John Neulinger does the same in *The Psychology of Leisure* (Springfield, IL: Charles C. Thomas, 1974).

SERIOUS LEISURE. See AMATEUR.

SERVICE AREA. 1. The geographic area surrounding a recreational facility that is served by that facility. 2. The area surrounding a recreational facility from which all (or a specified percentage) users are presumed to come. The extent of the service area may be based on either empirical research or on the basis of planners' intuition.

The concept of the service area of a facility derives from the observation that there appear to be distances beyond which potential users will not come. Among the first formal expressions of this concept were the central place theories of Walter Christaller (1933) and August Lösch (1944). These authors described the

formation of hinterlands around hypothetical central places (cities and towns) such that the hinterlands completely and efficiently fill the landscape. The size of the hinterlands is determined by the size of the central place and the population density surrounding the central place. Larger cities have larger hinterlands; smaller population densities in the surrounding area also tend to create larger hinterlands.

Central place theories were developed to explain the spacing of cities and towns, the range of economic services provided in cities of different sizes, and the number of cities and towns of different sizes. The theories were not originally applied to describing the hinterlands or service areas associated with specific types of business, although regional scientists and geographers subsequently extended these more general theories to individual businesses and public facilities.

In the case of recreation services and the LEISURE INFRASTRUCTURE, an early, explicit application of central place concepts to recreation facilities was formulated by Lisle Mitchell (1969). Mitchell defined a hierarchy of urban recreation facilities ranging from small vest-pocket PARKS and tot lots to large regional parks. He then demonstrated how the concepts of central place theory could be applied to define an ideal pattern for facility location and optimal size of service areas for each type of facility in the hierarchy. Each city would support, for example, a large number of tot lots distributed hexagonally (the most efficient pattern for filling space) with small hinterlands. In contrast, a city might have only one very large park offering a wide range of facilities and activities, serving the entire urban region. The actual number, spacing, and service area sizes are a function of the population density in the city or in each neighborhood.

While Mitchell's theoretical formulation of the pattern of service areas was one of the first applications of central place theory to urban recreation DELIVERY SYSTEMS, the concept of service areas had already been developed and applied independently by recreation planners. The National Recreation Association defined a series of STANDARDS to be used as guides in planning the number, size, and location of urban parks (Butler, 1959). The National Recreation Association's guidelines were adopted or modified by many cities for their use. The city of Dallas, Texas, for example, defined a set of service areas in terms of a "use radius"—the distance within which 80 percent of facility users would be expected to come (Doell and Twardzik, 1973:72).

Facility Type	Service Area
Playlot	One city block or 0.25 miles
Playground	0.50 miles (similar to area served by an elementary school)
Playfield	1.00 miles (similar to area served by a high school)
Large park	3.00 miles

Special parks and   Entire urban area
preserves

Regional recreation   Entire urban area
area

The explicit correlation between the service areas for Dallas playgrounds and playfields and elementary schools and high schools raises an important feature about service areas for public facilities. In the case of public schools, service areas are formally used to allocate children to specific facilities. The service areas of recreation facilities, however, are usually intended only to be descriptive. The assumption is that users will normally go to the closest facility, but they are free to select whatever facility they desire. The willingness of some users to travel beyond the nearest facility to a more distant facility, has been used as a basis for defining the relative ATTRACTIVITY of different facilities. Although more attractive facilities may be expected to exhibit greater service areas, the differences in quality or attractivity are normally not explicitly incorporated into the definition of service areas as used in recreation planning.

Michael Goodchild and Peter Booth (1980) provide an illustration of the differences between service areas defined in terms of the expected willingness to travel and service areas defined in terms of actual use patterns. In a study of swimming pool usage in London, Ontario, the authors first mapped each municipal pool's location on a base map of the city. They then drew a service area around each pool using the city's standard of 1.5 miles for municipal pools. Next, they conducted a survey among pool users and drew a convex curve around each pool on the basis of the most distant users for each pool. This type of service area is sometimes referred to as the catchment area. In general, the actual catchment areas were larger and significantly more irregular than the circular service areas suggested by the city's standard service radius of 1.5 miles.

John Wright, William Braithwaite, and Richard Forster (1976) have built on the concept of the service area by defining a measure of ACCESSIBILITY for individual households. This measure, known as the normal relative accessibility (NRA) is based on the distance between an individual household and a facility in comparison to the size of the standard service area for that facility:

$$NRA = 100 \times e^{-(d/r)^2}$$

where r = range or radius of service area for the facility
      d = distance between the household and the facility
      e = natural logarithm base (about 2.718)

In the case of a playground, with a service area of 0.5 miles (Doell and Twardzik, 1973) and a household located 0.5 miles away from the playground, the NRA is $100 \times e^{-(0.5/0.5)^2}$ = 36.8 percent. Wright, Braithwaite, and Forster (1976) suggest the following interpretation of the values of the NRA:

80–100%   Excellent accessibility

60–79%   Good accessibility

40–59%   Fair accessibility

20–39%   Poor accessibility

0–19%   Very poor accessibility

In the case of our hypothetical household located at the edge of the service area, its NRA of 36.8 percent implies poor accessibility as one might expect given the location of the household on the edge of the service area.

The use of the service area concept, as the use of standards generally, is out of favor in planning theory and philosophy. The objections include the fact that there is often little correlation between the actual catchment area and the specified service area. This, in turn, reflects the fact that the willingness of users to visit certain facilities is not just a function of distance but their own mobility, the quality of the facility, and many other social and physical factors in the community. The concept of the service area persists, however, because the notion that there is an upper limit to the distance people are willing to travel for any particular facility is still relevant and the concept of a service area reflects the desire of recreation planners to formalize this principle in their work.

REFERENCES

Butler, George. 1959. *Introduction to Community Recreation*. New York: McGraw-Hill. An early and influential text in recreation administration; a major advocate for the use of open space standards.

Christaller, Walter. 1933. *Die Zentralen Orte in Süddeutschland*. Jena: Gustav Fischer. The original formulation of central place theory; focus was on the number and spatial distribution of cities and towns serving a range of marketing, transportation, and administrative functions.

Doell, Charles E., and Twardzik, Louis F. 1973. *Elements of Park and Recreation Administration*, 3rd edition. Minneapolis: Burgess. A basic introductory text for park and recreation administration. Includes a section on the use of standards—and service areas—in park administration.

Goodchild, Michael F., and Booth, Peter J. 1980. "Location and Allocation of Recreation Facilities: Public Swimming Pools in London, Ontario." *Ontario Geography* 15:35–52.

Lösch, August. 1944. *Die Raümliche Ordnung der Wirtschaft*. Jena: Gustav Fischer. Builds on Christaller's central place theory, relaxing assumptions about uniform landscapes; emphasis is on distribution of industrial activity.

Mitchell, Lisle S. 1969. "Toward a Theory of Public Urban Recreation." *Proceedings of The Association of American Geographers*. 1:103–108. Demonstrates how the logic of Christaller's central place theory can be applied to predicting the location of urban recreational facilities.

Wright, John R., Braithwaite, William M., and Forster, Richard R. 1976. *Planning for Urban Recreational Open Space: Towards Community-Specific Standards*. Guelph, Ont.: Centre for Resources Development, University of Guelph.

SOURCES OF ADDITIONAL INFORMATION

Examples of standards, including service areas, are provided in most park-administration and park-planning textbooks. A typical example is Seymour Gold's, *Urban Recreation Planning* (Philadelphia: Lea & Febiger, 1976, esp. Chapt. 5). A technically more advanced example of the use of service areas is Isobel Robertson, "Planning the Location of Recreation Centres in Urban Areas: A Case Study of Glasgow" (*Regional Studies,* 12:419–427, 1978). Robertson uses a distance minimizing algorithm to define the optimal locations of recreation centers, with special attention given to the size of the resulting service areas. Louis Hodges and Carlton Van Doren, in "Synagraphic Mapping as a Tool in Locating and Evaluating the Spatial Distribution of Municipal Recreation Facilities" (*Journal of Leisure Research* 4:341–353, 1972), describe a computer graphics methodology for empirically estimating service areas.

A slightly different but related perspective on the topic of service area and the willingness of visitors to travel to recreation facilities is found in Stephen Smith, "Intervening Opportunities and Travel to Urban Recreation Centers" (*Journal of Leisure Research* 12:296–308, 1980). This paper compares the relative importance of distance versus INTERVENING OPPORTUNITIES (a measure of supply) as factors in determining the size of recreation facility service areas.

SOCIALIZATION. The process by which an individual learns values, skills, and attitudes considered by society to be appropriate and necessary for participation in social life.

The intellectual and emotional development of a human being occurs in two realms: social and psychological. Social development involves the learning of norms and knowledges that characterize an individual's CULTURE and that make the individual a functioning part of that society in ways or roles that the society deems appropriate. Psychological development involves the growth of a personality with an accompanying sense of identity and self-esteem within a social setting. Sociological, anthropological, and social psychological research on socialization attempts to develop an understanding of the processes and outcomes of both forms of development. RECREATION, LEISURE, SPORT, and PLAY settings are widely recognized as important contexts in which human socialization occurs throughout the HUMAN LIFE CYCLE. Furthermore, participation patterns in recreation, sport, and play are the result of socialization experiences (Kleiber and Kelly, 1980).

Research designs employed in the study of socialization reflect the two forms of human development. The earliest and dominant design is functionalism. Functionalism is a sociological tradition that emphasizes the relationships between social "facts" such as age, sex, and marital status and patterns of human behavior, such as social expectations or model roles. This tradition dates from the very beginning of sociology as a social science, in the late nineteenth century. [A good history of the beginnings of sociology and the importance of socialization in that beginning is found in William Wentworth (1980); portions of the following paragraphs are based on Wentworth's insights.] Socialization is a core issue in both functionalism specifically and sociology generally. Much of what sociologists have to say about forms of human behavior and social structure has its roots in socialization research.

The dominant social and philosophical view of human nature in the late nineteenth century was that of individualism, a popular belief that people had natures or personalities prior to and independent of social contact. In contrast, among the earliest tenets of sociologists were (1) that something called a society did really exist as a structure that was more than just the collectivity of several million individuals and (2) that this society shaped, in some way, human nature. A goal of the early sociologists was to be able to explain how human beings could overcome their differences to form groups that had a meaning and existence based on collective action and values. A sociological pioneer, E. A. Ross (1896) described the importance of studying the forces that shaped "the molding of the individual's feelings and desires, to suit the needs of the group"—this "molding" would soon be called socialization. In fact, only a year later, Franklin Giddings (1897) published one of the first formal studies of socialization, in which he used the term *socialization* and defined it as "the development of a social nature or character—a social state of mind—in individuals who associate."

In the beginning, socialization had a strong moralistic theme. The concept was based on the assumption that human nature had a wild and independent streak in it that required domestication to the standards of civilization. Indeed, socialization was seen as being identical with the creation of a civilized society. Albion Small (1905:363), another early sociologist put the point clearly, "At present we may use the terms 'socialization' and 'civilization' interchangeably." (Interestingly, "becoming socialized" emerged as a modern or scientific synonym for "becoming civilized" about the same time that "becoming cultured" declined as a philosophical or humanistic synonym for "becoming civilized.")

The key issue in the study of socialization was the question of how it was possible for a social order to emerge out of the interactions of countless individuals who, it was believed, tended to be driven largely by selfish concerns. James Dealey (1920:385–386) explained, "The process of socialization is difficult and contrary to crude human nature. Society must build up through social control and education a type of mind that will be individualistic through social service. . . . Men become socialized as they cease to war against society."

Sigmund Freud (1961:79), working in a different discipline with radically different assumptions and values, coincidentally proposed ideas about the socialization of the human personality that closely paralleled the early sociological notions of socialization: "In the course of human development a part of the inhibiting forces in the world became internalized; we call [this product] the Super-ego." Freud's notion of "internalization" would eventually become part of the functionalist's vocabulary in socialization research.

As noted previously, the initial theme—through the 1920s—of socialization research was how conflict and competition among individuals could be reduced so that a social order might emerge. In the 1920s, however, this conflict-reduction paradigm slowly changed to a focus on the refinement of the human personality. Edward Hayes (1921) provides an illustration of the emergence of this new paradigm. Whereas Dealey spoke of getting individuals to cease warring against society through socialization, Hayes (1921:264) saw socialization as providing the "social conditions necessary to human welfare," providing for the "intelligent utilization of the tendencies of human nature." Or as William Ogburn and Meyer Nimkoff (1940:131) were to put it a couple of decades later, "Socialization is how the individual is converted to a person."

One of the hidden casualties of World War II was the idea of autonomous human nature. For good or ill, people began to be viewed in the 1940s as the creation of the social forces surrounding them. Socialization was neither the taming of a wild human nature, nor the unleashing of human potentials, but the creation of a social personality: Socialization is "the taking over of another person's habits, attitudes, and ideas, and the reorganizing of them into one's own system" (Young, 1944:170) This view reached its culmination in the 1950s, with the work of Talcott Parsons (1951). Arguing from a "systems perspective," Parsons suggested that the critical question in socialization was not what must be done to socialize an individual, but how socialization worked to allow an individual to function as a human being in a social system. Socialization was, in Parsons' (1951:208) leaden prose, "the learning of any orientations of functional significance to the operation of a system of complementary role-expectations." In other words, socialization created social beings and helped society become a stable, self-perpetuating system.

In addition to advancing the notion that socialization virtually created the human personality, Parsons also argued for a distinction between "primary socialization" and "secondary socialization." Primary socialization was the social learning of children, while "secondary socialization" was the acquisition of specific professional roles by adults. This theme was further developed by Robert Merton (1957) in *The Student Physician*. Merton (1949) used the phrase *anticipatory socialization* to express the idea that adolescents and adults imitate and practice the actions and values of groups they hope to be able to join, such as a profession.

While Parsons, Merton, and their contemporaries helped to further refine the concept of socialization, the most important aspect of their work for the purposes of this definition was their promulgation of the functionalist viewpoint: the individual personality is shaped by external forces beyond its control. The functionalist notion of socialization is basically a mechanistic one. A person is buffeted by outside forces that shape his personality; the role of sociology is to be able to describe how these forces work. This viewpoint has generally been dominant not only in traditional sociology but also in recreation and leisure studies. From the early work of Catherine Patrick (1945) through the most recent studies, most recreation researchers are interested in how the forces of socialization affect what children do in their leisure, or how early childhood leisure socialization experiences carry through the human life cycle to influence adult leisure patterns (e.g., Yoesting and Christensen, 1978; Spreitzer and Snyder, 1983).

Although the functionalist viewpoint has been successful in providing insights into important social processes, it does have certain weaknesses. With respect to socialization, one of its major weaknesses is the image of human beings as being passive recipients (or victims) of external forces beyond their control. There is strong evidence that people can actively select, interpret, modify, control, or even reject social stimuli. Several schools of thought have developed in sociology that focus on how human beings respond to or interact with others. These include symbolic interactionism, exchange theory, and conflict theory. These diverse schools can be grouped together as part of an interactionist tradition as an antithesis to the functionalist tradition. George Herbert Mead (1962), Emile Durkheim (1961), and many contemporary feminist sociologists are examples of this tradition. Although many of their specific ideas and interests differ significantly, the unifying notion in their work is that individuals interact with each other through exchanges, negotiations, and conflicts (Homans, 1958). Although socialization has been less widely studied by most of the interactionists, it has received some attention. For example, Sam Sieber (1974) has examined how socialization forces can lead to the creation of multiple roles for any one individual, and the impact of the accumulation of different roles on the individual's levels of anxiety. Sheldon Stryker and Anne Macke (1978) have examined the problem of role conflicts and discrepancies between personal desires and social expectations in the socialization process.

In comparing the essential differences between functionalism and interactionism, Wentworth (1980) offered the following observations. Functionalists believe that society is dominant, and that society is the proper focus of study. Socialization is seen as a deterministic process explainable by stimulus-response or social learning theories. In contrast, interactionists believe the individual is dominant and is the proper focus of study. Socialization is a reciprocal process in which the individual actively influences his learning. While functionalists believe social structures create persons, interactionists believe that individuals shape and give meaning to social structures. Functionalists study how socialization processes work, and how people learn values generally or specific roles and skills. Functionalists study the effects of socialization on people and the strategies employed by individuals to manipulate or manage the socialization process.

Barbara Brown (1983) and Barry McPherson (1986) have examined the strengths and weaknesses of both the interactionist (sometimes called the "undersocialized model") and functionalist (the "oversocialized model") traditions from the perspective of sport sociology. They both conclude that the two approaches are overly simplistic. While they are unable to offer a practical prescription for what McPherson calls a "new wave" in socialization research, they do offer some useful suggestions for research design principles:

1. Recognize the distinction between socialization as a form of learning and socialization as a way of developing social relationships.

2. Study socialization from the viewpoint of an observer or disinterested third party, rather than the perspective of "society" or the individual being socialized.

3. Assume that the acquisition of social skills and role models for social life are the primary goals of socialization.

4. Pay greater attention to the contexts in which socialization occurs (e.g., family, sports teams).

5. Recognize that power and social control are essential concepts in the study of socialization, although they are not the goals of socialization.

6. Socialization is an ongoing, lifelong process.

7. Different forms of socialization are relevant at different stages in life. A functionalist model may be more appropriate in childhood, while an interactionist model may be more appropriate for adults.

Both authors also note that socialization research continues to be diffused, contradictory, lacking in any new conceptual developments since the 1950s, and often too closely tied to the researcher's personal beliefs about human nature. McPherson (1986) described the field as being eclectic in substance, theory, and methods. He attributed the eclecticism, which he considered a weakness, to (1) the lack of interest by many contemporary sociologists and social psychologists in pursuing socialization topics and (2) the growing interest of "novice investigators" from "emerging fields" (i.e., not mainstream sociology or social psychology) who McPherson alleged lacked knowledge of the literature, theory, and methods used by the older fields when they were still active in socialization research. Whether or not McPherson's accusations about the competence of social scientists outside traditional sociology and social psychology are accurate, another conclusion of his does seem legitimate. The field, he notes, still lacks "irrefutable postulates or laws" on which further empirical and theoretical advances can be based (McPherson, 1986:111). There are few reliable, nonrefutable conclusions about the processes, strategies, and outcomes of different forms of socialization. This lack of progress or indepth understanding is especially apparent in the sociology of recreation and leisure. There are also some unexplored contradictions between the belief that socialization is an important force shaping recreation and leisure (and that recreation and leisure are powerful socializing forces) and the idea that SELF-ACTUALIZATION, which implies the transcendence of socializing forces, is the goal of recreation and leisure experiences.

REFERENCES

Brown, Barbara A. 1983. Factors Influencing the Process of Withdrawal by Female Adolescents from the Competitive Age Group Swimmer. Unpublished Ph.D. dissertation, University of Waterloo, Department of Kinesiology. Applies various socialization concepts and models to the decision for females withdrawing from competitive swimming.

Dealey, James Quayle. 1920. *Sociology: Its Development and Application.* An early general text on sociology, with a discussion of the notion of socialization as a force for "civilizing" people.

Durkheim, Emil. 1961. *Moral Education*. New York: Free Press. A classic work in the sociology of education (first published in 1902); emphasizes an "interactionist" perspective in understanding how individuals learn values.

Freud, Sigmund. 1961. *Civilization and Its Discontents*. New York: Norton. A reprint of the 1930 edition; includes a discussion of the notion of the id, ego, and super-ego and the role of "internalization" of parental images as part of one's psychological development.

Giddings, Franklin Henry. 1897. *The Theory of Socialization*. New York: Macmillan. One of the first presentations of the concept of and possible mechanisms associated with socialization.

Hayes, Edward Cary. 1921. *Sociology and Ethics*. New York: McGraw-Hill. A functionalist examination of the issue of values formation and the development of ethical systems in society; illustrates a refinement in the definition of socialization beyond the original focus on socialization as a synonym for "civilization."

Homans, George C. 1958. "Social Behavior as Exchange." *American Journal of Sociology* 62:597–606. One of the first statements of "exchange theory"—the idea that social interactions can be analyzed as examples of material or nonmaterial exchanges.

Kleiber, Douglas, and Kelly, John R. 1980. "Leisure, Socialization and the Life Cycle." In *Social Psychological Perspectives on Leisure and Recreation*, ed. Seppo E. Iso-Ahola, 91–137. Springfield, IL: Charles C. Thomas. A good review of the research literature on socialization into and through leisure at various stages in the life cycle.

McPherson, Barry D. 1986. "Socialization Theory and Research Towards a 'New Wave' of Scholarly Inquiry in a Sport Context." In *Sport and Social Theory*, ed. C. Roger Rees and Andrew W. Miracle, 111–134. Champaign, IL: Human Kinetics Press. A critical review of the history of socialization research, with recommendations about the potentials and problems facing sport sociologists interested in socialization.

Mead, George Herbert. 1962. *Mind, Self, and Society*. Chicago: University of Chicago Press. A posthumous work based on Mead's earlier writings; represents a summary of many of Mead's insights into the reciprocal relationship between the human being and society.

Merton, Robert K. 1949. *Social Theory and Social Structure*. Glencoe, IL: The Free Press. A dated but important scholarly work that presents the case for a functionalist approach in sociology; based on a collection of papers originally published elsewhere and then collected and edited into a single volume.

Merton, Robert K. 1957. *The Student Physician*. Cambridge, MA: Harvard University Press. A functionalist's interpretation of the educational and socialization process of medical students.

Ogburn, William F., and Nimkoff, Meyer. 1940. *Sociology*. Boston: Houghton Mifflin. Presents a view of socialization that emphasizes the "refinement" of human nature and the "unleashing" of human potential.

Parsons, Talcott. 1951. *The Social System*. New York: Free Press. A systems-oriented, functionalist view of the development of society and of the individual's role in society.

Patrick, Catherine. 1945. "Relation of Childhood and Adult Leisure Activities." *Journal of Social Psychology* 21:65–79. An early examination of the relationship between childhood and adult recreation patterns; finds only a weak correlation.

Ross, E. A. 1896. "Social Control." *American Journal of Sociology* 1:513–535. Describes the importance of social control as a phenomenon of concern in developing a science of society.

Sieber, Sam. 1974. "Toward a Theory of Role Accumulation." *American Sociological Review* 39:567–578. Disputes the notion that an individual having to play many different roles experiences undue anxiety or "role conflict."

Small, Albion. 1905. *General Sociology*. Chicago: University of Chicago Press. Another early scholarly inquiry into the nature, methods, and scope of sociology; includes a discussion on socialization as the mechanism for "civilizing" people.

Spreitzer, Elmer, and Snyder, Eldon. 1983. "Correlates of Participation in Adult Recreational Sports." *Journal of Leisure Research* 1:27–38. Examined tournament racquetball players, competitive runners, and the general population to see if there was a relationship between childhood and adult participation patterns; found no strong association.

Stryker, Sheldon, and Macke, Anne. 1978. "Status Inconsistency and Role Conflict." In *Annual Review of Sociology,* Vol. 4, ed. R. Turner, J. Coleman, and R. Fox, 57–90. Palo Alto, CA: Annual Reviews Publishers. A literature review of recent research on role conflicts and status conflicts; the authors suggest these are specific instances of a more general phenomenon of interpersonal interactions.

Wentworth, William. 1980. *Context and Understanding: An Inquiry Into Socialization Theory*. New York: Elsevier. A good review of socialization research, including a critique of the functionalist tradition; promotes greater emphasis on "interaction theory" as a basis for understanding socialization.

Yoesting, Dean R., and Christensen, James E. 1978. "Reexamining the Significance of Childhood Recreation Patterns on Adult Leisure Behavior." *Leisure Sciences* 1:219–229. A test of the "carry-over" hypothesis of participation; the authors found only very weak support for a link between childhood and adult participation.

Young, Kimball. 1944. *Personality and the Problems of Adjustment*. New York: Crofts. Presents a definition of socialization as the adoption of a general social "personality" into one's own personality; written from a functionalist perspective.

SOURCES OF ADDITIONAL INFORMATION

A dated but classic critique of the functionalist approach to socialization is Dennis Wrong's "The Oversocialized Conception of Man in Modern Sociology" (*American Sociological Review* 26:183–193, 1961). Orville Brim provides an overview of "Socialization through the Life Cycle" in Orville Brim and Stanton Wheeler, eds., *Socialization after Childhood* (New York: Wiley, 1966). The relevance of socialization to THERAPEUTIC RECREATION is discussed by John Lewko in "Specialized Knowledge and the Delivery of Services to the Disabled" (*Leisure Sciences* 1:131–146, 1978). Dennis Orthner and Jay Mancini examine the relationships between one's childhood family patterns and marital family leisure patterns in "Parental Family Sociability and Marital Leisure Patterns" (*Leisure Sciences* 1:365–372, 1978). Role change and socialization is considered in Seppo Iso-Ahola and Kevin Buttimer's "The Emergence of Work and Leisure Ethic from Early Adolescence to Early Adulthood" (*Journal of Leisure Research,* 13:282–288, 1981).

A useful collection of readings on socialization is David Goslin's edited work, *Handbook of Socialization Theory and Research* (Chicago, Rand McNally, 1969). A more recent view of social psychological research in socialization is D. Baumrind, "New Dimensions in Socialization Research" (*American Psychologist* 35:639–652, 1980).

Examples of further research on socialization and children's play are Janet Lever's "Sex Difference in the Games Children Play" (*Social Problems* 23:478–487, 1976) and "Sex Differences in the Complexity of Children's Play and Games" (*American Sociological Review* 43:471–482, 1978); T. Wolfe, "Influence of Age and Sex of Model on Sex-Inappropriate Play" (*Psychological Reports* 36:99–105, 1975); and Lance Wuellner, "The Adult Inhibition and Peer Disinhibition and Preschool Group Play" (*Journal of Leisure Research* 13:159–173, 1978).

SPORT. A type of GAME characterized by COMPETITION based on physical skill, subject to established rules of PLAY, and governed through some form of institutionalization.

Sport, as a word, is an apheresis of the Middle English *desport,* a term that meant "to get carried away through amusement or enjoyment." The modern form appeared as early as the mid-1400s and was used especially with reference to erotic play. By the twentieth century the primary connotation of the word was that of athletic contests, although many of the earlier connotations such as amusement, teasing, and sexual play are still recognized as legitimate meanings of the word.

The contemporary social scientific study of sport is based primarily on psychology and sociology. Some geographers, political scientists, economists, economists, and historians have studied sport from the perspectives of their own disciplines, but the greatest volume of work is still psychological or sociological in content.

A common theme in the attempts by sport social scientists to define the concept is the relationship between sport and other forms of LEISURE, especially play and games. The most frequent argument is that sport is a type of game. John Loy (1968:12) defined sport as "any institutionalized game demanding demonstration of physical prowess." Kent Pearson (1975:1) suggested a more succinct view by noting that, for most authors, "sport is seen as a sub-class of games." Gunther Lüschen and George Sage (1981:5) offered a slightly more elaborate conception by considering sport to be any activity that is "playful, competitive, internally rewarding, and involves individuals and teams in a contest that is zero-sum in outcome."

A related but more critical argument about the relationship between sport and play was articulated by Johan Huizinga (1955) in *Homo Ludens*. Huizinga described sport as a type of playful competition that has lost much of its original playful qualities by virtue of the increasing seriousness society accords sport. Harry Edwards (1973) repeated the same theme nearly two decades later, noting specifically the overinstitutionalization of sport and the strong business ethic in much of professional sport. Kenneth Schmitz (1976) suggested that the pressures of modern athletes to achieve ever-greater physical skill was also a major cause of the loss of playfulness in sport.

More recently, Kendall Blanchard and Alyce Cheska (1985) acknowledged the growing seriousness associated with some aspects of sport, but argued that critics such as Edwards and Schmitz considered sport in an overly narrow context: university and professional leagues in modern Western societies.

The foundation of these authors' opinions is, of course, the notion that sport originally was and should ideally be a form of play. Most authors, however, also cite other characteristics of activities that qualify them to be labeled as sport, regardless of the level of seriousness. These characteristics are physical skill, competition, rules, and institutionalization.

In the context of sport definitions, physical skill refers to (1) one or more physical movements of the human body required by the sport, (2) movements that can be improved through practice, and (3) movement skills that can influence the outcome of the contest. The notion of physical skill can be deceptively simple. A foot race, for example, clearly is a sport because running is a physical skill that can be improved through practice and that determines the outcome of the race. Chess, on the other hand, clearly is not a sport because the physical skill in moving the chess pieces about the board is irrelevant in determining the outcome of the contest. In contrast to these simple examples, one can ponder whether physical skill and practice play significant roles in auto racing, horse racing, hunting, or fishing.

Competition, in the definition, refers to the effort by a participant to become a winner in a contest. The concept of competition in sport implies the existence of at least one other human participant who is also endeavoring to win and to force his opponent to lose. Lüschen and Sage (1981) used the term zero-sum to designate competition. Zero-sum, however, is not strictly accurate in the case of most sports. The sum of points earned in most sporting events is not zero. One team's points are not earned at the direct expense of points lost by other teams. The notion of a winner and loser is also overly simplistic. Many track and field events as well as other sports result in rankings of participants: first, second, third, and so forth.

Rules play the same roles in sport as they do in all games. They prescribe what actions are permissible as well as those that are not. Rules tend to establish a degree of inefficiency of action and of equality between opponents. Teams are required to have the same number of players; equipment and playing areas must conform to certain STANDARDS. Rules usually define how long the game is to be played or how it is terminated and how a winner is determined. An important characteristic of rules in sport is that they are standardized; they are not negotiated anew for every game occurrence. This quality of rule standardization is, in fact, an aspect of the institutional quality of sport.

The institutionalization of sport was identified by Paul Weiss in 1967 (quoted in Loy, 1968). Weiss (1967:82) suggested, ''a game is an occurrence; a sport is a pattern. The one is in the present, the other primarily past, but instantiated in the present. A sport defines the conditions to which participants must submit if there is to be a game; a game gives rootage to a set of rules and thereby enables it to be exhibited.'' Loy (1968) took this distinction further by arguing that sport, as a concept, should be defined at four different levels of institutionalization: (1) as a game occurrence, (2) as an institutionalized game, (3) as a social institution, and (4) as a social system.

Sport as a game occurrence, to Loy, has many playful qualities but is not simply a subset of play. Although some sports could be classified as play forms, other sports are too serious, too professional, or too highly organized to be considered as play.

As an institutionalized game, sport is an abstraction. Baseball, in this view is not an individual contest between two teams but a rule book, a league structure, sponsorship, and a sport governing body. Institutionalized games are not casual or even formal encounters between participants but an enduring structure that regulates and defines the conduct of countless game occurrences. The institution of sport also provides educational opportunities for the acquisition and improvement of physical skills by participants as well as sanctions for those who violate the rules of the sport.

The social institutional perspective of sport is even broader than that of sport as an institutionalized game. The social institution of sport (also referred to as the sport order) encompasses equipment manufacturers, facility owners and managers, teams, leagues, sport governing bodies, and even publishers and journalists. The sport order is, in brief, the totality of all individuals and organizations directly associated with sport. These individuals and organizations can be divided into four groups:

1. *Primary*. Participants in informal games.
2. *Technical*. Collegiate teams and leagues.
3. *Managerial*. Professional sport clubs.
4. *Corporate*. Sport governing bodies.

Loy's fourth and most general perspective on sport is that of the social system of sport. This concept refers to the social context or social situation in which people become involved directly or indirectly with sport. It encompasses individuals and organizations; social, economic, and political environments; the various cultural objects used in sport; the symbolism of sport phenomena; and the relationships among all these components of the sport system.

Although there is a body of literature (some of it quite theoretical as can be seen in Loy's work) devoted to defining sport, other authors have challenged the notion that sport can be or should be defined. First, they interpret the various definitions offered by different authors as reflecting fundamentally different perspectives on the nature of sport. Second, the existence of these different perspectives is empirical evidence that there is no consensus on what constitutes the essence of sport. And third, the lack of such a consensus despite the efforts of numerous authors of the last few decades is strongly suggestive that such a consensus is impossible and that further efforts to define sport are a waste of time (see, for example, Kleinman, 1968; McBride, 1975).

McBride concedes that it may be necessary to operationally define sport for the purposes of scientific research projects, but he also argues that these definitions are not the same as conventional dictionary definitions. Pearson (1975), however, suggests that the difficulty the "antiessentialists" (those who oppose the development of conventional definitions) experience in searching for a definition stems from their desire to be overly precise and to be able to accommodate every existing connotation within one standard definition. Pearson believes that definitions are both possible and mandatory if there is to be a cumulative social scientific study of sport. Definitions, to Pearson, can be based on the common characteristics of activities generally recognized as sport by most people: competition, rules, institutionalization, and physical skill.

REFERENCES

Blanchard, Kenneth, and Cheska, Alyce. 1985. *The Anthropology of Sport*. Boston: Bergin and Garvey. Examines sport as an anthropological phenomenon and promotes the study of sport in a multicultural context.

Edwards, Harry. 1973. *Sociology of Sport*. Homewood, IL: Dorsey Press. Presents an argument that sport is becoming "too serious."

Huizinga, Johan. 1955. *Homo Ludens: A Study of the Play Element in Culture*. Boston: Beacon Press. The classic study on the nature of play and sport.

Kleinman, Seymour. 1968. "Toward a Non-Theory of Sport." *Quest* 10:29–34. Argues that definitions of sport are not possible.

Loy, John. 1968. "The Nature of Sport: A Definitional Effort." *Quest* 10(May):1–15. A major theoretical statement on the nature of sport as a game and play form.

Lüschen, Gunther, and Sage, George. 1981. *Handbook of Social Science of Sport*. Champaign, IL: Stipes. A good sourcebook for definitions of sport as well as examples of sociological and psychological research on the nature of sport.

McBride, Frank. 1975. "Toward a Non-Definition of Sport." *Journal of the Philosophy of Sport* 2:4–11. Presents a formal argument that definitions of sport are illogical and a waste of time to pursue.

Pearson, Kent. 1975. "The 'At Leasts' of Games and Sport and a Model for Conceptualizing and Locating Games, Sports, and Forms of Athletics." Paper presented at the Conference on Sport, Society, and Personality. Bundoora, Australia: La Trobe University. A difficult-to-find paper describing some of the basic common characteristics of sport activities.

Schmitz, Kenneth. 1976. "Sport and Play: Suspension of the Ordinary." In (*Sport in the Sociocultural Process*, 2nd edition, ed. M. Hart, 35–48. Dubuque, IA: William C. Brown. Examines the nature of sport and the relationship between sport and play.

Weiss, Paul. 1967. Sport: A Philosophic Society. Unpublished manuscript. A theoretical and philosophical inquiry into the nature of sport; suggests that not all sports are play forms, although all sports are games.

SOURCES OF ADDITIONAL INFORMATION

Additional information on sport may be found in Bernard Jeu, "What is Sport?" (*Diogenes* 80:150–163, 1972); Robert J. Paddick, "What Makes Physical Activity Physical?" (*Journal of the Philosophy of Sport* 2:12–20, 1975); and Allen Sack, "Sports: Play or Work?" in Phillip Stevens, ed., *Studies in the Anthropology of Play* (West Point, NY: Leisure Press, 1977, 186–195). Klaus Meier, "On the Inadequacies of Sociological Definitions of Sport" (*International Review of Sport Sociology* 16:79–102, 1981) is another example of an author identifying problems with existing definitions of sport. Marie Hart and Susan Birrell, eds., *Sport in the Sociocultural Process* (3rd edition, Dubuque, IA: William C. Brown 1981) and John Loy, Gerald Kenyon, and Barry McPherson, eds., *Sport, Culture and Society: A Reader on the Sociology of Sport* (Philadelphia: Lee & Febiger, 1981) are collections of readings on the nature of sport.

STANDARD. A quantitative index specifying either a minimum or desired supply of open space or other recreation facilities for a community; usually expressed in terms of a per capita ratio.

Seymour Gold (1973:143) once observed, "no single concept or measure has had a more significant impact on the urban recreation experience than the RECREATION standard." Standards are generally used as a guide for specifying the amount of open space that should be dedicated for various types of PARK use, given a community's population. Other standards have also been developed, however. These include specifications for the percent of a municipal budget that should be allocated to recreation, the number and spacing of recreation facilities and equipment, operational estimates of CARRYING CAPACITY, and a minimum program or leader/staff provision for a given population. Architectural standards to ensure safety, ACCESSIBILITY, and use efficiency have also been developed and, in some cases, have the force of law (such as those designed to eliminate BARRIERS for users with physical disabilities) or to insure EQUITY.

Recreation standards as open space guidelines have been part of the American recreation movement since its inception at the beginning of the twentieth century. As a result, many recreation professionals tend to think of standards as an American invention. In fact, however, William Theobald (1984) has traced their roots back to the mid-nineteenth-century in England. Theobald (1984:193) quotes Charles Smith, for example, who in 1852, criticized the plans of the city of London for expanding its park system by adding to large suburban parks. Smith suggested, "if, instead of enlarging the parks to the extent of 150 to 270 acres, and placing them at considerable distances, they had confined them to 80 to 100 acres at one-half the distance, and had multiplied them proportionally, they would have easily procured a sufficient quantity of ground near and more accessible to all classes of the inhabitants." Although Smith's suggestion was not as formal a standard, it did reflect a dawning awareness of the need for guidelines about planning the size and location of public open space.

Perhaps the first formal statement of a recreation standard was the suggestion by the Earl of Meath in 1883 that "a public open space for recreation should be within a quarter mile of everyone's door" (Theobald, 1984:193). Theobald also cites the suggestion by Robert Hunter (1891) that new towns be required to dedicate 5 percent of their area of public open space.

In the same decade the London school board began to address the problem of providing adequate PLAY space at schools for children. In 1891, the board's Department Committee of Playgrounds specified a "minimum size of a site [playground] should ordinarily be one-quarter of an acre for every 260 children" (Theobald, 1984:194). This was modified in 1893 to a minimum of 30 square feet of play space per child. It was this standard that was first imported to the United States by the National Playground Association of America for use in planning American playgrounds. Through the 1920s and 1930s the standard was revised several times, each time recommending greater space for children's play.

By the 1940s, the neigborhood playground began to be recognized as a resource important for all people living in a neighborhood, not just children (Butler, 1948). This changing perception of the neighborhood park resulted in not just another expansion of the standard but also its modification to apply to the general population. This new standard called for 1 acre per 1000 people—a ratio still widely considered appropriate for neighborhoods today.

During the 1960s, the recreation movement began to be increasingly concerned about the provision of adequate RESOURCES for society's recreation needs (Gold, 1973:146). The result of this concern was a reaffirmation of the use of standards (National Recreation and Park Association, 1967; Bureau of Outdoor Recreation, 1967) but without a serious rationalization, testing, or critiquing of the indexes used as standards.

In 1969, the National Recreation and Park Association released the proceedings of a national forum on standards, *National Park, Recreation and Open Space Standards* (Buechner, 1971) which clearly urged municipalities to use standards, particularly for the provision of open space at the neighborhood and subneighborhood level. Furthermore, standards were to be considered as guidelines for minimum levels of provision. Although released two decades ago, this report still adequately represents the "state of the art" of standards in North America, in both its philosophy and contents.

Virtually every author who has written on standards has warned of the need to consider them as guidelines only, not as rigid specifications (Gold, 1973; Wilkinson, 1985). Yet these authors also fear that recreation planners tend to use them uncritically and without making any allowances for community variations. "Planners have tended to adopt standards as . . . absolute rather than as guidelines that must be applied with discretion" (Wilkinson, 1985:194).

Tests of the apparent use of standards by municipalities, however, fails to provide adequate evidence to support the assertion that municipal recreation planners and professionals actually are guilty of the uncritical use of standards. Carlton Van Doren (1973) examined patterns of open space provision in American cities in 1955 and 1965; Leslie Lynch (1965) examined patterns in 1960; and Arthur Haley (1979, 1985) analyzed data for the years 1965, 1975, and

1980. All three authors found significant variations in the ratio between designated open space and a city's population. Haley also noted substantial variations between central cities and their suburbs, and marked differences over the years he examined. These authors did not interview planners as to their perceptions or interpretations of standards—so their results cannot be considered a direct refutation of Wilkinson's charge that planners view standards as "absolute." However, the finding that the great majority of cities either fall far short or greatly exceed formal standards does suggest that standards are not widely used as "absolutes" in planning.

In the 1970s and 1980s, some attention was given to the development of community-specific standards (Wright, Braithwaite, and Forster, 1976). The basic idea behind community-specific standards is that the sociodemographic, housing, and morphological characteristics of a community would somehow guide the development of a set of standards for each community. In this case, a community might actually be individual neighborhoods or other planning units within a larger urban area. The ideal of developing community-specific standards, however, has not yet been achieved. One possible reason for this is that traditional standards are simple to understand and appear impartial. Community-specific standards, while overcoming some of the criticism of traditional standards that they fail to account for local conditions, can be challenged on the grounds that they lack objectivity, a scientific base, and wide professional acceptance.

One possible compromise between the use of traditional objective standards and the idiosyncratic community-specific standards was proposed by Stephen Smith (1975). Smith developed and applied a classification algorithm for groups of cities that produces relatively homogeneous clusters on the basis of cities, social, economic, demographic, and political characteristics. It is conceptually possible to modify existing standards to better reflect the needs of a group of similar cities, without being subject to criticisms that the standards are so unique to specific communities that they lack impartiality. However, Smith did not extend his work beyond the development of a classification methodology.

Standards, in practice, appear to be used more as a political or policy tool than as a formal planning tool. They are in particular, cited by funding agencies to justify decisions (typically negative decisions) about the provision of funding to recreation agencies. In this context, standards are sometimes interpreted as a type of normative NEED—as an "absolute" as Wilkinson would suggest. But in practice, standards appear to be more of a political convenience to support an unpopular but politically necessary decision. In other cases, political considerations may totally override standards in the allocation of funding or resources.

The fact that standards have been developed through consensus by a professional association and sometimes given official sanction by a public agency not responsible for local budgetary decisions is both the great strength and great weakness of standards. They are generally seen as being neutral and objective. An agency or citizens' group can appeal to standards as an impartial and "scientific" argument that may support their cause. On the other hand, by their very nature, standards do not reflect local situations that may require special political or planning considerations. Standards are a tool most professionals find useful on some occasions, but which have inherent and obvious weaknesses, can be easily overridden by politics, and which can be turned around or interpreted and used against a recreation agency to justify a negative decision not to support some proposal.

Recreation standards are a well-established part of the professional literature. They are sometimes used in planning and policy applications, and are favorite targets for academic criticism. Although some authors have suggested abandoning standards altogether, Thomas (Tim) Burton (1967) concluded that standards are probably necessary and are likely to stay. The use of standards in the recreation profession will benefit from further research. Fortunately, the topic appears to continually attract attention by a variety of researchers, policy analysts, and planners that will eventually produce further improvements in our use and understanding of standards.

REFERENCES

Buechner, Robert D. (Ed.). 1971. *National Parks, Recreation, and Open Space Standards*. Washington, DC: National Recreation and Park Association. One of the "standard" references for standards in parks and recreation.

Bureau of Outdoor Recreation. 1967. *Outdoor Recreation Space Standards*. Washington, DC: U.S. Government Printing Office. Essentially a restatement of the NRPA's views on standards.

Burton, Thomas L. 1976. *Making Man's Environment: Leisure*. New York: Van Nostrand Reinhold. A general conceptual discussion of open space and recreation planning; argues that standards are "here to stay."

Butler, George. 1948. "Standards for Municipal Recreation Areas." *Recreation* 42 (July/August): 20–22. An influential article promoting the use of open space standards.

Gold, Seymour M. 1973. *Urban Recreation Planning*. Philadelphia: Lea & Febiger. An excellent survey of the concepts and practices of urban recreation planning; includes an entire chapter on the history and application of standards.

Haley, A. J. 1979. "Municipal Recreation and Park Standards in the United States: Central Cities and Suburbs." *Leisure Sciences* 2:277–290. Examines space per capita and budget ratios for seventy-six central cities and their suburbs.

Haley, A. J. 1985. "Municipal Recreation and Park Standards in the United States: Central Cities and Suburbs, 1975–1980." *Leisure Sciences* 7:175–188. Updates his 1979 article; notes several significant historical changes.

Lynch, Leslie. 1965. "Recreation Area Standards: The City." *Recreation* 18(1):20–21. A brief review of open space per capita ratios for fifty cities in the United States.

National Recreation and Park Association. 1967. *Outdoor Recreation Space Standards*. Washington, DC: National Recreation and Park Association. Presents an argument for and examples of open space standards, but failed to justify the specific standards in common practice.

Smith, Stephen. 1975. "Similarities between Urban Recreation Systems." *Journal of Leisure Research* 7:270–281. Describes and applies a factor-clustering methodology for defining groups of relatively homogeneous cities; could be used as a basis for developing standards that are specific to types of community, rather than general to all communities or specific to individual communities.

Theobald, William. 1984. "A History of Recreation Resource Planning: The Origins of Space Standards." *Leisure Studies* 3:189–200. A descriptive review of the development of space standards, emphasizing their British origins.

Van Doren, Carlton. 1973. "Urban Recreation and Park Standards in the United States." *Proceedings of the Association of American Geographers* 3:266–271. Examines open space ratios and selected other measures of resource allocation for recreation in fifty-four cities.

Wilkinson, Paul F. 1985. "The Golden Fleece: The Search for Standards." *Leisure Studies* 4:189–203. A response to Theobald's history; takes a more critical view of the use of standards by the profession.

Wright, Jack; Braithwaite, William; and Forster, Richard. 1976. *Planning for Urban Recreational Open Space: Towards Community-Specific Standards*. Toronto: Ontario Ministry of Housing. A conceptual argument for community-specific standards; fails to provide practical guidelines for actually developing them, however.

SOURCES OF ADDITIONAL INFORMATION

The literature on standards is fairly large, and good bibliographies may be found in the works by Gold, Theobald, and Wilkinson (cited in the references). Some basic works include George Butler, *Standards for Municipal Recreation Areas* (New York: National Recreation Association, 1962); George Hjelte and Jay Shivers, *Planning Recreational Places* (Cranbury, NJ: Fairleigh Dickinson University Press, 1971); W. F. Lever, "Recreational Space in Cities: Standards of Provision" (*Journal of the Royal Town Planning Institute* 59, 1973); and the Ontario Ministry of Culture and Recreation, *Guidelines for Developing Public Recreation Facility Standards* (Toronto: Ministry of Culture and Recreation, 1976).

SUBSTITUTION. The process of switching one activity (or site) for another when the original activity (or site) becomes unavailable.

This apparently simple concept is an important topic in leisure research. The substitution of activities and sites (site substitution is also known as DISPLACEMENT) may be necessary when personal or management factors such as increased cost of participation, overuse of a site, the depletion of a particular resource, crowding, or user conflicts eliminate access to a particular activity or site. Applied research into identifying what activities or sites may be substituted for others can pay useful dividends in terms of more efficient and responsive management and increased user satisfaction. Furthermore, the long term success of this applied research depends on the development of a solid basis of theoretical research into the motivations for and the satisfactions derived from leisure behavior. Substitutability, therefore, is a potential source for advancements in both applied and basic research. Because the greatest volume of work as well as the most significant work on substitution has been devoted to activity substitution, that will be the focus of the following discussion. Site substitution, nonetheless, remains an important topic in its own right and one deserving greater inquiry.

Research in this area has grown from a series of early empirical studies of ACTIVITY CLUSTERS such as Charles Proctor's (1962), Doyle Bishop's (1970), and Thomas (Tim) Burton's (1971) factor analytic studies of leisure behavior. These and other authors speculated on the potential for substituting one activity for another among those activities that clustered together on statistically derived factors. One such cluster might be "Outdoor Activities," consisting of hunting, fishing, camping, and hiking. The premise behind these speculations was that if one activity becomes unavailable—perhaps hunting because licenses are issued through a lottery system and some would-be hunters are denied access to hunting because of the luck of the draw—they could participate in fishing, camping, or hiking and still derive similar satisfaction from participation. Among the first authors to formally describe the management implications of factor analysis research of activities and substitutability were John Hendee and Rabel Burdge (1974).

Their work prompted a critique by Jay Beaman (1975) who confirmed the potential significance of research on substitution. He noted, however, that there were some technical problems associated with the use of factor analysis to derive activity clusters. He also warned that it is difficult, if not impossible, to distinguish between substitutability and COMPLEMENTARITY when analyzing aggregate patterns of participation. Finally, Beaman advised researchers interested in substitution to base their research in a more precise social and management context.

Although it has been the dominant research design used in studying substitutability, factor analysis of participation patterns is not the only research design employed. Robert Baumgartner (1978) and Jerry Vaske (1980) developed clusters of activities on the basis of specific activity characteristics. Neil Cheek (1971) and Dominic Dottavio, Joseph O'Leary, and Barbara Koth (1981) used the social grouping context of participation in leisure activities to define similarities among activities. John Hendee, Richard Gale, and William Catton (1971) as well as David Chase and Neil Cheek (1979) explored the use of expressed preferences for activities as a basis for activity clustering. And Brent Ritchie (1975) and Boris Becker (1976) experimented with recreationist-defined measures of similarity for defining clusters.

In 1977, James Christensen and Dean Yoesting (1977) surveyed existing research on substitutability and noted that insufficient attention had been paid to empirically testing many of the underlying assumptions of the concept. They were particularly concerned about the implicit assumptions that there are no differences (1) among individuals' willingness to substitute activities and (2) in the substitutability of different types of activity. To test the validity of these assumptions, they developed a questionnaire to examine the willingness of different socioeconomic groups to substitute different activities (grouped into four categories: hunting and fishing, nature appreciation, games and sports, and motorized activities). Their results suggested that, contrary to the implicit assumption of no differences, significant differences did exist. Senior citizens, for example, were less willing to substitute activities in three of the four activity categories than younger adults. On the other hand, individuals with lower incomes were willing to substitute activities in all categories except for sports and games.

Robert Baumgartner and Thomas Heberlein (1981), expanding on Baumgartner's (1978) earlier work, explored the possibility of defining activity clusters on the basis of elements of the recreation experience itself, rather than on the basis of participation patterns or the psychological needs of the participant. Using Marion Clawson and Jack Knetsch's (1966) five-stage model of a recreation experience, they derived a series of five activity elements: (1) preparation for the activity, (2) social interaction that accompanies the activity, (3) the participation process, (4) the presence or absence of a goal in participation, and (5) postexperience reflections. Baumgartner and Heberlein then constructed a series of hypotheses relating the substitutability of different activities to their different patterns associated with these five elements. Their results suggested that there is some degree of association between activity characteristics and the potential for finding a substitutable activity. For example, an activity that offers a high degree of social interaction (e.g., hunting in a group) is less susceptible to successful substitution than solitary activities (fishing by oneself). On the other hand, activities with low goal orientation (e.g., hiking) are more amenable to substitution than those with high goal orientation (e.g., trophy fishing).

The authors also noted that it was important for researchers to specify activities as precisely as possible when doing substitutability research. They found, for example, significant differences in the degree of substitutability between deer hunting and goose hunting. Simply studying "hunting" as a discrete activity would miss many important variations among different hunting specializations.

A fundamental issue in determining whether activities are substitutable is, of course, the degree of similarity between activities. A question implicit in this issue is who is to decide on the degree of similarity. Jerry Vaske, Maureen Donnelly, and Dan Tweed (1983) examined this question in a project comparing recreationist-defined and researcher-defined similarity judgments. Comparing these different judgments to observed substitutions confirmed the authors' beliefs that recreationists' judgments of similarity may be a more reliable and valid measure of activity substitutability than researchers' judgments.

The majority of the studies mentioned previously have been empirical. The two exceptions, Hendee and Burdge and the critique of their article by Beaman, were commentaries on the topic rather than theoretical contributions. One of the few theoretical statements on substitutability that has appeared in the leisure studies literature in Seppo Iso-Ahola's (1986) outline of a "theory of substitutability." He defined the phenomenon to be a psychological process based on the loss of access to some activity. The potential for substituting one activity for another is influenced by two forces: (1) the individual participant's perception of why the substitution is necessary—in other words, why has access to an activity been lost or denied and (2) the individual's perception of the psychological qualities of the original activity and available alternatives. Iso-Ahola then derived a number of hypotheses (which were not tested). These include the predictions that the acceptability of a substitute activity is directly associated with (1) the feeling of freedom in making a substitution, (2) the perceptions of fairness in the reasons for losing access to an activity, (3) the degree of advanced notice of the need to find a substitute, and (4) the similarity of the benefits received from participation in alternative activities.

Much more work needs to be done on the topic of substitutability, including testing and refinement of Iso-Ahola's theory. The record of research, however, demonstrates a growth in our understanding of substitutability, increasing precision and detail in empirical studies, and a growing theoretical interest in the concept. This work, if it is combined with applications and testing of models in management settings can produce exciting and useful results in the future.

REFERENCES

Baumgartner, Robert. 1978. Recreation Substitutability: An Empirical Investigation of Goose Hunting at the Horicon Marsh. Unpublished Master's thesis. University of Wisconsin, Madison, Department of Rural Sociology. Examines substitutability in terms of elements of participation.

Baumgartner, Robert, and Heberlein, Thomas A. 1981. "Process, Goal, and Social Interaction Differences in Recreation: What Makes an Activity Substitutable?" *Leisure Sciences* 4:443–458. Authors advocate using elements of recreation experience as basis for defining similarity; illustrate approach with data from deer and goose hunting.

Beaman, Jay. 1975. "Comments on the Paper 'The Substitutability Concept: Implications for Recreation Research and Management' by Hendee and Burdge." *Journal of Leisure Research* 7:146–151. A methodological critique of Hendee and Burdge's research overview of substitutability.

Becker, Boris W. 1976. "Perceived Similarities among Recreational Activities." *Journal of Leisure Research* 8:112–122. Uses recreationists' perceptions of activity similarities to define activity clusters.

Bishop, Doyle W. 1970. "Stability of the Factor Structure of Leisure Behavior." *Journal of Leisure Research* 2:160–170. Compares activity clusters in four communities.

Burton, Thomas L. 1971. *Experiments in Recreation Research*. Totowa, NJ: Rowman & Littlefield. An early methodological text in leisure studies; includes an example of factor analysis of activity participation.

Chase, David R., and Cheek, Neil H. 1979. "Activity Preferences and Participation: Conclusions from a Factor Analytic Study." *Journal of Leisure Research* 11:92–101. Authors define activity clusters on the basis of stated preferences for participation.

Cheek, Neil H. 1971. "Toward a Sociology of Not-Work." *Pacific Sociological Review* 14:245–258. Describes the significance of social context in the analysis of recreation behavior.

Christensen, James E., and Yoesting, Dean R. 1977. "The Substitutability Concept: A Need for Further Development." *Journal of Leisure Research* 9:188–207. Overview of substitutability research; examines socioeconomic correlates of participants' willingness to substitute activities.

Clawson, Marion, and Knetsch, Jack L. 1966. *Economics of Outdoor Recreation.* Baltimore: Johns Hopkins University Press. The well-known study of outdoor recreation economics; includes a description of a five-stage experience model widely used in leisure studies.

Dottavio, F. Dominic, O'Leary, Joseph T., and Koth, Barbara. 1981. "The Social Group Variable in Recreation Participation Studies." *Journal of Leisure Research* 12:357–367. Surveys use of social context in empirical studies of recreation behavior.

Hendee, John C., and Burdge, Rabel J. 1974. "The Substitutability Concept: Implications for Recreation Research and Management." *Journal of Leisure Research* 6:157–162. Describes concept of substitutability as well as planning and management implications of the topic.

Hendee, John C., Gale, Richard P., and Catton, William R. 1971. "A Typology of Outdoor Recreation Preferences." *Journal of Environmental Education* 3(1):28–34. Authors define activity clusters on the basis of stated preferences for participation.

Iso-Ahola, Seppo E. 1986. "A Theory of Substitutability." *Leisure Sciences* 8:367–390. One of the first theoretical examinations of substitutability; views the concept as a psychological process.

Proctor, Charles. 1962. "Dependence of Recreation Participation on Background Characteristics of Sample Persons in the September 1960 National Recreation Survey." In *National Recreation Survey ORRRC Study Report 19*,77–94. Washington, DC: U.S. Government Printing Office. The first published factor analytic study of recreation participation.

Ritchie, J. R. Brent. 1975. "On the Derivation of Leisure Activity Types: A Perceptual Mapping Approach." *Journal of Leisure Research* 7:128–140. Uses recreationists' perceptions of activity similarities to define activity clusters.

Vaske, Jerry J. 1980. An Empirical Comparison of Methodological Approaches to Recreation Substitutability. Unpublished Ph.D. dissertation, University of Maryland, College Park, Department of Recreation. Uses elements of recreation experience as basis for defining similarities.

Vaske, Jerry J., Donnelly, Maureen P., and Tweed, Dan L. 1983. " Recreationist-Defined Versus Researcher-Defined Similarity Judgments in Substitutability Research." *Journal of Leisure Research* 15:251–262. Compares two different methods for assessing similarity of activities.

SOURCES OF ADDITIONAL INFORMATION

Human response to forced change is a fundamental issue in the study of substitutability. A useful reference for understanding this issue is Jack Brehm's *A Theory of Psychological Reactance* (New York: Academic Press, 1966). Ronnie Bulman and Camille Wortman also examine this issue in "Attributions of Blame and Coping in the 'Real World': Severe Accident Victims React to Their Lot" (*Journal of Personality and Social Psychology* 35:351–363, 1977). John Harvey, Richard Barnes, Dwight Sperry, and Ben Harris, "Perceived Choice as a Function of Internal-External Focus of Control" (*Journal of Personality* 42:437–452, 1974) and John Harvey and Sharon Johnston, "Determinants of the Perception of Choice" (*Journal of Experimental Social Psychology* 9:164–179, 1973) are also useful sources for research into the perception of freedom and choice.

Sources on substitutability and the psychology of leisure behavior include Seppo Iso-Ahola's *The Social Psychology of Leisure and Recreation* (Dubuque, IA: William C. Brown, 1980) and Howard Tinsley and Robert Kass, "Leisure Activities and Need Satisfaction: A Replication and Extension" (*Journal of Leisure Research* 10:191–202, 1978).

T

THERAPEUTIC RECREATION. 1. A professional specialization whose goal is to help individuals with any type of limitation or disadvantage to develop and enjoy an appropriate leisure lifestyle. 2. A professional specialization whose goal is to use recreation activities as part of an overall treatment strategy to ameliorate physical, mental, or emotional disorders.

Precedents for the use of RECREATION as part of the promotion of health and well-being are ancient. Elliott Avedon (1974) and Richard Kraus (1978) cite examples of the use of leisure activities as part of health practices in ancient Greece, Rome, China, and India. Most societies through the ages, to varying degrees, have recognized the benefits of providing some form of leisure activity to help individuals suffering from any of a wide range of physical, mental, emotional, and social problems. These activities run virtually the entire range of possibilities from passively listening to music or storytellers to active participation in physically challenging outdoor experiences. It can be argued that the belief in the potential of recreation to contribute to human development and well-being was the driving spirit that gave rise to the modern recreation movement. David Gray (1969:23), in fact, observed, "The recreation movement was born with a social conscience. It grew up with the settlement house movement, the kindergarten movement, and the youth movement that fostered the great youth agencies of the nation. Its earliest practitioners had a human welfare motivation in which the social ends of human development . . . were central."

In the early years of the recreation movement, many groups actively promoted recreation as a tool for the betterment of the human condition. In addition to the early Boston sand gardens and school playgrounds, recreation facilities and programs were provided in hospitals and residential institutions. One serendipitous discovery of the value of recreation grew out of an experience at the Manhattan State Hospital East in New York City in 1901 (Caplan, 1967). The hospital's administration moved an overflow of psychiatric patients into tents set up on the hospital's grounds. The attending physicians noted a marked improvement in the physical and mental well-being of the patients in the tents and concluded that the camping environment was responsible. A program of "tent treatment"—regular camping and outdoor activity—was developed at the hospital and spread to other institutions. The use of camping continued for several decades, and eventually merged philosophically with the OUTDOOR EDUCATION movement (that had begun independently in the 1860s). By the 1940s, residential camps had been established across the United States and Canada to serve the needs of individuals with special needs. Many of these camps are still in operation.

Wars also were indirectly responsible for the growth of therapeutic recreation services. Hospitals serving veterans discovered that RECREATION PROGRAMMING contributed significantly to the morale and occasionally the physical and mental recovery of military personnel. Among Florence Nightingale's numerous contributions to nursing and patient care in the nineteenth century was the development of recreation programs in veteran's hospitals during the Crimean War. Both World Wars in the twentieth century also saw the expansion of recreation services in military and veterans hospitals as part of the daily regimen for patients.

During the first decades of the twentieth century, other social changes were occurring that would have an impact on the development of therapeutic recreation. In particular, concepts of the human personality and of the individual's relationship with society (see SOCIALIZATION) were evolving. Although the full extent of these changes is too complex to cover here, one important development was the acceptance of the idea that recreation is intrinsically important and rewarding. It is not just a means to an end, but an end in itself. The concept of SELF-ACTUALIZATION, especially, helped to establish and reinforce the importance of transcendent and intrinsically rewarding experiences such as recreation and leisure.

Thus during the first half of the twentieth century, two broad and divergent views of recreation shaped the development of the recreation profession: (1) the socially conscious notion of recreation as a tool to promote health, reduce juvenile delinquency, help people acquire social and vocational skills, and solve other problems and (2) the idea that recreation and leisure are intrinsically worthwhile and essential experiences that individuals have a right to enjoy. While these notions are not inherently contradictory, they have the potential to create misunderstanding between professionals who operate from a value base founded on the two different views. And this happened in therapeutic recreation.

In the 1950s, a group of hospital workers, recognizing how recreation improved the overall quality of life of patients in hospitals—although recreation did not necessarily directly contribute to their physical recovery—formed the Hospital Recreation Section, under the auspices of the American Recreation

Society, to promote hospital-based recreation programming. Approximately the same time, another group, recognizing that recreation could be used along with other forms of therapy to treat various disorders, formed the National Association of Recreation Therapists (NART). Their goal was to further the application of recreation as a formal therapy in a clinical setting. And it was in this clinical sense that the term, therapeutic recreation, first appeared in the literature in an article by Verna Rensvold, Beatrice Hill, Elizabeth Boggs, and Martin Meyer (1957).

Through the 1960s, recreation professionals alternately debated the different perspectives and attempted to reconcile them. Finally, in 1969, the Southern Region Institute of Therapeutic Recreation proposed the following definition: Therapeutic recreation is "a process which utilizes recreation services for purposive intervention in some physical, emotional and/or social behavior to bring out a desired change in that behavior and to promote the growth and development of the individual" (Kraus, 178:3). This definition was widely accepted for a decade because it implicitly combined both views of therapeutic recreation. This success, however, came at the price of vagueness. As Kraus noted, key terms such as *change* and *growth,* were left undefined. The criteria for determining which changes were "desired," and who had the power to decide what was "desired" was unspecified. This had the potential for producing debates among administrators, recreation professionals, advocates, and clients/participants, as to the content and even ultimate goals of therapeutic recreation programs and ADVOCACY efforts.

This definition was eventually superseded by one that the National Therapeutic Recreation Society (NTRS), (a branch of the National Recreation and Park Association, the successor to the American Recreation Society) issued in 1982: The goal of therapeutic recreation is "to facilitate the development, maintenance, and expression of an appropriate leisure lifestyle for individuals with physical, mental, emotional, or social limitations . . . through the provision of professional programs and services . . . eliminating BARRIERS to leisure, developing leisure skills and attitudes, and optimizing involvement" (Peterson and Gunn, 1982:321). This definition makes a stronger statement than the 1969 definition about the FACILITATOR role of the therapeutic recreationist. This is in marked contrast to the clinical or interventionist role envisioned by some therapeutic recreationists in the 1950s and 1960s.

The NTRS philosophy, sometimes known as the leisure ability philosophy, has a number of implications. Professional programs and services represent a continuum of services ranging from traditional therapy (a concession to the clinical viewpoint), through LEISURE EDUCATION, to recreation participation (including activities provided through ADAPTIVE PROGRAMMING). The notion of a leisure lifestyle is also central to this philosophy. Carol Peterson and Scout Gunn (1982:4) define leisure lifestyle as "the day-to-day behavioral expression of one's leisure-related attitudes, awareness, and activities within the context and composite of the total life experience."

The leisure ability philosophy also stresses DEINSTITUTIONALIZATION and MAINSTREAMING. Therapeutic recreationists, to Peterson and Gunn, should strive to provide recreation experiences in the least restrictive environment possible so that the individual can enjoy as fully as possible the benefits of leisure experiences.

While few professional recreationists would challenge this as a laudable goal, it still leaves latent the controversy over the role of recreation as therapy. Lee Meyer (1981) revived the debate when he argued that the three components of service envisioned by Peterson and Gunn are still only two: treatment and recreation. Therapy and leisure education, to Meyer, are simply alternative forms of treatment, and should not be separated as distinct forms of service. Meyer's two service components—treatment and recreation—of course, are the same two faces of therapeutic recreation that were present when the American Recreation Society and the National Association of Recreation Therapists were pressing different philosophies and practices.

At present, the debate concerning the interpretation of the term therapeutic recreation can be summarized as follows. On one hand, if the goal of therapeutic recreation is to facilitate the development and enjoyment of a leisure lifestyle for people, most of whom have been socialized or mainstreamed into community life, these individuals may find the notion of providing them with "therapy" to be inappropriate if not offensive. Furthermore, the provision of services for leisure lifestyles has traditionally been the mandate of community recreation leaders. In other words, the Peterson-Gunn philosophy can logically lead to the position where there is no need for a distinct professional orientation called therapeutic recreation. The real need is not to train therapeutic recreationists but to train community recreationists to be able to respond to the NEEDS of all people.

On the other hand, there still appear to be some individuals for whom general public community programs will likely never be appropriate: inmates of correctional institutions, patients in hospitals or chronic-care facilities, and individuals with severe motor or mental limitations. They have a right to recreation as an intrinsically rewarding activity, as any other person does, but they may require specially adapted or programmed activities. Furthermore, individuals with special needs may also receive nonrecreation benefits from therapeutic programs that include the use of leisure activities. The recognition of this separate issue—of the "special needs" of "special populations"—led a group of professional recreationists to create the American Therapeutic Recreation Association as a clinically oriented alternative to the lifestyle philosophy of NTRS. The argument for the distinction between a lifestyle approach and a clinical approach is more fully developed in Dan Kennedy, David Austin, and Ralph Smith (1987).

The central issues of the two philosophies: (1) the assertion that "recreation is good" and (2) the search to discover and apply the answer to "what is recreation good for?" will continue to dominate recreation professional thinking. It is unlikely that any debate between the two philosophies will ever be won. And, in fact, the notion of a debate between the two philosophies is dysfunctional.

Both are legitimate, albeit divergent, views of how the term therapeutic recreation is used.

REFERENCES

Avedon, Elliott M. 1974. *Therapeutic Recreation Service: An Applied Behavioral Science Approach*. Englewood Cliffs, NJ: Prentice Hall. Provides a link between concepts and principles of the behavioral sciences and therapeutic recreation; offers a particularly good discussion of ACTIVITY ANALYSIS.

Caplan, Richard. 1967. "Tent Treatment for the Insane." *Hospital and Community Psychiatry* 18:145–146. Includes a description of the early use of tents and camping as a treatment of psychiatric patients.

Gray, David E. 1969. "The Case of Compensatory Recreation." *Parks and Recreation* 4(4):23, 24ff. Presents a view of recreation as a force for social development and justice.

Kennedy, Dan W., Austin, David R., and Smith, Ralph W. 1987. *Special Recreation*. Philadelphia: Saunders College. The authors argue for the distinction between therapeutic recreation services (as a form of general recreation programming) and "special recreation" or the provision of specialized services to particular client groups.

Kraus, Richard. 1978. *Therapeutic Recreation Service*, 2nd edition. Philadelphia: Saunders College. An excellent introductory text for therapeutic recreation; includes extensive discussion of its history and theoretical rationale.

Meyer, Lee E. (1981) "Three Philosophical Positions of Therapeutic Recreation and Their Implications for Professionalization and NTRS/NRPA." *Therapeutic Recreation Journal* 15(2):7–16. A critique of alternative views of therapeutic recreation including the NTRS (Peterson-Gunn) model.

Peterson, Carol Ann, and Gunn, Scout Lee. 1982. *Therapeutic Recreation Program and Design: Principles and Procedures*. Englewood Cliffs, NJ: Prentice Hall. Considered by many to be the best therapeutic recreation text available; based on a "leisure ability" or lifestyle philosophy.

Rensvold, Verna, Hill, Beatrice H., Boggs, Elizabeth, and Meyer, Martin W. 1957. "Therapeutic Recreation." *Annals of the American Academy of Political and Social Science* 313(Sept.):87–91. Probably the first published use of the term; presents a rationale for the clinical application of recreation services.

SOURCES OF ADDITIONAL INFORMATION

A standard source of information anyone interested in therapeutic recreation should consult is the *Therapeutic Recreation Journal*, published by the National Recreation and Park Association. NRPA also published a variety of monographs on therapeutic recreation under the title *The Masters Series*. Volume I of this series was called *Philosophy of Therapeutic Recreation: Ideas and Issues* and was edited by Charles Sylvester (Alexandria, VA: National Recreation and Park Association, 1987). A few other general NRPA publications relevant to therapeutic recreation include *Guidelines for Administration of Therapeutic Recreation Service in Clinical and Residential Facilities* (1982) and *Standards of Practice for Therapeutic Recreation Service* (1980).

Stuart Schleien and M. Tipton Ray cover strategies for integration in *Community*

Recreation and Persons with Disabilities (Baltimore: Paul Brookes, 1988). An important conceptual statement arguing the need for integration and mainstreaming is Wolf Wolfensberger, *Normalization: The Principle of Normalization in Human Services* (Toronto: National Institute on Mental Retardation, 1972).

Three authors that address therapeutic recreation from the perspective of psychotherapy include Joan Erikson, *Activity, Recovery, Growth: The Communal Role of Planned Activities* (New York: Norton, 1967); Linda Finlay, *Occupational Therapy Practice in Psychiatry* (London: Croom Helm, 1988); and Moya Wilson, *Occupational Therapy in Short-Term Psychiatry* (London: Churchill Livingstone, 1984).

TIME. A fundamental property of the universe that permits the possibility of change or of two objects occupying the same position; it is revealed and measured through the sequence of events.

Of all the concepts covered in this dictionary, time was the most difficult to write. There are several reasons for this. First, the literature on time is vast. Many of the great (and not-so-great) philosophers as well as thousands of scholars in the biophysical and social sciences and in the humanities have written on the topic. Besides the sheer volume of literature, each discipline has distinctive perspectives and vocabulary used to discuss time. For example, physicists tend to view time as a mathematical variable, sometimes interdependent with the three dimensions of space. Psychologists focus on the perception and experience of time. Theologians view time as a problem in ontology: the study of meaning and purpose in God's creation. Horologists see time as a measurement problem. Economists, when they think about time at all, tend to think of it as a scarce RESOURCE. Sociologists are interested in time as an artifact of social values and, conversely, as a force shaping social structures such as work patterns. The attempt to summarize and compare these various perspectives within the very severe space restrictions posed by this dictionary inevitably meant oversimplification of complex ideas and the omission of many important topics that inform our understanding of time.

Finally, the topic itself is frustratingly imprecise. Some scholars, particularly sociologists and anthropologists, appear to focus on the *language* of time even though they suggest that they are examining time per se. Thus one can read about how the Hopi do not share our conception of past, present, and future because they do not have verb tenses reflecting the past, present, and future (Whorf, 1950). Whether this finding tells us more about the Hopi conception of time or more about Hopi grammar is moot. Certainly the Hopi, like individuals in other CULTURES, understand and experience succession and change in their lives even if their language does not directly express it. An analogy may be found in Japanese: the Japanese language does not have a word for *me,* but the Japanese do understand and experience the concept of *self.*

Thus a fundamental problem faced by sociologists and anthropologists who hope to examine how different cultures view time is that the main source of their information is that culture's language. Their analysis of a foreign language's time vocabulary is typically conducted through the use of their own language. Their language, which is English in our case, is implicitly used as a metalanguage for the study of time, although it is as much a cultural artifact as any other language. Some attempts have been made to develop a formal metalanguage for the analysis of time vocabulary such as Arthur Prior's (1971) symbolic tense logic. His work, however, is difficult for the nonexpert and still focuses on the language of time rather than time per se, which is our topic.

The following discussion of the concept of time begins with a brief overview of some mythological notions about time. We then consider, in a highly abbreviated fashion, the evolution of philosophical ideas about time, since philosophers tend to have the most general interest in time. This is followed by an equally abbreviated discussion of time as a physical reality—specifically the existence of "arrows of time" that provide evidence for the linear view of time common to the industrialized world. Finally, we look at some of the major social science perspectives on time.

Human interest in time is ancient. Many of the earliest myths about the creation of the universe include metaphors for time. Greek mythology, for example, described the universe as being bounded by a circular river. The river, known variously as Oceanos or Chronos, represented the circular flow of time—of which the cycle of the sun across the sky was visible evidence. Later, Chronos became associated with Kronos, the father of Zeus and a primal creative spirit in the universe. Ancient Chinese, Japanese, Indian, Egyptian, Norse, and Native American religions have images or models of time and how it shapes human experience and the prospects of future life. For many of these, time is associated with a deity and often had cyclical or self-renewing properties. Judaism, Christianity, and Islam, in contrast, place their God outside of time. The universe was created as a discrete event, in which time began. The universe is now unfolding until the end of time. For Christians, Jesus lived and died once, but redeemed mankind for all eternity.

The distinction between the circular and linear models of time is often a matter of degree rather than of kind. For example, Buddhists' notions of reincarnation allow a soul to eventually end the cycle by achieving a timeless nirvana. On the other hand, Judeo-Christian linear time is organized in a series of cyclical events including a recurring sabbath and an annual cycle of liturgical or religious holidays. Our contemporary model of time mixes both cyclical and linear images. Minutes, hours, days, weeks, and months are cyclical—they repeat themselves. Yet years, decades, and centuries and other epochal measures are linear.

Turning now from mythological questions of time to ontological questions, it may be useful to review some of the major philosophical views of time. The following paragraphs are based, in part, on Cornelius Benjamin's (1966) review of the history of ideas of time.

Heraclitus, one of the sixth-century B.C. pre-Socratic Hellenistic philosophers, built his philosophy on the concept of change as evidenced through the passage of time. His world was in a constant state of "becoming" rather than "being." Only change, flow, and motion were "real." His ideas, however, were contested by other pre-Socratics, notably Parmenides and Zeno. These philosophers asserted that only those things that were enduring and stable were real. Change was illusory. Zeno expressed his arguments in a series of famous paradoxes that can challenge us even today. Typical of these is the paradox of the race. One cannot possibly complete a foot race, Zeno argued, for the following reason. Before you reach the end of the race, you must cover half the distance. After running half the distance, you must run half the remaining distance. And then you must run half that distance ad infinitum. Because there are an infinite number of "halves" to run, one can never complete the race in a finite time.

Benjamin (1966:9), in relating this story in his review, also recalled that Zeno allegedly presented this argument to Diogenes and challenged him to refute. After thinking for a minute, Diogenes stood up and walked away without uttering a word. Diogenes's point was that Zeno's argument denied the possibility of such movement, and one way of refuting such an idea was by demonstration of movement. However, Zeno did not deny the appearance of motion, only its reality. So Diogenes's response could be dismissed as simply an illusion. On the other hand, one wonders how Zeno—who denied the possibility of change—would have responded to Diogenes's agreeing that Zeno's arguments had indeed *changed* his mind.

Plato was interested in the debate between Heraclitus and Zeno. He believed that any model of the universe had to account both for the appearance of change as well as stability of being. His solution was to bifurcate reality. All things had two aspects: their essence or "form" (which was eternal and unchanging) and their physical manifestation or "individuality" (which is temporary and changeable). Thus Heraclitus was a man who was born, grew old, and died as a real man—but he was also an aspect of the essential man, which is unchanging and eternal.

Aristotle approached the question of time more directly and analytically than his predecessors. He proposed an operational definition of time as the "number of motion" in respect of "before" and "after" (Aristotle, 1942:219). This requires a bit of explanation. Aristotle's idea of motion was broader than our contemporary idea of motion. It included (1) changes in the appearance of condition of an object (such as ice melting), (2) changes in size (such as a child growing into an adult), and (3) changes in location (which is what we would normally consider to be motion). Time is not synonymous with motion, but is a measure of the quantifiable change from "before" to "after."

Aurelius Augustinus, better known as Saint Augustine, examined the nature of time in a remarkable passage in Book IX of *Confessions* (Saint Augustine, 1951). He was unable to adequately resolve the question of what time was and summarized his frustration in a lament that speaks for anyone who has wrestled with the topic: "And I confess to Thee, O God, that I yet know not what time

is, and again I confess unto Thee, O Lord, that I know that I speak this in time, and that having long spoken of time, that very 'long' is not long, but by the pause of time. How then know I this, seeing I know not what time is? Or is it perchance that I know not how to express what I know? Woe is to me, that do not even know, what I know not. . . . Courage, my mind, and press on mightily'' (Saint Augustine, 1951:232–234).

During the Middle Ages few philosophers added substantially to inquiries into the nature of time (although some mystics such as Plotinus and theologians such as Thomas Aquinas did discuss time in their religious reflections). Although the subject of time did not receive substantial attention from philosophers during this 1000-year period, the human experience of time changed dramatically: first through the spread of The Rule of St. Benedict and then the gradual improvement of the technology of timekeeping. We shall return to these two matters shortly.

By the seventeenth century, philosophers began to once again include the nature of time in their speculations. John Locke (1894), a British empirical philosopher, was interested in how people developed ideas and came to possess knowledge about the world. In contrast with philosophers such as Plato who believed that man had innate ideas that existed independent of experience, Locke argued that ideas are acquired through the senses. We receive various experiences from the world around us, reflect rationally upon those experiences, and then generate complex ideas. The proper role of ''natural philosophers'' (scientists) is to use empirical methods to study ideas that are ultimately derived from external sources. Locke used the example of the human experience of sequential events, such as night following day, as the basis for our idea of time. From this experience, we not only develop the idea of time, but we can even extrapolate our experience to generate the idea of an eternity.

Isaac Newton, who lived approximately the same time as Locke, directly questioned the nature of time. Although Newton is remembered as the inventor of calculus and as a great scientist, he was also an intensely (almost fanatically) religious individual. To him, the existence of God required the existence of an absolute time and space that were direct emanations from God. Absolute time, to Newton, ''flows equably without relation to anything external, and by another name is called duration: relative, apparent, and common time is some sensible and external (whether accurate or unequable) measure of duration by means of motion, which is commonly used instead of true time, such as an hour, a day, a month, a year'' (Newton, 1947:6). Newton's conception of time differed from Locke's in that he did not accept the assertion that time could only be understood in relation to other sensory experiences. Although both accepted the notion of absolute time, ''for Newton this [absolute time] is 'in the world' and is discovered; for Locke it is 'in the mind' and is manufactured'' (Benjamin, 1966:600).

While we may use other sensory experiences to estimate or measure time, Newton believed in an absolute time beyond our ability to directly monitor it. He also believed in the strict separation of time and space. Either could be studied without reference to the other; and both ensured that there were absolutely correct answers about questions concerning location, movement, duration, and the sequence of events.

Gottfried Wilhelm von Leibniz not only paralleled Newton's mathematical creativity by independently inventing calculus, he also proposed a conception of time similar to Newton's. Although he did not share Newton's intense religiosity, he did accept the idea that there was an eternally true and stable flow of time that existed independently of sense experiences. Leibniz did not go quite as far as Plato, for example, in stating that the mind has innate thoughts or ideas, but he did describe a model of the mind that hypothesized the existence of inherent "principles" that were made conscious thoughts through experience. Time was just such an example. An "ideal time" existed, which permitted the succession of events. The human mind has the inherent potential to interpret succession as evidence of this ideal time—which it does once we experience succession. Although their ideas parallel each other there are certain differences. G. J. Whitlow (1980:42) summarized their differences succinctly as: "According to Newton the universe *has* a clock, whereas according to Leibniz *it* is a clock."

Immanuel Kant's philosophy, sometimes known as apriorism and described most formally in *Critique of Pure Reason* (Kant, 1929), is the opposite of Locke's empiricism. Although Kant discussed the nature of time as an example of what he called a "category" (or a metaphysical concept), his discussion of the nature of time is considered to be confused and the weakest aspect of his philosophy (Smith, 1918:137). Time and other concepts including things such as "substance" and "causality" do not really exist in the world but are the product of pure reason. We perceive the reality of time because our minds are constructed so as to necessarily generate the concept of time. In other words, we impose the concept of time on the world just as a person wearing red-tinted glasses imposes the color red on the world (Benjamin, 1966:23).

Henri Bergson (1912), a French philosopher working around the turn of the century, was influenced by Darwin's theory of evolution. Bergson's central interest was understanding the stream of thought and how original ideas and creativity emerged from the internal conversation the mind had with itself. Although he is usually associated with the "stream of consciousness" literary movement, Bergson did attempt to explain the nature of time. His solution included a division of time into two aspects: (1) duration or flow, which is an idealized form of time and (2) "spatialized" time, which is a practical estimation of time obtained by focusing on empirical events and relationships in the universe.

Samuel Alexander (1966), a contemporary of Bergson, was even more interested in the nature of time. He found his inspiration in the work of Hermann Minkowski (1923) on the four dimensions of the space-time continuum in the theory of relativity. Alexander felt that Minkowski was on the right track, but did not go far enough. Minkowski, as many physicists still do, considered the dimensions of space and time to be essentially mathematical entities and not necessarily something "real." The four dimensions proved themselves useful in developing mathematical models of the universe that produced verifiable hypotheses—but did not necessarily provide the basis for making ontological statements about reality. Alexander felt they did. He particularly believed that the mathematical equality between space and time was ontologically real. Furthermore, he proposed a metaphysical hierarchical view of the universe in which the space-time continuum formed the base and God resided at the summit.

The twentieth century has seen a steady increase of interest by philosophers in the meaning and applications of the discoveries and models of relativity and quantum physics. While some of this work has been thoughtful and well-considered, some has bordered on the puerile. A number of popular books have attempted to meld quantum physics with Westernized notions of Eastern philosophies. An understanding of quantum physics requires a high level of mathematical ability that even many scientists do not possess. Accordingly, we will not even pretend to summarize the ways in which time is conceptualized in either relativity or quantum physics. It is appropriate, however, to mention briefly the notion of "arrows of time"—empirical evidence for the independent existence of a forward-flowing linear time.

The significance of these arrows can be appreciated by recalling that many models of the universe, from Newton's classical mechanics to quantum mechanics, permit time to flow forward or backward. Time could reverse itself without violating most of the laws of physics—with certain notable exceptions. These exceptions are the arrows of time. Tony Rothman (1987) has provided a highly readable summary of these arrows; the following paragraphs are based on his review.

The first arrow is ordinary human experience. People do not remember the future; we remember only the past.

The second arrow is found in the behavior of electromagnetic radiation. Radio waves radiate away from an antenna; no one has ever seen them generated out in space and then converge concentrically on an antenna. Or to use a more familiar example, when we drop a stone in a still pond, concentric waves radiate outward from the impact point. No one has ever seen concentric waves generated in the form of a large circle that then shrinks and closes in on an impact point.

Arrow number three comes from the peculiar world of quantum mechanics. If one could apply quantum equations to the toss of a coin, the equations would describe the coin as 50 percent heads and 50 percent tails while it was in the air. As soon as it hits ground, it changes to 100 percent heads or 100 percent tails. There is no way for the process to reverse so that a coin that is 100 percent heads becomes 50 percent heads and 50 percent tails.

Evidence of the fourth arrow comes from kaon decay. The kaon is an unstable subatomic particle. Like all unstable particles, it has a distinctive half-life. Mathematical analysis of the decay of the particle has revealed that the half-life is different for kaons decaying forward in time than backward. Because the difference in half-life is never observed, we have another arrow.

Time's fifth arrow is found at the other end of the spectrum of physical size:

the behavior of black holes in the universe. Black holes are so powerful they swallow even light, hence their blackness. If time could flow in either direction, one would expect to find black holes "running in reverse"—white holes spewing out massive quantities of light and other forms of radiant energy. No white holes have ever been observed and until one is, their absence may be another arrow.

The sixth arrow involves a controversial reasoning about the universe. It is generally accepted by most physicists that the universe is expanding. What happens if the universe eventually begins to contract? A once-popular hypothesis was that time would run backward. But this would imply that an individual would enter life by "undying," and then "youthen" to the point where his life would end when he entered his mother's womb. Snow would appear through the sublimation of running water and then fall up into clouds. Ashes would slowly ignite and burn backward into logs. The absurdity of such notions seems to be another example of the essential linearity of time regardless of whether the universe is expanding or contracting.

The seventh arrow of time is entropy. The laws of thermodynamics require that entropy in the universe is always increasing. If one lights a match and then allows it to burn out, there is no way to get the molecules of the match to reorganize themselves to relight the match again. The inevitable increase in entropy in the universe—its slow progression toward a state of maximum disorder—appears to be yet another bit of evidence of the one-way flow of time.

Recently, an eighth arrow of time has been proposed by Ilya Prigogine and Isabelle Stengers (1984). These authors, through their work on chaos theory and self-organizing systems have argued that the inevitable tendency of certain types of system to produce order in themselves (this is not a violation of the laws of thermodynamics because the increase in order within these systems is obtained at the expense of greater disorder elsewhere in the universe) may be a further example of linear time.

Barbara Adam (1988:24) notes that Prigogine and Stengers's work may have profound implications for better incorporating the concept of time into models of social behavior, because much social behavior appears to be an example of a self-organizing system. As yet, however, social scientists have not explored the implications of the arrow of time in self-organizing systems and have relied on more traditional perspectives on time. And it is to these perspectives we now turn.

Social scientists, unlike philosophers and physicists, have been less interested in understanding the nature of time and more interested in how time shapes human behavior and how, in turn, human (or social) behavior shapes time. Such an orientation is not surprising because questions of human behavior and social organization are more fundamental to the social sciences than the nature or meaning of the universe. Psychologists, for instance, tend to concern themselves with questions about human perception of time, the way in which people learn about time, and how time influences their behavior. William James (1890:624), who worked in psychology at the time when it was striving to emerge from philosophy as an independent and empirical discipline, described a fairly common psychological experience: "In general, a time filled with varied and interesting human experiences seems short in passing, but long as we look back. On the other hand, a tract of time empty of experience seems long in passing, but in retrospect short."

Time also played a role in shaping Sigmund Freud's psychoanalytic research. He became convinced that past experiences could be responsible for various neuroses that people experienced in the present. This notion, commonplace to us, presented Freud with an intellectual problem. In one sense, past events are no more real than future events because they do not exist in the present. How can an unreal event have a real effect on present mental states? His solution was to conceive of a subconscious that operates outside of time. Past experiences, especially those from our childhood, exist in a type of timeless "now" deep in our minds. For certain psychological phenomena, time might be said to simply not exist.

The perception of time was also of interest to empirical psychologists, such as Henri Pieron (1923), who examined the psychophysical bases for the perception of time and to developmental psychologists interested in the intellectual growth of the child. Jean Piaget (1946) considered the acquisition of a time-sense as part of his research into the developmental states of the human being. In one experiment, for example, Piaget had young children watch two toy trains. Although both trains were started and stopped simultaneously, one ran slower and thus covered a shorter distance. Children younger than five years of age routinely said that the train that had covered the shorter distance stopped sooner, even though it stopped simultaneously with the other, faster train. This answer suggested to Piaget that young children confused space and time. In other studies he noted that children under five often confuse height and age, and could not grasp the relationship between birth order and age. These findings supported his contention that an awareness of time is a cognitive skill that was not acquired until a child was approximately school aged.

This conclusion, though, may push the results too far. Although children under five have problems with the language and logic of time, any parent can attest to the development of a sense of time even in very young children. For instance, enjoyment of a game of peek-a-boo requires that the infant have at least a rudimentary understanding of past, present, and future. An infant can not only tolerate the temporary disappearance of his parent, but find it fun because he knows his mother or father will return in the very near future to make silly faces and noises.

Some particularly dramatic work has been done on the impact of sensory deprivation on perceptions of time. One recent study in 1989, involved a volunteer, Stefania Follini, who spent four months in a New Mexico cave. Living in an environment devoid of cues about the progression of time in the external world allowed an innate biological clock to govern her activities. After some initial disorientation (including the ceasing of her menstrual cycle), she settled into a thirty-five-hour "day": twenty-five hours of activity followed by ten hours of sleep. As a result, she believed she had spent only two months in the cave when, in fact, she had spent twice that.

Psychologists have also examined other factors that can distort the perception of the passage of time such as various drugs or mental illness (Yaker, Osmond, and Cheek, 1972), as well as intense psychological involvement in activities in a phenomenon known as FLOW (Csikszentmihalyi, 1975). Another aspect of the psychological response to time is the development of the individual's ability to comprehend a future time horizon. Very young children are usually limited to a future time horizon of a few minutes. But by the time the child is seven or eight, he can comprehend the notion of history and is beginning to realize he has a distant future that will include career choices and the possibility of a family. Some of the personal factors that shape the development of the time horizon were explored in pioneering work by Robert Kastenbaum (1961).

The notion of the time horizon is also a social psychological and anthropological phenomenon. Whorf's (1950) work on the Hopi is considered a classic in the field. The various mythological and religious models of time can be interpreted as attempts to help the individual believer develop an appropriate (usually eternal) time horizon, as dictated by the tenets of faith.

Sociologists tend to be particularly concerned with how different societies organize their time. The organization of time may be examined on at least two different levels. The first is the creation of the familiar categories of time: the hour, day, week, and so on. Virtually all societies have time categories corresponding to a night and day cycle. And most societies also have some form of time unit based on the phases of the moon. In addition to these, many societies have artificial time units consisting of a period between four and ten days (a "week") which is usually based on a marketplace or religious cycle. Still longer periods of time are based on the cycle of seasons (the year) and epochal events such as the birth or death of a political or religious leader.

The study of the organization of time also focuses on more subtle but powerful aspects of organization—the way in which time is incorporated into social values and the process of SOCIALIZATION of individuals. The social organization of time at this level is so important in our understanding of the human response to time that some sociologists, ranging from Emile Durkheim (1915) to Robert Lauer (1981), have asserted that all time is "social time." Social time is a conception of time defined by the rhythms of social life as reflected in HOLIDAYS, TIME BUDGETS, and other social phenomena. This view is essentially a form of neo-Kantism in that it posits that time is a category that exists solely in the human mind instead of as an independent reality. Such a view, if taken literally, is indefensible. Without the existence of billions of years of time independent of human cognition, human life, including sociologists, could have never evolved to debate the subject. This is not to argue against the legitimacy of the concept of social time, but only to make explicit the fact that time is a physical reality.

Adam (1988: 198), a sociologist who reviewed social research perspectives on time once commented, "social scientists must get to know physical and biological time."

Durkheim (1915), Carlo Cipolla (1967), Eviatar Zerubavel (1981), Lewis Mumford (1934), and Nigel Thrift (1988) are just a few examples of sociologists who have examined the long-term impact of models of social time on social structure. One of the historically most important models of social time in the Western world was the Rule of Saint Benedict, developed in the sixth century A.D. It came to exercise a powerful influence on the daily lives and annual calendar of Medieval Europe. Benedict developed a conception of monastic life in which no real distinction was made between secular and sacred activities. Work was considered as much a form of prayer as reciting psalms—a view that became a cornerstone of the WORK ETHIC. The Rule, however, had a significance beyond just establishing the dignity of labor in religious life. Benedict laid out a firm schedule of activities for his communities. The schedule included both an annual calendar of required activities (ranging from a liturgical calendar of annual feasts to the scheduling of when monks should be bled). Monthly calendars specified times for cleaning and maintenance. Daily schedules specified the sequence and timing of prayers, meals, work, and rest. Days were organized into canonical "hours" that had specified psalms to be read or sung. Bells were rung in a tower to call the devout to worship in from the fields and workshops. The ringing of bells was initially tied to water clocks or other crude time-keeping devices that were set according to sunrise or sunset. This resulted in substantial variation in the daily schedules among various monasteries as well as a change in the length of the canonical hours from summer to winter, as the length of daylight changed. By the thirteenth century, however, mechanical clocks had begun to replace water clocks for timing the ringing of the bells. This permitted greater uniformity and regularity in the pace of daily life.

The bells not only set the pace for monastic life, they also guided life in nearby towns. The opening and closing of shops, work in the fields, mealtimes, and many other aspects of social and family life became regulated by the monastic temporal order. This socialization of urban European life to daily routines governed by a communal clock helped to set the stage, first, for a shift to a capitalist economy and eventually the Industrial Revolution (Weber, 1958; Mumford, 1934; Dillistone, 1973). Max Weber, Lewis Mumford, Frederick Dillistone, and other sociologists and philosophers have commented on the central importance of precise, mechanized time in governing the pace of industrialized life. The regimentation of time and its ascendancy in shaping the demands of the workplace was the inspiration behind Frederick Taylor's (1911) time-and-motion studies and the rise of time budget research in both the Soviet Union and Western societies. The primacy of the clock is dramatically demonstrated by the development of automotive assembly lines by Henry Ford. This phenomenon, once called "Fordism," had several major social impacts. On the positive side, it helped to produce vast quantities of relatively reliable manufactured goods at reasonably low prices for the majority of consumers. America's genius in mass production arguably helped the Allies win both world wars.

On the negative side, assembly line work bred discontent and boredom among workers. The lines became a symbol for the transmogrification of a human being into a cog in a giant machine. The powerful socialization forces that made punctuality and time regimentation a major social virtue in support of industrial society spilled over into other aspects of our lives, just as the peel of the monastery bells spilled over into nonmonastic life. Sebastian de Grazia (1962) is typical of many contemporary authors who lament the loss of what they see as a "natural" rhythm in life, and criticize mankind's willing acceptance of the tyranny of the clock.

Such criticism of the pervasiveness and precision of industrial time is partially correct, but not completely fair. While starting times are rigidly controlled for many workers by a punch clock, the same clock sets them free at the end of the day. A cost born by many students, university professors, self-employed business people, and executives whose workdays are free of the clock is that their work tends to spill over into evenings, weekends, and holidays. The clock controls the impact of time even more than it controls human lives.

Precise measurement and coordination of time is essential in the production of many commodities that enhance the quality of life or in the case of medical goods and services, may even make life possible. Rapid long-distance communication could not occur without the precise global coordination of time. Long-distance navigation would be impossible.

As a social science, leisure studies involves many of the same questions about time: perception, allocation, use, and structure. One of the more common ways in which the topic of time enters research on recreation and leisure is through an examination of the allocation of time as a scarce resource. This work is usually based on time budgets or other social surveys (Cheek and Burch, 1976). A question of particular concern regarding the allocation of time is whether the amount of LEISURE is increasing or decreasing. Staffan Linder (1973) presented a provocative argument in the early 1970s why the eagerly anticipated "age of leisure" was a myth. In 1989, a survey conducted for Hilton Hotels discovered that many people were spending an increasing amount of time on chores and family matters, especially on the weekends. The result was a steady erosion in the amount of leisure time, including vacations away from home and on weekends. A poll for Lou Harris, in the same year, found that the average workweek had grown by 15 percent since 1973 (the 1989 average workweek was 46.8 hours), with only 16.6 hours of leisure per week (down by 37 percent from 1973). Not surprisingly, then, time is often cited as the main BARRIER to participation in preferred leisure activities.

Another context in which leisure researchers consider time is the definition of leisure. As noted in the section on leisure in this dictionary, some authors reject a time-based definition in favor of a "state of mind" definition, whether that state be PERCEIVED FREEDOM or OPTIMAL AROUSAL. These definitions are essentially neo-Kantism. Leisure is viewed as a mental category, so to speak, rather than as an empirical phenomenon. Other authors, including the author of this dictionary, prefer a more objective and empirical view (roughly paralleling Locke's philosophy). The proper study of social scientists is, to this group, phenomena that can be studied objectively and empirically. A time-based definition of leisure fits this criterion more closely than the subjective view of the neo-Kantists.

As with St. Augustine, we are still uncertain as to what time is. We tell time; we keep time; we kill time; we save time. We lose it; we find it. We measure and mark time. We ask What is the time? and then, hearing the answer, lament that "time has flown." But we are still hard pressed to define it in such a way as to avoid paradoxes and contradictions. We often sense that time speeds up or drags by. This implies the existence of some absolute time of the sort that Newton believed in and that Einstein disproved.

Time presents us with three relatively unambiguous categories: past, present, and future. These categories are reflected in our verb tenses, but they are not the creation of our language. Rather, our language attempts to reflect the linear flow of time. Of these three, the "present" is the most difficult to understand yet, ironically, it is the only aspect of time we directly experience. "Now" is the dimensionless boundary between past and present. It is ever fleeting, yet always present. Paul Fraisse (1963) was the first to present evidence that the psychological experience of "now" covers several seconds. But to a computer, whose operations are measured in nanoseconds, "now" is much shorter. Some physicists have speculated on whether there is a quantum of time: some discrete but finite unit in which time is packaged. All forms of energy, from light to gravity, are now recognized as coming in quanta; the notion that time is not a smooth, infinitely divisible flow is not beyond the realm of imagination.

Time permits creativity and change, yet must allow for apparent stability. While you have this dictionary in your possession, it remains essentially unchanged, yet your use of it (it is to be hoped) results in change in you. Does time, therefore, exist for you but not the dictionary? Of course, the dictionary is also experiencing change—oxidation of its pages, for example—yet at a much slower rate. Does time move at a slower rate, then, for the book?

Faced with such questions and possible paradoxes, Mary Frances Cleugh (1937:233) quoted Jacques Maritain in her reflections on the nature of time: time is "a place where we put our blackest contradictions out to pasture." Such sentiments are widely held by many philosophers of time. Alfred North Whitehead (1920:73), however, felt something more akin to awe than frustration in contemplating the nature of time: "It is impossible to meditate on time and the creative passage of nature without an overwhelming emotion at the limitations of human knowledge."

REFERENCES

Adam, Barbara. 1988. "Social Versus Natural Time, A Traditional Distinction Re-examined." In *The Rhythms of Society,* ed. Michael Young and Tom Schuller, 198–226. London: Routledge. A critique of the frequent distinction made between the physical and the social conceptions of time; she argues that the distinction is sometimes overdrawn, and that social scientists need to understand natural time better.

Alexander, Samuel. 1966. *Space, Time and Deity*. London: Macmillan. A lengthy and thorough examination of the concept of time, allegedly based on an empirical approach, although the book frequently involves abstraction of the evidence; a highly dogmatic book.

Aristotle. 1942. *The Student's Oxford Aristotle,* trans. William D. Ross. Oxford, England: Oxford University Press. A good accessible translation of some of Aristotle's writings on the nature of reality, including his views on time.

Benjamin, A. Cornelius. 1966. "Ideas of Time in the History of Philosophy." In *The Voices of Time,* ed. J. T. Fraser, 3–30. New York: George Braziller. An excellent, brief overview of some of the major philosophical views on the nature of time.

Bergson, Henri. 1912. *Introduction to Metaphysics,* trans. T. E. Hulme. New York: Putnam. This work includes a discussion of the nature of time as an agent for change and human creativity.

Cheek, Neil H., and Burch, William R. 1976. *The Social Organization of Leisure in Human Society*. New York: Harper & Row. A sociological analysis of the structure of leisure in the modern world; includes data on time budgets.

Cipolla, Carlo M. 1967. *Clocks and Culture: 1300–1700*. London: Collins. A history of the changes in the conception and measurement of time in Medieval Europe.

Cleugh, Mary Frances. 1937. *Time and Its Importance in Modern Thought*. London: Methuen. A review of images and models of time and their influence on contemporary world views and philosophies.

Csikszentmihalyi, Mihaly. 1975. *Beyond Boredom and Anxiety*. San Francisco: Jossey-Bass. Presents the author's notions of "flow" as a form of intense psychological involvement; a loss of an awareness of the passing of time is a distinctive feature of "flow."

de Grazia, Sebastian. 1962. *Of Time, Work, and Leisure*. New York: Twentieth Century Fund. A lengthy study of changes in attitudes toward time, work, and leisure; proposes a view of leisure that is independent of time; criticizes the modern acceptance of the "tyranny" of the clock.

Dillistone, Frederick W. 1973. *Traditional Symbols and the Contemporary World*. London: Epworth. Another example of the hypothesis that precise and regular time measurement is essential to the modern industrial world.

Durkheim, Emile. 1915. *The Elementary Forms of Religious Life: A Study in Religious Sociology,* trans. J. W. Swain. London: Allen & Unwin. An early and major sociological study; includes a discussion of the role of time in the development of Christianity and the ways in which people are socialized.

Fraisse, Paul. 1963. *The Psychology of Time*. New York: Harper. An empirically based examination of the human experience and perception of time.

James, William. 1890. *Principles of Psychology*. New York: Smith. One of the first texts on psychology as a social science; generally considered a classic in the field.

Kant, Immanuel. 1929. *Critique of Pure Reason,* trans. Norman Kemp Smith. London: Macmillan. One of the important and more difficult philosophical works on the nature of human thought and awareness; the treatment of the concept of "category" of time is particularly difficult.

Kastenbaum, Robert. 1961. "The Dimensions of Future Time Perspective: An Experimental Analysis." *Journal of General Psychology* 65:203–218. Describes some of the factors shaping the development of a "time horizon" or awareness of the future.

Lauer, Robert Harold. 1981. *Temporal Man: The Meaning and Uses of Social Time.* New York: Praeger. An extensive discussion of the concept of social time; argues that all time is social time.

Linder, Staffan. 1973. *The Harried Leisure Class.* New York: Columbia University Press. A provocative book that argued that time and labor-saving devices when combined with certain value trends in society would result in even further shrinking of leisure time—not an increase.

Locke, John. 1894. *An Essay Concerning Human Understanding,* annoted by Alexander Campbell Fraser. Oxford, UK: Clarendon. A reprint of Locke's major philosophical work; this edition includes annotations and commentary.

Minkowski, Hermann. 1923. *The Principle of Relativity,* ed. W. Perrett and G. B. Jeffrey. London: Constable. An early and mathematical interpretation of the notion of the space-time continuum and the theory of relativity.

Mumford, Lewis. 1934. *Technics and Civilization.* New York: Harcourt. A sweeping history of technology and civilization; changes in time measurement are given particular attention.

Newton, Sir Isaac. 1947. *Sir Isaac Newton's Mathematical Principles of Natural Philosophy and His System of the World,* trans. Andrew Motte. Berkeley: University of California Press. A translation and revision of Florian Cajori's 1729 translation of Newton's great classic.

Piaget, Jean. 1946. *Le developpement de la notion de temps chez l'enfant.* Paris: Universitates de Paris. Describes Piaget's research into how children develop an awareness of time.

Pieron, Henri. 1923. "Les problemes psychophysiologiques de la perception du temps." *Annee psychologique* 24:1–25. An early examination of the psychophysical basis for the perception of time.

Prigogine, Ilya, and Stengers, Isabelle. 1984. *Order out of Chaos.* London: Heinemann. The authors describe some recent developments in chaos theory, paying particular attention to the operation of self-organizing systems.

Prior, Arthur N. 1971. "Recent Advances in Tense Logic." In *Basic Issues in the Philosophy of Time,* ed. Eugene Freeman and Wilfrid Sellars, 1–15. Lasalle, IL: Open Court. A review of tense logic, a form of symbolic logic used to examine sentence structure.

Rothman, Tony. 1987. "The Seven Arrows of Time." *Discover,* Feb., 63–77. A popularly written discussion of the evidence for linear time in the physical sciences.

Saint Augustine. 1960. *The Confessions of Saint Augustine,* trans. Edward B. Pusey. New York: Washington Square Press. An English translation of one of the major personal religious statements in the history of Catholicism.

Smith, Norman Kemp. 1918. *A Commentary to Kant's "Critique of Pure Reason."* London: Macmillan. Smith's scholarly analysis of Kant's major work.

Taylor, Frederick. W. 1911. *The Principles of Scientific Management*. New York: Harper & Row. An influential model for industrial management; based, in part, on time-motion studies of manufacturing processes.

Thrift, Nigel. 1988. "*Vivos Voco*: Ringing the Changes in the Historical Geography of Time Consciousness." In *The Rhythms of Society,* ed. Michael Young and Tom Schuller, 53–94. London: Routledge. The author maps and describes the spread of mechanical clocks in churches in medieval England and comments on the associated social changes.

Weber, Max. 1958. *The Protestant Work Ethic and the Spirit of Capitalism*. New York: Charles Scribner's Sons. A scholarly inquiry into the origins of the work ethic and the capitalist economy, with particular attention given to the role of Christianity in establishing social structures conducive to the capitalist economy.

Whitehead, Alfred North. 1920. *Concept of Nature*. Cambridge, UK: Cambridge University Press. A thoughtful reflection on the nature of the universe and the role of time in it; written by a noted philosopher of science.

Whitrow, G. J. 1980. *The Natural Philosophy of Time,* 2nd edition. Oxford, UK: Clarendon. A review of some classical philosophical explanations of time.

Whorf, Benjamin L. 1950. "An American Indian Model of the Universe." *International Journal of American Linguistics* 16:67–72. Suggests a model of the Hopi world view on the basis of their vocabulary for time; notes that their verbs do not have tenses in the same sense that English verbs do.

Yaker, Henri, Osmond, Humphry, and Cheek, Francis. 1972. *The Future of Time*. New York: Anchor. A collection of essays examining time from social, anthropological, psychological, and biological viewpoints; includes several papers on mental illness and time.

Zerubavel, Eviatar. 1981. *Hidden Rhythms*. Chicago: University of Chicago Press. An introduction to the sociology of time; places special attention on the rational organization of time in society.

SOURCES OF ADDITIONAL INFORMATION

Gary Machils and Ellen Wenderoth looked at different forms of social time in their study of "Cultural Variation in the Use of Leisure Time: Foreign Tourists at the Grand Canyon" (*Leisure Sciences* 6:187–204, 1984). Some other examples of sociological inquiries into time, as a social variable, include Max Heirich, "The Use of Time in the Study of Social Change" (*American Sociological Review* 29:386–397, 1964); Wilbert E. Moore, *Man, Time, and Society* (New York: Wiley, 1963); and John Robinson and Philip Converse, "Social Change Reflected in the Use of Time," in Angus Campbell and Philip Converse, eds., *The Human Meaning of Social Change* (New York: Russel Sage Foundation, 1972). Alexander Szalai has edited a major time-budget study, *The Use of Time: Daily Activities of Urban and Suburban Populations in Twelve Countries* (The Hague: Mouton, 1972).

An excellent review of ancient theories of time is provided in Richard Sorabji, *Time, Creation, and the Continuum* (Ithaca, NY: Cornell University Press, 1983). Some theological perspectives are covered in William Hasker, *God, Time and Knowledge* (Ithaca, NY: Cornell University Press, 1989). G. J. Whitrow covers a broader historical perspective of time in *Time in History: The Evolution of Our General Awareness of Time and Temporal Perspective* (London: Oxford University Press, 1988).

TIME BUDGET. A log describing the nature, sequence, and duration of the uses of TIME by an individual, usually on a twenty-four hour basis.

The beginnings of time budget studies are obscure, but precedents for the methodology can be traced back to Friedrich Engels's (1845) work *The Situation of the Working Class in England,* in which he examined selected time use patterns by English laborers. Time-and-motion studies pioneered by Frederick Taylor (1947) as part of his "scientific management" philosophy at the end of the nineteenth century also employed a time diary design in his study of time usage during working hours. The first fully developed time budget study was arguably that by George Bevans (1913) in his examination of American workers' use of leisure.

Little research was done in the United States on time uses for a decade or so after Bevans's work, however. It was Soviet social scientists, instead, that made the initial sustained push in conducting time budget studies, and who have been responsible for much of the work done during the first half of the twentieth century on this topic. A pioneer among the Soviets was Stanislav Strumilin, whose work in the 1920s was intended to contribute to the development of a comprehensive, rational plan for industrial development in the Soviet Union. This initiative was specifically related to the institution of the "New Economic Policy" announced in 1921 at the Tenth Congress of the Communist Party in an attempt to infuse economic policy with greater efficiency, based on economic and statistical research. Jiri Zuzanek (1980) provides an excellent insight into the history of Soviet time budget studies.

Although most of the early time budget studies were conducted in the Soviet Union, some American researchers did eventually pick up on the work initiated by Bevans. Of particular note was a series of studies detailing the use of time by farm women and rural homemakers conducted by the Bureau of Home Economics (a division of the U.S. Department of Agriculture) in the 1920s. A bibliography of these studies is provided in Pitirim Sorokin and Clarence Berger (1936:16). Two more major studies were released in the 1930s: George Lundberg, Mirra Komarovsky, and Mary Alice McInerny (1934) on suburban leisure patterns and Sorokin and Berger's (1939) comprehensive look at uses of time including "physiological and economic activities," "cultural activities," and "love and pleasurable activities."

After a hiatus caused by World War II, time budget studies were again conducted in many countries, particularly with an interest in understanding consumer behavior and mass media (television) habits. By the mid-1960s, the common divisions of activities and the basic methodologies for collecting data were sufficiently standardized that the United Nations organized a twelve-nation comparative time budget study (Szalai and Converse, 1972).

Time budget studies continue to be an active area of research among sociologists as well as some geographers (Elliot, Harvey, and Procos, 1976). One reason for the popularity and significance of time budget research is the obvious fact that all individuals are allotted the same amount of time a day. The allocation of that time to various uses is an observable result of each individual's subjective determination of the VALUE of various uses of time. Time budgets provide unique "hard evidence" of human preferences and values that most forms of behavioral research cannot provide. More time spent at work or relaxing, for example requires an equal diminution of the time devoted to other activities. While motivations, attitudes, and various behavioral constraints may remain hidden, time budgets do provide a potentially unambiguous look at the results of these forces.

Time budget data, however, can be difficult and expensive to obtain. Three sources are commonly used: (1) self-maintained diaries, (2) recall questionnaires, and (3) recorded observations by another observer. The first method is generally considered to be the most reliable and least subject to memory lapses. It does require, though, an enthusiastic, willing, and reasonably literate subject. The recall questionnaire requires less commitment on the part of the subject but is obviously vulnerable to forgetfulness. The third method—use of an observer— can be especially costly and virtually eliminates the privacy of the subject. The observer, as one would expect, may distort the actions of the subject in unknown ways.

Assuming data can be reliably collected, time budget studies are still subject to several difficulties. One of the most important is that the nearly infinite range of human behaviors must be collapsed into a relatively small number of discrete activity groupings. These groupings are based on the manifest characteristics of human behavior, but not necessarily on the meaning of those behaviors to the individual. A simple walk around the block, for example, may be the occasion for exercise, relaxation, meditation, time with a friend or family member, or an attempt to change one's mood.

Time budget studies can provide a fascinating glimpse into how individuals (and groups) use and structure their time. They can also offer intriguing insights into cross-cultural differences and patterns of social change over time. They are, however, costly, difficult to administer, and may produce relatively shallow and theoretically unimportant findings if the researcher fails to explore the deeper meanings and social contexts of the various uses of time.

REFERENCES

Bevans, George Edras. 1913. *How Workingmen Spend Their Spare Time*. New York: Columbia University Press. Perhaps the first "modern" time budget study; focused on uses of free time exclusively.
Elliott, David H., Harvey, Andrew S., and Procos, Dimitri. 1976. "An Overview of the Halifax Time-Budget Study." *Society and Leisure* 8:145–159. A description of a time budget study done in Canada; included an examination of spatial variations in human activity around the city over the course of a typical day.
Lundberg, George A., Komarovsky, Mirra, and McInerny, Mary Alice. 1934. *Leisure:*

A Suburban Study. New York: Columbia University Press. An early and major time budget study examining the use of free time during the Great Depression.

Sorokin, Pitirim A., and Berger, Clarence Q. 1939. *Time-Budgets of Human Behavior*. Cambridge, MA: Harvard University Press. One of the first comprehensive American studies of the use of time; included a section on the attempt to predict time use patterns given certain personal and social characteristics of the individual.

Szalai, Alexander, and Converse, Philip (eds). 1972. *The Use of Time: Daily Activities of Urban and Suburban Populations in Twelve Countries*. The Hague: Mouton. Probably the largest and most important time-budget study yet conducted; involved a series of specific projects in a wide range of countries around the world.

Taylor, Frederick. 1947. *Scientific Management*. New York: Harper. A reprint of Taylor's work on "shop management"; based on time-and-motion studies.

Zuzanek, Jiri. 1980. *Work and Leisure in the Soviet Union: A Time-Budget Analysis*. New York: Praeger. One of the few examinations of patterns of work and leisure in the Soviet Union available to Westerners; includes an excellent history of time budget studies in the USSR.

SOURCES OF ADDITIONAL INFORMATION

Philip Converse provides a good overview of the uses and limitations of time budget studies in his entry, "Time Budgets" in the *International Encyclopedia of the Social Sciences,* Vol. 16 (New York: Crowell Collier and Macmillan, 1968, 42–47). Gary Machlis and Ellen Wenderoth compare uses of time by Japanese and various European visitors to the Grand Canyon in "Cultural Variations in the Use of Leisure Time" (*Leisure Sciences* 6: 187–204, 1984). Ronald Cosper and Susan Shaw examined the validity of time budget studies comparing a time budget diary and a leisure time recall questionnaire in their "The Validity of Time-Budget Studies: A Comparison of Frequency and Diary Data in Halifax, Canada" (*Leisure Sciences* 7:205–225, 1985).

Two studies that provide a geographic perspective on time use are Don Janelle and Michael Goodchild, "Diurnal Patterns of Social Group Distributions in a Canadian City" (*Economic Geography* 59:403–425, 1983) and "The City Around the Clock: Space Time Patterns of Urban Ecological Structure" (*Environment and Planning A,* 16: 807–820, 1984) by the same authors.

More general studies illustrating the usefulness of time budget research include John Robinson and Philip Converse, "Social Change Reflected in the Use of Time" in Anges Campbell and Philip Converse, eds., *The Human Meaning of Social Change* (New York: Russell Sage, 1972) and Eviatar Zerubavel, *Hidden Rhythms: Schedules and Calendars in Social Life* (Chicago: University of Chicago Press, 1981).

TOURISM. 1. The act of travel and set of actions engaged in by people during the trip to places away from their home environment. 2. The aggregate of all businesses that directly provide goods or services to facilitate business, pleasure, and LEISURE activities away from the home environment. 3. The combination of these two phenomena.

Tourism is derived from the Greek *torus,* a tool used to inscribe a circle (like the common drafting compass). The essential notion here is that of the circle—of leaving and then returning. By the early 1700s, at the latest, the notion of a tour in the sense of a temporary circuitous journey was well-established in the English language. Daniel Defoe (1971), for example, wrote an early travel guide first published in 1724, *A Tour through the Whole Island of Britain*. Touring in the eighteenth and the first part of the nineteenth century was a respectable, upper-class activity. It was a particularly important part of a young gentleman's education in the form of the grand tour through Europe. The term *tourism* itself seems to have appeared shortly after 1800. The *Oxford English Dictionary's* (1989) earliest citation of tourism is 1811, from England's *Sporting Magazine*.

The invention of mass tourism in the mid-nineteenth century is usually credited to (or blamed on) Thomas Cook, who developed and sold prepackaged tours on the newly developed steam train system throughout Britain. It was not long after the development of these inexpensively priced tours for the working and middle classes that the social elite began to disparagingly refer to mass travelers as "Cookites" (Swinglehurst, 1974). *Cookite,* as a term, however did not endure and was eventually replaced by TOURIST as a generic and sometime pejorative term for travelers.

Traditionally, tourism has referred to the act or experience of touring. Since the end of World War II, however, with the virtual explosion of tourism as an activity of significant economic, environmental, and social impacts, the term has also been applied to the travel industry. This trend has also been furthered by the creation of public agencies, industry associations, and visitor and convention bureaus concerned with promoting the interests of tourism businesses or of REGIONS that have the potential to draw tourists.

One result of the growth of divergent interest in travel-related phenomena has been a concomitant growth in divergent definitions of tourism. An example of this divergence may be found in the results of a 1977 study by the U.S. Department of Commerce. Tourism representatives from fifty states and 130 cities were asked to identify which of five definitions best described the travel-related phenomena they were most concerned with. Although nearly 70 percent of the 186 individuals responded, no one definition emerged as preferred. And, in fact, nearly 20 percent disliked all five definitions.

In reviewing the state of tourism definitions, Neil Lieper (1979) suggested that the myriad published definitions could be meaningfully reduced to three categories: "economic," "technical," and "holistic." While his notion that the hundreds of published definitions can be usefully summarized into a relatively small number of categories is correct, there are a couple of problems with the categories he selected. Economic definitions, according to Lieper, actually focused exclusively on the industrial or supply perspective. DEMAND-related definitions were not included, although demand is as much an economic concept as is supply. Lieper's technical definitions tended to actually be definitions of tourist, not tourism, per se. A better classification system, then, might employ the categories: demand-based definitions, supply-based definitions, and integrated definitions.

Demand-based definitions are those that emphasize tourism as a human activity. A typical demand-based definition is that used in the U.S. *National Tourism Policy Study Final Report* (Committee on Commerce, 1978): Tourism is "the action and activities of people taking trips to a place or places outside of their home communities for any purpose except daily commuting to and from work." The authors of this definition also explicity indicated their belief that tourism and travel were synonymous terms. (Although one can still find instances in which the terms are treated synonymously, the trend in the latter part of the 1980s has been to use tourism in the context of the above definition. "Travel" is increasingly being relegated to the specific connotation of human movement, usually by vehicle, regardless of purpose.)

Demand-based definitions, of course, ignore supply-side or industry-related aspects of tourism. Another common problem with this type of definition is the lack of precision about what actually constitutes "outside of their home communities." The usual solution to this is to impose an artificial technical requirement on the more general conceptual definition. Technical requirements typically involve a minimum distance that one must travel away from one's permanent and usual residence and/or length of stay away from one's residence. Conceptually, one could also allow individual travelers to indicate when they were outside of their home communities, and thus qualified to be called tourists. This self-classification has the advantage of accommodating different lifestyles and travel experiences. Some very mobile individuals, for example, may view "their home community" to be much larger than someone who has traveled very little. In practical terms, however, the use of such a subjective definition presents formidable measurement problems.

Supply-based definitions emphasize the provision of services to tourists. Drawing on work by the Canadian National Task Force on Tourism Data, Stephen Smith (1988:183) defined tourism as "the aggregate of all businesses that directly provide goods or services to facilitate business, pleasure, and leisure activities away from the home environment." An important advantage with this type of definition is that it defines tourism in terms consistent with how other industrial sectors are defined: by focusing on the commodities provided. As Smith (1988:183) notes in commenting on shortcomings in demand-based definitions, defining tourism "in terms of tourists' 'actions and activities' or their motivations and behaviors is comparable to defining the health care industry by defining a sick person."

Supply-based definitions, however, also have several limitations. As with demand-based definitions, they focus on only one aspect of a much bigger phenomenon. Furthermore, one must still develop some additional technical requirements to indicate when one is "away from their home environment."

The third category of tourism definitions—holistic definitions in Lieper's terminology—or integrated definitions combine both supply and demand sides of tourism. Because of their greater scope, integrated definitions also show greater variation in their content. A 1942 Swiss definition (Hunziker and Kraph), cited by A. J. Burkart and S. Medlik (1974:40) suggested that tourism was "the sum

of the phenomena and relationships arising from the travel and stay of nonres-
idents, in so far as they do not lead to permanent residence and are not connected
to any earning activity.'' The definition implicit includes both supply and demand
phenomena, as well as the impacts of tourism. It has subsequently been adopted
by the International Association of Scientific Experts in Tourism. Lieper
(1979:404), however, criticized this definition on the ground that the exact
identity of "the phenomena and relationships" is not specified.

Another commonly cited integrated definition is that by Jafar Jafari (1977:6):
"Tourism is the study of man away from his usual habitat, of the industry which
responds to his needs, and of the impacts that both he and the industry have on
the host's socio-cultural, economic, and physical environments." This definition
makes more explicit the notion of demand, supply to meet the demand, and
impacts resulting from both. It also recognizes the concept of flow from an origin
to a destination, although like most other definitions it fails to precisely define
the extent of the tourist's "usual habitat." The definition also avoids any mention
of motives or purpose of travel; this may be viewed as either a strength or a
weakness depending on one's own preferences for extending the term "tourism"
to cover nonleisure travel such as business, convention, or religious travel.

Jafari's definition has been used as the guiding definition for the *Annals of
Tourism Research* and has been repeated by Jafari and Brent Ritchie (1981) as
the basis for defining a university curriculum in tourism studies.

Perhaps the most comprehensive and complicated integrated definition of tourism is Lieper's (1979:403–404) own suggestion that tourism be considered as:

the system involving the discretionary travel and temporary stay of persons away from
their usual residence for one or more nights, excepting tours made for the primary purpose
of earning remuneration from points enroute. The elements of the system are tourists,
generating regions, transit routes, destination regions, and a tourist industry. These five
elements are arranged in spatial and functional connections. Having the characteristics
of an open system, the organization of five elements operates within broader environments:
physical, cultural, social, economical, political, technological with which it interacts.

Even this definition, however, is not totally adequate. Its sheer length discourages
its widespread use. The reference to five elements and an open system begs even
further elaboration. The phrase, tourist industry, is left undefined (but presumably
refers to those phenomena described in supply-based definitions). Finally, the
restriction of travel to stays of one night or more is arbitrary. In particular, no
justification is made for excluding day trips from the concept of tourism, despite
the fact that many people routinely make day trips covering several hundred
miles away from home.

It is unlikely that any single, widely accepted, and workable definition of
tourism will ever be developed. The concept is too broad for consensus to ever
be achieved. It may be more realistic to accept the existence of a number of
different definitions, each designed to serve different purposes.

REFERENCES

Burkart, A. J., and Medlik, S. 1974. *Tourism*. London: Heinemann. A British overview of the nature of tourism, with particular emphasis on industry characteristics.

Committee on Commerce, Science and Transportation. 1978. *National Tourism Policy Study Final Report*. Washington, DC: U.S. Government Printing Office. A set of recommendations for the development of a national strategy for tourism, commissioned by the U.S. Senate.

Defoe, Daniel. [1724] 1971. *A Tour through the Whole Island of Britain*. Harmondsworth, U.K.: Penguin. One of the earliest tour books published in the English language.

Jafari, Jafar. 1977. "Editor's Page." *Annals of Tourism Research* 5:6–11. A statement of the editorial perspective of the journal.

Jafari, Jafar, and Ritchie, J. R. Brent. 1981. "Toward a Framework for Tourism Education: Problems and Prospects." *Annals of Tourism Research* 8:13–34. Presents an outline for a curriculum in tourism studies based on Jafari's definition of tourism.

Lieper, Neil. 1979. "The Framework of Tourism." *Annals of Tourism Research* 6:390–407. Examines existing definitions of tourism and reviews their weaknesses; then outlines a "tourism system" and constructs a definition based on elements of that system.

Oxford English Dictionary, 2nd edition. 1989. J. A. Simpson and E. S. C. Weiner (preparers). Vol. 18, 306. Oxford: Clarendon Press. An extended definition of "tourism," based on etymology and historical precedents.

Smith, Stephen L. J. 1988. "Defining Tourism: A Supply-Side View." *Annals of Tourism Research* 15:179–190. Presents an argument for the importance of supply-based definitions and illustrates how such a definition can be developed and applied.

Swinglehurst, Edmund. 1974. *The Romantic Journey: Thomas Cook and Victorian Travel*. New York: Harper & Row. A history of the early days of Thomas Cook's organized tours; provides a good discussion of the social context of the rise of mass tourism in England.

U.S. Department of Commerce. 1977. *Analysis of Travel Definitions, Terminology, and Research Needs among States and Cities*. Washington, DC: U.S. Travel Service, Research and Analysis Division. A survey of terminology used by various public agencies with respect to tourism and travel.

SOURCES OF ADDITIONAL INFORMATION

Many texts on tourism usually include a definition of the term. A few references that provide a more extended discussion of the problems and issues in defining tourism include Neil Leiper's inquiry into the history of the word, "An Etymology of Tourism" (*Annals of Tourism Research* 10:277–281, 1983). Stephen Smith discusses a variety of definitional issues in Chapter 2, "Defining and Describing Tourism," in *Tourism Analysis* (London: Longman, 1989). Robin Chadwick provides an excellent review of both conceptual and operational definitions of the term as well as other related terms in "Concepts, Definitions, and Measures Used in Travel and Tourism Research," in Brent Ritchie and Charles R. Goeldner, eds., *Travel, Tourism, and Hospitality Research* (New York: Wiley, 1987; Chapt. 5).

TOURIST. An individual traveling away from his usual place of residence for less than one year and for any purpose other than routine business commuting.

Tourist as a word probably predates the appearance of TOURISM by approximately a decade. The *Oxford English Dictionary* (1989) cites use of the term by a Samuel Pegge about 1800 as a neologism synonymous with traveler. The notion of a tourist as a traveler or as one who goes on a tour has remained essentially unchanged since 1800. There has been, however, substantial discussion about how the term should be operationally defined.

One of the first formal operational definitions of tourist was presented in the appendix to the 1937 Report of the Committee of Statistical Experts of the League of Nations (quoted in World Tourism Organization, 1981:ii). They proposed a definition of a tourist (in an international context) as "any person travelling for a period of twenty-four hours or more in a country other than that in which he usually resides." This definition explicitly included travel for pleasure, business, health, domestic, and educational reasons as well as excursionists from cruise ships that visited a country during a port call, even though the stay in port might be less than twenty-four hours. Individuals arriving in a country to start a business, attend school, or who were just passing through the country without stopping were not considered to be tourists (World Tourism Organization, 1981).

This definition was reviewed and accepted in 1950 by the International Union of Official Travel Organizations (IUOTO), but was subsequently modified by IUOTO in 1957 to exclude excursionists and to include students. The World Tourism Organization (WTO) (1981) reviewed a number of other international definitions, most of which were similar to the 1937 definition. WTO's own definition involves a comparison of visitors, tourists, and excursionists. An international visitor is an individual entering a country that is not his usual place of residence and who is not:

1. Intending to emigrate or to obtain employment in the destination country.

2. Visiting in the capacity of a diplomat or a member of the armed forces.

3. A dependent or anyone in the above two categories.

4. A refugee, nomad, or border worker.

5. Going to stay for more than one year.

But who is or may be:

6. Visiting for purposes of RECREATION, medical treatment, religious observance, family matters, sporting events, conferences, study, or transit to another country.

7. A crew member of a foreign vessel or aircraft stopped in the country on a layover.

8. A foreign commercial or business traveler staying for less than one year, including technicians arriving to install machinery or equipment.

9. An employee of international bodies on a mission lasting less than one year, or a national returning home for a temporary visit.

International tourists are visitors who spend at least one night in accommodation in the destination country; international excursionists are visitors who do not spend at least one night.

Most countries accept formally or implicitly the WTO definition of tourist for international travel studies and statistical purposes. There is, however, no real consensus on definitions of domestic tourists. WTO (1981) has suggested some guidelines for how domestic tourists might be defined. Any domestic definition should, according to the WTO:

1. Not make a distinction between citizens and foreign nationals resident in a country.

2. Exclude travel associated with the pursuit of employment, such as commuting.

3. Make a distinction between extended migration and short-term migration or travel.

4. Make a further distinction between stays of more than twenty-four hours and less than twenty-four hours.

Stephen Smith (1989) has surveyed a number of domestic tourists definitions and observed that not all conform to the WTO guidelines. Some examples of different definitions include the following:

1. The 1973 National Tourism Resources Review Commission defined a tourist as anyone who traveled 50 miles one way for any purpose other than to commute to work.

2. Florida defines a tourist as anyone from out of state who spends at least one night while on a pleasure trip.

3. Ontario uses a 40 kilometer one-way distance criterion to define a tourist.

4. British Columbia considers a tourist to be anyone spending the night away from his home, regardless of the distance traveled.

Some of these jurisdictions have separate definitions for visitors, excursionists, and resident and nonresident travelers depending on other criteria such as place of residence, distance traveled, or length of stay.

The lack of consistency in definitions of tourist, even between states or provinces of one country has given rise to problems of a lack of comparability of data and confusion over the actual number of tourists that visit a given destination. Although a variety of task forces and working groups, such as Canada's National Task Force on Tourism Data, have made recommendations about how domestic tourism statistics and definitions could be made more consistent, few successes have been achieved. Interagency and interregional politics as well as budget limitations inevitably complicate changes in the collection and reporting of tourism statistics. Until the unlikely day that common operational definitions are developed for *tourist* and related terms, researchers, planners, and policy analysts must exercise care in interpreting and reporting statistics from different agencies or jurisdictions.

REFERENCES

Smith, Stephen L. J. 1989. *Tourism Analysis*. London: Longman. Chapter 2, "Describing and Defining Tourism," provides a good overview of a variety of definitional issues.

Oxford English Dictionary, 2nd edition. 1989. J. A. Simpson and E. S. C. Weiner (preparers). Vol. 18, 306. Oxford: Clarendon Press. An extended definition of "tourist," based on etymology and historical precedents.

World Tourism Organization. 1981. *Technical Handbook on the Collection and Presentation of Domestic and International Tourism Statistics*. Madrid, Spain: World Tourism Organization. The definitive work on international tourism statistical data collection; includes guidelines for domestic tourism statistics.

SOURCES OF ADDITIONAL INFORMATION

Many general tourism textbooks address the problems and approaches in defining a tourist; published sources of tourism statistics should also include a discussion of the definitions used in the preparation of those sources. Two sources of particular relevance to this topic include Robin Chadwick, "Concepts, Definitions and Measures Used in Travel and Tourism Research," in Brent Ritchie and Charles R. Goeldner, eds., *Travel, Tourism, and Hospitality Research* (New York: Wiley, 1987, Chapt. 5); and Raymond BarOn, *Travel and Tourism Data* (London: Euromonitor, 1989).

TRAVEL COST METHOD. A method for driving a DEMAND curve for a RECREATION site based on variations in the travel costs paid by visitors to that site; an estimate of the value of the site (consumer surplus) may be calculated from the demand curve.

The travel cost method (TCM) is one of three standard methods approved by the U.S. Senate in 1973 for estimating public resource VALUE in resource development plans. The two other methods are the UNIT DAY VALUE METHOD (U.S. Congress, 1962), and the CONTINGENT VALUATION METHOD, approved in 1979.

The basic notion underlying the travel cost approach is that the price paid for a private good (travel costs) as a prerequisite for consumption of a public good (a recreation site) may be interpreted as a surrogate of the price of the public good in a demand analysis of that good. Thus one replaces price on the vertical axis of a traditional demand curve by travel costs (sometimes inferred directly from distance traveled). Consumption, along the horizontal axis, is measured in terms of the number of trips made by visitors who have incurred various levels of travel costs (or who have traveled specified distances).

A key measure that may be derived from the travel cost approach is consumer surplus. Consumer surplus is the difference between what a consumer actually pays for some commodity, and what he would be willing to pay. This difference, the surplus value of the commodity provides a measure of the marginal value of the resource for policy and planning purposes.

The development of the travel cost method is usually associated with Marion

Clawson (1959), although Clawson gives credit to Harold Hotelling for some unpublished suggestions about using travel costs as a surrogate for market price. In the original formulation of the travel cost approach Clawson collected data from an on-site survey of visitors. The survey provided him with an estimate of the total number of visitors as well as information on their origins. These data were grouped into a series of origin zones (defined as the county of residence). The number of people from each county was plotted against the straightline distance (as a measure of travel costs) between the county seat and the recreation site. This graph represents the aggregate response of all people in the market area to the effects of distance (or travel costs) on their willingness to visit the site in question. Using this graphic relationship, Clawson then simulated the response to hypothetical fee increases by assuming people would respond to a change in the fees the same as they would to a change in travel costs. As the fees increased, the number of trips decreased in a predictable pattern, until some maximum fee was reached when all travel ceased. Clawson summarized this information by plotting the decreasing numbers of trips against simulated fee increases (as a surrogate for price). Because this new curve represents the willingness of recreationists to absorb travel cost to a site beyond what they actually paid, the area under the curve represents the consumer surplus of the site. The consumer surplus of a site is a measure of the value of that site.

While Clawson's original zonal version of the travel cost method is conceptually valid, it does have several problems that other researchers were soon to point out. One basic problem is that the decrease in the willingness of people to travel with increasing distance is a function not just of travel costs, but also of travel time (Cesario and Knetsch, 1970). Clawson and Jack Knetsch (1966) also noted that the number of alternative sites increases as distance increases. Thus declining attendance at any specified site is likely due to a combination of greater travel costs, greater travel time, and increased competition.

A key assumption of the travel cost approach is that a visit to a single, specific site is the sole purpose of that trip. In fact, federal guidelines advise that the method be used exclusively for single-destination trips. This assumption has been tested by Abraham Haspel and Reed Johnson (1982). They concluded that acceptable estimates of the value of individual sites visited on a multistop trip can sometimes be obtained by dividing travel costs proportionately among all stops.

Another development in application of the travel cost model is experimentation with a variation of the approach, known as the HEDONIC TRAVEL COST MODEL (Brown and Mendelsohn, 1984; Brookshire, Thayer, Schulze, and d'Arge, 1982).

Still other developments in the travel cost approach include modifications in how the market area is operationally defined. For example, the Army Corps of Engineers has suggested limiting the analysis to those closest distance zones that account for the origin of 95 percent of all users. The 5 percent excluded come from the most distant origins, and are considered to be potentially distorting. Whether this is an acceptable solution for all forms of outdoor recreation is still open to examination.

There are also some unresolved questions about the proper inclusion of other forms of costs, including the perennial concern about the value of travel time (Cesario, 1976), as well as accommodation costs for overnight trips (Walsh, 1977).

Richard Walsh (1987) noted that the travel cost approach not only has been tested and refined over the last twenty-five years, so that it is generally accepted as a reasonably accurate method, but that it has provided a very useful stimulus for cumulative research in resource economics. Starting with Clawson's original zonal model, successive waves of researchers have critiqued and refined the travel cost method, building on existing research. While one can still cite weaknesses and unsolved problems in connection with this approach, it is well-established in the resource and recreation economics fields and has resulted in important methodological and conceptual contributions to our understanding of the use of recreational resources and of pleasure travel.

REFERENCES

Brookshire, David S., Thayer, Mark A., Schulze, William D., and d'Arge, Ralph D. 1982. "Valuing Public Goods: A Comparison of Survey and Hedonic Approaches." *American Economic Review* 72:165–177. A description of the hedonic approach and its contrasts with the contingent valuation approach.

Brown, Gardner, and Mendelsohn, Robert. 1984. "The Hedonic Travel Cost Method," *The Review of Economics and Statistics* 66:427–433. One of the first explanations of this model in recreation economics.

Cesario, Frank J. 1976. "Value of Time in Recreational Studies," *Land Economics* 52:32–41. Examines methods for assessing dollar value of time in recreation travel settings.

Cesario, Frank J., and Knetsch, Jack L. 1970. "The Time Bias in Recreation Benefit Estimates." *Water Resources Research* 6:700–704. Examines effect of value of travel time on estimates of consumer surplus.

Clawson, Marion. 1959. *Methods of Measuring Demand for, and Value of Outdoor Recreation*. Washington, D.C.: Resources for the Future. One of the first formulations of the travel cost approach.

Clawson, Marion, and Knetsch, Jack L. 1966. *Economics of Outdoor Recreation*. Baltimore: Johns Hopkins University Press. The classic text on recreation economics.

Haspel, Abraham E., and Johnson, F. Reed. 1982. "Multiple Destination Trip Bias in Recreation Benefit Estimation." *Land Economics* 58:364–372. Tests the assumption that the travel cost method should be limited only to single-destination trips.

U.S. Congress, U.S. Senate. 1962. *Supplement No. 1, Evaluation Standards for Primary Recreation Benefits, Policies, Standards, and Procedures in the Formulation, Evaluation, and Review of Plans for Use and Development of Water and Related Land Resources*. 87th Cong., 2nd sess., May 29, S. Doc. 97. Established procedures for estimating non-market value of recreation resources. Subsequent supplement approved the use of the travel cost approach.

U.S. Army Corps of Engineers. 1974. *Estimating Initial Reservoir Recreation Use*. IWR Research Report 74-R1, vol. 2. Fort Belvoir, VA: U.S. Army Engineer Institute for Water Resources. A technical manual used for forecasting water-based recreation at Corps projects.

Walsh, Richard G. 1977. "Effects of Improved Research Methods on the Evaluation of Recreational Benefits." In *Outdoor Recreation: Advances in Applications of Economics*, comp. Jay M. Hughes and R. Duane Lloyd. general technical report WO-2, 145–153. Washington, DC: U.S. Forest Service. Reviews status of research on various supplements to travel costs such as value of time, costs of accommodation, and equipment expenditures.

Walsh, Richard G. 1987. *Recreation Economic Decisions*. State College, PA: Venture. A good overview of demand analysis as well as a variety of valuation techniques; see especially Chapter 8 and the bibliography.

Wilman, Elizabeth A. 1980. "The Value of Time in Recreation Benefit Studies." *Journal of Environmental Economics and Management* 7:272–286. Examines the value of time spent in travel as well as in recreation participation in the context of consumer surplus estimation.

SOURCES OF ADDITIONAL INFORMATION

The literature on the travel cost approach is rather extensive, but many of the reports are published in obscure sources such as agency technical reports. Some articles or chapters that have appeared in more widely available research journals and books are cited here. Examples of applications of the travel cost approach may be found in Charles Cicchetti, Anthony Fisher, and Kerry Smith, "An Econometric Evaluation of a Generalized Consumer Surplus Model: The Mineral King Controversy" (*Econometrica* 44:1259–1276, 1976); Jack Knetsch, "Outdoor Recreation Demands and Benefits" (*Land Economics* 39:386–396, 1963); Jack Knetsch and Robert Davis, "Comparison of Methods of Recreation Valuation," in Allan Kneese and Stephen Smith, eds., *Water Research* (Baltimore: Johns Hopkins Press, 1966); Andrew Trice and Samuel Wood, "Measurement of Recreation Benefits" (*Land Economics* 34:195–207, 1958); and John Loomis, "Use of Travel Cost Models for Evaluating Lottery-Rationed Recreation: Application to Big Game Hunting" (*Journal of Leisure Research* 14:117–124, 1982).

Other articles that address more technical issues in the travel cost approach include Geoffrey Allen, Thomas Stevens, and Scott Barrett, "The Effects of Variable Omission in the Travel Cost Technique" (*Land Economics* 57:173–180, 1981); Daniel Stynes, George Peterson, and Donald Rosenthal, "Log Transformation Bias in Estimating Travel Cost Models" (*Land Economics* 62:94–103, 1986); Rod Zeimer, Wesley Musser, and Carter Hill, "Recreation Demand Equations: Functional Form and Consumer Surplus" (*American Journal of Agricultural Economics* 62:136–141, 1980); Michael Bowes and John Loomis, "A Note on the Use of Travel Cost Models with Unequal Zonal Populations" (*Land Economics* 56:465–470, 1980); and Kerry Smith and Raymond Kopp, "Spatial Limits of the Travel Cost Recreational Demand Model" (*Land Economics* 56:64–72, 1980). David Seckler's, "On the Uses and Abuses of Economic Science in Evaluating Public Outdoor Recreation" (*Land Economics* 42:485–494, 1966) is slightly dated but still a provocative look at the use of willingness to pay models and the potential confusion between willingness to pay and ability to pay.

U

UNIT DAY VALUE METHOD. A method of estimating the VALUE of a recreation day produced at a recreation site that utilizes expert judgment and occasionally site rating scales.

The unit day value method was the first method approved by the federal government (U.S. Congress, 1962) for estimating the value of public RESOURCES for development plans and policy analysis. The other two methods are the TRAVEL COST METHOD (TCM), approved by the Senate for use in 1973, and the CONTINGENT VALUATION METHOD (CVM), approved by the Senate for use in 1979.

The basis of the unit day value method is the use of expert opinion to assign a value to a recreation-day produced by a specific site. The value determined through this method is considered to be an estimate of the average willingness to pay by consumers for a day of recreation at the site. Multiplying the unit day value by the number of visits to the site yields an estimate of total willingness to pay; this is equivalent to the consumer surplus of the site. Different values may be assigned for different types of RECREATION at any given site.

Determination of the value of a site is based on five criteria (Walsh, 1987):

1. The quality of the recreation experience is influenced by crowding at the site.
2. The quantity and quality of substitutable sites.
3. The CARRYING CAPACITY of the site as determined by the level of facility development.
4. The ACCESSIBILITY of the site as determined by road capacity and parking lots.
5. General environmental quality of the site.

Some agencies have developed scales to operationally define each of these criteria. The site under study is assigned a series of scores reflecting its performance on each criterion. These scores are summed to give an aggregate score, which is converted into a dollar-and-cents value, based on conversion rates established by the agency conducting the valuation. For example, the U.S. Forest Service specifies a range of unit day values for its recreation sites in the Southeastern Region ranging from $12.95 per twelve-hour visitor day for a high quality recreation site in a semiprimitive, nonmotorized zone (defined in the RECREATION OPPORTUNITY SPECTRUM or ROS) in a rural environment. Other values are assigned to each of the ROS zones for each Forest Service planning region.

Although the unit day valuation approach has the longest history of the three valuation techniques used by federal agencies, it also has the most problems. In addition to the inherent weakness that all values are ultimately based on opinion rather than theory or empirical analysis, the method is often criticized on three other grounds. First, the value produced does not reflect the law of diminishing marginal returns. The value of a recreational experience for any particular individual is implicitly assumed, in the unit day valuation method to be the same regardless of how many times the individual participates in the activity. This is, of course, contrary to typical human behavior.

Furthermore, the U.S. Forest Service scale used to assess the effect of crowding on the quality of a recreational experience requires that more users always lowers the quality of a recreational experience. This may be true for some recreation activities and for certain levels of use, but numerous exceptions can be found.

Another problem is that the Forest Service scale used in assessing the effects of nearby sites is based on the assumption that adjacent sites always compete. In fact, some adjacent recreation sites can provide a complement to each other, increasing their mutual ATTRACTIVITY.

Finally, the unit day value method does not take into account the distribution of users surrounding the site. A site close to a large population will normally be more valuable than one that is remote.

For these reasons and the availability of two alternative valuation methods, the unit day valuation approach is becoming less frequently used in policy analysis. Senate guidelines now suggest using this method only when the cost of using either of the alternatives is too high and when the site to be evaluated is small—producing fewer than 750,000 recreation days per year.

REFERENCES

U.S. Congress, U.S. Senate. 1962. *Supplement No. 1, Evaluation Standards for Primary Recreation Benefits, Policies, Standards, and Procedures in the Formulation, Evaluation, and Review of Plans for Use and Development of Water and Related Land Resources.* 87th Cong. 2nd sess. May 29, S. Doc. 97. This Senate document established the unit day valuation approach as the first nonmarket method for resource valuation in recreation planning. Subsequent supplements added the travel cost approach and the contingent valuation approach as alternatives.
Walsh, Richard G. 1987. *Recreation Economic Decisions.* State College, PA: Venture.

Provides a good overview of all valuation techniques; see Chapter 8, "Measures of Benefit," in particular.

SOURCES OF ADDITIONAL INFORMATION

Further discussion of the use of this method may be found in the U.S. Water Resources Council report, *Economic and Environmental Principles and Guidelines for Water and Related Land Resource Implementation Studies* (Washington, DC: U.S. Government Printing Office, 1983) and in the *Federal Register,* "Water Resources Council Guidelines" (Dec. 14, 1979, Pt. IX). Cindy Sorg and John Loomis illustrate how empirical research and expert judgment can be combined to arrive at day unit values in *Empirical Estimates of Amenity Forest Values: A Comparative Review* (general technical report RM107, Fort Collins, CO: Rocky Mountain Forest and Range Experiment Station, 1984).

V
_____

VALUE. A conception, measure, or expression of the preferences or ideals of an individual or group, particularly with respect to human behavior or choices among alternatives.

Value is a key concept for a number of fields of inquiry, including recreation and leisure studies. The breadth associated with the study of value is illustrated by the several hundred separate citations in Nicholas Rescher's (1969) text, *Introduction to Value Theory*. In addition to the breadth of interest in the topic, Rescher notes its extended history. Economists have written on the topic since before Adam Smith, while philosophers have concerned themselves with values from before Aristotle.

While the interest of the two disciplines just cited—economics and philosophy—might appear to represent radically different conceptions of value, numerous scholars have suspected that there are fundamental themes that link the diverse connotations of value. The interest in what might be termed a grand unified theory of value derives from the work of the German philosopher, Rudolph Herman Lotze (Rescher, 1969). Rescher describes Lotze's work as marking the beginning of the ''value-with-a-capital-V'' movement. This grand synthesis, however, has not yet been achieved in the eyes of most scholars. The growing use of value as a social, political, and behavioral concept by social scientists may mean that there is more confusion and ambiguity in the use of the term than ever before.

The numerous definitions of value may be grouped into two very broad and general categories: preferential definitions and nonpreferential definitions. The definition suggested above is an example of a preferential definition. Basically, professional definitions denote value in terms of human ideals, choices, or priorities. Most recreation and leisure scholars use the term in this general sense; in so doing, they stand in direct contrast to nonpreferential definitions. There are two common types of nonpreferential values. The first is the mathematical denotation of the value of a variable. (It should be acknowledged, of course, that one can find many examples in statistical analyses of leisure where reference is made to the value of a variable or of a significance test, but this does not represent the dominant use of the concept.) The second nonpreferential use of value concerns what Richard Andrews and Mary Jo Waites (1978) call functional value relationships. An example of this type of value is the value of a saltwater marsh to an inshore game fishery. One of the fundamental distinctions between the social sciences and the biophysical sciences, in the view of Thomas Brown (1984) is that the former are generally more concerned with preferential values while the latter are more concerned with nonpreferential, functional values.

Brown identifies three realms in which social scientists and humanists discuss preferential values: (1) the conceptual realm, (2) the relational realm, and (3) the object realm. Within the conceptual realm, values represent human ideals governing modes of behavior (e.g., COMPETITION), end states (e.g., pleasure), and qualities (e.g, beauty). These values are sometimes referred to as held values, reflecting the fact that they are fundamental preferences or ideals held by an individual.

Values in the relational realm arise from the conceptual preferences a person holds for one entity over another. These entities may be tangible objects, political systems, religions, modes of behavior, or any other discrete (but not necessarily tangible) phenomenon or object. When expressed overtly through choice, behavior, or some other objective measure, the values pass into the object realm and become what Brown terms an assigned value. Assigned values are expressed through overt actions such as voting behavior, religious observances, career selection, or market choices.

In casual discussions of values, the distinctions among the three realms of values are often blurred. For example, a director of a municipal recreation organization may talk about the value of liability insurance. In this case, the value may be either the limit of financial coverage (object realm) or the importance of liability coverage as part of an overall risk management strategy by the municipality (conceptual realm). Some CONSERVATION advocates appear to be referring to the relational realm when they argue that natural objects have an intrinsic value independent of human preferences or actions (Stone, 1974 and Ehrenfeld, 1976). For other conservationists, the value of RESOURCES may be expressed in terms of market prices and economics (object realm). The differences between these groups of conservationists probably stem from differences in their conceptual values.

Another aspect of the difference between the various realms of values is illustrated by a distinction often made in economics: use value versus exchange value. Use value refers to the conceptual importance of a resource or commodity. The use value of water, for example, is very high. Exchange value, however, reflects the interaction of supply and DEMAND. The use of value of diamonds is relatively modest, but their exchange value is very high, because the supply of diamonds is rigidly controlled by an international cartel. The exchange value of water, on the other hand, is very low because its supply is relatively abundant.

In empirical leisure research, assigned values (object realm values) are of particular importance. These are measured through words or actions and thus are open to scientific inquiry. Common forms of observing or estimating assigned values include the commitment of time to an activity, responses to questionnaires, the exchange of money for a commodity, or the explicit conservation or preservation of some resource.

Assessments of assigned values may be made by either an individual or a group for either themselves or for another individual or group. The purchase of an item for personal use or the response to an opinion poll reflects the values of an individual assigned to himself. An elected official casting a vote in city council about a proposed recreation budget represents an individual assigning a value for a group. A decision by a university tenure and promotion committee concerning tenure for a professor of leisure studies represents a group's assessment of the value of an individual's productivity and academic suitability. Finally, the joint deliberations of a grants program review panel about the optimal allocation of research funds among a large number of proposals illustrate a group valuation process applied to a group.

One special context in which valuations are made is in the allocation of resources, whether the resources are public or private. In the case of privately owned and controlled resources, a common measure of their value is market price. For example, a potential consumer is interested in acquiring a sailboat. The price asked by the dealer represents a complex interplay of supply and demand forces including the factors (e.g., material, labor, transportation, capital costs) that were required to produce the sailboat and deliver it to the point of purchase as well as to the existing level of demand, and the supply of boats from competitors. The price the potential consumer is willing to pay represents an equally complex interplay of individual factors including his ability to pay; the recreational preferences of family and/or friends; his basic demand for sailing; and whether or not he already owns a boat.

A full explanation of price theory is beyond the scope of this dictionary, but a basic principle of market place economics that should be mentioned is that market prices provide an objective measure of the value of privately owned resources in various uses. Price is, in effect, a rationing mechanism that directs the supply of resources or commodities to the place where they are most valued, i.e., where they can command the highest price for the seller. At the same time, of course, potential purchasers are attempting to get suppliers to compete against each other by lowering the asking price in order to actually close a deal. The final sale price theoretically represents some form of equilibrium among all the forces affecting supplier and buyer, and thus some general social assessment of the value of a resource in a particular use.

The dynamics of a free market work well in many circumstances to insure an adequate supply and reasonable allocation of many types of resources. There are circumstances, however, in which the results of a market place allocation of resources or commodities produces results that are not socially or politically acceptable. As a result, virtually all societies have decided that some commodities will be allocated through some type of nonmarket mechanism. In the United States these commodities include elementary and secondary education, national defense, highways, and certain recreational resources such as public PARKS.

Even though these commodities are not allocated through the market place, some form of allocation mechanism is still needed because the supply of resources used to produce these commodities is not sufficient to meet all possible demand. For example, a ten-acre plot of publicly owned land in a large metropolitan area may be the object of competition by home builders, a mall developer, a utility company, and the municipal recreation and parks department. Among the techniques available to public planners in determining the value of a public resource in a recreational application are the so-called shadow pricing tools: the CONTINGENT VALUATION METHOD, the TRAVEL COST METHOD, and the UNIT DAY VALUE METHOD.

It should be emphasized that the type of value derived through these estimation procedures is intended to be analogous to market value. There are other types of value provided by recreation resources, including nonpreferential functional values (such as the value of a forested park in flood control) as well as more specialized types of value such as option value (the value of a type of a recreation resource), preservation value (the philosophical and scientific value of a resource), and bequest value (the amount current users are willing to pay to ensure that future users will have access to recreational resources).

Regardless of what method is used to determine values, the discussion and comparison of values in recreation and leisure studies is an emotionally laden topic. Some of the reasons for debates in valuation studies or statements include differences in (1) how groups perceive the entity to be valued, (2) their held values and implicit preferences, (3) the social contexts in which different groups make judgments, (4) conditions internal to the groups making those judgments, (5) differences in the forms that the groups believe the valuations should be expressed or the consequences of different valuations, and (6) the constituency of the valuation, including whether the constituency is the group itself or another group they represent. And finally, misunderstandings and arguments arise not only from these differences, but even from differences in understanding how the term *value* is defined.

REFERENCES

Andrews, Richard N., and Waites, Mary Jo. 1978. *Environmental Values in Public Decisions: A Research Agenda.* Ann Arbor: University of Michigan, School of Natural Resources. Includes a discussion of the definition of values; introduces the distinction between preferential values and functional nonpreferential values.

Brown, Thomas C. 1984. "The Concept of Value in Resource Allocation." *Land Economics* 60:231–246. An excellent review article on various concepts of value and their implications for the study of economics.

Ehrenfeld, David W. 1976. "The Conservation of Non-Resources." *American Scientist* 64:648–656. An essay promoting the notion that natural objects have an intrinsic value regardless of their usefulness to human beings.

Rescher, Nicholas. 1969. *Introduction to Value Theory*. Englewood Cliffs, NJ: Prentice Hall. A good survey of the variety of uses of the term, "value"; examines how different disciplines have studied the concept. Describes basic principles and relationships among connotations of value.

Stone, Christopher D. 1974. *Should Trees Have Standing? Toward Legal Rights for Natural Objects*. New York: Avon. An essay promoting the belief that natural objects have intrinsic value that should be given legal status.

SOURCES OF ADDITIONAL INFORMATION

The article by Thomas Brown and the text by Nicholas Rescher, cited in the Reference list provide numerous useful references. Some other good sources dealing with values, particularly as they affect public policymaking, are B. M. Anderson's *Social Value* (New York: Augustus M. Kelley, Reprints of Economic Classics, 1966) and Samuel Bailer, *A Critical Dissertation on the Nature, Measure, and Causes of Value* (New York: Augustus M. Kelley, Reprints of Economic Classics, 1967). Another classic text is Samuel Hart's *Treatise on Values* (New York: Philosophical Library, 1949). Kenneth Boulding has examined the "Contributions of Economics to the General Theory of Value" (*Philosophy of Science* 23:1–14, 1956). A valuable collection of readings on value may be found in Ray Leply, ed., *Value: A Cooperative Inquiry* (New York: Columbia University Press, 1949).

Some texts that examine the variety of meanings of value include Charles Morris's *Varieties of Human Value* (Chicago: University of Chicago Press, 1956); Ralph Perry Burton, *Realms of Value: A Critique of Human Civilization* (Cambridge, MA: Harvard University Press, 1954); and Karl Scheibe, *Beliefs and Values* (New York: Holt, Rinehart, & Winston, 1970). Finally, a good introduction to price theory and values is Jack Hershleifer, *Price Theory and Application* (Englewood Cliffs, NJ: Prentice Hall, 1980).

VOLUNTEERISM. The combination of volunteer activity, the management of volunteers, and the philosophy behind volunteer service as a social activity.

Volunteerism emerged as a distinct concept during the 1960s. During this decade many social agencies significantly increased the use of volunteers to meet their program objectives in areas ranging from literacy programs through environmental projects to rape crisis centers. "Voluntarism" has also been used with the same connotation as the above definition; however, voluntarism properly denotes any theory that emphasizes the role of free will in mental processes or in decisions about behavior in contrast to theories of determinism. It has no direct connection with volunteering.

Virtually all research on volunteerism has approached the topic from the perspective that volunteering is unpaid work. Robert Stebbins (1982), while asserting this viewpoint, did acknowledge that volunteering might be viewed as a special form of "serious" LEISURE, along with hobbyism and AMATEUR sport/ science/art. Given the popular view that volunteering is a form of work, it is not surprising that research on volunteers has tended to adopt models and concepts from research on paid workers. The most common research topic has been the general question of the motivation of volunteers. Several different approaches have been used to study volunteers' motivations.

A popular belief about the motivations of volunteers is that they are somehow highly altruistic people. David Smith (1981) has argued that this popular view is incorrect. The reasons behind volunteering are complex he suggests, but altruism is not especially strong. In fact, Smith challenges the idea that anything is done for purely altruistic reasons. The decision to volunteer is based on the probability of obtaining some form of personal reward or meeting some personal NEED. Rewards from volunteering may be in the form of material rewards (such as obtaining access to services), "solidarity" rewards (such as developing friendships), or purposive rewards (such as helping to achieve a goal that the volunteer personally believes is important). Smith's ideas are essentially the same as the tenets of social exchange theory. Social exchange theory interprets human interactions as exchanges in which an individual gives up something of value, such as time and energy for volunteering, in return for some form of payment, perhaps friendship or social status.

Dorothy Briggs (1982) attempted to apply motivation-hygiene theory (Herzberg, 1976) to volunteer activity. The basic idea of motivation-hygiene theory is that satisfaction and dissatisfaction in a job are not opposite ends of one continuum but separate continua. Motivation factors are those forces or conditions that, when present, provide job satisfaction. These factors include opportunities for achievement, recognition, advancement, personal growth, and the intrinsic satisfaction of a job done well. Hygiene factors produce dissatisfaction when absent or unsatisfactory. These include general working conditions, relations with peers and supervisors, company policies and administrative procedures, job security, safety conditions, and pay. While there is empirical support for the relevance of motivation-hygiene theory to motivating paid employees, Briggs found the model failed to explain the levels of motivation and satisfaction among volunteers.

Another approach toward analyzing volunteers' motives has been the notion of sufficiency of justification, which comes from studies on INTRINSIC MOTIVATION. Barry Staw (1974) hypothesized that individuals in a job or other obligatory setting will experience COGNITIVE DISSONANCE if the associated extrinsic and intrinsic rewards are too high ("overjustified") or too low ("underjustified"). In the case of overjustification, Staw suggested that individuals will downplay the importance of intrinsic rewards, while keeping the extrinsic rewards important. On the other hand, in the case of underjustification, individuals will emphasize in their own minds the importance of the intangible intrinsic rewards to compensate for the lack of extrinsic motivations. He tested his hypothesis with a sample of Reserve Officer Training Corps (ROTC) volunteers before and after a draft lottery and found support for his model.

Jone Pearce (1983) attempted to replicate Staw's work using a sample of volunteer and paid firefighters. She failed to find support for Staw's hypotheses and concluded, in particular, that the presence or absence of extrinsic rewards had no regular impact on the levels of intrinsic motivation.

The issue of the relative importance of extrinsic and intrinsic motivation as it applied to volunteers has also been examined by Eva Schindler-Rainman and Ronald Lippitt (1975) and Lynn Miller (1985).

Craig Pinder (1985) proposed using an EXPECTANCY-VALENCE MODEL to explain why some people become volunteers and others do not. He developed a series of three general questions as a model of the decision-making process of the potential volunteer: (1) If I attempt the volunteer activity, will I succeed? (2) If I succeed, what will it do for me? (3) How much satisfaction or dissatisfaction will I derive from the consequences? If acceptable answers are not found for all three questions, the individual elects not to volunteer.

Still another approach has been proposed by Robert Flashman and Sam Quick (1985), as an answer to Smith's (1981) cynicism toward altruism. Using a logic roughly parallel to Herzberg's separation of satisfaction/dissatisfaction from one continuum into two, Flashman and Quick suggest that self-centeredness/altruism are not the poles of one continuum, but rather separate continua: selflessness/selfishness and self-care/self-neglect. They propose that the best volunteers score high on both self-care and selflessness—a form of "enlightened self-interest."

One of the few researchers that has examined volunteering as a form of leisure rather than as a form of work is Karla Henderson (1981). Working with a group of 4-H volunteers, Henderson found that the overwhelming majority felt that their volunteer service was either equally work and recreation or just recreation.

Research on volunteerism, especially the motives of volunteers, is not only of scholarly interest but of practical relevance. A better understanding of the values and interests of volunteers may help agencies recruit, retain, and reward volunteers. Furthermore, such knowledge may help provide greater insight into the nature of leisure, and why some individuals freely give up the opportunity for other recreation activities in order to do volunteer work. Some further, specific suggestions for research needs in volunteerism are given by Susan Ellis (1985).

REFERENCES

Briggs, Dorothy L. 1982. "On Satisfying the Volunteer and the Paid Employee: Any Differences?" *Volunteer Administration* 14(4)1–14. An examination of motivations of education volunteers versus those of general employees using a motivation-hygiene research perspective.

Ellis, Susan J. 1985. "Research on Volunteerism: What Needs to Be Done." *Journal of Voluntary Action Research* 14(2/3):11–14. A brief inventory of suggested research topics, based on the author's personal opinions.

Flashman, Robert, and Quick, Sam. 1985. "Altruism Is Not Dead: A Specific Analysis of Volunteer Motivation." In *Motivating Volunteers,* ed., Larry F. Moore, 154–170. Vancouver, B.C.: Vancouver Volunteer Centre. A retort to the position of David Smith using anecdotal evidence; proposes a "double bar" continuum model of altruism.

Henderson, Karla. 1981. "Motivations and Perceptions of Volunteerism as a Leisure Activity." *Journal of Leisure Research* 13:208–218. One of the few studies that examines the leisure-related aspects of volunteer activity.

Herzberg, Frederick. 1976. *The Managerial Choice: To Be Efficient or to Be Human?* Homewood, IL: Dow-Jones-Irwin. The standard reference for the motivation-hygiene model of management.

Miller, Lynn E. 1985. "Understanding the Motivation of Volunteers: An Examination of Personality Differences and Characteristics of Volunteers' Paid Employment." *Journal of Voluntary Action* 14(2/3):112–122. An examination of volunteers from several social service agencies to test the hypothesis that volunteering meets unsatisfied "growth needs."

Pinder, Craig. 1985. "Beliefs, Expected Values, and Volunteer Work Behavior." In *Motivating Volunteers,* ed. Larry Moore, 31–60. Vancouver, B.C.: Vancouver Volunteer Centre. Proposes an application of the expectancy-valence model for modeling the decision to volunteer.

Pearce, Jone L. 1983. "Job Attitude and Motivation Differences between Volunteers and Employees from Comparable Organizations." *Journal of Applied Psychology* 68:646–652. A replication of Staw's research hypotheses, with opposite results.

Schindler-Rainman, Eva and Lippitt, Ronald. 1975. *The Volunteer Community: Creative Use of Human Resources,* 2nd edition. San Diego, CA: University Associates. A broad look at motivating, managing, and utilizing volunteers.

Smith, David Horton. 1981. "Altruism, Volunteers, and Volunteerism." *Journal of Voluntary Action* 10(1):21–36. One of a series of articles by the author on the nature of volunteering; includes a brief discussion on defining *volunteers.*

Staw, Barry M. 1974. "Attitudinal and Behavioral Consequences of Changing a Major Organizational Reward: A Natural Field Experiment." *Journal of Personality and Social Psychology* 29:742–751. Presents and tests a "sufficiency-of-justification" model relating the relative importance of intrinsic and extrinsic motivations in ROTC volunteers.

Stebbins, Robert. 1982. "Serious Leisure: A Conceptual Statement." *Pacific Sociological Review* 25:251–272. Describes volunteerism, amateurism, and "hobbyism" as forms of "serious leisure."

SOURCES OF ADDITIONAL INFORMATION

The Journal of Voluntary Action Research contains many articles on all aspects of volunteerism, and is an important source of information for research on this topic. David Horton Smith and Jon Van Til edited *International Perspectives on Voluntary Action Research* (Washington, DC: University Press, 1983), which contains a number of papers on volunteerism from several countries. Another collection of papers, predominantly political in orientation, may be found in John Harman's edited volume *Volunteerism in the Eighties* (New York: University Press of America, 1982).

A more specific recreation-related article on managing volunteers is "Effective Management of a Volunteer Corps" (*Parks and Recreation* Feb., 55–59, 70, 1984) by Ted

Tedrick, William W. Davis, and Gerald J. Coutant. Steve Dennis and Ervin H. Zube have looked at members of voluntary outdoor recreation associations in "Voluntary Association Membership of Outdoor Recreationists: An Exploratory Study" (*Leisure Sciences* 10:229–245, 1988).

W

WILDERNESS. 1. A large tract of land that retains its natural primeval quality and that is free of observable human impact. 2. Such a tract of land officially designated as "wilderness" by a public agency.

There are two different issues that may be addressed when discussing the concept of wilderness. The first is the denotation of the term: its technical or general definition. The popular usage of the word, land untouched by human hands, is essentially the same as when the word first appeared in English—the first appearance was in *Layamons Brut,* a thirteenth-century poem (see Madden, 1847:217). Scientists and politicians still debate operational and legal definitions, but the essence of wilderness as large tracts of an unspoiled ENVIRONMENT enjoys a stable consensus. The other issue is the connotation of wilderness: its social VALUE, and whether society views wilderness as good or bad. Roderick Nash (1967:1) alluded to the distinction between these issues in the opening paragraph to *Wilderness and the American Mind:* " 'Wilderness' has a deceptive concreteness at first glance. The difficulty is that while the word is a noun, it acts like an adjective. There is no specific material object that is wilderness. The term designates a quality that produces a certain mood or feeling in a given individual and, as a consequence, may be assigned by that person to a specific place."

The mood, feelings, and qualities evoked by wilderness are nearly as diverse as the range of human emotions. Over history, they have ranged from terror to religious ecstasy, with artistic appreciation, economic greed, and scientific curiosity thrown in for good measure.

The recognition that lands that have been settled and cultivated are somehow fundamentally different from lands that have been unmodified is probably as old as civilization itself. Titus Lucretius Carus, the great first-century B.C. Roman poet cited the existence of uncultivated wild lands (Latin lacks a direct equivalent for *wilderness*) as evidence that "the universe was certainly not made for us by divine power, for it is too full of faults." These faults included regions "held by greedy mountains and dense forests," "wild beasts' haunts," "crags and desolate marshes," and "lands uninhabited because of scorching heat and ever-falling frost" (Lucretius, 1965:141–142).

John Wycliffe, in his fourteenth-century translations of the Greek texts of the Bible (Joseph Hall, 1901 and W. A. Craigie, 1925), selected *wilderness* to refer to the uninhabited desert lands where much of the story of the Bible unfolds. Prophets searched for their God in the wilderness. Moses and the Hebrews wandered in the wilderness for forty years as penance for doubting God. John the Baptist and Jesus went into the wilderness to pray and to be purified. The wilderness was demanding and punishing, but it did have, literally, redeeming properties.

Early Christian religious figures also went into the wilderness, either as hermits or, as Saint Basil did, to start religious communities. Although his contemporaries considered the wilderness to be dangerous, Basil found not only peace and solitude, but beauty. In a letter to Gregory of Nazianus, Basil describes in almost poetic detail the site he has chosen for his house. He concludes his description with the observation, "even Kalypso's isle, which Homer seems to have admired above all others for its beauty, is insignificant as compared with this" (Saint Basil, 1926:109).

Although rare individuals can be found in every age who appreciated the beauty of wilderness, the dominant view of Europeans through the Middle Ages and the Renaissance was that wilderness was something to tame if you could or shun if you could not. This attitude was imported by the early colonists into North America. Their trials—and frequent deaths—reinforced their fear of wilderness.

It was not until the nineteenth century that a significant number of individuals began to view wilderness in a more favorable light. The change in perception was due in large part to the emergence of the American Transcendentalist Movement. Wilderness, to the Transcendentalists such as William Cullen Bryant, Ralph Waldo Emerson, and Henry David Thoreau, was a source of sublime inspiration and an antidote to the spiritual illness of civilization (in their view).

Other writers and artists shared many of the views of the Transcendentalists, although they were not formally a part of the movement. The painter George Catlin, who was one of the first Americans to explore the west for the sake of curiosity and pleasure, painted many scenes of the western wilderness as well as Indian life in the 1820s and 1830s. Catlin argued for the establishment of a national park to protect the wilderness and Indian cultures a generation before Yellowstone would be set aside for the first NATIONAL PARK (Catlin, 1841). Other writers and artists joined Catlin in arguing for the need to protect the disappearing wilderness; these included John James Audubon, Thomas Cole, and James Fenimore Cooper. Their contributions, as well as those of their contemporaries, are described in Nash (1967).

The most articulate and influential advocate of wilderness in the late nineteenth and early twentieth centuries was John Muir. Muir's extensive writings (such as *Gentle Wilderness: The Sierra Nevada,* 1967), public-speaking engagements, and debates with Gifford Pinchot about the proper orientation of the CONSER-VATION movement generated substantial interest and support (as well as strong opposition) for the wilderness preservation movement. Muir's values continue to exercise a strong influence in the preservation movement through the orga-nization he founded, the Sierra Club.

In the first half of the twentieth century, Aldo Leopold (1921) and Robert Marshall (1930) further refined the popular and scientific understanding of the importance of wilderness. Leopold, in particular, was instrumental in establishing a legal precedent within the U.S. federal government for protecting wilderness. In 1921, he proposed the designation of a section of the Gila National Forest in New Mexico and Arizona as the "Gila Wilderness Area." Although his proposal initially received little interest, the district forester eventually agreed and set aside a section of the forests as the first administratively designated Wilderness Area in 1924. Since then, dozens of areas within the National Forests have been reserved as wilderness areas. This work also helped to set the stage for the establishment of the Wilderness Act.

A bill proposing the creation of a national system of wilderness areas was tabled in Congress in 1957. After seven years of hearings, debates, and modi-fications, Public Law 88–57, the Wilderness Act of 1964 was passed. The Wilderness Act was not only the culmination of a long evolutionary process in the connotation of wilderness as a disappearing valuable RESOURCE, but also represented the emergence of a consensus on technical definitions of wilderness in the United States. Leopold (quoted in Nash, 1967:187) suggested that wil-derness be considered as a contiguous area preserved in its natural state; open to hunting and fishing; devoid of roads and buildings, and other human alterations; and capable of absorbing a two weeks' pack trip. This definition was used as the basis for defining the area of the Gila National Forest Leopold wanted protected as a wilderness area. In 1962, the Outdoor Recreation Resources Review Commission (ORRRC) defined wilderness to be public land of at least 100,000 acres, with no roads useable by the public, within a reasonably unified boundary configuration, no significant ecological disturbance, and the presence of humans was not obvious with the exception of livestock grazing (in the West) or early-day timber harvesting (in the East). The authors of the ORRRC definition noted that this was not intended to be a recommended legal definition, but only a working premise for their discussion of wilderness area issues and supply.

Growing from the initial establishment of a wilderness area in the Gila National Forest, the U.S. Forest Service developed a series of administratively defined areas that served wilderness purposes: primitive areas, wilderness areas, wild areas, and canoe areas. "Wilderness areas" had to be a minimum of 100,000 acres and essentially devoid of human impact, and were managed with very restrictive guidelines. Primitive areas had fewer restrictions on use and management, while wild areas were equivalent to wilderness areas except they could be as small as 5,000 acres. Canoe areas—of which the Boundary Waters Canoe Area in northern Minnesota is the only example—provided for the protection of natural beauty along canoe routes, but permitted timber harvesting at some distance from the water's edge.

Under the terms of the Wilderness Act, wilderness is undeveloped federal land that retains its primeval character without evidence of human impact, provides outstanding opportunities for solitude or primitive RECREATION, is at least 5000 acres or of sufficient size to ensure its preservation and use in an unimpaired condition, and may also contain areas of ecological, geological, educational, scenic, or historical significance.

Preservation of public lands as wilderness is now well established as a philosophical and legal principle. Contemporary work on wilderness issues is now focused on narrower (but not necessarily less difficult) issues of whether specific areas should be designated as wilderness, the extent to which legal definitions may need to be modified to accommodate contemporary society (e.g., whether the presence of aircraft flying over wilderness areas violates the wilderness quality of the area), and how specific areas are to be managed and protected.

REFERENCES

Catlin, George. 1841. *North American Indians,* 2 vols. London: George Catlin. A compilation of letters written by Catlin in the 1830s detailing his travels and ideas about the American West, particularly his relationships and observations with American Indians.

Craigie, W. A., ed. 1925. *Legends of the Saints in the Scottish Dialect,* 18:52. Edinburgh: William Blackwood and Sons. This is a collection of saints' stories translated by John Wycliffe into 14th-century English dialect; a passage on page 52 illustrates his use of "wilderness."

Hall, Joseph, ed. 1901. *The New Testament in Scots: Being Purvey's Revision of Wycliffe's Version Turned into Scots by Murdoch Nisbet c. 1520/ edited from the unique ms. in the possession of Lord Amherst of Hacnkney by Thomas Groves Law.* Edinburgh: William Blackwood and Sons. A Celtic translation of the New Testament.

Leopold, Aldo. 1921. "The Wilderness and Its Place in Forest Recreational Policy." *Journal of Forestry* 19(7):718–721. An early and influential essay promoting the legal designation of sections of the national forests as wilderness areas; written at the time Leopold was pressing for protection of sections of wilderness in the Gila National Forest.

Lucretius. 1965. *On the Nature of the Universe,* trans. James H. Mantinband. New York: Frederick Ungar. A translation of the classic first-century B.C. didactic poem on nature and creation.

Madden, Frederick (trans). 1847. *Layamons Brut, or Chronicle of Britain.* Osnabruck,

Germany: Otto Zeller. A translation of the thirteenth-century Saxon poem; perhaps the earliest appearance of *wilderness* as a word in an English dialect.

Marshall, Robert. 1930. "The Problem of the Wilderness." *Scientific Monthly* 30:142–143. A brief essay on the importance of wilderness in modern society; argues that man has a psychological need for wilderness.

Muir, John. 1967. *Gentle Wilderness: The Sierra Nevada.* San Francisco: Sierra Club. A reprint of Muir's classic apologia for the wilderness; based on his extensive travels in the Sierra.

Nash, Roderick. 1967. *Wilderness and the American Mind.* New Haven, CT: Yale University Press. Probably the most thorough and scholarly study of the evolution of the concept of wilderness in the United States.

Outdoor Recreation Resources Review Commission. 1962. *Wilderness and Recreation— A Report on Resources, Values, and Problems.* Washington, DC: U.S. Government Printing Office.

Saint Basil. 1926. *Saint Basil: The Letters,* Vol. 1, trans. Roy J. Deferrari. London: William Heinemann. A translation of the letters (originally written in Greek) of Saint Basil to his contemporaries.

SOURCES OF ADDITIONAL INFORMATION

An excellent overview of recreation and leisure uses of the wilderness is provided in Frank Brockman, *Recreational Use of Wildlands* (3rd edition, New York: McGraw-Hill, 1979). Lloyd Irland examines some economic issues of wilderness in *Wilderness Economics and Policy* (Lexington, MA: Lexington Books, 1979); ecological and management issues are covered in William Hammit, *Wildland Recreation* (New York: Wiley, 1987). The history of wilderness preservation is covered in Michael Frome, *Battle for the Wilderness* (New York: Praeger, 1974). Legal issues and challenges associated with preservation are found in Corry McDonald, *The Dilemma of Wilderness* (Santa Fe, NM: Sunstone Press, 1987).

Problems in wilderness management and policy issues are examined in two good texts, Michael Frome, *Issues in Wilderness Management* (Boulder, CO: Westview Press, 1985) and Douglas Wellman, *Wildland Recreation Policy* (New York: Wiley, 1987). Craig Allin discusses political issues in greater depth in *The Politics of Wilderness Preservation* (Westport, CT: Greenwood Press, 1982).

WORK ETHIC. The belief that work is inherently good and ennobling, and that it is the source of one's personal and social identity.

Although the phrase work ethic is a part of popular vocabulary, the term is used in two very different ways. One denotation of the term is represented by Irving Siegel's positive or nonnormative definition of the concept: a work ethic is "a value or belief concerning the place of work in one's life that either (a) serves as a conscious guide to conduct or (b) is simply implied in manifold attitudes and behavior" (Siegel, 1983:28–29). Everyone, according to Siegel, has a work ethic—some value work, others despise it, but they all have a view of where it fits into their life. The second use is as a normative term. In this case, work ethic refers to a specific attitude about work, usually some variation on the theme that work is good and the source of one's identity. In this latter sense, the work ethic is sometimes known as the Protestant (work) ethic. A dated but classic study of the rise and importance of the Protestant work ethic in Western countries is Max Weber's (1958) *The Protestant Ethic and the Spirit of Capitalism*.

Precedents for the Protestant work ethic are found as early as the writings of the Talmud and Old Testament. God is frequently characterized as a worker—who labored so hard He had to rest on the sabbath. Many of the Old Testament leaders such as Saul and David were depicted as coming from a working-class (usually agricultural) background. Numerous Old Testament passages praise work, such as Proverbs 22:29, "Seeist thou a man diligent in his business? He shall stand before kings."

Work continued to hold a position of honor in the New Testament. Jesus, of course, came from a working-class family, as did all of His apostles. Paul, in particular, pushed the inherent goodness and virtue of work. In 1 Corinthians 7:20, for example, he wrote "Let every man abideth in the same calling wherein he was called," an assertion that each person has a job to do and should devote himself to it. Paul was particularly critical of idleness, as seen in II Thessalonians 3:10, "If any would not work, neither should he eat."

Other early Church leaders such as Basil and Augustine also preached on the value of work. It was Benedict, however, who perhaps had the strongest and most direct impact on the development of a work ethic. In the establishment of his religious order of monks, Benedict set out a set of rules in which manual labor and spiritual labor alternated with time for rest and relaxation. His brothers were not excused from physical labor so that they might spend their TIME solely in prayer. They were required to engage in all forms of manual work for the sake of their community as well as their own souls. Benedict's rules eventually became the norm for most Christian monastic orders.

By the time of the Protestant Reformation, Martin Luther (who had a monastic background) could cite many examples of corruption and decay in monastic and religious ideals within the Church. He continued, however, to respect the tradition of work that had long characterized monastic orders. The Council of Trent, called to internally reform problems within the Church, ordered significant changes in the monastic orders but retained and reinforced the importance of physical work in religious life.

Luther was especially influenced by Paul's notion of a "calling," *beruf* in Luther's German. The ideal of a calling was that each Christian was given a particular responsibility or task by God to perform for the Christian community. This task or assigned work was seen as central to each person's life. Work, to Luther, was not inherently good; rather, God called on people to do certain jobs. Accepting that call and doing one's proper job was a virtue. This qualification of only certain types of work as proper was clearly expressed in a passage from Luther's letter to Pope Leo X, "The Freedom of a Christian": "any work that is not done solely for the purpose of keeping the body under control or of serving one's neighbor is not good or Christian.'' Thus work for self-profit, the exploitation of others, or work that promoted sin or vice (or was based on sin) was unacceptable—regardless of how hard one worked.

John Calvin, drawing on the writings of Luther and the Swiss reformer Zwingli, further refined the merging Protestant work ethic. While Calvin believed that the fate of one's soul was predestined, and that work could not merit one's salvation, work did impose meaning and order in life. Work was a "calling" to Calvin (1953) as it was to Luther: "Finally, this point is to be noted: the Lord bids each one of us in all life's actions to look to his calling. . . . Each individual has his own kind of living assigned to him by the Lord as a sort of sentry-post so that he may not heedlessly wander about through life.'' The essential point to note is that work was given by God to man to provide meaning and order to his existence.

Roughly the same time as the Protestant reformation began, the European economy was slowly moving from the old feudal barter-based economy to a mercantilistic, money-based economy. By the time that Calvin was promoting his vision of a work ethic, the rise of the capitalism system was already under way. Calvin and the other Protestant reformers were not consciously responsible for creating the work ethic to help support the new economic order; however, the emerging work ethic could be used to inculcate values among workers that would strengthen a capitalistic economy.

The work ethic began in a religious context. It was seen as essentially a mandate—or perhaps a gift—from God that provided order, discipline, and meaning in life. By the nineteenth century, however, the religious view of the work ethic had been dramatically replaced by a political-economic philosophy. Workers rationally chose their calling and had an obligation to work hard, not for themselves, but for their employers and for their country's economy. The extent to which ordinary workers actually accepted this version of the work ethic can be debated. Sebastian de Grazia (1962:143) asserts, "among workmen the work ethic never existed.'' De Grazia suspected that the ethic, if it was truly believed by anyone, was probably accepted mostly by Protestant professionals and business people. Even among nineteenth-century professionals, there was significant variation in acceptance of the work ethic, especially along religious lines—Catholics appeared to have placed less emphasis on work as the key social virtue than did Protestants (de Grazia, 1959:146).

The work ethic, to most contemporary scholars, usually implies one or more of the following beliefs (Cherrington, 1980:20):

1. People have a religious and moral obligation to work hard.

2. People are supposed to spend most of their time at work, and not in leisure.

3. A worker should be prompt.

4. A worker should be productive.

5. A worker should take pride in his work and should do his job well.

6. Employees should be loyal to their employers.

7. Employees should strive for promotion and advancement through hard work, and should admire those who have achieved success in work.

8. People should build wealth through work, and should not spend money on too many luxuries.

These various beliefs have been used by Herbert Mirels and James Garrett (1971) to develop an attitude instrument to measure the strength of one's "Protestant ethic." The range of values on this Protestant ethic scale form a continuum from "Workaholic" (someone who works through the desire to remove guilt or fear); through several degrees of "work ethic" (such as the individual who finds self-esteem and status in his work); the "LEISURE ethic" (where work is seen as merely providing the resources necessary to pursue nonwork activities); to the extreme belief that all work is punishing and should be avoided.

REFERENCES

Calvin, John. 1953. *Institutes of the Christian Religion,* Book III, Chapter 10, Section 6, trans. Henry Beveridge. Grand Rapids, MI.: Eerdmans.

Cherrington, David J. 1980. *The Work Ethic: Working Values and Values That Work.* New York: AMACOM. As the title suggests, a value-oriented look at the role of work in society; Chapter 2 describes a continuum of work ethic values.

de Grazia, Sebastian. 1962. *Of Time, Work, and Leisure.* New York: Twentieth Century Fund. A major scholarly examination of changes in attitudes toward work and leisure; based on an elitist perspective of leisure.

Mirels, Herbert L., and Garrett, James B. 1971. "The Protestant Ethic as a Personality Variable." *Journal of Consulting and Clinical Psychology* 36:40–44. Describes a series of questionnaire statements that can be used to measure the strength of one's Protestant work ethic.

Siegel, Irving H. 1983. "Work Ethic and Productivity." In *The Work Ethic—A Critical Analysis,* ed. Jack Barbash, 27–42. Madison, WI: Industrial Relations Research Association. Suggests a nonnormative definition of work ethic as a basis for examining the relationship between commitment to work and quantitative measures of productivity (further argues that the perceived decline in American productivity is a myth).

Weber, Max. 1958. *The Protestant Ethic and the Spirit of Capitalism,* trans. Talcott Parsons. New York: Charles Scribner's Sons. A classic study of the origin of the Protestant work ethic and its impact on Western economies.

SOURCES OF FURTHER INFORMATION

A popular accounting of attitudes toward work (now dated, but still enjoyable reading) is Studs Terkel, *Working* (New York: Avon Books, 1972). A collection of more scholarly analyses of the work ethic is Jack Barbash, Robert Lampman, Sar Levitan, and Gus Tyler, eds., *The Work Ethic—A Critical Analysis* (Madison, WI: Industrial Relations Research Association, 1983). Veronique de Keyser, Thoralf Qvale, Bernhard Wilpert, and S. Anotionia Ruis Quintanilla have edited an international collection of articles on technological aspects of the work ethic, *The Meaning of Work and Technological Options* (New York: Wiley, 1988). An historical perspective on the subject is covered in Patrick Joyce, ed., *The Historical Meanings of Work* (Cambridge, UK: Cambridge University Press, 1987).

Other attitude scales measuring aspects of the work ethic have been developed by Stephen Wollack, James Goodale, Jan Wijting, and Patricia Smith, "Development of the Survey of Work Values" (*Journal of Applied Psychology*, 55:331–338, 1971) and Milton Blood, "Work Values and Job Satisfaction" (*Journal of Applied Psychology*, 53:456–459, 1969).

X

XENOPHOBIA. Fear or extreme distrust of strangers, particularly tourists.

Although xenophobia traditionally referred to a relatively rare psychological condition in which a person became incapacitated by fear of strangers, the term is now frequently used in TOURISM to refer to dislike or hatred by local residents toward visitors or TOURISTS. Alister Mathieson and Geoffrey Wall (1982: 140–141) suggests that xenophobia results when the social CARRYING CAPACITY of destination regions is exceeded. Manifestations of xenophobia range from vocal expressions of resentment by locals to their political leaders to outbursts of physical violence.

REFERENCE

Mathieson, Alister, and Wall, Geoffrey. 1982. *Tourism: Economic, Physical, and Social Impacts*. London: Longman. An excellent overview of the various impacts of tourism on destination regions; includes a brief discussion of the phenomenon of xenophobia.

SOURCES OF ADDITIONAL INFORMATION

Jafar Jafari examines some of the cultural forces contributing to the development of xenophobia in ''The Socioeconomic Costs of Tourism to Developing Countries'' (*Annals of Tourism Research* 1: 227–262, 1965). Richard Butler describes problems arising from xenophobia in a Scottish setting in ''The Impact of Recreation on Life Styles of Rural Communities: A Case Study of Sleat, Isle of Skye'' (*Studies in the Geography of Tourism and Recreation* 1: 187–201, 1978). Although he doesn't use the term explicitly, George Doxey has developed a model forecasting the evolution of hosts' attitudes from one of a warm welcome to xenophobia in ''A Causation Theory of Visitor-Resident Irritants: Methodology and Research Inferences'' (*Proceedings of the Travel Research Association*, 6th annual conference, 1975).

Name Index

Subject Index

Bold page numbers refer to main entry.

About the Author

STEPHEN L. J. SMITH is Professor and Chairman of the Department of Recreation and Leisure Studies at the University of Waterloo, Canada. He is the author of *Recreation Geography* and *Tourism Analysis,* and has written numerous articles and technical reports for journals such as *Leisure Sciences, Journal of Leisure Research,* and *Annals of Tourism Research.*